UNDERSTANDING
Orchids

BOOKS BY
WILLIAM CULLINA

Wildflowers
Native Trees, Shrubs, and Vines
Understanding Orchids

A FRANCES TENENBAUM BOOK

Houghton Mifflin Company
BOSTON NEW YORK 2004

UNDERSTANDING
Orchids

*An Uncomplicated Guide to Growing
the World's Most Exotic Plants*

WILLIAM CULLINA

For information about permission to reproduce selections from this book,
write to Permissions, Houghton Mifflin Company, 215 Park Avenue South,
New York, New York 10003.

Visit our Web site: www.houghtonmifflinbooks.com.

Library of Congress Cataloging-in-Publication Data is available.
ISBN 0-618-26326-8

Book design by Anne Chalmers. Typefaces: Minion, The Sans, Bellevue

Printed in the United States of America
RMT 10 9 8 7 6 5 4 3 2 1

Uncaptioned photos:
page i, *Sophronitella violacea;* ii–iii, *Osmoglossum pulchellum;* iv–v, *Epidendrum capricornu;* vi left, *Dendrobium pseudoglomeratum;* vi right, mounted orchids; vii top left, *Encyclia alata* 'Sunset Valley Orchids'; vii top right, *Oncidium* Twinkle; vii bottom, *Encyclia vitellina;* viii–ix, *Oncidium* hybrid; x–1, *Trichopilia suavis;* 38–39, *Encyclia* Atropine 'Montclair'; 100–101, *Paphiopedilum rothschildianum* hybrid; 128, *Bulbophyllum* Frank Smith 'Sunset Valley Orchids'; 228–29, *Doritaenopsis* Purple Gem 'Sparkler'

Acknowledgments

I AM INDEBTED once again to my lovely and very patient wife, Melissa, who gave up family time while I typed ceaselessly on the computer or drove off to do research. At last it's party time, family! I am equally in debt to my tireless editor, Frances Tenenbaum, not only for suggesting this project but also for helping me stay focused during the two very hectic years it took to write it, and to Peg Anderson and the editorial staff at Houghton Mifflin for taking it from raw text to finished book. I'm grateful as well to David DeKing, Cayte McDonough, and the staff at the New England Wild Flower Society for their support and encouragement while this text took shape.

This book is greatly enhanced by the wonderful images contributed by the master orchid photographer Charles Rowden — thank you, Charlie, for the integral part you played in making this project a reality. Thanks as well to Darrin Norton for his beautiful images and the time he let me spend photographing his collection. Kudos as well to my friends Carol Yee, Alan Wachtel, Sandy Ek, and the crew at the University of Connecticut Greenhouses, and to Cordelia Head, Marguerite Webb, and Lucinda Winn, owners of J & L Orchids, for allowing me to photograph their collections. Everyone needs heroes and mentors, and the owners of J & L are certainly three of mine. Many of my first plants came from their tremendous collection, and the diversity of plants within their greenhouse walls is a continuing source of wonder and amazement to me. Of equal importance on this journey of exploration have been my friends Ann and Phil Jesup — orchid growers extraordinaire and genuinely kind and generous people in word and deed. I was fortunate to learn from other legendary figures in the orchid world, including the late Gustav Mehlquist and Benjamin Berliner, to whom I owe special thanks.

Finally, thanks to the plants themselves — especially those I have killed through inexperience or ineptitude. I hope I don't make the same mistakes again!

Contents

Part 1
Setting Up the Orchid Environment

Part 2
Care and Feeding

Part 3
Orchid Reproduction

Part 4
Common Orchid Genera from A to Z

Introduction

LEARNING TO GROW ORCHIDS and understand their idiosyncrasies is a true journey. The sheer number of orchid species—estimates range from 25,000 to 35,000 worldwide, not to mention some 40,000 hybrids—means there will always be new plants to explore, new friends to make. You could start acquiring an orchid a day when you were twenty and still not have grown them all when you turned eighty! No other family of plants offers us inquisitive humans such overwhelming diversity. Orchids are a world unto themselves, and I think the almost limitless potential for discovery is one key to their phenomenal popularity. Even after twenty years of growing orchids, whenever I see a new one or a particularly well grown specimen, I still get that spine-tingling, toe-tickling feeling of WOW that hooked me in the beginning. If you are just starting out with orchids, you are in for quite an adventure.

How to Use This Book

My goal is to lead you on that adventure, and because I am writing for orchid lovers at every level of expertise, from absolute beginner to experienced grower to expert, you may find that some parts of the book are not pertinent at this time. Here's how the text is organized.

Part One contains all of the information you'll need to choose a place where your plants will grow well, whether on a windowsill, under lights, in a greenhouse, or outdoors. Here you'll learn about light, temperature, and humidity, the basics of good orchid culture. I have tried whenever possible to explain concepts in a straightforward way in plain English. However, I recommend that you become familiar with some of the terms listed in the glossary, which are in bold type the first time they're used in the text. After a while, the meaning of words like "pseudobulb" and "velamen" and "footcandle" will become second nature to you.

Part Two, "Care and Feeding," delves into the topics of watering, potting, fertilizing, and dealing with pests and diseases, as well as troubleshooting when your plants have problems. All of this information will help you keep your orchids thriving for years to come.

Part Three, "Orchid Reproduction," covers more specialized topics. Although you don't have to understand the mechanics of evolution, pollination, and hybridization to grow orchids, these chapters give you more background and context about this amazing family.

Part Four focuses on one hundred of the most commonly grown groups (genera) of tropical orchids, covering in detail the general cultural advice given in Parts One and Two. From *Angraecum* to *Zygopetalum,* this section describes each genus, explains which species are easiest for beginners, and includes anecdotes and growing hints that will help you decide which orchids are right for you.

The appendixes at the back of the book contain useful information about botanical terminology, orchid resources on the Web and orchid organizations, and awards. There is also a glossary of terms and a list of books for further reference.

This book is based largely on my own experience, along with that of people who, in person or in print, have been my mentors over the years. I cringe to think about it, but I always learn as much from my mistakes as from my successes. I truly hate to kill an orchid, partly because each one is so darned expensive, but mostly because I probably could have saved it had I known a bit more. With that in mind, I offer here what I have learned, in the hope that you will be able to learn from my mistakes as well as my successes.

No doubt some people will take exception to my advice, for there is more than one way to pot an orchid. Take my words as a guide or a starting point, but, most of all, be observant, patient, and caring, and the orchids will teach you well. Of course I am biased, but I think you will find that there is no more magical, fascinating, and only occasionally frustrating family of plants than the Orchidaceae. I raise my watering can to you and offer this toast: "May your roots be long, your pseudobulbs fat, and your flowers all the colors of the rainbow."

PART ONE

Setting Up the Orchid Environment

CHAPTER 1

Getting Started: Your First Orchid

LOOKING BACK, I realize that I fell into orchid-growing by accident. My first orchid was a rootless *Dendrobium phalaenopsis* hybrid that was on the brink of dying in a crowded greenhouse of a small local nursery. I bought it because I thought I could save it. But try as I might, I could not get the orchid to form any roots, and I watched helplessly as its **pseudobulbs** began to crease and wrinkle, then gradually deflate as it used up the water stored inside. In desperation, I placed the plant in a pail of water for twenty-four hours, enclosed it in a plastic bag with some damp moss (a trick that has worked for me since), and danced around it three times waving a chicken bone and muttering "Unwitherus pseudobulbis rehydratus novum immediatum!" and other spells. All was for naught, and the plant dropped its last remaining leaves and slowly faded to brown.

Had I known then what I know now, I might have been able to save the plant, but even so, starting out with a cheap, weakened plant, I was hooked. Once it was obvious that my first

plant was a terminal case, I bought a *Phalaenopsis* in **spike** (flowers developing), and it bloomed! I purchased some books on orchids, and soon the bay window in my apartment was screened off with plastic and humming with the soft whoosh of an electric fan and a small humidifier.

At that point, orchids stopped living with me, and I began to live with orchids. Their next home was an enclosed box under fluorescent lights in a spare bedroom. This setup saved the floors and satisfied me for a time, until I decided that high-intensity lights—the kind you see in warehouse stores that blind you if you stare at them—would be just the thing for my burgeoning collection. So I took my orchids down to the basement, first constructing a plastic box with a single light fixture and later wrapping a corner of the basement in plastic sheets and growing the plants on benches in an artificially lit **grow room**. Later still I went on to manage a conservatory collection of orchids as well as thousands of other tropicals. Now, a greenhouse is the holy grail of most serious orchidophiles, but in all honesty, some plants did better back on the windowsill than they ever did in the greenhouse. In part it's a question of numbers. It is easier to give plants individual attention when you have fifteen than when you have fifteen hundred. Furthermore, not all tropical orchids are **rain forest** plants. Many grow in seasonally dry environments, and

Dendrobium King Dragon 'Montclair' HCC/AOS

Slc **Wasp Nest 'Sunset Valley Orchids'** HCC/AOS is a compact, easy-to-grow, free-flowering hybrid.

the ever-present humidity of a greenhouse is just not to their liking. Believe me when I say that you don't need a greenhouse to grow orchids. You just need to pick plants suited to your space.

Buying Your First Orchid

Unless you are as obstinate as I am, I don't recommend beginning with a plant that is knocking on heaven's door even before you bring it home. Start with as healthy a specimen as you can find. My best advice is to visit a nursery that specializes in orchids (to find a nursery, contact your local orchid society or search on the Internet) and ask the proprietor for recommendations based on your growing space. Some orchids need a bright, south-facing window; others will thrive in a shaded east- or north-facing one. Even the temperature at which you set your thermostat during the winter has a bearing on the type of orchids you should start with. Of course, many people receive their first orchid as a gift or pick one up on impulse at the supermarket or home store. These inexpensive, plastic-sleeved plants may do just fine, but look up the genus in Part Four to learn about its light and temperature requirements.

What to Look For

There are basically two kinds of orchids—those that have a camel's hump of sorts for storing water (either a swollen stem called a pseudobulb or fleshy, thickened leaves) and can thus withstand occasional droughts, and those without a pseudobulb or fleshy leaves that require more consistent moisture. If cacti thrive in your care because you are forgetful about watering or you travel quite a bit, the first type is a better bet. Orchids in this category include species of *Cattleya, Oncidium, Dendrobium, Laelia, Encyclia, Brassavola, Cymbidium, Coelogyne,* and many other genera. If your apartment is full of ferns and African violets and you are happiest when you are carrying a watering can, try the more water-demanding but generally easy and shade-tolerant *Paphiopedilums* and *Phalaenopsis.*

Look at the orchid you are planning to buy. Are the stems, leaves, and pseudobulbs plump and unwrinkled? Do most or all of the stems have a good complement of leaves? Examine the roots if they are visible. They should be white or pewter-colored when dry, and green or silvery green when wet. The root tips should be pointed and bright green. The longer the green tip, the faster the root is growing. Dead roots are dull tan when dry, brown when wet, and the tip is usually broken or chaffy. If some of the roots have crept up and over the lip of the pot, that's okay, but the plant should feel firmly anchored in the pot, with no wobble; look to see if it is clipped or wired in place, and if possible, lift the clip off to check for wobbliness.

It is tempting to buy plants in flower, but flowering is stressful for the plant, and the added stress of having to acclimate to a new environment may cause the flowers to drop prematurely, especially the unopened flowers and developing flower spikes. I prefer to buy a plant that is in active vegetative growth. Unlike mature leaves, immature ones can adapt to changes in light and humidity when the orchid moves into its new home. If you choose a healthy plant suited to your conditions, it will be better able to cope with the stress of flowering when that time comes.

Cultivated tropical orchids are commonly potted in several different materials, but with very few exceptions they should never be potted in soil. The reason is that most orchids are **epiphytes**; that is, they grow naturally in trees. They are adapted for life in the branches of the rain forest or cloud forest, where air circulates around their roots all the time. Thus they need a potting mix that breathes, and they will quickly decline in soil that smothers their roots. Most likely your first orchid will be potted in a material that looks like the bark mulch used in landscaping, but it's a screened and graded Douglas fir **bark** specifically manufactured for orchids. The mix may contain additional ingredients such as **perlite, charcoal,** and **lava rock** (see Chapter 8, pp. 68 and 71). More and more commonly, inexpensive orchids are potted in what are called peat-lite mixes, which contain **peat moss** and perlite or other additives. What all these mixes provide is good drainage—a very critical requirement for most orchids.

Figure on watering your plant thoroughly once or twice a week—basically once the surface of the growing mix has dried out and turned a lighter color. The best way to water is to take it to the kitchen sink and douse it with the spray hose, making sure a torrent of water flows out of the drain holes. Check the pseudobulbs and/or leaves, which should remain stiff and unwrinkled. About once a month, mix a teaspoon of a good liquid fertilizer into the water. Most orchids grow in places where the humidity remains fairly high, at least during the growing season. Therefore, in the very dry atmosphere of a heated house in winter, they will benefit from a daily misting and will need more water than they do during the summer, when humidity is higher, though air conditioning also dries out the air. In Part Four I indicate orchids that are more tolerant of lower humidity and thus good candidates for windowsill culture.

When the orchid is in bloom, it is okay to display it on an end table for a week or two, but for its permanent home, choose a sunny window. I shouldn't say permanent, for the best way to assure that the orchid has a long and happy life is

to put it outdoors in light shade during the summer. A few rainstorms will wash away all the dust and salts accumulated indoors. Even if you cannot put it outdoors, the stronger sun and warmer temperatures of the summer months will trigger the plant to grow. Those with pseudobulbs will send up a new set of leaves from the base of one pseudobulb, which should continue to grow and then bloom in season. A *Phalaenopsis* will simply produce a new leaf or two. If the new growth or leaf is markedly smaller than the previous one but overall the plant looks plump, take it as a sign that it needs more light or fertilizer. A new crop of roots should sprout from the developing pseudobulb as well. Actively growing roots have a green tip and a silvery or bright white **velamen** (jacket) that helps them sop up water.

Bulbophyllum **Frank Smith 'Sunset Valley Orchids'**

Getting Started: Your First Orchid   5

Orchids have two distinct patterns of growth—**sympodial** and **monopodial**. All orchids with pseudobulbs and some without are sympodial growers, sending up successive leafy growths or vertical stems along a creeping horizontal stem called a **rhizome**. Roots also emanate from the rhizome, especially at the juncture with a vertical stem.

You can tell quite a bit about a particular plant from the relative sizes of the various growths along the rhizome. Ideally, starting when the orchid is a seedling or tissue-cultured plantlet, each new growth produced by the rhizome should be larger than the last until the plant reaches its genetically determined maximum size. If you examine a sympodial species such as a *Cattleya, Oncidium, Dendrobium, Cymbidium,* or even *Paphiopedilum,* the newest stem/pseudobulb and leaf—that is, the one at the growing tip of the rhizome—should be at least as large as those trailing it. The rhizomes of most orchids creep along on top of or out of the potting mix, so they are easy to spot and trace. If the newest growth is actively developing—that is, if the leaves are still expanding and the pseudobulb (if present) is still growing—look at the one directly behind or below it on the rhizome for comparison. The successive increase in size is your best indication that the plant is healthy and vigorous and, if it is of blooming size, that it will bloom in season. If the newest growth is smaller than the preceding one, it means the plant has recently suffered a setback caused by some trauma, such as division, root loss, or a major change in growing environment. I would avoid buying that plant, for it is already weak and may not bloom for a few years. If the newest growths are smaller than the oldest but show a positive increase in size, the plant is recovering and, though it may take a year to bloom, should be adequately healthy. Buy it if the price is right.

Monopodial orchids lack pseudobulbs and rhizomes. Instead, they have a vertical stem lined with alternating leaves and, lower down, roots. *Phalaenopsis* and *Vanda* are common monopodials. You can look at the relative length of newer versus older leaves the same way you examine the growths of sympodial orchids to judge the plant's health, but ignore the newest-growing leaf or leaves. Expanding leaves should have a zone of lighter green at their base. Monopodial orchids produce new leaves continually, so if the highest or youngest leaf lacks this light green zone, it could mean the plant has been shocked into **dormancy.** Don't select it.

Rhizome

Actively growing lead growth, with new roots erupting from the rhizome

Old pseudobulb

Oncidium sphacelatum has a clearly sympodial growth habit. The long rhizome allows the plant to climb a tree but makes it difficult to contain in a pot. This one is mounted on a piece of cork.

Though they lack pseudobulbs, *Paphiopedilums* are sympodial orchids, with a short, creeping rhizome hidden down in the pot. Each fan of leaves grows from the previous fan. The old flower stem just to the right of center arose from the center of the older fan after all the leaves had expanded.

The fantastic pseudobulbs of *Ionobulbum munificum* are ringed with bristly hairs instead of papery sheaths. The purpose of the hairs is a mystery.

Leaf loss is often a natural part of an orchid's growth cycle. This *Dendrobium cruentum* hybrid had shed the leaves on its oldest canes to reduce water loss during winter dormancy. The old canes, still green, are alive and photosynthesizing and should not be removed.

Old, leafless cane used primarily for water and food storage

Young, actively growing cane

Last year's cane, which has shed its lower leaves. The papery gray coverings are the old leaf bases, which help protect the cane.

Aerial roots are physiologically different from roots that develop inside a pot. Their thick white velamen protects them and sponges up water or mist in the air.

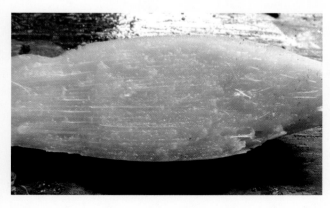

A *Brassia* pseudobulb cut open to show the succulent water-filled cells inside. Vertical fibers give rigidity to the structure, which expands when water is plentiful and contracts when it is scarce.

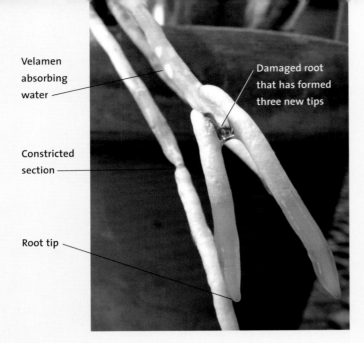

Velamen absorbing water

Damaged root that has formed three new tips

Constricted section

Root tip

Long green tips are a sign of healthy roots in active growth. The spongy white velamen that surrounds the mature root forms just behind the tip. The constricted section of root on the left and the damaged tip on the right, which has branched into three new tips, are signs of some trauma, such as dryness or overfertilization, that the roots have recovered from.

Dendrobium kingianum produces new plantlets, or keikis, instead of flowers from some of its flower buds. Keikis can be removed after they have formed at least two pseudobulbs or, in the case of monopodials, three leaves and a few roots. This keiki is still too small to be separated.

This *Ascocenda,* a monopodial, has a vertical stem lined with alternating leaves. Roots grow out from the bases of the oldest leaves.

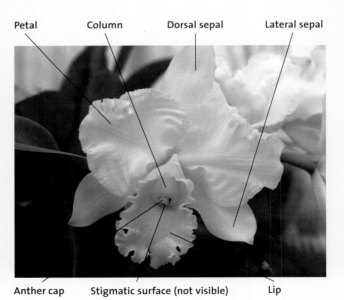

Petal   Column   Dorsal sepal   Lateral sepal

Anther cap   Stigmatic surface (not visible)   Lip

A beautiful white *Cattleya* flower

CHAPTER 2

Where to Grow Your Orchids

YOU CAN GROW ORCHIDS in many places, from the kitchen window to a state-of-the-art greenhouse or, if you live in the tropics, a tree in your backyard. I'm assuming that like mine, your first tropical orchids were (or are) set on a windowsill in your home, so I'll start there and work toward more complex setups like grow rooms and greenhouses.

On the Windowsill

The old-fashioned double-hung windows in my house were not designed for horticulture. They are standard-sized windows — 4 feet high by 2½ to 3½ feet wide, with sills too small to accommodate anything wider than a picture frame. At least they don't have triple-track storm windows and screens, which are hard to clean and greatly reduce the amount of light getting through. The house runs north to south, with most of the windows facing east and west. The only south-facing win-

ABOVE: *Brassavola nodosa* is a rugged, drought-tolerant species with intoxicating night-scented flowers. It thrives on a sunny windowsill in a small pot or on a mount.

dow is behind the armchair in the living room, and it is so shaded by the big pines that line the street that it might as well be facing north. In winter, when the deciduous trees around the house lose their leaves, the east-facing kitchen and living room windows receive only about one and a half hours of direct, low-angled sun. My house is small and quite dark, and it's so full of furniture and baby apparatus that very little floor space is unused, so I understand how hard it can be to find the perfect place for plants. I have not always been so unfortunate. When I really came down with the orchid bug, I was living in a house with a big floor-to-ceiling, southeast-facing bay window that received four hours of sunlight even in the heart of winter but was shaded by the time the summer sun really got cooking around one in the afternoon. By pulling a drape around the plants in the evening during winter, I could cool them down about 10 degrees below the room's temperature, and the drapes helped retain some of the humidity generated by the plants and my little humidifier. Later I moved into a big Victorian with three southeast-facing bay windows. I wonder sometimes if that serendipity played a part in my interest in orchids.

So what window should you choose? Many books consider a north-facing window that receives no direct sunlight adequate for shade-tolerant *Paphiopedilum* and *Phalaenopsis,* but

I am skeptical of this claim. Maybe if you live in the Sunbelt and have a big sliding glass door open to the sky, your north window would be all right. In my experience, though, even the most shade-adapted orchids benefit from a few hours of direct sunlight on a windowsill. A clean pane of glass transmits only about 85%–95% of the light trying to pass through it, and the percentage is lower if the glass is dirty or if you have storm windows, screens, or double or triple glazing. Triple-track windows that are reasonably clean and include a storm window and a screen cut the amount of light down to 65%–75% of full strength. The sunlight itself is obviously weaker during winter—much weaker when you live as far from the equator as I do. So choose a southeast or, less ideally, a south or west window for your plants, one that is not shaded by overhanging trees, neighbors' houses, or that two-story abstract sculpture on the lawn that your spouse or partner is so proud of.

If you grow other houseplants, a window where African violets flower well should be all right for *Phalaenopsis,* and one where Christmas cacti bloom profusely would probably be suitable for a *Dendrobium* or *Cattleya.* If you have a window where the sun beats in and fades the fabric on the new sofa, that would be a good place to grow some of the real light-loving orchids. Keep an eye on your plants for cues that they are receiving adequate light. Good signs are blooming, of course, some red or maroon pigment in the leaves, leaf bases, pseudobulbs, and even root tips, and sturdy, medium green foliage. In most places the plants will benefit from spending the summer outdoors to fortify them for the winter; see p. 22.

BELOW: On a bright, southeast-facing window, orchids grow with other houseplants in year-round profusion.

SOME EASY ORCHIDS FOR A SUNNY WINDOWSILL

Ascocentrum species and hybrids

Barkeria species

Brassavola nodosa

Brassia hybrids

Catasetums and relatives

Cattleya bowringiana

Cattleya aurantiaca

Cattleya skinneri

Cattleya hybrids (especially the "mini-cats" involving
   RUPICOLOUS *Laelia* and *Sophronitis* species)

Cymbidium (miniature types)

Dendrobium kingianum

Dendrobium phalaenopsis hybrids

Dendrobium nobile hybrids (they need a cool, dry rest period)

Encyclia, especially *E. cochleata*

Epidendrum porpax (also grows well on a mount)

Galeandra species

Laelias, especially *L. anceps* and related Mexican species and
   RUPICOLOUS types like *L. flava, liliputana, and lundii*, as
   well as *L. pumila*

Leptotes bicolor

Lycaste (Central American species)

Miltonia spectabilis and hybrids

Oncidium (EQUITANT) hybrids

Oncidium ornithorhynchum

Oncidium sphacelatum hybrids (the big yellow ones commonly
   sold as florist plants)

Polystachya species

SOME TO TRY ON A SHADY WINDOWSILL

Masdevallia floribunda and *infracta*

Paphiopedilum sukhakulii and *callosum* (also its hybrid Maudiae)

Phalaenopsis equestris and the myriad *Phalaenopsis* hybrids

Pleurothallis grobyii

Restrepia species

LEFT: The cartoon-elephant flowers of warm-growing **Paphiopedilum bellatulum** are beloved by many. This mottled-leaved species is one of the better choices for a shady window.

and add humidity. It is still best to water your orchids over a sink or bucket, though, so that you can drench them thoroughly to wet the medium and **leach** salts. When my collection had grown to twenty-five plants, lugging each one to the sink one to three times a week became a big chore, so under the slatted trays I rigged up some rubber dish rack mats that tilted into a gutter feeding into a bucket. Then I could (with care) drench the plants in situ. It took a bit of engineering to get it right, but then it saved a lot of time.

Under Artificial Lights

Satisfying some or all of your plants' light requirement with artificial lights is an excellent option for the home orchid grower. When I ran out of good windowsill space, it didn't take me long to move my growing collection and put it under fluorescent fixtures. Under lights the plants never have a dull day, and it is possible to grow many species that just don't receive enough natural light on most sills. In fact, my plants started growing so well that they rivaled specimens raised by friends with greenhouses. Having a dependable year-round light source means no short, dark winter days. And you won't

Because epiphytic orchids typically need watering more frequently than houseplants growing in soil, and because their potting **media** drain most of the water you apply, I suggest you set up a water-catching tray under the plants (not individual plant saucers, though, which limit air movement into the pot). I built a slatted tray of ³/₄-inch-wide cedar strips with ³/₄-inch spaces, which I fitted over a gravel tray to catch water drips

bulbs are also very inefficient at converting electricity to light, turning most of it into heat instead. Even the 75- and 150-watt incandescent spotlight-type grow lights, with spectral characteristics specifically designed for plants, put out a lot of heat and not many **lumens** (see Chapter 3). They are really useful only as a supplemental source of light on a windowsill, not as a plant's primary light source.

FLUORESCENT FIXTURES

Fluorescent bulbs are much, much better than incandescents in the quality, quantity, and cost of the light they produce, and they have long been the standard for indoor growers. They are very inexpensive to set up and operate, and many orchid species thrive under them. Their main disadvantages are disposal of the bulbs and headroom. Fluorescents have to be changed about once a year to keep up the light output, and if you have more than a few fixtures, changing them and, more important, disposing of the old bulbs becomes a chore; many

lie awake on frigid nights, worrying that the heat in your greenhouse has quit. The main drawback of lights compared with a greenhouse (besides taking up your living space) is that it's usually harder to achieve the 10°–15° F nighttime temperature drop that some orchids need for blooming.

The cost of electricity, which varies from region to region, is certainly a factor to consider. All in all, I think the cost will be reasonable unless you light up your whole cellar. For example, a four-tube fluorescent fixture uses 160 watts. At my current electricity rates, it costs 28 cents to run this fixture for sixteen hours a day, or about $8.50 a month. Selling off a few extra plants at an orchid society meeting covers my bill. A 400-watt high-intensity-discharge (HID) fixture costs me an average of 71 cents a day, which adds up to $21.30 a month.

Indoor growers use three types of lights: incandescent, fluorescent, and **HID** fixtures.

INCANDESCENT BULBS

Standard incandescent light bulbs are not suitable for plants because the light they cast is very yellow; it doesn't include the red and blue light that plants need for photosynthesis. These

municipalities won't take the bulbs as standard household trash. As to headroom, the intensity of the light from fluorescents drops quickly with distance from the fixture, so the plants need to be within a foot of the bulbs for optimal growth. Watering, grooming, and enjoying your plants require some gymnastics when you have to operate in such a tight space.

Fluorescent lights work by passing an electric current through a pressurized gas that causes a coating on the inside of the glass tube to fluoresce and give off visible light. For the fixtures to work effectively, the electricity level must be carefully controlled; this is accomplished by a ballast, which meters out the juice so that the bulbs fluoresce evenly. Still, they do pulse and flicker a bit even when they're working right.

You can pay a lot of money for tiered prefab fluorescent light setups, but I have always used cheap, 4-foot-long "shop lights," which you can buy at your local home center for about $15 apiece (in an interesting example of anti-inflation, when I bought my first set twenty-four years ago, they were the same price). Get the two-tube, 40-watt fixtures, which include a ballast, wires, reflector, and chain. If you are not good at assembly, have the store or a competent friend or family member put it together for you. There is a multiplying effect when you

Orchids thrive under fluorescent lights, and a two-tier light table makes caring for them easy. The grower has closed off a section of the basement to raise the humidity around the plants. Enclosing just the table would have the same effect.

LEFT: Breeders have paired the easy culture of *Cattleyas* with the compact size of *Sophronitis* to produce this award-winning hybrid "mini-cat," *Sophrolaeliocattleya* **Isabelle Stone 'Mem. Enza Wilson'** HCC/AOS.

combine fixtures, since proportionally less light is wasted along the edges. I always hang two or three two-tube fixtures side by side to create a nice, bright growing area. This arrangement makes it a bit harder to work on the plants in the middle, but it's easier to contain light and humidity than it is if you string the fixtures end to end. These fixtures are 4 feet long, and you should hang them so that their reflectors almost touch, so light doesn't bleed out between them. A three-fixture, six-tube setup would thus cover a space 4 feet long by $2^{1}/_{2}$ feet wide. I can fit about a hundred miniature orchids in such a space.

Because light output drops off quickly, set the bulbs 6–8 inches above the tops of the plants. The orchids can even touch the bulbs, and light-loving types will try to do so, but this makes caring for them difficult unless the lights are on a pulley that can be raised and lowered easily. Light intensity is highest at the center of the bulbs and lower toward the sockets, so put your most light-demanding plants in the middle. I set smaller plants on overturned pots (lining up the drainage holes) to keep them from getting shaded by taller neighbors.

Standing less than 3 inches tall, this marvelous specimen of *Cadetia chionantha* — a relative of *Dendrobiums* —is a perfect size for culture under fluorescent lights.

Many types of fluorescent bulbs are available, both in size and in the quality of light they produce. As a general rule, the longer the bulb, the more light it generates per watt of electricity used. I feel that fixtures shorter than 4 feet do not generate bright enough light. If you have a small space to illuminate, you can buy U-shaped 4-foot bulbs that will fit into a 2-foot space, and two of these are better than four 2-foot bulbs. Eight-foot fixtures are brighter still, though a bit unwieldy to handle. There are also special high-output and very-high-output (HO and VHO) fluorescent fixtures that use bigger ballasts, more electricity, and special bulbs to generate light levels approaching HIDs in intensity. But unless you want to open a tanning salon on the side, if higher light output is your goal, it is simpler and cheaper to use HIDs.

By changing the fluorescing powder, manufacturers can alter the color of the light the tube emits. The bulb that puts the white in a white collar and drains the color from your skin is the ubiquitous cool white bulb, which emits a bluish white light. Warm white bulbs are closer to incandescents, with a pinkish orange color that includes the red wavelengths. Since plants need both red and blue light for photosynthesis, you can combine warm and cool white bulbs to get a fairly well balanced light for plant growth. I usually combine them in a

1:1 ratio, though others suggest 2:1 red to blue (red is used a bit more in photosynthesis) if you have more than four tubes in your setup. Other colors are available, such as soft white, but I usually stick with the warm and cool (these are usually the cheapest, too).

You can purchase bulbs designed specifically to emit light that is very high in the photosynthetically active red and blue wavelengths and that also usually has some purple thrown in to enhance the plants' appearance (similar to the aquarium bulbs used to brighten the colors of tropical fish). I'll be honest; some flowers—especially red and purple ones—never appear as vibrant and lustrous in natural light as they do under these grow lights. I remember the first time my red *Dendrobium cuthbertsonii* came into flower under these lights —it looked like sumptuous red velvet fit for a queen's robe! Of course, as soon as you take the plant into natural light, the color returns to its less penetrating but still beautiful normal hue. These spectrum-optimized bulbs, which are of higher quality than many fluorescents, undoubtedly provide some growth enhancement along with color enhancement, so they are worth the extra cost.

Because of the push to save energy as well as reduce manufacturing costs, it has become difficult to find true 40-watt,

4-foot warm or cool white fluorescent tubes unless you go to a wholesale supplier or specialty store. Tubes available at the home center are often 34 watts (about 15% less light than a 40-watt tube) or even 25 watts (37% less light). Also, although cheap fluorescent tubes have changed little in price since the early 1980s, their quality has declined. You can expect these inexpensive bulbs to last about one year, though there is a significant decline in output after six months. Accordingly, many serious under-lights growers buy the more expensive bulbs, such as Grolux, that attempt to match the spectrum of sunlight. A 40-watt Grolux or similar bulb costs about three times as much as a cheap cool white tube ($10 to $12 versus $3 to $4), but it will last twice as long and put out as much as 45% more usable light. Philips sells the Ultralume bulb (F40/50U is the 4-foot, 40-watt model), which produces light close to sunlight, and though it costs $16—about 50% more than a standard grow light—it emits about twice the usable light, so you can get away with half the fixtures and save quite a bit in electricity costs.

High-Intensity-Discharge (HID) Fixtures

Thanks mostly to the burgeoning indoor marijuana-growing market, reasonably priced prewired and preassembled HID fixtures have become much more easily available to home orchid growers. Despite several reports years ago of Drug Enforcement Agency personnel showing up at an orchid grower's door and asking about that glow coming from the cellar, these extremely bright fixtures have been embraced by many people growing legal plants, such as orchids, cacti, and bromeliads. HID fixtures have been used for years to light streets and factories and as supplemental lighting in production greenhouses, but those are big, unwieldy things that have to be wired professionally and are really cumbersome to use for orchid-growing. The newer consumer-friendly models (available from mail-order suppliers, which advertise through the American Orchid Society and in many horticultural magazines) are more compact, fitted with proper reflectors, and ready to plug in and use.

I was a bit intimidated by HIDs at first, because of my experience with the big greenhouse fixtures, but I took the plunge after my collection grew beyond my two fluorescent setups and I got tired of the cramped headroom. I have been very pleased with the result. Their big advantage is that the light is much stronger and is still very bright even 4 feet from the bulb, so you can work among your plants as you would in a greenhouse. The lights are efficient, too, though they do use more electricity than a four-tube 4-foot fluorescent rig. However, because their light is stronger, you can grow many more plants under HIDs than you can with the equivalent number of fluorescents. HIDs are point-source fixtures like standard light bulbs, so they are smaller and simpler to hang. You still have to change the bulb once a year, despite what the manufacturers tell you, but doing it is as fast as screwing in a light bulb (wear gloves to avoid getting skin oils on the bulb). The cost of one bulb is about the same as or a bit more than that of the equivalent bundle of fluorescent tubes. Their disadvantages are that the fixtures initially cost about three times more than fluorescents, and they give off such a bright light that they really need a room of their own. It's hard to coexist with an HID without feeling like you're part of some light-therapy experiment. Many people wear sunglasses or at least a brimmed hat when working under the lights, and you shouldn't look directly at a lit bulb. I do think all that light helps cure my winter blues, though.

HID lamps look like giant incandescent light bulbs. The three types (each of which needs specific ballasts and sockets, so make sure you buy the appropriate one) are mercury vapor, sodium, and metal halide. Mercury-vapor lamps, used most commonly for street lighting, produce the familiar silvery blue color that brightens the suburban night. Their light is unsuitable for plants. Low-pressure sodium lamps, also used for night lighting, emit a pink-orange light. These are also unsuitable for plants, but high-pressure sodium (HPS) lamps, with their white-orange light, are excellent. The other type used in horticulture is metal halide (MH), which gives off a bluish white light. HPS and MH lamps are equivalent to warm and cool fluorescents; the first is richer in red, the second in blue. In practice, it is rather difficult to combine the two, as the fixtures must be mounted some distance apart and thus their light doesn't overlap. You can buy a rotating arm that moves the two lamps around slowly to disperse the blue and red light more evenly, but that requires considerably more capital outlay. When I purchased my HIDs, I opted for metal halide because it has a more balanced spectrum overall and the bluish light is easier on the eyes than the orange-pink of the sodium (MH lamps do appear to wash out all the reds and yellows in flowers). If you have an HPS fixture, for about 25% more you can buy special bulbs with enhanced blue that are designed for plants.

Both HPS and MH fixtures are available in 250-, 400-, and 1,000-watt sizes. The 250-watt units usually have the ballast housed next to the reflector and bulb, but the more powerful models made for home use usually have remote ballasts that can sit on the floor; they are too heavy to hang from a ceiling hook. The ballasts generate quite a bit of heat, so it's a good idea to keep them out of the way. I started with the 250-watt size, which was enough to illuminate a 3 × 4 × 4-foot case with plants hung on the sides and back as well as on "egg crate" (the gridded plastic stuff sold to cover recessed fluorescent fixtures) at the bottom. With the added wall space made possible by the greater headroom, I have about 50 square feet of grow-

Long-blooming **Dendrobium petiolatum** relishes the bright light and cool temperatures of my basement HID cabinets. The flowers of this showy Papua New Guinean species last for months.

ing area per case contrasted with at best 15 square feet with the six-tube, 240-watt fluorescent setup I had before. When I moved again, I bought a 400-watt MH fixture and decided to make a grow room in a corner of the cellar. With a 6 × 6-foot tabletop plus 100 square feet of wall space, I gained about two and a half times the space of one 250-watt fixture. (I have to admit that writing about my progression from windowsill to fluorescents to a brightly lit grow room makes the whole orchid-growing thing seem a bit obsessive, but I assure you, each step seemed logical at the time—manifest destiny for the orchid grower. At least I know I'm writing to a sympathetic audience.) I never did make the jump to 1,000 watts; I was under one once and felt as if I were staring into the white-hot core of the sun.

Another new product is the Envirolite (www.fearlessgardener.com), which is made to replace an HID fixture. It is a mega version of the U-shaped, screw-in fluorescent with built-in ballast that is used as a replacement for an incandescent bulb. The Envirolite has a 125-watt bulb that can fit into an HID-type reflector (you will need a special socket, though), and it generates about 12,600 lumens (one-third the light of a 400-watt MH bulb). They cost about $75 each, which includes the ballast but not the reflector (about $25). The advantage of the Envirolite is much lower heat output and the more even spread of light in the growing area (using multiple bulbs). They are a bit cheaper in the short term than the equivalent in HID fixtures, but more expensive in the long term because replacement bulb prices are higher.

SAFETY

Obviously, mixing water and electricity is a dangerous business. Make sure that all your light fixtures are properly grounded. If your house has two-prong rather than three-prong grounded plugs, ground your unit either to the center screw on the wall-socket cover plate or, in a cellar, to a copper water pipe. I always replace the outlets in my growing area with ground-fault circuit-interrupter (GFCI) outlets (the ones you find in bathrooms with the little test and reset buttons). They are designed to trip when they detect a short circuit, saving you from a nasty shock should you drop your hair dryer into the tub or douse your portable heater with the hose. If you are at all unsure about wiring, have a licensed electrician hook these up for you. One GFCI will protect all the outlets run on the same circuit beyond it, so you can have one put in at the circuit breaker box to protect the whole circuit.

You don't want to splash water on a fluorescent bulb, but you definitely don't want to get water anywhere *near* an HID lamp. The cold water hitting the hot lamp will cause it to explode, sending hot bits of glass and metal everywhere. I strongly recommend spending the extra money on a tempered-glass reflector cover when you buy an HID lamp. This will both shield the bulb from water and contain it if it does break. Even with fluorescents, I like to hang a sheet of acrylic (Plexiglas)—which you can get at any home store—between the bulbs and the plants. I mist the plants liberally, and the shield prevents the fixture from getting wet. Remember to clean the acrylic regularly (and the bulbs, for that matter), because the residues and dust that build up really lower light transmission.

I use the inexpensive in-line lamp timers that turn lights on and off automatically when you're not home. Buy the three-prong, slightly heavier-duty timers. These are rated for the number of watts and amps they can handle; it's important not to overload them. I use one timer for each HID fixture or bank of up to eight 40-watt fluorescents, and this is fairly conservative. If you have a great many lights and too many timers, have your electrician hard-wire a real heavy-duty timer into a circuit or part of a circuit to turn on and off everything plugged in after it. That is how I have wired the HID lights in the greenhouse.

ENCLOSED LIGHT CHAMBERS AND GROW ROOMS

Growing orchids under lights allows you to control more than the light itself, because your plants can be easily enclosed with plastic, acrylic, wood, metal, or glass to create a miniature greenhouse in which humidity, temperature, and air movement can be significantly increased. You can certainly grow orchids under lights in an area open to the room at large, but taking the extra step of enclosing it will allow you to grow many species and hybrids that are unsuitable for windowsills. Even plants that do well on a windowsill will do spectacularly in an enclosed environment. I admit that from the outside, a growing chamber or room doesn't look like much, and it isolates the plants from view, but when you look inside, it's like seeing a little **cloud forest**, complete with mosses, gentle breezes, and pleasantly humid air (I have even known spring peeper frogs to take up residence in such an enclosure). It is a pleasure to sit next to one on a dry, cold winter day.

There are many ways to enclose your plants, keeping in mind the main purpose, which is to let light into the space while containing water, both to keep the air inside humid and to keep the fixtures as well as the floor dry. I'll describe what I have done and leave the rest to your ingenuity.

My first growing chamber was simply a $2^1/_2 \times 4^1/_2 \times 1$-foot box made from pressure-treated 2×4s, which stood on legs at table height in a corner of our spare room. Three 4-foot fluorescent shop lights hung from beams across the top of the box, separated from the plants by a sheet of Plexiglas. Because acrylic is expensive and I was in school at the time, I used pieces of $^1/_8$-inch-thick paneling to form the sides of the box, then wrapped the sides and bottom in clear 6-mil polyethylene plastic sheeting that was stapled to the frame. I painted the

Though it casts a yellowish light, a 400-watt high-pressure sodium fixture is intense enough for most orchids that demand bright light. Plants that need the brightest light are hung near the bulb, and less demanding specimens inhabit the benches below.

inside with flat white exterior paint for reflectivity (white is almost as reflective as foil, and it's a lot easier on the eyes). The plants rested on egg crate, which is better than galvanized hardware cloth in that it is reasonably rigid and needs less support underneath to keep it from sagging. The lights hung about 12 inches above the egg crate, and hardware cloth was attached to the back and sides of the box for hanging some mounted plants. To gain access to the box, I set two sheets of acrylic into an aluminum track across the front to create sliding cabinet doors. The double-thickness plastic sheeting slung across the bottom caught and held irrigation water in a reservoir, which overflowed into a bucket. I set two 3½-inch "pancake" fans (the square fans sold at electronic stores for cooling equipment) in the front corners below the egg crate and slanted them down to blow across the water reservoir. This provided all the moisture necessary to keep the interior above 70% relative humidity. I did add one more fan in the back corner when the case became full, to maintain good air movement. The whole contraption was certainly a function-before-form solution, but with that basic idea you can create something much more stylish, such as an elegant **Wardian case**, which is like a piece of fine furniture.

HID fixtures can be mounted above such a chamber, and the stronger light allows greater headroom. For my 250-watt metal halides, I constructed a frame out of ¾-inch galvanized electrical conduit called EMT, which is available everywhere. It's very cheap, strong, lightweight, and rust-resistant. With an inexpensive C-clamp-style pipe cutter and a drill to make the holes for bolts, you can build a 3 × 4 × 4½-foot box in an afternoon. I have installed these structures in a high-ceilinged basement, a cramped eighteenth-century farmhouse cellar, and even the deepest part of a crawlspace. Cut the posts and crosspieces, then cut a diagonal support for each side and the back; the diagonals, run from corner to corner, give the structure rigidity. I found that pounding the ends of the tubing flat with a 3-pound sledgehammer makes putting the parts together much easier. After attaching hardware cloth to the back and sides, wrap all but the top in white (or clear) 6-mil polyethylene and secure it to the frame with clamps made from an old garden hose cut to the right lengths and slit along one side. A sheet of acrylic across the top, another that swings down on hinges to make the front, and egg crate for the bottom complete the box. A box this size needs four pancake fans hung in various places to keep the air moving. You can adjust them over time to eliminate dead spots. About once a year it's necessary to take the plants out and scrub down the chamber with disinfectant to control the algae that luxuriate in all that humidity.

When I bought my 400-watt HID fixture, I made an 8 × 8-foot, plastic-enclosed room in my cellar by simply building a frame of 2 × 4s nailed to the joists above and a sill of 2 × 4s on the floor. I stapled plastic sheeting to the frame and the ceiling, overlapping the two ends of the sheeting but leaving them unfastened to make a curtain door. I made benches from wood and hardware cloth, and along the sides, hung from the ceiling, I placed EMT frames covered in hardware cloth. The light fixture was inside this grow room, so I installed a protective glass cover and was extra careful to keep water away from the bulb. A console humidifier and an oscillating pedestal fan set on high provided humidity and air movement. Rolling the edges of the plastic before stapling kept the moisture pretty well sealed in, and I didn't find dampness developing on the floor joists above the room. The concrete floor underneath the plants did need an occasional scrubbing to remove algae. I constructed rooms like this in two different houses. The first had a sump drain nearby to catch irrigation water; in the second, I had to be more careful with watering to prevent a flood. Many cellars have a threaded faucet (for a washing machine or the drain for a well-pressure tank) to which you can attach a garden hose for watering. When you are used to the slow trickle of water from a can or sink, using a garden hose feels liberating, but it's easy to overdo it and flood the basement. When water control is an issue, I find that a 1½- to 3-gallon pump sprayer sold for pesticide application makes a dandy watering device, and if you use rain water or reverse-osmosis (RO) water, it provides an easy way to deliver it to the plants. You can also add dilute fertilizer to the tank as needed.

In the Greenhouse

Unless you live in a tropical climate, a greenhouse is the ultimate home for orchids and, just as important, for the orchid grower. While a good artificial light setup can provide everything the plants need, nothing beats spending a sunny winter day in a warm glass room filled with the colors and sweet, musky fragrance of orchids in bloom. Not surprisingly, most serious orchid growers dream of building a greenhouse for their plants, and for good reason. Orchids can be grown satisfactorily on a windowsill and very well under lights, but in a well-designed, well-maintained greenhouse they positively thrive. If you are thinking of taking the plunge, though, weigh the decision carefully. Tending a greenhouse full of orchids is like raising a child in that it requires constant supervision and years of daily commitment. One heatless night in winter can destroy your entire collection, as can one unvented summer day. When the temperature plummets or a windstorm comes up, prepare to spend some sleepless nights listening for the startling beep of the temperature alarm or the splintering crash of a tree limb hitting glass. Plants in a greenhouse need daily watering or at least checking, and as the collection will surely enlarge to fill the space, it will require more yearly maintenance as well. Going on vacation (or even a weekend getaway) means that you have to hire a plant-sitter to water and be on call should there be a temperature emergency. If your enthusiasm is not the least bit dampened after reading these caveats, I understand. I have managed six different greenhouses professionally, and I know how much of a pain in the neck they can be, yet I still plan to build my own as soon as I possibly can!

This book is not the place for an in-depth tutorial on greenhouse design and construction, but I will provide a brief overview of the various options available to you. Once you decide on one, the manufacturer and distributor can help you design, build, and outfit the structure to your specifications. Your local agricultural extension service is a good source of information, as are hobby greenhouse associations.

In essence, a greenhouse is any structure with a translucent or transparent roof designed primarily for growing plants under controlled conditions. (A sunroom, designed primarily for human comfort, is more like a brightly lit interior room than like a greenhouse and can be a great place for orchids that do not require high humidity.) A true greenhouse can be as simple as a sheet of clear plastic stretched over a frame or as elaborate as a Victorian glasshouse, complete with domes and minarets, or even a "phytotron," in which the environment is controlled precisely with computers. For orchid hobbyists, the reality is likely to fall somewhere in the middle.

Although you can build a greenhouse from pressure-treated or rot-resistant wood, I personally think this is a bad idea in the long run. A wood-frame greenhouse, though inexpensive and fine as a temporary structure, is just not durable enough to withstand constant moisture without careful maintenance. Also, in order to withstand snow and wind loads, it must be overengineered, with a big, heavy, light-blocking roof, which seems overpowering to me. I would suggest a tube-steel or truss-steel and/or aluminum-alloy frame instead.

Quonset-style greenhouses made of tubular steel have been the standard commercial structure of choice for the past thirty years. Compared to truss frames, they are cheap to buy and set up. They require minimal footings and no foundation, so many towns treat them as temporary structures for tax purposes. You can choose various widths, but I recommend a building at least 25 to 30 feet wide. A narrower house has too low a peak and knee walls—meaning no headroom. If you have good technical skills, you and a few assistants can set one up easily enough in a week or two, because they are quite forgiving. Many companies will set up the structure for you at an additional cost. Tubular steel greenhouses came into their own with the invention of inexpensive corrugated fiberglass and polyethylene plastic sheeting. Louvered glass, once the only option for covering greenhouses, is completely impracti-

The tables in the cool greenhouse at J & L Orchids overflow with plants. *Draculas* hang in baskets above the tables, and mounted plants are hung on wire mesh on the exterior walls. Fans draw air through cooling pads set into an end wall to chill and humidify it.

cal for a curved Quonset-style frame, but plastic sheets are easily slung over the smooth, arching ribs. I'll be the first to admit that a plastic-covered tube-steel greenhouse has about as much architectural appeal as a metal storage shed, but if low cost, not aesthetics, is your primary concern, this is the best option.

In the past, one of the problems with standard plastic-skinned Quonsets was their lack of roof vents and thus the need for large fans, which were usually mounted on the gable ends. But depending on fans can be disastrous if the power fails on a hot day and you don't have a backup generator. However, the newer tube-steel greenhouses have optional ridge vents at the peak that alleviate heat buildup, and I strongly recommend spending the extra money for one with a manual override. Attaching the plastic around a ridge vent is a bit more difficult, but it's still straightforward. You can cut down on heat loss by 30% if you use double poly (see p. 21). You can also cover tube-steel frames with pricier polycarbonate or acrylic panels, which look a bit nicer than poly sheeting, and you don't have to replace them nearly as often (every ten to fifteen years as opposed to every two to four). Be sure to purchase a frame engineered for the snow and wind loads in your area. Gothic-arch ribs are stronger than half rounds, and I think they look better, too.

A tube-steel greenhouse with fans, benches, wiring, grading, heaters, and so on, will cost about $10–$17 per square foot (the high end if you use polycarbonate glazing). The cost of heating and cooling a greenhouse varies tremendously according to your climate and the cost of electricity and fuel. However, you should budget $1–$4 per square foot for annual utility costs. I discuss heating, cooling, and humidification systems for greenhouses separately in the following chapters.

Steel-truss greenhouses were originally designed to support louvered-glass roofs. In fact, the form of the classic glasshouse was largely dictated by the limitations of the small glass planes available in Victorian times. Though glass is still best for light transmission, few people today build a greenhouse with traditional overlapping single-glass panes. The costs of heating such a poorly insulated structure are astronomical unless you live in a very mild climate. However, modern energy-efficient glazing, using polycarbonate, insulated glass, or acrylic, can be fitted to a traditional peaked-roof structure made of steel or, more commonly, aluminum. These greenhouses need a poured concrete foundation or at least footings, and their overall cost will be about twice that of a tube-steel structure (roughly $15–$30 dollars per square foot). But their attractiveness may make it easier to get approval from the planning and zoning boards. Many manufacturers sell both complete kits and custom frames. Be wary of bargain structures, which are designed more for starting vegetable seedlings than for permanently housing orchids.

And be sure to ask about shipping and setup charges when soliciting bids.

A greenhouse can be built onto an existing structure or erected as a free-standing unit. You can attach one at the gable end of your house or garage so it juts out like an addition, or you can attach it to the long wall as a lean-to greenhouse, which is basically half a greenhouse cleaved along the peak. It is usually easier to get water and electricity to an attached greenhouse, and if your household furnace is large enough, you can heat the greenhouse from it by having a plumber install a separate zone. Access to the greenhouse is also easier —a plus on rainy or cold days. On the downside, water and humidity can endanger the rest of the house if the greenhouse is not carefully isolated with vapor barriers. An attached greenhouse will block views, and maintenance of both parts may be more difficult. A free-standing greenhouse lets in more light and won't create problems in your house or garage, but

Even a spacious greenhouse, like this one at Mountain Orchids, will fill up with plants eventually. Here are stock plants used in breeding work as well as specimens grown for exhibit. Watering so many plants is tricky, but the impression is one of junglelike exuberance.

because it's exposed on all sides, it's more costly to heat and cool and even—to some extent—to build.

Another possibility, especially if you are planning to pour a foundation, is to build a pit greenhouse, which is simply a greenhouse roof erected on a cellarlike foundation. Because the floor is belowground, a pit is far better insulated than a typical greenhouse. The earth keeps the temperature more stable, meaning warmer in winter and cooler in summer. We have a small pit greenhouse at the New England Wild Flower Society, and even though it is not heated, it rarely freezes in winter. Heating costs being as high as they are, the extra cost of concrete and excavation will pay for itself quickly. The disadvantages of a pit are that it gets less light—ours has a higher north and a lower south wall to partially offset this problem—and has more likelihood of flooding and excessive humidity.

No matter what type of greenhouse you construct, I recommend putting in a 1-foot layer of coarse gravel for the floor instead of poured concrete. Gravel allows water to evaporate from the ground underneath, which helps keep the humidity high enough without using misting equipment—at least when the vents are closed. It is not easy to keep gravel clean, though, so consider adding some flagstone walkways.

Greenhouse Size

The size of your greenhouse is important in terms of both cost and space. If you have been growing orchids indoors, even a small greenhouse will seem incredibly spacious at first, but as your collection expands, space will become tight. It is possible to add another bay or two to a greenhouse—especially a tube-steel type—as long as your heating and cooling system is large enough for the final structure. It's a good idea to buy one with excess capacity at the outset, then heat only as much space as you need. It should be noted, though, that the smaller the greenhouse, the more difficult it is to achieve a stable atmosphere. Smaller spaces heat up and cool down faster, and humidity is quickly lost when the vents are open. I have seen orchids growing well in a 6 × 10-foot homemade greenhouse with a 7-foot peak in which I felt cramped, but I recommend starting with at least a 10 × 16-foot structure, though 15 × 30 or even 20 × 48 will give your collection much more room to expand. The wider the greenhouse, the higher the peak, so while a 10 × 16-foot structure may have an 8-foot peak, a 25 × 48 might be 13 feet at the peak. This extra headroom will mean a more stable atmosphere and a wonderful feeling of space inside. It also means higher sides, so you won't bump your head when watering along the knee wall. A 25 × 48-foot greenhouse with 1,200 square feet of usable floor space is probably sufficient for even the most ardent collector or small orchid business. You can fit a lot of plants in that area, more than one person can easily keep up with, in fact. You can

always close off part of a larger greenhouse with sheets of plastic at first so you don't have to heat the entire structure.

Greenhouse Glazing

As I have briefly mentioned, clear polyethylene sheeting is the least expensive covering in the short term. Greenhouse suppliers sell it in a variety of lengths and widths, and greenhouse-grade poly has ultraviolet (UV) inhibitors so that it will last several seasons. You will have to replace it every two to four years, but if money is tight initially, you can use it until you can afford a more expensive option. A four-season greenhouse should be covered in double poly—two sheets that are sealed along the edges and the space between them inflated with a small blower fan. The air space affords surprisingly good insulation—roughly equal to that of two panes of glass. A double layer of poly (with a 6-mil sheet outside and a 4-mil sheet inside) costs about 20 cents per square foot. If you are considering using polyethylene, be sure to buy a frame that will accept it. Many aluminum or steel-truss structures are difficult to cover with it.

Polycarbonate (Lexan) and acrylic are ten times as expensive as polyethylene, but these materials are available in flexible panels that can be fitted to nearly any structure. They are usually guaranteed for ten years, but the two-layer polycarbonate on our greenhouse is seventeen years old and still in great shape. Although not shatterproof, it is much less likely to fail than polyethylene. You can get both polycarbonate and acrylic in single-, double-, or triple-layer sheets. The triple-wall type has a much higher insulation value than the other types and is really the only good choice if you live in a cold winter climate. The main drawback to these materials compared to glass is their opacity. While you can get single-wall corrugated sheets that are almost transparent, the double-wall panels are about as opaque as glass bricks, so you can't really see out or look in through them. Manufacturers are making improvements, however, and nearly transparent triple-wall polycarbonate will be available before long. Though polycarbonate is more expensive than polyethylene, its long-term benefits in lower maintenance costs and heat savings certainly outweigh the initial cost.

Corrugated fiberglass panels were an early substitute for glass, and they are as strong and long-lived as polycarbonate, but even the newer fiberglass resins turn yellow and lose transparency with age. Old yellow fiberglass looks like moldy toenails—not a pretty sight!

Glass is a popular choice, though pricey. Even with all the synthetic products currently available, nothing is as transparent or long-lived as tempered glass. You can get it in wider panes than the Victorians could, and a roof of wide glass panes and aluminum trusses barely looks like a roof at all. Glass is heavy, so beyond the cost of the glazing itself is the higher cost of the structure needed to support it. Double-pane (float) glass costs about ten to fifteen times more than double polyethylene. Large-panel tempered double glass is the most expensive, at up to forty times the cost of polyethylene.

When you order your greenhouse, be sure to purchase shade cloth, which will be fitted to your structure and thus will take a few weeks to arrive. The standard shade cloth for orchids allows in 60%–70% of the natural light. The black or green cloth (really an indestructible woven plastic fabric) is attached on the outside, while heat-reflective aluminized fabric can be used on the inside or outside.

The Great Outdoors
PUTTING ORCHIDS OUTDOORS FOR THE SUMMER

Orchids relish being outdoors, even for an occasional bath on a rainy day. The fresh air, light, and evening dew will revive plants that are forlorn after a long winter indoors. Even if you have just a few plants on a windowsill, putting them outdoors for two or three months—after nighttime temperatures are above 55°F—is probably the best thing you can do for them, except in areas like the desert Southwest, where the summertime relative humidity is too low. That time outdoors can make the difference between plants that just survive and plants that thrive indoors for the rest of the year. The extra photosynthesis allows them to build reserves for later bloom, and summer showers help leach away salts that build up around the roots. The UV wavelengths in natural unfiltered sunlight can even kill bacteria and fungi that plague the plants. I strongly encourage everyone—but especially windowsill growers—to put their plants outdoors for the summer.

The transitions between indoors and outdoors can be traumatic for the plants if not handled carefully. Remember that leaves formed in dim light will not be able to withstand a sudden blast of strong light. Conversely, leaves used to the bright light outside will be inefficient at photosynthesis when brought in to a dim window. Try to situate your plants so that the light intensity is similar to what they are accustomed to. Even if the light intensity is the same, the light will last longer outdoors in a spot open to the sky than in a window. Dappled shade under tall trees, where sunlight and shadow flicker across the ground, is a good place for most orchids, and it simulates the conditions they would experience in nature. Monitor the spot on the first sunny day to make sure no plants are in a canopy gap, where the light streams through unimpeded for more than ten minutes, at least from midmorning to midafternoon.

If your yard has no suitable natural shade, you can erect an inexpensive lath house for your plants. A lath house is an open structure with a flat roof made from strips of wood spaced to allow some sunlight to get through. The laths are typically 1½ inches wide and made from a rot-resistant wood like cedar, cypress, or pressure-treated pine. If you make the gaps between each strip as wide as the lath, you will block 50% of full sunlight. If you make the gaps three-quarters the width of the strips, you block 75%, which is about right for most orchids. A lath house made from 1-inch lath with ¾-inch gaps will work well. Many narrow strips are better than fewer wide ones, as the sunlight will be more evenly distributed. If you live in a nearly frost-free climate, a lath house that can be quickly covered with a tarp during cold snaps may be all the greenhouse you need.

One of the nice things about summering your plants outdoors is ease of watering. The natural rainfall in most of Canada, the United States, and Europe is not usually enough to completely satisfy your plants' watering needs, but it is easy to run the hose over them outdoors. Once, when I was headed off to Bolivia for a few weeks in summer, I bought an inexpensive irrigation timer at the home center and hooked it to an oscillating sprinkler, which rained water down on the plants for a few minutes each morning and again for half an hour every third day. I have seen lath houses equipped with mist nozzles that can be run automatically or manually to water and refresh the plants on dry or hot days.

OUTDOORS IN THE TROPICS

No part of the continental United States, Canada, or Europe is technically tropical. The tropics are truly frost-free (except at high elevations), and temperatures remain fairly constant year-round, dipping down into the high 40s or low 50s only occasionally. Extreme southern Florida and parts of coastal California are subtropical (nearly tropical); and Hawaii, the Caribbean, and Mexico escape the threat of cold weather completely. Orchidists in South Florida have to deal with frost perhaps once every five years; they can attach plants to trees and protect them with blankets or tarps during freeze warnings.

In some ways, you have to be even more selective about orchids that live outdoors year-round than you do for indoor or greenhouse culture. You have less control over temperature and humidity, so choose plants wisely. You will probably have to fertilize and repot more often than you would farther north, but there is no doubt that tropical orchids really look their best in a climate that comes close to tropical. Not surprisingly, most orchid nurseries are located in the subtropics and tropics. Many people build inexpensive lath houses for larger collections raised in pots or baskets.

For the rest of us, though, it is more practical to put the plants outdoors after all danger of frost has passed and lug them indoors again in autumn when temperatures regularly dip below 50°F at night.

CHAPTER 3

Light

THE FUNDAMENTAL MIRACLE of life—the process that makes it all possible—is photosynthesis, that ability of plants to transform the energy in sunlight into stored chemical energy. Aside from a few bacteria and the deep sea organisms around volcanic vents, all living things on earth depend directly or indirectly on this basic process. Plants photosynthesize by collecting sunlight and channeling it to chloroplasts in leaves and stems —and even roots in the case of many orchids. Through a series of chemical reactions, water molecules are split into oxygen and hydrogen, and the hydrogen combines with carbon obtained from CO_2 to form sugar and, from that, everything else the plant needs. Chlorophyll molecules and photosynthetic enzymes within the chloroplasts operate most efficiently at certain temperatures and light intensities, using mostly the red and blue parts of the visible spectrum.

When temperatures and light levels are too low, photosynthesis never really gets going, and when temperatures are too high and light too strong, the reactions speed up so much that

ABOVE: *Phragmipedium besseae* '**Don't Know**'.
It takes a tremendous amount of energy to produce the dazzling flowers of this South American slipper orchid.

the molecules and even the cells themselves are at risk of destruction. Plants that evolve in a particular average temperature range develop enzyme systems that work most effectively at those temperatures. This is the main reason for providing the proper temperature range for the plants you grow.

Orchid species that have evolved in high light have also developed ways to shield their chloroplasts from the worst of the sun's radiation by burying them deep in the spongy tissues of the leaves, by surrounding them with red or yellow pigments that act almost like sunglasses, and by orienting leaf surfaces so that sunlight enters at an angle, not full on. As individual leaves mature on a plant, they adapt to the light levels they experience. Once a leaf is mature, it cannot adjust easily to a big change in light intensity or orientation. In the wild, tropical orchids don't experience much change in light conditions from month to month, unless they are growing on deciduous trees that go dormant during the dry season. The sun's position and intensity, as well as day length, are fairly constant through the year near the equator, with changes mainly from the incidence of cloud cover during rainy and dry seasons. Thus not only does the successful plant germinate and establish itself in a spot that receives adequate light and proper temperatures, its individual leaves develop to be maximally efficient in their place on the plant or in the clump.

In temperate regions away from the equator, the position and intensity of light increase and decrease dramatically over the course of the year, and it is difficult for mature leaves to adapt to the changes completely. However, while mature orchid leaves cannot grow thicker or change their orientation, they can infuse themselves with more masking pigments as the light gets more intense or more chlorophyll as it dims—as long as the change is gradual. Unless you are growing orchids under artificial lights, you can never achieve the constancy they experience in the tropics. Luckily, though, they are an adaptable group, and as long as change is gradual and kept within certain limits, the orchids will thrive.

Light is as quantifiable as water or heat. The traditional way to measure it has been the **footcandle** (fc), defined as the amount of light one candle casts 1 foot away. It's sort of a quaint measurement, like horsepower or knots, that harks back to a simpler age, and like those units, the footcandle is still widely used. The other unit you need to know is the **lumen**, which is the light of 1 footcandle spread over 1 square foot. A standard 75-watt light bulb produces about 1,100 lumens, so if you concentrated all that light on 1 square foot of tabletop, it would receive 1,100 fc. If you put this same bulb in a reflector and illuminate a 10 × 10-foot area—100 square feet—each square foot would be receiving only 11 fc. That amount of light is plenty for us to see by but far too little for even the most shade-tolerant orchid to survive under.

Highly shade-tolerant orchids—those with big, flat, deep green leaves designed for maximal light capture, like *Phalaenopsis*, will do well if they receive about 1,000 footcandles on average for eight hours or so. *Cattleyas* and the majority of epiphytic orchids require 2,000 to 4,000 fc. That's about 20% of the intensity of tropical sunlight, just about as much as would filter down through the upper tree canopy. True light-loving species such as *Broughtonia* and some *Vandas* require as much as 7,000 fc to bloom properly. It's important to understand that while the plants may grow decently under suboptimal light, they will rarely bloom well. Blooming requires a large expenditure of energy, and perennial plants will bloom only if they have been able to stock up enough energy to "spend" on flowering. Too little light is the primary reason that otherwise healthy orchids don't bloom.

You can easily measure the amount of available light in any situation if you have or can borrow a decent 35 mm camera that lets you set the film speed, shutter speed, and f-stop manually. Set the film speed (ASA) to 200 and the shutter speed to $^1/_{125}$ second. Now set a piece of white paper down where you would put the plants and aim the camera at it perpendicularly, then focus and adjust so that all you see in the viewfinder is white paper. If the light meter recommends setting the f-stop to 2.8, then you're getting a measly 32 fc; 4 = 64 fc; 5.6 = 125 fc; 8 = 250 fc; 11 = 500 fc; 16 = 1,000 fc; 22 = 2,000 fc; 32 (if your lens stops down that much) = 4,000 fc. Take readings several times during a sunny day and repeat it several times over the course of the year to see how the light changes. Nowadays I don't run around with a light meter, taking readings all the time, but this method did help me get a frame of reference for how bright 1,000 or 2,000 fc really is.

As an example, below I give some light meter readings taken around noon on a cloudless day in late April in Massachusetts. In order to get the higher readings, I set my camera's ASA to 50, which means I could quadruple the fc number for a particular f-stop. That is, at ASA 50, with the shutter speed set to $^1/_{125}$ second, if the camera recommends an f-stop of 32, this translates into roughly 12,000 fc. Using the lower ASA setting is also handy if your lens goes only to f 8 or f 16.

Outside in full sun: 12,000 fc
Inside greenhouse with double-wall polycarbonate:
    6,000 fc
Inside greenhouse covered with 60% shade cloth: 3,000 fc
Through a south-facing double-pane window: 2,000 fc
    (lens aimed skyward)

As I mentioned, for optimum performance a *Phalaenopsis* requires about 1,000 fc for eight hours or so. My guess is that especially in winter, few places in your house get that kind of light naturally for eight hours (in Massachusetts in December it's hardly even light for eight hours!). Fortunately, several things are operating in your favor. First, plants can store some

The short, cool days of winter are necessary to "ripen" the flower buds of spectacular *Coelogyne multiflora* **'Sunalda'** CBR/AOS, which appear along with the new leaves as the days lengthen in spring.

brown, especially where it receives the maximum amount of light, such as the topmost part of a curved leaf, the tip of a vertical one, or the exposed side of a pseudobulb or stem, it might need more shade. If the leaves are firm and thick and you see some red or purple pigment developing in the most exposed areas, but overall the color is a grassy green, and especially if the plants grow and bloom well, then they are getting the right amount of light.

Since light intensity changes so much from winter to summer, if your orchids are in a very sunny south-facing window, sunroom, or greenhouse, you should shade the glass from about March or April until October. Again, you want to apply just enough shading to reduce light levels to the range your orchids can tolerate. A sheer curtain indoors or a 50%–70% shade cloth on or in the greenhouse will do the trick. In the greenhouse, a cloth or curtain that can be opened by hand or automatically on a cloudy day is ideal. (The drawback to automatic shade curtains, as I mention in the section on greenhouse cooling [page 30], is that because they are usually inside the glazing, they let more heat build up inside than shade cloth draped over the exterior or whitewash applied to the glazing.)

Day Length or Photoperiod

Plants have different ways of "telling time" in order to coordinate their growth, flowering, and dormancy with the natural rhythms of the climate. Few places on earth—even in the tropics—have such a steady and predictable climate that plants can grow and bloom at any time of the year. They have to deal with cold or cool weather, seasonal drought, heat, and monsoons. Everywhere except directly on the equator, day length changes through the year with great regularity, unlike patterns of temperature and precipitation. Therefore, it is not surprising that plants have seized on day length—or, in horticultural terms, the photoperiod—to help them tell time. Here in Massachusetts, at a latitude of 42° N, the photoperiod at the winter solstice on December 21, the shortest day of the year, is just over 9 hours, and on June 21, the longest, it's a whopping 15½ hours. Away from the equator, most plants time their growth and flowering at least in part by this seasonal clock, with summer-blooming species termed long-day plants, and spring- or fall-blooming species called short-day plants. Temperature patterns and rainfall interact with day length, *but if you keep a long-day plant growing under short-day*

of the energy they make to use on a rainy (or winter) day. If your plants have been happily photosynthesizing all spring, summer, and fall, they can spend some of their energy stores to get through the winter or even to bloom then. Since footcandles received convert directly into energy stored, if your plants receive an hour at 2,000 fc, two at 1,500, and five at 600, this still averages to 1,000 fc over eight hours. If you grow under lights, you can get away with 500 fc over sixteen hours, which is one of the reasons we leave the lights on so long.

If all this calculating and fussing over light levels is turning you off, don't worry. Once you get to know your plants, you can tell just by how they look and bloom whether the light is right or not. If your plants are healthy and well watered and fed, but the leaves are thin, floppy, and dark green, try putting them in a brighter spot, especially if they are not flowering. Remember, too little light is the number one cause of failure to bloom. On the other hand, if a plant is turning yellow or

Cymbidium **'Sussex Down'** blooms with abandon during the dark days of winter.

light conditions, it is unlikely to flower, regardless of variations in temperature and moisture. The same can be said for short-day plants growing under consistently long days; a poinsettia kept in the living room will not rebloom because the lights you leave on at night fool it into thinking it is still summer.

In Quito, Ecuador, which sits a stone's throw south of the equator, the photoperiod varies by only 3 minutes over the course of the year, from 12 hr 6 min at the winter solstice to 12 hr 9 min at the summer solstice. Even plants cannot read that small a change, so as you might expect, Ecuadorian orchids time growth and flowering more by seasonal variation in rainfall, humidity, and associated temperature fluctuations than by day length. In Port Moresby, Papua New Guinea, which sits at about 10° S latitude, days range from 11 hr 31 min to 12 hr 44 min, a change of 1 hr 15 min—certainly not much, but enough for an orchid to sense. In São Paulo, Brazil, at 23.5° S latitude, just a hair south of the Tropic of Capricorn, day length ranges from 10 hr 45 min to 13 hr 32 min, or a change of 2 hr 45 min, and orchids native to this region are likely to be more photoperiod-sensitive than those found closer to the equator.

Since day length can influence both flower bud initiation and blooming, it is an important factor—especially if you grow Brazilian or Central American *Cattleyas,* Australian *Dendrobiums,* or any orchid native to an area about 10° north or south of the equator. In a greenhouse, as long as you don't regularly turn on the lights at night, the plants will respond naturally to the progressive seasonal changes in day length. (Even turning on a 75-watt light bulb for ten minutes during the night is enough to reset the plants' day-length clock.) Commercial nurseries fool plants into blooming in a different season by either lighting them at night or covering them with a blackout curtain in the late afternoon. To initiate flowering, day length must reach a certain minimum (or maximum) length for a certain number of days. The good news is that since day length is more extreme at temperate latitudes, your plants will have days that are plenty short enough in winter and long enough in summer.

If you use artificial lights, day length is whatever you want it to be. Thus you have quite a bit of control over flowering—or, more to the point, flower prevention—if you don't take day length into consideration. When I first set up my lights, everyone I talked to seemed to have a different idea about how long to leave them on. I ended up modeling the natural yearly day length at a latitude similar to São Paulo's. A good schedule is to set your lights for sixteen-hour days during June (to maximize total footcandle exposure) and shorten one hour a month to eleven-hour days by December, then lengthen by one-hour intervals starting in January. This is easy enough to do with automatic timers, and if you forget a month, you can change it by two hours the next month without harm.

Of course, changes in temperature are also important to trigger flowering, as we will see in the next chapter.

CHAPTER 4

Temperature

LIKE THE EARLY VICTORIAN orchid enthusiasts, I once imagined that the plants needed a steaming hothouse environment to survive. Before I went there, I pictured the tropics as giant saunas complete with palm trees, orangutans, and umbrella drinks. The reality, of course, is that not all tropical areas are swelteringly hot and humid. Lowland rain forests generally are, but high-elevation cloud forests remain downright chilly most of the time. Subtropical areas can be quite cool in winter and very hot in summer. Thus it is possible to select tropical orchids that will be comfortable at temperatures as low as 45°F for a few days and others that revel in 90°-plus heat. Remember, though, that every orchid is adapted to a particular temperature range, and staying within that range as much as possible will keep the plant at its best. A plant that prefers warm conditions will slowly decline if it's always cool, and a cool-growing species will "melt down" after

ABOVE: Orchids that have evolved in high-elevation cloud forests require cool temperatures for proper growth and flowering. This bicolored form of the miniature *Dendrobium cuthbertsonii* is happiest at temperatures between 50° and 75°F.

weeks of high temperatures. Blooming may also be adversely affected by temperature. Life is a series of chemical reactions, and the speed of these reactions as well as the efficacy of the enzymes that catalyze them depends on temperature. A plant that has evolved in a warm climate has an enzyme system and metabolism geared to those temperatures. Put such a plant in cool conditions and it's like trying to start an old car on a cold winter morning—the engine won't turn over, and the plant slowly runs out of energy. The converse happens to cold-adapted plants. They have very sensitive enzyme systems and fast metabolisms to help them cope with cool temperatures. In warm conditions, these systems go into overdrive and may burn themselves out like an overheated car in the desert.

Another important point about temperature is *fluctuation.* Ideally, nights should be 5°–15° cooler than days, and for some species seasonal variation is beneficial too, with more warmth in summer and less in winter. Diurnal and/or seasonal temperature fluctuation is one of the three cues orchids use to time growth and flowering (the others are day length and rainfall/humidity changes). Many orchid species require a

Cycnoches Cygnet (top right), *Angraecum* Ol Tukai (left), and *Cattleya* Lodiaca (bottom right) thrive at intermediate to warm temperatures.

lower temperature—say, 55°F—for several weeks or months during fall or winter in order to initiate flower buds or growth. If the temperature doesn't fall to the necessary range, blooming will be delayed or prevented. The drop in temperature also helps slow down the plant's metabolism. Cool-growing orchids can tolerate warm days much better if the night temperature falls below 65°, and flowers will last longer, too. No matter what their preferred range, keeping your plants at a constant day/night temperature may compromise blooming and growth.

In a greenhouse it is pretty easy to achieve a nightly drop in temperature as the sun warms the interior during the day and heat is lost at night. Invest in a thermostat or thermostat/timer combination that can be set to lower the nighttime temperature automatically. Some fairly cheap computer systems will do this if you want to get fancy. In a basement like those I have raised plants in, the temperature remains much more constant because of the insulating effects of the earth surrounding it. However, in an enclosed growing space some of the heat generated by artificial lights can be used to raise the temperature by 5° during the day even in winter without resorting to additional heaters. Some species (*Mediocalcar decoratum, Maxillaria sophronites,* and a few *Bulbophyllums* come to mind) refuse to bloom with such a small diurnal variation, but plenty of others will. On a windowsill, if you turn your heat down at night during winter and leave the window open at night in summer, you should be able to lower the nighttime temperature sufficiently. Also, sandwiching the plants between the window and a curtain will lower the temperature markedly during winter. Just be careful on very cold nights, as it may fall to close to freezing behind a curtain.

To make things easier for all of us, orchid reference books rate species and hybrids by their temperature preferences using three categories—*cool, intermediate,* and *warm.*

COOL GROWERS are mostly those that are native to high-elevation cloud forests and delight in temperatures between 50° and 75°. Winter lows of 50°–55° and summer highs below 80° (with a few days up to 85°) are ideal. Unless you live somewhere like San Francisco, the primary challenge is keeping the plants cool enough.

INTERMEDIATE GROWERS like temperatures about 5°–8° warmer than cool growers on average: 58°–62° for winter lows and 80°–82° for average summer highs with an occasional spike to 85° or 90°.

WARM GROWERS prefer winter lows in the 65°–70° range and summer highs around 85° with spikes up to 90° or 95°.

When buying plants, pay attention to their temperature preferences and select those that fit your conditions. In the

A maximum/minimum thermometer accurately records high and low temperatures and is easy to reset.

coastal Northeast, we have relatively cool summers and cold winters, so it is difficult to keep warm-growing species comfortable in a greenhouse without running up an enormous heating bill, but they will be fine on a windowsill if you keep the room reasonably warm. Intermediate growers are quite easy to grow here, and cool growers are fine except during the one or two weeks (sometimes more) of hot and humid weather we get during the summer, which they barely muddle through. When I lived in central North Carolina, I desperately tried to keep my cool-growing miniatures happy with air conditioning during the summer, but they suffered, and I lost more plants than I'd like to admit. The hot, humid summers in the Southeast are perfect for warm growers, and the mild winters make heating less costly. It's a good idea to group plants with similar requirements together. If you have both cool and warm growers, consider putting the former in the cellar and keeping the latter on an upper floor. Many greenhouse growers put in two heating zones, so that they can accommodate cool to intermediate and intermediate to warm growers in the same structure.

Keeping your plants warm enough is pretty straightfor-

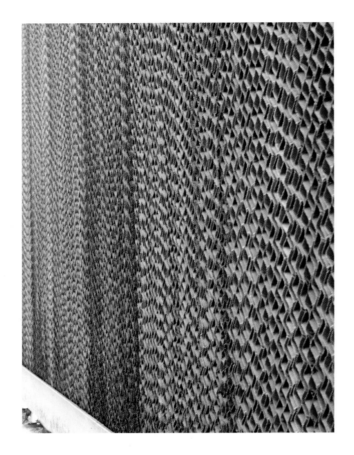

Cooling pads soak up water trickling down from a perforated tube. A fan draws outside air through the wet pads to humidify and cool the air. This is the most economical way to cool a greenhouse in summer, though it is most effective when the outside humidity is low.

ward, because home and greenhouse heaters are much the same, and I don't need to use space describing them. Cooling systems, though, are a bit different and deserve mention, especially if you are interested in the cool cloud forest species. Air conditioning, the standard method for cooling homes, has several disadvantages for orchids. It dehumidifies the air, which is good for people and furnishings but hard on moisture-loving plants, and it is very expensive to operate. If you already have central air conditioning, you can simply enclose the indoor orchid-growing space in plastic and humidify it. Some growers use an air conditioner tied to an evaporative humidifier to supercool and rehumidify the air, and this system will work even in a greenhouse if you can afford it.

In a greenhouse, it's more common to lower the temperature with a fan and a swamp or evaporative pad. This is simply a big spongy pad made from excelsior (wood shavings) or synthetic fibers built into one wall of the greenhouse over which water constantly drips; an exhaust fan at the other end

of the greenhouse pulls outdoor air through the pad. Evaporation of the water uses heat energy, thus cooling as well as humidifying the air, which is drawn through the greenhouse and out the other end. As long as the dew point (the point at which the air becomes saturated with water) is at least 10° lower than your target temperature, these pad and fan coolers are quite effective. On a very humid day, though, their efficacy drops off considerably. Still, they are the method of choice for greenhouses. You can get a small, self-contained unit about the size of a large air conditioner that will work for a small hobby greenhouse. A fog humidification system can achieve similar results when used in conjunction with an exhaust fan. Keeping the plants well shaded and damp but not soaked can also help them weather a heat wave. On a hot day, if you can get temperatures down to the mid-60s or lower at night, the cooler-growing orchids will fare much better.

The type of shading you use on your greenhouse influences heat buildup. It is always better to hang or apply a shade cloth on the exterior to deflect heat before it enters the glass. The interior shade/energy-saving curtains that open and close in the eaves of the greenhouse allow the heat to build up above them, which inevitably raises the temperature around the plants as well. Old-fashioned whitewash does a decent job of reflecting some of the sun's heat before it enters, and special metal-coated shade fabric reduces temperatures within the greenhouse by several degrees more than heat-absorbing black shade fabric. And believe me, the fabric is far easier to apply and remove than whitewash.

Odontioda **Thomas Gettel 'Sunset Ruby'** will suffer when the temperature rises above 80°F.

CHAPTER 5

Humidity and Air Movement

Relative Humidity

THE TERM "HUMIDITY" is short for relative humidity (RH). Air can hold only a certain amount of gaseous water (water vapor), and that amount is relative to the air temperature, thus the term "relative humidity." Humidity is very important in orchid culture, so it merits some further explanation.

If you remember your high school physics, air in our atmosphere is not emptiness but rather a jumble of gas molecules (mostly nitrogen, oxygen, and carbon dioxide, as well as water vapor) floating around and banging into each other. As air warms up, the molecules move around faster and allow room for more water to enter the atmosphere. Cooling has the opposite effect, forcing some of the H_2O molecules out of the atmosphere as they lose heat energy. On a rainy day, the air becomes completely saturated with water molecules, at which point you can say that the relative humidity is 100% (or that the dew point has been reached), and no more water can

ABOVE: Orchids respond well to high humidity, especially when combined with strong air movement. Though you cannot turn your living room into a cloud forest, a small room humidifier will add enough water to satisfy the plants. Misting the plants daily is also beneficial.

evaporate. Think of trying to air-dry a bath towel on a rainy day. If the saturated air warms and expands just a bit, there will be more energy ("room") for more water vapor, so the RH drops to, say, 90%, allowing a bit more water to evaporate. If the saturated air cools, though, some water vapor is forced out as liquid—in the form of fog, dew, or raindrops.

In the humid tropics, where most epiphytic orchids grow, the air is usually very humid, at least at night, when it cools a bit and fog forms as the dew point is reached, as well as during frequent thunderstorms and rain showers. The orchids depend on this high relative humidity to slow their transpiration rate—the rate at which water is lost when leaves open their pores, or stomata, to let in carbon dioxide and expel oxy-

Some orchids require the very high humidity possible in an enclosed light box, grow room, or greenhouse. This **Lepanthes tsubotae,** with its diaphanous flowers and frail stems, would quickly shrivel up on a windowsill.

gen, the same way we lose water as we exhale. The high humidity also slows the evaporation of water from the bark, moss, or other surface that the roots are clinging to. If the relative humidity becomes too low for an extended period, the orchid loses water from its stomata faster than it can be replaced through the roots, and drought stress sets in. The orchid will close its stomata—in a sense, it will stop breathing —or, if the air becomes very dry, the plant will shed some or all of its leaves and go dormant until the rains return. Epiphytic orchids are more vulnerable to desiccation than many terrestrial plants, so they are especially fond of high humidity.

Orchid diversity is highest in mountainous regions of the wet tropics, for reasons related indirectly to humidity. Rather than boring you with more physics that I don't completely understand, suffice it to say that as warm, humid air rises, it cools and thus cannot hold as much water vapor, so some is forced out as fog and dew. That is how clouds form, and if a mountain juts up high enough, its top will frequently be covered in clouds. Because the air in tropical lowlands starts out so warm, even after the air has risen to 4,000 or 5,000 feet and cooled off, with water vapor condensing into clouds, it may still be 50° or 60°F, which is warm enough for some orchids to grow. On the upper slopes of the Andes, and in other high tropical mountain ranges, cloud forests are almost constantly bathed in cool, saturated air; the relative humidity hovers near 100% most of the time. In a cloud forest, the mornings usually start out foggy, but as the sun rises and warms the air, the fog burns off until afternoon, when warm air rising from the lowlands begins condensing again. By late afternoon it starts raining, and the night remains dripping wet and foggy until the following morning. So although the RH may drop to 50% for a short time around noon, the plants and mosses are still damp from the night before. What a place for an epiphyte! In the tropical cloud forests, orchids, bromeliads, ferns, and many other plants hang from every branch. Cloud forest orchids like *Masdevallia, Lepanthe, Telopogon,* and the like, are very intolerant of low humidity and warm temperatures, even less tolerant than their lower-elevation counterparts. If your house gets so dry in winter that an open box of crackers doesn't go stale for weeks, you need to look for species or hybrids that are less amphibian in temperament. Start with the list of good windowsill orchids in Chapter 2. But if you really want to grow cloud forest species, you can take some steps to raise the humidity either in your whole house or just in the area around the orchids.

If you live in a humid temperate climate, as I do, during some of the spring and fall and most of the summer, the relative humidity outdoors ranges between 40% and 100%. The lower end of the range may not be ideal for the fussiest cloud forest orchids, but it's acceptable for many of the commonly grown genera. Inside, though, whenever the heat is running, making the indoor air temperature higher than it is outdoors, the relative humidity will necessarily drop. If the RH outdoors is 55% and the temperature is 45°F, the RH of this same air indoors will drop to 20%–30%. In the winter the outside air is drier to start with than it is in summer, and indoor relative humidity below 20% is common in my house on a cold winter night. Such very dry air is hard on us as well as on the orchids. We develop stuffy noses, irritated eyes, and an unquenchable thirst, but the orchids suffer in silence. Some houses have humidifiers built into the heating system, but unless you have one of these or live in a very humid climate, like that of coastal Washington State, if you are going to grow orchids successfully indoors during the winter, plan to use some sort of humidification. You and your orchids will be much better off. If you run air conditioning in summer, your indoor air will be drier, but usually not to the extremes found in winter.

When you humidify the indoor air in winter, there is a risk of this air moving out through the walls and condensing on the cold inner surfaces of the exterior siding, causing damage to the house. And when the moist air hits the windows and cools, they fog up and weep condensation down into the frame and mullions. If you are going to humidify a room or the whole house, 40%–50% humidity is about the maximum that's safe for the structure. This should be fine for most of the commonly grown genera like *Cattleya*, *Oncidium*, and *Phalaenopsis*. If you choose orchids that come from seasonally dry climates, such as Australian *Dendrobiums*, Brazilian rupicolous *Laelias*, or *Catesetums*, a lower humidity (35%–40%) should be fine. However, if you want to grow cloud forest plants like *Draculas* or *Masdevallias*, which require humidity levels closer to 70%–80%, you will have to construct some sort of structure — a Wardian case, a plastic-wrapped grow room, or a greenhouse — that can be humidified without endangering the house or windows.

MEASURING RELATIVE HUMIDITY

While you can safely assume that the heated air in your home is probably too dry for orchids, you'll need some way to measure the humidity to be sure you have adjusted it correctly. Of course, you could just set up a humidifier and adjust it so the air feels "spring morning fresh." But it's useful to know the numbers. For less than $50 you can buy something called a sling psychrometer, which consists of two thermometers mounted side by side in a case attached to a handle. One thermometer bulb has a little cotton sock around it that you wet with distilled water (the salts in tap water can throw the readings off), and the other bulb is dry (no sock). You simply swing the gadget around like one of those New Year's noise-

A sling psychrometer in action. After wetting the cotton sock attached to the "wet" thermometer bulb, I swing the gadget around until the mercury in both thermometers has stopped moving. Comparison of the wet and dry readings against a scale on the cover gives an accurate reading of relative humidity. Digital hygrometers are fast replacing this old-fashioned technology.

makers until the temperature on both thermometers has stabilized. Because evaporation cools the wet bulb in direct proportion to the humidity of the air, the bigger the difference between wet and dry, the lower the humidity. My psychrometer has a handy sliding scale for reading the humidity once I get the wet and dry readings. I have had this one for twenty years, and as long as I keep the sock clean, it works flawlessly. Meters that read humidity are called hygrometers (or humidistats if they are attached to a switch that activates a humidifier); they aren't as accurate as a psychrometer, but they work more quickly and are easier to read. They contain a strip of plastic or a hair (from a horse or a human), or some other material that expands and contracts with the humidity level, connected to a needle and dial for reading the relative humidity. However, once you get an idea of what "proper" humidity feels and smells like, you won't need any equipment beyond your nose and skin.

TYPES OF HUMIDIFIERS

There are four types of humidification for use in a house or greenhouse: passive evaporation, forced evaporation, steam or warm-vapor humidifiers, and cool mist or fog (including ultrasonic humidifiers).

PASSIVE EVAPORATION SYSTEMS are the easiest way to raise RH in the home and can be as simple as a tray of pebbles filled with water. The water evaporates from the water surface and pebbles as convection currents slowly circulate the air. Pebble trays don't add a lot of water to the atmosphere, though, and it is doubtful that they will have much effect unless you scatter them all over your house. A fan blowing air over the tray will increase the rate of evaporation, and this is how I maintain humidity in my enclosed artificial-light chambers (see Chapter 2).

FORCED EVAPORATION SYSTEMS use the principle of a fan forcing a high volume of air over a wet surface to raise humidity. Inexpensive cool-moisture humidifiers consist simply of a wicking filter that draws water from a reservoir and a fan that pulls or pushes air through the filter. On the same principle, larger console humidifiers have a revolving treadmill-type pad that runs through a water reservoir before moving in front of the fan. I have had good results with one of these larger units, although the tank and pad are difficult to clean. Its advantages are the big tank, which can run for days without refilling, and the capacity to humidify large areas. Because it takes heat energy to evaporate water, forced evaporative systems can markedly cool the air as they humidify. The console-type humidifiers are really small evaporative coolers like those used in greenhouses. Since you are likely to run the humidifier only during the heating season, though, remember that it will be working against your furnace. Believe me, a big evaporative humidifier can really send out a chilly draft.

WARM-VAPOR HUMIDIFIERS are popular, in part because they don't cool the air. This type generates steam the way a pot boiling on the stove does. This also means it evaporates easily without a fan, so warm-mist units are quieter than cool ones. Older models created steam with a heating element set into a water tank. These always seemed dangerous to run unattended, but they have been improved quite a bit in recent years, and I have been very happy with one of the newer models. It certainly puts more moisture into the air than an equivalent cool type does, and it is very quiet. The heat it generates actually warms the air a bit, too. The big disadvantage that this and all small units have is that the reservoir needs frequent refilling. During the middle of winter, a one-gallon tank has to be refilled two or three times in twenty-four hours.

ULTRASONIC HUMIDIFIERS were all the rage ten years ago, yet now it is difficult to find one anywhere, perhaps because of health concerns related to the way they work. Ultrasonic units have a small, vibrating disk that breaks up water into microscopic droplets—fog, basically, which is blown out of a spout with a small fan. The fog is cool, unlike the steam from warm-

mist humidifiers, but so fine that it quickly evaporates without cooling the air too much or leaving a puddle of water around the humidifier. A small unit set on high can quickly humidify a room. The disadvantage is that, unlike evaporative or steam systems, which put pure water into the air, these units use tap water, and if your water is hard, a fine calcium dust will settle on your furniture after a while. For a time supermarkets were installing larger units in the produce section to keep the lettuce crisp, but their maintenance proved too costly. I know of several people who bought the supermarket discards, which they use in greenhouses or grow rooms to produce a velvet fog.

All humidifiers need regular maintenance to keep them running well. Filters, tanks, and reservoirs should be cleaned to remove mineral deposits and bleached to destroy any bacteria that have become established, which might pose health problems if unchecked. Most humidifiers in the middle to upper price range come with a built-in humidistat to turn off the unit when the desired humidity is reached, but they are generally inaccurate, though they can give you an approximate reading.

So which type is best? To humidify one or two rooms in your house, I would choose a good warm-mist unit because it is quiet and doesn't cool the air. Buy one that is rated to humidify more square footage than you will use it for. For an enclosed growing area, a console type or cool-moisture unit is preferable, as it can provide some cooling in summer, and the fan provides extra air movement, which is good for the orchids.

GREENHOUSE HUMIDIFICATION

Since a greenhouse is designed as a "wet" structure, it is easier to humidify than a house. Though a gravel floor is harder to clean than concrete or stone, it acts as a giant pebble tray, allowing irrigation water to evaporate and keeping the structure very humid as long as all windows and vents are closed. However, even a gravel floor will not maintain high humidity on a warm, dry day when the vents are open for cooling or on a very cold night when the heat runs nonstop. Thus, it's a good idea to have some sort of supplemental humidification. The options are basically mist, fog, or swamp coolers. Swamp coolers, discussed in Chapter 4, p. 30, are very effective in the summer, but obviously cannot be used on a cold night.

I have installed a simple mist system in two greenhouses, hanging PVC plastic pipes under the benches to deliver water to nozzles that spray a fine mist when a solenoid connected to a humidistat kicks on. The nozzles are available from greenhouse suppliers. I use as fine a nozzle as I can (one with a rated output of less than 2 gallons per hour at standard household water pressure) that won't clog easily; it's worth installing an inexpensive water filter after the solenoid, though, to prevent small particles from clogging the nozzle orifices. Look for the nozzles that are sold for greenhouse mist propagation. There are basically two types: the oil-burner type, which sprays out mist in a cone pattern, and the anvil or deflection type, on which the mist shoots out of the orifice and is deflected when it hits a metal pin. Most people prefer the anvil type for under-bench mist, as it lessens the amount shooting up through the bench mesh. The anvil nozzles also have larger orifices and thus don't clog as easily, and you can get plastic ones for pennies apiece. You can hang these upside down or string them along a series of risers from a pipe run along the ground. I have used the oil-burner type effectively by pointing the nozzles down toward the floor. This system is simple because it needs only household water pressure; the downside is that the droplets don't stay airborne for long, so you need a fan to distribute the mist. Furthermore, if the mist does waft up onto plants, it can keep their leaves wet, encouraging diseases.

A fog system produces very fine water droplets that, like natural fog, stay suspended in the air for a long time—really until they evaporate. A fog system lets you come closest to creating natural cloud forest conditions in your greenhouse—it's wonderful to walk into a greenhouse on a bright, cold day and be enveloped in a warm, dry fog. Perfection comes at a price, though; these systems are more complicated and require higher maintenance than mist systems. Several systems—high-pressure, ultrasonic, and centripetal—will produce true fog, defined as water droplets under 20 microns in size.

High-pressure systems are the most costly to install, as they require a compressor that generates water pressure at up to 1,000 pounds per square inch (psi) and rugged piping built to withstand such pressures. However, it is reasonably quiet, and because it uses a number of small nozzles, it fills the greenhouse quickly with fog. Several manufacturers will design a system to fit your needs. Ultrasonic systems are a bit different from the type sold for home humidification, and I have installed one of these in the greenhouse I use currently. The advantage of this type is much lower cost (depending on the compressor you buy, about a sixth to a quarter of the cost of a high-pressure fog system), and you can build it yourself, as it operates at 30 psi—roughly household water pressure. The heart of the system is a special nozzle with a port for pressurized air and one for water. (Dripsafe Airjet nozzles are made by Spray Systems Co.: www.spray.com/.) The air enters a resonating chamber, which creates sound waves that atomize the water streaming in from the other side. Each nozzle can produce quite a bit of fog, so I have only two in a 350-square-foot greenhouse, and they can generate a pea-soup fog in a matter of minutes. The drawback is that you need an air compressor, which is very noisy. I bought a big one at the local home store and it has worked fine, but it's hard to be in the same room with it. If possible, house the compressor in a soundproofed shed. Besides the compressor, you need to install solenoids on the water and air lines, both connected to the same humidistat, and a filter on the water line. Because the orifice is relatively large, though, clogging is not a real problem.

Low-cost greenhouse foggers designed for hobbyists cool as well as humidify. This ¼-horsepower unit emits a high-pitched whine like an ultralight airplane engine, but it is a vast improvement over earlier models. This is a centripetal system that uses air turbulence to break up water particles into a fine fog that quickly fills the greenhouse. The fan can be mounted on an oscillating base to improve the fog distribution.

Centripetal humidifiers use a very fast fan with nozzles mounted on or in front of its blades to atomize water. This is the least costly and simplest system to install—you just hang the fan, tap into a water line, and hook up a humidistat—and I installed one in an orchid greenhouse with good results. Their drawback is mainly noise. The fan has a high-pitched whine that sounds like the propeller on an ultralight aircraft. The unit I installed was 1 horsepower, but the manufacturer now has smaller, oscillating 1/4-hp models with improved blades that can easily humidify a 1,000-square-foot greenhouse, and the noise is bearable because it runs only occasionally. The only other problem with this system is that you get some fallout of larger droplets in the area in front of the fan.

So there is no ideal way to humidify a greenhouse. Gravel floors work well during most of the year. Mist systems are cheap to install and maintain, but fog has the advantage of humidifying without wetting foliage and actually cools the air quite well, too. If you combine fog with a ventilation fan, you can lower the temperature in the greenhouse by 5° to 15°F, depending on the outdoor humidity.

Air Movement

Orchids appreciate moving air; after all, the majority of them evolved as epiphytes high in the tree canopy, where winds are much stronger than they are on the ground. Assuming you have achieved the proper humidity and light levels, adding ventilation will aid gas exchange through leaf pores and, more important, around the rhizome and roots and through the potting mix. Good air movement is the best defense against fungal and bacterial diseases. If you grow orchids on a windowsill, supplemental air movement is really not a major consideration. Even when I had a collection of thirty plants on and near a windowsill, the air from my cool-moisture humidifier provided enough circulation in winter, and an open window did the same in summer. When I put the plants outdoors, of course, there was plenty of wind and breezes. However, in an enclosed grow room or greenhouse, fans are essential to good orchid health.

I find that sufficient air movement is the environmental factor least understood by orchid growers. Air turbulence is especially important as the relative humidity rises. For example, in an enclosed 3 × 4 × 3-foot case or light box with an average RH of 50%, one 3 1/2-inch pancake fan is probably adequate to keep the plants healthy. However, for every 10% rise in average humidity, I would add an extra fan. Thus, at an average 80% RH, I'd have four fans scattered around the case to move the damp air. I really think the ideal condition for most tropical orchids is high humidity (about 70%) coupled with high turbulence. Most growers respond to outbreaks of fungal or bacterial diseases by lowering the humidity, but I think the best solution is to increase air movement. Some of the healthiest plants I have seen were growing in saturated environments with lots of fans. Roots grow magnificently and water doesn't collect in the leaf and flower sheaths, so rot cannot get started and the plants thrive just as they would in the rain forest. I think orchids in the cloud forests thrive in nearly constant fog because breezes constantly rise from the lowlands on convection currents. Put those same plants in a greenhouse with too little air movement, and they'll succumb to rot at much lower humidity levels. Remember, though, you always have to strike a balance between airflow and humidity. If the humidity is too low, fans can quickly desiccate the orchids.

How do you decide how strong your airflow should be? I think of it in this way. If your humidity is 50%–60%, aim for the equivalent of a 5-mile-an-hour gentle breeze. If the greenhouse, grow room, or case is closer to 80%–90% RH, then you need a 10–15 mph breeze (if you don't know what 15 mph feels like, it's enough wind to fly a kite). I know one grower who runs his humidity close to 100%, and the wind in his greenhouse blows over 20 mph!

But for enclosed light boxes or cases, the little pancake fans work well, as you can tuck them into corners away from plants and watering hose. For bigger grow rooms, oscillating fans are better, because they distribute the air and give the plants a breeze, then rest, breeze, then rest, the way they experience wind in the wild. In greenhouses, ceiling or horizontal airflow (HAF) fans, possibly combined with oscillating fans, are best.

Watch the plants. Are they drying out too much? Or is rot setting in? If you have the first problem, try raising the humidity or, if you can't, redirect the fans so that they blow around but not on the plants. If rot is a problem, try increasing airflow or redirecting the fans to blow more directly on the plants. I like to set the fans so that the air moves up from below or down from above, working its way through the pots and the crowns of the plants.

LEFT: *Phalaenopsis* Betris 'Logan Vesquez' HCC/AOS. Not all orchids require high humidity. If you pay attention to watering, most *Phalaenopsis* will grow and bloom under household conditions.

PART TWO

Care and Feeding

CHAPTER 6

Watering

HOW MUCH AND HOW OFTEN should I water my orchids? This basic question has no simple answer. I know from years of working in nurseries that beginners want easy instructions like "once a week," but it is never that straightforward, is it? I've often thought that someone could make a bundle inventing a little water-minder along the lines of those pop-up sensors that let you know when the turkey is cooked. A little device in the pot that would chime "warning, warning, water wanted" or play a snippet of "Singin' in the Rain" would be just the thing. While hand-held water sensors are available for houseplants, they are not really effective with orchids because the potting mixes are so physically different from the potting soil to which the sensors are calibrated. Orchids are also not like typical houseplants such as peace lilies or philodendrons, which wilt quickly when they're dry. Some orchids need fairly constant moisture, but others like to go bone-dry between waterings. On the whole, tropical orchids are at least moderately drought tolerant, so the cues they give are far more sub-

When I say water, I mean *water!* A thorough drenching flushes excess salts from the potting mix and assures that the mix and this *Cattleya*'s roots are adequately wetted. The kitchen sink is the best place to drench your plants indoors.

tle than rapid wilting or yellowing. Learning to read these subtle cues takes time and involves understanding the different languages of the pot, the potting medium, and the plant itself, but these signs are as effective as the most sensitive moisture meter, and far more practical. Once you have learned the correct schedule for your plants, watering will become second nature.

Watering Orchids in Pots
TYPE OF POT

Unglazed terra-cotta pots are porous, and when water is freely available they wick it from the potting mix. So when the exterior of the pot is dark, clammy, or cool to the touch, you can assume that the potting mix and roots inside the pot are sufficiently damp. As the contents dry, the pot dries as well, becoming lighter in color at the top and progressing down the sides toward the bottom. If you are growing orchids like equitant *Oncidiums,* which like to dry out between waterings, let the pot surface go completely dry before irrigating. Moisture-loving *Masdevallias,* on the other hand, should be watered just as the pot surface begins to lighten or when the area near the rim is dry. Remember that dry clay will pull moisture from the mix until it is rewetted, so you may need an extra pass with the hose to slake its thirst. (If you dunk a dry clay pot in water, it will bubble and hiss as water is absorbed and air displaced. It is amazing how long it takes a dry pot to stop bubbling.)

Plastic, glazed earthenware, and stoneware pots are nonporous, so unlike terra cotta, they do not give visible clues about soil dampness, though you can lift them up and check the condition of the mix protruding through the drainage holes. Water tends to pool in the bottom of plastic pots, so the lower third of the mix stays damp much longer than the upper portion (the wicking action of terra cotta helps negate this reservoir effect). If you examine just the top surface of plants potted in plastic, it is easy to underestimate the dampness of the lower portion of the mix and thus overwater the orchid. Use the drainage holes and the condition of the mix protruding through them to gauge dampness.

TYPE OF MIX

One of the main reasons to find a potting mix you like and stick with it is that every mix dries at a different rate and in a

visibly different way. If you keep your orchid collection in a variety of different concoctions, it is hard to standardize watering, so you're more likely to overwater or underwater some plants. Every mix changes in color as it dries, and if you get to know a particular type, you can tell at a glance whether a plant needs water. *Without exception, water makes any mix appear darker.* When well wetted, fir bark or lava rock is dark reddish brown, long-fibered sphagnum is a deeper tan, gravel is a glossier, richer russet or gray, and tree-fern fiber is a more saturated black. Since the upper surface dries quickly, let your eyes travel to the cracks or crevices where moisture persists longer. As you are learning to judge dryness, poke the mix gingerly with your finger to gauge whether an inch or two down it's still damp. Lift the pot up and look through the drainage holes. With practice, you'll be able to gauge moisture content by the subtle changes in the color of the mix. Also, water will make any medium heavier. This may seem obvious, but relative weight is an extremely valuable indicator since it directly correlates with the amount of water. Lightweight, absorbent media such as New Zealand sphagnum, lightweight expanded clay, and even old fir bark show the most noticeable differences in dry versus wet weight, but it is possible to sense the weight change in gravel or lava rock as well. One trick I use when learning about a new mix is to fill several different-sized pots with it, add water, and then, a few days later, pick them up, estimate their weight, and dump out the mix to see how wet it is at the core. After doing this a few times you'll get a feel for it.

TYPE OF ORCHID

The plants themselves can give you both short-term and long-term feedback as to the efficacy of your watering. Orchids in active growth should have plump pseudobulbs and/or leaves. Pseudobulbs and fleshy leaves are the plant's water tanks, and though it can draw them down occasionally, they need to be refilled afterward. When dry, roots exposed to air will be white, but they should quickly turn green when watered. Healthy root tips are bright green; the longer the green portion, the faster the root is growing. Depending on the species, $1/8$–1 inch of green tissue may be exposed to the air. Roots grow only when there is enough water. Do the roots burrow quickly into the potting mix? If instead they die when they hit the mix, it could be a sign of overwatering or salt buildup. It is natural for older leaves to fall after one to three years (except in deciduous species like *Catasetum* and *Barkeria*). If the leaves fall sooner, you may not be watering enough. Remember, though, that chronic overwatering results in root loss, and the symptoms can mimic those of underwatering. The only way to tell for sure is to carefully unpot the plant and look at the roots. If they appear solid and alive, then a thirty-

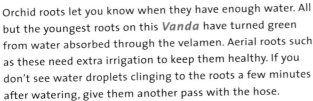

Orchid roots let you know when they have enough water. All but the youngest roots on this **Vanda** have turned green from water absorbed through the velamen. Aerial roots such as these need extra irrigation to keep them healthy. If you don't see water droplets clinging to the roots a few minutes after watering, give them another pass with the hose.

Masdevallias lack pseudobulbs and are thus very susceptible to desiccation. This poor plant is shedding older leaves in a desperate attempt to survive. I could tell that it was underwatered rather than overwatered because the roots were still alive and firmly knitted in place. Drenching it and keeping it in a large, clear plastic bag away from strong sunlight for a few days might allow it to recover.

minute soaking once a day for a week may be all that is required to rehydrate the plant. If overwatering is the problem, you probably should repot the plant and check the condition of the roots again later.

Because orchids are sensitive to the salts in tap water, be sure to thoroughly flood the pot so that water comes pouring out the bottom, then flood it again. When I had just a few orchids, I would take them to the kitchen sink and water them with the sprayer hose. I even gave them a warm shower once in a while. If possible, water the plants with cool or tepid water. Especially in winter, cold-water pipes along outside walls can get very chilly, and water that cold can shock the plants. Whatever you do, don't leave the plants in a saucer or larger pot that lacks drainage holes. These not only keep the mix wet, they prevent flushing of salts and will cause your plants to decline rapidly. Placing the pots on little risers above a pebble tray will catch runoff and add humidity, as long as the

pots don't come in contact with the water. (The exceptions to this are certain genera, such as *Phragmipedium* and *Disa*, which do well in a saucer of water *as long as the water is very pure*. See caption on opposite page.)

Watering Mounted Orchids

Mounted plants (orchids growing epiphytically on slabs or sections of tree branch) are both easier and harder to water than potted ones. You aren't likely to overwater them, but it is far easier to underwater them. Remember that roots exposed to light and air are physiologically different from those growing in the dark recesses of a pot. There is much more velamen —that water-absorbing outer layer—on aerial roots, and they are adapted to the cyclical drenching and drying they would experience during intermittent rainstorms. In the wild, orchids are bathed in showers of raindrops that may last min-

RIGHT: *Phragmipedium sedenii* flower

BELOW: Moisture-loving orchids such as this *Phragmipedium sedenii* do well if the pot is placed in a shallow dish of water — no more than one third the depth of the pot. Use rainwater or distilled water and flush the pot in the sink once a month to leach fertilizer salts. An inorganic potting medium such as Aliflor is a good choice for this sort of semihydroponic culture, as it will not decay when constantly wet.

utes, hours, or even days. In this situation the roots continually absorb water as needed, replenishing stores in pseudobulbs and leaves and encouraging new root growth in a way that is impossible to simulate indoors without an automatic irrigation system. Even if you live in a temperate climate, take your mounted orchids outdoors just before a rainstorm and let them get water the natural way. (This is also a great way to leach salts from the mount or potting medium.)

If you're growing orchids in a greenhouse, enclosed cabinet, or grow room equipped with floor drains, watering the mounts is simply a matter of drenching them every day or every few days with a hose or pressure sprayer. You should water them enough to flood the whole root area and, ideally, enough that water droplets remain clinging to roots and mount for a while after you finish. If a permeable mount like tree fern becomes dry, it should be drenched a few times to rewet the core, and even mossy cork or tree-branch mounts may need a few passes with the hose several minutes apart. If the plants are looking water-stressed, dunk the whole plant and mount in a five-gallon bucket of water and let it soak for ten to thirty minutes. It's remarkable how soaking will rehydrate a dry plant if its root system is healthy.

As I discovered myself, a windowsill is not the best place for mounted orchids. I ruined the varnish on the hardwood flooring below the windows in two apartments despite trying to be careful when I watered. After watering, let the plant drip-dry before replacing it on the windowsill. If you have a few mounted orchids, the shower may be the best place to water them, though it's time-consuming.

Watering   43

After a two-week vacation, I returned to find my *Phalaenopsis* quite dry — notice the shriveled, limp leaves. After a half-hour soak for three consecutive days, the plant largely recovered and did not abort the bloom spike already well under way here. Because the root system was large and healthy, the plant rebounded swiftly.

Catasetums evolved in seasonally dry climates, so they shed their leaves naturally in the fall. Decrease watering slowly once new growths mature, and restrict water severely after all the leaves have fallen to give the plant a dry rest. Overwatering a fully dormant orchid will rot its roots.

Automatic Watering

Inevitably, there will come a time when you have to leave your plants with no one to water them. Most orchids can stand a long weekend without attention, but what about a week? When I had just a few orchids, I simply placed them in a dry cleaner's bag when I was away as long as a week. I made sure they were damp but not wet going into the bag, and they did fine. In the winter, simply turning the heat down to 55° will slow water loss markedly.

When my collection had grown and my job took me away regularly during the week, I had to work out a more elaborate solution. By this time my plants were in the cellar, where water

on the floor wasn't so much of a problem, so I bought an irrigation timer used for lawn watering (about $40) and rigged it up to a solenoid valve. These systems are a lifesaver in my nursery operations, and they can easily be adapted to home use. The solenoid opens when the timer says so, allowing water into hoses connected to mist nozzles, which I mounted on PVC pipe and aimed so that the mist would cover all the plants. I made sure to set the water timer to come on well before the lights did so that any stray mist would not contact a hot bulb. It took a bit of tinkering to get the watering system right; I set it so that mounted plants were on a separate solenoid for more frequent watering. I used oil burner–type nozzles for the mounts and anvil misters for the bench-top plants, and the mist came on every one to three days and ran for ten to fifteen minutes. Eventually I added a third solenoid and hose that ran into my console humidifier to fill it automatically as needed. All in all, the system worked very, very well. As long as I checked for clogged nozzles and for wet or dry areas on the weekend, I was able to maintain my plants like this for a year without problems. While automatic watering can never substitute for careful hand-watering, I think such a system has its place as a backup for greenhouses, grow rooms, and possibly even enclosed cases. You can get even more elaborate by adding additional zones to create wetter and drier microhabitats within the larger environment.

Watering Plants That Need a Dry Rest

Tropical orchids native to seasonally dry habitats often require an annual period of dormancy in the fall or winter in order to flower and resume growing the following season. *Catesetums, Cycnoches,* and some *Dendrobiums* and *Lycastes,* among others, drop all their leaves when they enter their resting phase. Watering dormant orchids is tricky, because you don't want to let them either get too desiccated or end their dormancy prematurely. Overwatering dormant plants can also quickly lead to root rot, which is a serious threat. Check the condition of the pseudobulbs (if present) to gauge whether the plant needs water. Completely deciduous species should be allowed to dry to the point that their pseudobulbs have shriveled to about a third or a half of their full size. I think a heavy misting once every five to ten days (depending on temperature and humidity) is better than an occasional heavy drenching, as it more closely simulates the dews and fogs the plants would experience in the wild. Most deciduous orchids want it cool (50°–60°) during dormancy, and the lower temperature will lower the evaporation rate, so watch the mix or feel the weight of the pot and water only when the medium has completely dried out. Bring the plants out of dormancy slowly (usually

How dry is too dry? Dormant deciduous orchids can look pretty awful, but they will plump up in no time once watering commences in late winter or spring. Check the condition of the pseudobulbs to gauge when to water during dormancy. The older pseudobulb *(left)* on this **Lycaste deppei** is very wrinkled, but the newest one *(right)* is still quite plump. In a few days I'll water it lightly.

about mid-February, when the sun is getting stronger). A good soaking in a bucket, followed by several days of drying off, will usually wake them up. Increase watering enough that the pseudobulbs regain their plumpness. Many species begin flowering as they come out of dormancy, and their initial water needs may be higher.

Many nondeciduous species benefit from a less severe rest period, again typically in fall or winter, to harden off new growth and initiate flowering. Because they are evergreen, they may need only a less drastic cutback in watering, coupled with a moderate drop in temperature. There is no hard and fast rule, but in general a 30% decrease in watering frequency for a month or two should suffice for many *Bulbophyllums,* the Australian *Dendrobiums, Coelogynes,* and some *Cattleya-*alliance species, to name a few. As temperatures cool, it is prudent to reduce watering anyway, as transpiration rates slow and the risk of root rot increases.

Water Quality

As I have stressed, epiphytic orchids are not like typical land plants. They have evolved to cling to tree branches or rock, and the only water they are exposed to is fairly pure rainwater and dew. Rainwater is not completely pure; usually it contains some dissolved solids (human-made and natural pollutants picked up as gases in the clouds), and it also accumulates some organic acids and nutrient ions as it washes through the tree canopy and down branches—or, for that matter, down your roof and through the gutter. But rainwater is far purer than groundwater, which picks up dissolved solids or salts from organic and mineral sources in the soil. It stands to reason that epiphytic orchids (and also semiterrestrials such as *Paphiopedilums*) love pure water or, more accurately, are *intolerant of any water not approaching the purity of the rainwater they experience in the wild.*

Most of us do not collect rainwater for household use, relying instead on either well water or city water for ourselves and our plants. These groundwater sources can't approach the purity of rainwater, though if you are lucky enough to have very pure tap water, I'm sure your orchids show their appreciation. I have grown orchids in twelve different apartments, houses, and greenhouses in four states over the past twenty years, and I have had both very good and very bad water for orchids. Nothing is more disheartening than moving from a place with clean water to one with salt-laden effluent (I'm exaggerating, of course). It takes some time for the orchids to

Excess salts in poor-quality irrigation water tend to accumulate at leaf tips. *Sobralias* are particularly sensitive to salty water.

start showing it, but after a while you may see root loss, yellowing leaves, or even dead plants. When everything except the water has remained the same, you may feel bewildered. Poor-quality water is insidious; it raises the salt levels that the roots are exposed to and alters the pH of the mix as well as the solubility of and need for various fertilizers. Now, like many of the topics I cover in this book, worrying about your water can drive you to drink (pun intended). If you are just beginning with orchids and have a few plants on your living room windowsill, focus first on getting the watering routine and light level right—don't worry about water quality. However, if you feel that you have mastered the basics of watering, fertilizing, and light exposure, then you should pay some attention to the quality of your water. Pure water can clearly make the difference between surviving and thriving plants.

If you are on town or city water, the officials may be able to provide you with a water report, since they have to test the supply regularly. Be sure to ask if the town uses more than one well or reservoir to supply your home. One source can vary greatly from another, and you will need all pertinent analyses

to correctly determine the quality of your water. If you are on a private well or are having trouble getting a water report from your municipality, then it's worth paying for a commercial water quality analysis. The company will provide you with a container for the sample and instruct you on how to handle it correctly. Explain that you need to know the pH and the TDS (total dissolved solids), as well as total dissolved sodium and, if they can give it to you, the amounts of other dissolved minerals, such as calcium, magnesium, and iron. The TDS reading is the sum of all the ions floating around in your sample, and it is the ions—especially sodium and potassium—that stay behind as salts in the mix and roots after the water evaporates. Thus the higher the TDS, the poorer your water is for orchids. The reading is given as a percentage, expressed as parts per million (ppm) or the equivalent mg/l, of dissolved salts in a given volume of water.

Rainwater collected from a roof has an average TDS of 10–20 ppm. If your water tests below 60 ppm, then it should be fine for your orchids. A TDS of 60–120 ppm is a bit high, but if the sodium tests below 10 ppm, the water quality should be all right. You probably should repot more frequently, and it is important to flush the pots thoroughly at every watering. Also avoid heavy doses of fertilizer to keep the ppm of nitrogen (N) below 100. Water with a TDS over 120 ppm is really unsuitable for orchids, especially if the sodium is above 10 ppm. Even at a TDS of 150 ppm, the water probably won't taste salty to you. To give you some perspective, drinking water is considered "safe" with a TDS lower than 500 ppm. Swimming-pool water may have a TDS of 1,000–2,000 ppm, mostly from the chlorine, and seawater weighs in with a whopping average TDS of 34,200 ppm! So you can see, it doesn't take much salt to make water too salty for orchids.

By the way, since tap water varies from week to week, some especially diligent orchid growers invest in a fairly inexpensive (less than $100) electrical conductivity or EC/TDS meter and test their own water. These meters work on the principle that pure water is a less effective conductor of electricity than salty water, so the higher the conductivity, the higher the level of salts or solids. Meters read in microsiemens or millisiemens, although the less expensive ones convert this reading into ppm. While some accuracy is lost in the translation, the reading will give you a fairly close approximation of your TDS, provided you accurately calibrate the meter and test at the temperature indicated by the manufacturer.

So if your water fails the test, what to do? If you have just a few plants, you can buy jugs of distilled water at the supermarket and mix this in equal parts with your tap water. If your test showed a TDS of 175 ppm, adding a half gallon of distilled water (with a TDS below 5) to a half gallon of tap water will give you a more respectable 90 ppm. Be sure to get distilled rather than spring water, which may have a higher TDS than

Paphiopedilum **Mt. Toro**, like all *Paphiopedilums*, indicates its dislike for salty water with leaf-tip dieback; see photo, p. 98.

your tap water (many spring water sources are prized for their mineral content, and some producers even add mineral salts for flavor). The other options are to collect rainwater or purify your tap water. Either way, the switch from salty to pure water may elicit some quick responses from your orchids—healthier root and leaf tips, less flower-bud blast.

COLLECTING RAINWATER

From both a cost and an environmental point of view, collecting your own rainwater is an excellent choice. This is what I have done when I have been faced with poor water quality. It is amazing how much water you can collect off a roof during even a minor shower. The roof area of a 1,700-square-foot house is roughly 2,100 square feet, depending on the roof pitch. You can calculate the volume of water that runs off this roof with this simple equation:

(Rainfall in inches × square footage) ÷ 12 × 7.48 = no. gallons

So a modest $1/2$ inch of rain yields almost 655 gallons of water: $(0.5 \times 2,100) \div 12 \times 7.48 = 654.5$. Over the course of an average rainfall year in Massachusetts, that roof will collect and discharge the incredible total of 54,978 gallons of water.

Rainfall harvesting, as it's called, is becoming more popular in dry climates, and the equipment is much more readily available than it was ten years ago. The cost to install a collection system using existing rain gutters is roughly 50 to 75 cents per gallon capacity of your tank if you buy an off-the-shelf tank, pump, and hoses. For a few dozen plants, a few lidded plastic garbage cans (each holding about 30 gallons) is enough. I place a 30-gallon container under a gutter spout, then use an inexpensive water pump to deliver it into the cellar and onto the plants. A friend in Vermont buried a 1,000-gallon plastic tank under his greenhouse, and that meets most of his water needs. In a drier climate than New England's, you would need a bigger tank (3,000–10,000 gallons). Even in winter, some of the snow on a roof usually melts off, so you can collect water year-round (in a pinch I have even shoveled snow into a barrel and let it melt). If you switch from tap water to rainwater you will see tremendous positive effects on your orchids and the mosses that grow with them. With rainwater I have even kept lichens growing on the bark of branches I cut for mounts (though fungicides will kill the lichens). If you are interested in collecting rainwater, try searching the Internet for rainwater harvesting equipment dealers to design a system that works for you.

REVERSE OSMOSIS

If collecting rainwater is not feasible for you, there are other options. Reverse osmosis, or RO, has become very popular among orchidists, mainly because of the low-cost home units advertised widely in orchid magazines. RO systems are, in effect, very fine filters. Water is forced under pressure over the filters, which allow a portion of the water molecules through while most of the water and the dissolved solids stay behind. Whatever passes through collects in a tank for later use. RO water is as pure as or purer than rainwater (the TDS will average 6–10 ppm for a standard RO system, depending on water pressure and temperature, and assuming you are not starting with seawater). However, for every gallon of purified water, you'll have one to three gallons of waste water to discharge into your sewer, septic system, or the ground. The inexpensive units run close to 3:1 waste to pure water; more expensive, high-efficiency models get almost 1:1. RO water is so pure that it is almost caustic—it will eat through copper pipes to replace the dissolved solids it has lost. It is a good idea to treat your filtered water with a bit of dilute fertilizer while it's still in the collection tank. You will need a fertilizer balanced for RO water that has all the macro and micro nutrients and is pH buffered, because ordinary soluble fertilizers can make very pure water extremely acidic; pure water lacks the buffering capacity of water with more dissolved solids.

WATER SOFTENERS

Calcium and magnesium, two of the most soluble cations (positive ions), are abundant in some types of bedrock. Consequently, well water often contains high levels of both. Such water is termed "hard." Hard water can be a problem for plumbing, because the calcium and magnesium precipitate out as scale (really a limestone-like residue) that can gum up pipes (not to mention shower stalls). Hard water also has a high pH, which reduces the efficacy of soaps and detergents. Thus many people with hard water put in water-softening systems, which remove the calcium and magnesium and replace them with sodium ions. The softener filter is filled with little beads covered in sodium ions, and as the hard water passes over them, the sodium swaps with the other ions, which cling to the beads. Every so often the system pumps highly saline water over the beads to wash off the calcium and magnesium and coat them with more sodium. The waste water is pumped into the septic or sewer system. As you can imagine, water laced with fairly high levels of sodium is terrible for orchids. I have grown thousands of orchids in hard water with very few problems. So if your house has a water-softening system, I recommend that you have a plumber put in a bypass pipe to draw off unsoftened water for garden and orchid use or use rainwater on your plants. Also, RO filters can be used to remove salts from the softened water. Our house has a water-softening system that works the same way to remove iron, and I avoid watering plants (or drinking) the softened water.

CHAPTER 7

Fertilization and Nutrition

I FIND FERTILIZING plants satisfying. Watering and repotting are important tasks, but they seem like chores — maintenance activities necessary for the plants to live. But mixing up a bucket of a good soluble "plant food" and dunking the roots in it goes beyond maintenance; it's a sign of *caring*.

Most epiphytic orchids and, for that matter, the majority of terrestrial ones as well, need far less fertilizer for adequate growth than house or garden plants do. Because they are very frugal in consumption of nutrients, they can survive in places where few other plants could. Let's face it: few places are less fertile than the end of a twig or a bare outcropping of rock, yet orchids survive in just such inhospitable places. Still, surviving is different from thriving, and a little bit of extra nutrition can make a big difference. You can easily spot the orchids that are getting all the nutrients they require; they are the ones getting all the attention on the show table at the monthly orchid society meeting. In sympodial types, the newest pseudobulb or

ABOVE: *Slc* (Lc Ann Akagi × Sc Beaufort), a complex *Cattleya* hybrid, grows and blooms throughout the year. Ideally, it should be fertilized regularly all year long.

stem will often be markedly larger than the previous ones. In monopodials, the newer leaves will be longer or wider than the older ones. Leaf color will be a strong green, and the plant will hold on to many of its older leaves. Good nutrition encourages rhizome branching, so there will be many new leads, especially on sympodial plants. Root growth, too, if you can see it, will be prolific and vigorous. Balanced nutrition also gives the plant greater resistance to disease. Add all this up and what do you get? Flowers, flowers, and more flowers! When a plant is producing more and bigger leads, it will produce more and bigger flowers as well. So you can see that once you get the basics of light, air, and water under control, fertilizing your plants adequately can elevate them quickly from good to fantastic.

Okay, so what's the catch? I admit I am sometimes overly exuberant when it comes to fertilizing, a fact that has given me the somewhat dubious nickname "Mr. Fertility" (as regards plants only, I assure you). You can certainly overdo it with fertilizer, and this may have grave consequences for your orchids in several ways: salts build up, excess nutrients accumulate in plant tissues, and the medium breaks down too quickly. Fertilizer is basically salts. Not table salt, which is sodium, but ions such as potassium, calcium, and sulfur dioxide, plus magnesium, ammonium, and phosphate, which bind together in the dry state as salts. Salt attracts water, which is why it is used to preserve fish and meat, and it can draw water from a plant's roots on the same principle, of osmosis.

If you remember your high-school chemistry, osmosis is merely the movement of a fluid or solvent (in this case water) from an area of higher concentration of solute to an area of lower concentration. If you have two equal-sized pools of water separated by a semipermeable membrane, one very salty and the other relatively salt free, water will flow from the less salty pool until the two are equally salty. Because the salts cannot flow back through the membrane, the salt-free pool dries up as all its water rushes to the salty side. Plants absorb water through their roots in just the same way, accumulating higher concentrations of solutes in their root tissues than are found in the soil (or in rainwater). Water is "pulled" across a membrane called the casparian strip into the root cells. However, if the water in the soil or potting medium becomes excessively salty, the reverse happens, and water is literally sucked out of the roots, which can damage or kill them. Plants like mangroves that are adapted to saline environments have ways of dealing with salty soils, but orchids—especially epiphytic orchids used to a diet of pure rainwater—are easily injured when salt levels around the roots get too high, as I discussed in "Water Quality" in Chapter 7.

Besides the problem of salt accumulation, excessive fertilization can cause other health problems in orchids. We humans evolved on a diet that was low in fats and sugar and high in fiber, but we crave fatty and sweet foods because of their nutritional value and former scarcity. However, a diet of French fries, cheeseburgers, and milkshakes, while tempting, has obvious negative consequences for our waistline and lifespan. In a similar fashion, orchids (and most plants, for that matter), evolved in environments where some or all nutrients were in limited supply, so they are programmed to scavenge all they can find. In our land of plenty, where fertilizer flows in great blue (or green) rivers from the watering can, they don't

A balanced, soluble fertilizer contains roughly equal amounts of the three major nutrients: in this case, nitrogen 15%, phosphorus 16%, and potassium 17%. Micro or trace nutrients are listed below the big three.

15-16-17
(For Continuous Liquid Feed Programs)

F1143

Guaranteed Analysis	
Total nitrogen (N)	15%
3.05% ammoniacal nitrogen	
8.04% nitrate nitrogen	
3.91% urea nitrogen	
Available phosphate (P2O5)	16%
Soluble potash (K2O)	17%
Magnesium (Mg) (Total)	0.117%
0.117% Water Soluble Magnesium (Mg)	
Boron (B)	0.02%
Copper (Cu)	0.0075%
0.0075% Chelated Copper (Cu)	
Iron (Fe)	0.075%
0.075% Chelated Iron (Fe)	
Manganese (Mn)	0.042%
0.042% Chelated Manganese (Mn)	
Molybdenum (Mo)	0.0075%
Zinc (Zn)	0.01215%
0.01215% Chelated Zinc (Zn)	

Derived from: ammonium phosphate, potassium and sodium nitrate, urea, magnesium sulfate, boric acid, copper EDTA, manganese EDTA, iron EDTA, zinc EDTA, sodium molybdate.
Potential acidity: 196 lbs. calcium carbonate equivalent per ton.

know when to stop, absorbing the fertilizer ions in excessive quantities, which can lead to flaccid or distorted growth, clogged cells, and increased susceptibility to disease. Too much of a good thing, whether fast food or soluble fertilizer, has its consequences.

If you are using an organic potting mix (bark, sphagnum moss, coconut fiber, tree fern), fertilizing will speed the breakdown of the mix as microorganisms take advantage of the influx of nutrients to consume it. With very light fertilization, organic mixes will last twice as long as they would with moderate fertilization.

So how do you know what is enough and what is too much? Before I answer that question, I must digress a bit and provide some basic facts about fertilizer. Everyone uses the term "plant food" to describe fertilizer, but it is not food in the sense that a tuna sandwich is food for us. Fertilizer does not provide the plant with energy that it can use to drive metabolism. It gets energy from the sun (or artificial light). Fertilizer provides the plant with the minerals it needs for cell growth, biochemical reactions, osmosis, protein synthesis, and so on. The list of minerals on the label of your own vitamin and mineral supplement probably includes calcium, manganese, potassium, phosphorus, iron, boron, and zinc—many of the same minerals found in a complete fertilizer. (In our less sanitized past, we obtained these minerals from the foods we ate and also from the soil that clung to them and our unwashed hands. Now we get them as supplements and "fortification" in cereals and juice.) In the wild, plants obtain nutrient minerals from the soil, mostly from decaying organic material and minerals dissolved out of bedrock. In an artificial potting mix for plants indoors or in a greenhouse, we need to provide supplements in the form of fertilizer. It's basically the same reasoning behind your taking a vitamin/mineral supplement. We are supplying what we no longer get naturally.

People long ago figured out that putting animal manures or other organic wastes around crop plants increased yields, but it was not until the nineteenth century that scientists figured out what the magic ingredients in these materials were. The big three plant nutrients, the ones needed in the greatest amounts and whose scarcity in nature is most limiting to plant growth, are nitrogen (N), phosphorus (P), and potassium (K). The fertilizer label is required to spell out the percentage by molecular weight of the big three in that order. Thus a fertilizer whose analysis reads 30-10-10 contains 30% N, 10% P, and 10% K. The other 50% by weight consists of other nutrients, impurities, dyes, chelates (chemicals that help increase solubility at less than the ideal pH), and "carrier" molecules that have no nutritive value.

Some chemical fertilizers, especially those designed for use on plants growing in soil, contain only the big three. These fertilizers are inadequate for orchid culture, because they lack what are called the minor nutrients or micronutrients—the minerals sulfur (S), calcium (Ca), magnesium (Mg), iron (Fe), manganese (Mn), boron (B), copper (Cu), zinc (Zn), molybdenum (Mo), and chlorine (Cl). Plants need smaller quantities of these than of N, P, and K, but deficiencies can still lead to problems. Fertilizers that contain all these minerals are called complete formulations (or the label may read "with minors" or "includes micronutrients"). Even though the plant may be getting some or all of them from well water if you use it and to a lesser extent from the decay of organic ingredients, like bark, or inorganics, like charcoal or lava rock, in the potting mix, I feel it is always a good idea to use a complete formulation on orchids. And a complete, balanced fertilizer is especially important if you grow in rock wool, Turface, sponge rock, or another inert mix, or if you use RO water.

Because fertilization can have such pronounced positive effects, many growers develop a near-religious devotion to a certain brand or regimen. As with potting mixes, it is tempting to search for the magic fertilizer that will produce lush verdure and a bounty of flowers on your windowsill or in your grow room. However, though not all fertilizers are created equal, I honestly don't believe there are huge differences in results between comparable complete, balanced blends. The larger difference is between one water source and another. A fertilizer that works splendidly for your buddy may yield dismal results for you if your water is of much poorer quality.

The key point is that plants can absorb nutrients through their roots or leaves only in the form of dissolved ions in a water solution. Sorry to subject you to more chemistry, but this is important. When you dump a salt, be it table salt or a fertilizer salt like ammonium phosphate, in water, it dissolves and "breaks apart"; that is, the ammonium separates from the phosphate, and they float around separately as ions. What kept them together as a salt was the sharing of electrons; when they dissolve, the phosphate takes the electron, which has a negative charge, giving the molecule itself a negative charge. Since the ammonium loses the electron, it takes on a positive charge. The plant then sops up these positively or negatively charged ions through special cell pumps in the roots. The plant can absorb only free ions, not salts per se or larger organic compounds.

In water-soluble fertilizers (the kind you scoop into the watering can and drench the plants with), the nutrients instantly dissolve into ions when added to water, so they can be immediately assimilated by the plant. Those ions that are not sopped up right off by leaves or roots will (a) be held temporarily on the electrically charged surfaces of certain colloidal minerals like clay, vermiculite, or organic compounds that form as organic materials decay; (b) be assimilated by microorganisms such as bacteria or fungi in the media; or (c) be flushed out of the mix and down the drain. Since many orchid mixes contain high percentages of fairly decay-resistant noncolloidal inorganic materials, such as perlite or Turface, and similarly decay-resistant organic materials, like sphagnum moss, tree fern, or coconut fiber, the chances are that most of the soluble fertilizer you apply will be washed out of the pot's drain holes. Accordingly, using a highly concentrated soluble fertilizer risks root injury and excessive consumption by the plant—and it's simply a waste. Also, all that fertilizer may contribute to the contamination of water supplies.

Therefore, I stick by the adage "weakly weekly" as far as fertilizer goes. Professional growers calculate fertilizer concentrations based on the ppm of nitrogen, since it is the most important nutrient. Obviously, most hobbyists are not going to bother figuring the ppm N. You can approximate the same result with teaspoons (tsp) and tablespoons (tbsp) per gallon. So if you are using a fertilizer whose analysis reads 20-20-20, for most orchids you can figure 1 tbsp/gal, equivalent to about 250 ppm N, to be a *strong* dose; 1 tsp/gal, equal to $^1/_3$ tbsp, or 83 ppm N, to be a *moderate* dose; $^1/_2$ tsp/gal (42 ppm N) to be a *light* dose; and $^1/_4$ tsp/gal (21 ppm N) to be a *weak* dose. The dosage strengths are relative to the concentration by weight of the major nutrients. If your fertilizer analysis is 10-10-10, then 2 tbsp would be a strong dose, 2 tsp moderate, and so on. If it's 5-6-4, 1 tsp would be a weak dose. I rarely use a strong dose of fertilizer on orchids, though a strong drenching maybe once or twice a year when new growth begins can work wonders for "greedy" genera like *Lycaste* or *Catesetum*. If you fertilize once every two to four weeks, a moderate dose should suffice. If once a week, go with a light dose, and if you want to feed every time you water, use a weak or very weak dose (say, $^1/_4$ tsp/2 gal water for a 20-20-20 fertilizer). In nature, orchids receive a constant very dilute supply of nutrients in rainwater, which picks up residues as it runs through the tree canopy and over bark and moss, so I feel that the best practice is constant-feeding with very dilute fertilizer or feeding at every other watering—especially if you use rainwater or purified water. That way, you get in the habit of using fertilizer, so you're less likely to forget. I don't know about you, but I find it hard to remember when I fertilized last if I do it only once a month or so. If you elect not to constant-feed, try to follow the "weakly weekly" adage as best you can. This will minimize problems with salinity, excess consumption, and media breakdown.

Fertilization and Dormancy

Plants need fertilizer mostly when they are in active growth. Orchids like *Cycnoches* or *nobile*-type *Dendrobiums,* which go completely dormant for part of the year, benefit little from fertilization when they're at rest. In fact, fertilization at these times can interfere with dormancy and thus flowering, as well

as contributing to salt buildup in the potting mix. Most **pleurothallids**, on the other hand, are in active growth year-round, so they will benefit more from a constant program. Also, cool or excessively warm temperatures, the low light at northern latitudes during winter, or stress brought on by poor culture or disease all greatly decrease the need for fertilizer and increase the chance of negative consequences. In general, use the plant's growth as a guide. When it is growing actively and is otherwise healthy, regular fertilization is appropriate; when it is overly stressed or resting, curtail or eliminate fertilizer.

Fertilization and Flowering

Fertilization can certainly be fine-tuned for a particular species to optimize growth and flowering. Quite a bit of research has been done on nutrition for high-value florist crops such as mums and poinsettias. Now that orchids are capturing a larger market share, research on their needs has also expanded. Certain ratios of major and minor nutrients will enhance vegetative growth, while other proportions promote flowering. Bloom-boosting fertilizers are available, but the problem is that very few hobbyists are raising just one particular orchid. Most of us have mixed collections of species and hybrids with very different yearly growth cycles and slightly different nutrition needs. So trying to fine-tune fertilization in a mixed collection is darn near impossible. Unless you specialize in a particular genus, I recommend that you use a complete, balanced fertilizer year-round and just vary the frequency of application. If you see a plant in spike, skip the fertilizer for a few weeks; fertilization during flower development can lead to bud drop.

Types of Fertilizer
SOLUBLE FERTILIZERS

You'll find many soluble fertilizers to choose from, and of course each brand is promoted as "better than the rest." But as far as the plant is concerned, one potassium ion is as good as another, and if the fertilizer is complete—that is, it contains the minor nutrients—and you use it correctly, it should perform well. The most important factor is how a particular brand interacts with your irrigation water. The levels of some ions, like calcium, magnesium, iron, or sulfur, in your water will affect the way other nutrients go into solution. My home well water is so high in iron and sulfur that we have to soften it so that it doesn't stain the bathroom fixtures. Iron and sulfur make for a very low—acidic—pH, which alters the solubility of some nutrients in solution. The well water at the New England Wild Flower Society is full of calcium and magnesium, meaning the water is sweet or alkaline in pH, which makes some minerals (like iron) less soluble. The phenomenal

Nitrogen is a mobile nutrient, meaning that a plant can move it from older leaves into the newest ones, where it will be most needed. Though partially caused by bright light, the yellowing of the older leaves of this *Laelia spectabilis (praestans)* may also indicate a slight nitrogen deficiency.

results some growers get with certain formulations have more to do with their water quality than with anything inherent in the fertilizer itself.

If a water test reveals low levels of calcium in your water or if you use rainwater or purified (RO) water, you may want to try a fertilizer that includes calcium. (Many soluble fertilizers do not, for unless it is formulated very carefully, the calcium will displace phosphorus, causing the phosphorus to precipitate out so it cannot be adsorbed.) If your water is naturally high in calcium, you might try a fertilizer slightly higher in phosphorus to counter precipitation problems. However, I have grown hundreds of species in a greenhouse where the water had enough lime (calcium and magnesium) to leave a white scale on the leaves, and a standard, complete 20-20-20 fertilizer (or one with roughly those proportions) worked very well, mainly because calcium and magnesium are relatively insoluble in water, so only small amounts are present in solution.

Another debate that continues to rage among orchid growers is the best form of nitrogen to look for in a fertilizer.

Nitrogen can be absorbed by the plant as either ammonium (NH_{4+}) or nitrate (NO_{3-}) ions, and fertilizer analyses break down the percentage of each one. There is some evidence (although it's controversial) that orchids and some other families of plants that have evolved in low-fertility environments are sensitive to large amounts of ammonium ions, resulting in a condition known as ammonium toxicity. Therefore, a fertilizer containing two to three times as much nitrate as ammonium is considered ideal for orchids. (The plants absorb and utilize the two forms differently, and both are necessary.) In reality, though, if you fertilize weakly, chances are pretty slim that you will ever see ammonium toxicity develop. It is more common in floriculture operations where heavy doses of fertilizer are regularly applied to crops like poinsettia to maximize growth.

Related to this is the question of urea, which is a synthetic form of organic nitrogen that must be broken down into ammonium by microorganisms around the roots of plants or by the plants themselves before it can be absorbed. Urea is added to soluble fertilizers because the nitrate and ammonium are so soluble that they readily leach out of the pot. Urea is in effect a timed-release form of nitrogen that makes ions available over several weeks, so if you apply fertilizer only occasionally, the plants won't be starved of nitrogen. The problem for orchids—especially epiphytic species growing on mounts—is that conditions are not ideal for breaking down urea. In a pot of soil or in the ground, where moisture and temperature are more constant, microorganisms can do their work more efficiently. An organic, water-retentive mix like Pro-Mix would also provide conditions in which urea could be utilized. On a slab of cork, however, conditions are obviously different. Though bacteria are likely to be living in the **rhizosphere** (the microscopic zone around a root where leachates, mostly sugars, oozing from the root foster colonies of microorganisms that help the root scavenge nutrients), my guess is that most of the urea gets washed away before it can be absorbed. This is obviously wasteful, so check the label to make sure you're getting a low-urea formulation. Some fertilizers sold specifically for orchids state that they are low in urea.

Controlled- or Timed-Release Fertilizers

In the perennial nursery at the New England Wild Flower Society, we rely heavily on controlled-release fertilizers (CRFs) to administer a constant supply of nutrients to the plants as they grow. There are several brands on the market, including Osmocote and Nutricote; to oversimplify, they work by gradually releasing liquid fertilizer from coated pellets over a period of time (given on the bag as a number of days). Release is temperature-dependent, with optimal release around 70° or 75° *on average.* Cool or cold weather slows or stops release, while hot weather speeds it up. Some orchid growers use these fertilizers effectively, but I cannot claim to be one of them. When I experimented with CRFs on epiphytic orchids growing in bark, I discovered that the media broke down rapidly and that roots were easily burned. Perhaps with a more "terrestrial" mix like Pro-Mix, such problems would be lessened, but in my opinion, these fertilizers are simply not formulated for light-feeding, salt-sensitive plants such as orchids. So try them with caution—especially during hot weather.

Organic Fertilizers

The term "organic fertilizer" includes everything from composts and manures to fish emulsion, blood meal or cottonseed meal, and ground crab shells. Most of the nutrient ions they contain are bound up in the complex organic molecules used to build the organism they are derived from. In order for these ions to become available to the plant, the complex compounds must be broken down by soil microorganisms. This means that organic fertilizers are weaker and slower to release nutrients than soluble chemical fertilizers. But, as with urea, it's doubtful that much decomposition takes place on an orchid mount or even in a pot filled with something like lava rock or sphagnum. Most organics do contain low levels of *soluble* nutrients and other compounds, as well as most of the micronutrients that the orchids would be exposed to in the wild, so some very accomplished growers swear by organics. While there are many types that can be used in gardens outdoors, only a few soluble types are suitable for orchids. Fish emulsion made from ground-up fermented fish waste smells as bad as you are imagining, but it is an old standby that can be added to water as needed. I do find the smell hard to take, though. Manure teas are another old solution, and these are much less odoriferous. To make manure tea, cut off a foot from an old pair of pantyhose and fill it with 1 cup of dehydrated (not composted) cow manure. Tie off the open end with a rubber band and put the bag into a 1-gallon jug of warm water. Let the tea steep for twenty-four hours or until it turns a deep brown. Dilute 1 cup of this concentrate in 1 gallon of water and use it to fertilize orchids in active growth once every ten to fourteen days.

With the boom in organic farming in the past ten years, a number of proprietary soluble organic fertilizers have hit the market. There is a bit of snake oil salesmanship about some of these products, which are touted as restoratives as much as fertilizers, and it is hard to say whether they have benefits other than straight nutrition. Honestly, the ones I have tested on orchids performed no better than inorganic soluble fertilizers. One of the oldest proprietary concoctions is Superthrive, which is not technically a fertilizer but rather an additive, used in addition to fertilizer. The ingredients are secret, but the main ones are obviously B-complex vitamins, because it smells just like a bottle of those vitamins you'd buy at a health food store. B-complex vitamins (B_{12} in particular) seem to have some benefits for plants. I have revived highly stressed, dehydrated orchids by soaking them overnight in a solution made from two crushed B complex vitamins in a gallon of water, and I have used Superthrive in the same way. These were not controlled experiments, though, so soaking in plain water may be just as effective.

Fertilizer and RO Water

Remember that distilled water and RO water are very pure, lacking any of the trace minerals found in well water, municipal water, and even rainwater collected from a hot tin roof. Since many "complete" fertilizers are technically incomplete if they do not contain calcium or magnesium, your plants may develop deficiencies unless you alternate with a cal-mag fertilizer every few feedings.

CHAPTER 8

Potting and Dividing

TAKE ONE "o" away from "root" and you are left with "rot." Leave a plant in its pot too long, and the effect will be the same. Regular repotting keeps the medium around the roots fresh and the plant growing vigorously. The irony is that it is better to repot your orchids before they need it, when the mix is still in good condition and the plants are growing lustily. So here is the rub: repotting an orchid carries certain risks. It is, in effect, a form of preventive surgery and, as with any surgery, there is a chance—often a very small chance—that the patient will die. Being risk-averse by nature, I tend to postpone orchid surgery, especially when the plant shows no outward signs of problems, until its condition has deteriorated so much that the plant has a far poorer prognosis and the procedure itself is more complicated.

So let's get to the heart of the matter: when to repot? There

ABOVE: Though an epiphytic orchid can be simply suspended from a wire, it's easier to keep it adequately watered in a pot.

Orchids should be repotted just as they put out a new flush of roots to ensure that they reestablish quickly. This ***Eria convallarioides*** certainly needs a new pot, and if the plant is handled gingerly, its healthy crop of new roots will be undamaged. A few of the young root tips are turning brown as they contact the rim of the pot, a sign that the clay has absorbed dangerous levels of soluble salts.

You can learn much about the health of a plant by examining its roots. The roots of ***Dendrobium alaticaulinum*** are rich in red pigment, which is masked by white velamen when the roots form in air. Here the thick nest of live roots spreading through the NZ sphagnum is a testament to the benefits of irrigating solely with rainwater.

is no question that the best time is when the plant is beginning a period of active root growth. With most orchids, a new flush of roots coincides with or directly follows new top growth. New roots may be either secondary—that is, initiated along older roots (not all orchids can produce secondary roots)—or primary, beginning from the tip of the rhizome at the base of the new leaf (or leaves) or pseudobulb. Seasonal cues help determine when most orchid species begin growth and flowering (see "Day Length or Photoperiod" in Chapter 3). Many growers like to keep to a yearly schedule, doing all their potting at an opportune time, say, in spring just as the plants are surging into growth or, in the case of cool-growing species, in fall or winter when heat stress will be minimal during the recovery period. If you have just a few plants, you can be even more precise, waiting until you notice the faint green swellings of new roots at the base of the lead growth. A section of rhizome has a finite number of preformed root **initials** scattered along its length. When the roots begin growing, they are first visible as bright green "pimples" along the rhizome (usually the lower half), just underneath the new leaf or pseudobulb in the case of sympodial types and in the axils of older leaves for monopodial ones. Once they begin to elongate, these new

roots are obviously fragile, so if you can time your potting to coincide with the first signs of swelling, you will be less likely to damage them, and the plant will be poised to surge ahead in its new medium.

Whether or not your plants will need repotting annually depends on a few variables, including the medium's rate of decay, the quality of your water, the frequency of fertilization, and the growth rate of the plants themselves. Any organic potting medium will begin to decay as soon as the plant is potted and watered in. The *rate* of decay is determined by five factors: the medium's decay resistance, the amount of water available, the level of nutrients in the water, the average temperature, and the available oxygen. All else being equal, a grower in Singapore will have to repot more frequently than one in Alaska simply because the warmer climate will speed up the rate of decay. So while once a year is a good approximation to start from, experience will help you determine the ideal interval in your situation. If you don't fertilize heavily and aren't heavy-handed with the watering wand, repotting once every two or even three years may suffice. Your experience with a particular mix over several years will help you decide.

The physical decay of the potting mix is dangerous to

orchid roots primarily because as the mix breaks down into smaller pieces, the pore spaces, which allow the all-important gas exchange, get smaller, retaining more water and less oxygen than they did originally. However, even an inorganic medium like rock wool or a very decay-resistant organic material like tree-fern fiber must be replaced periodically for an important reason: all potting materials build up levels of soluble salts (present in fertilizers and in all but the purest water) that will eventually lead to root death (see "Water Quality" in Chapter 6). Also, many orchids will simply outgrow their pots and, in the case of species with long rhizomes, even "walk" right out of the container before the mix has broken down so much that repotting is needed.

Repotting an orchid is not like repotting a standard houseplant in certain critical ways. First, the potting medium acts quite different from potting soil. Second, it is very risky to plunk the whole root ball with its old medium into a bigger pot and backfill around the edges. The insidious hazard of simply "stepping up" the whole plant in this way is that the core of the root ball—the mix of older roots and potting medium—will begin to decay even faster in the dark, sweaty interior of the new pot. Not only will the core decay, it can become a source of disease and rot that will spread throughout the pot. New roots coming from the rhizome will run into this dark secret heart of decay and go no farther, and before long the only live roots will be in the air or on the surface or the inner rim of the pot.

To avoid this problem, I like to remove all of the old mix and dead roots from the plant when I repot. For a large, thick-rooted *Cattleya* or *Phalaenopsis* potted in chunks of bark, this is usually a fairly straightforward procedure, but fine-rooted and miniature species are a bit more complicated. To get the dead roots and mix out of the core, you often have to divide the plant and shake or tease out decayed material from the thick tangle of roots. It's necessary to learn the skill of plant division for simple reasons of space. Healthy orchids grow quickly, and unless you divide them occasionally and give the extras to your friends, you will soon find yourself lost in a tangled jungle of exuberant plants. Many orchid businesses have started as a byproduct of successful cultivation. Selling or trading extra divisions or seedlings is a wonderful way to meet other growers and increase the diversity of your collection.

Pots and Other Containers

Theoretically, you can use any container that will hold a potting mix and that has drainage holes in the bottom. In practice, though, an old shoe or your child's cracked beach pail are not the first containers that come to mind when you're searching for something to put an orchid in. Plastic or terra cotta—unglazed earthenware—pots are by far the most common. Which type you should use for a particular plant or for the collection depends on both the mix you use and how heavy-handed you are with the watering can. Unglazed red clay pots

Timely repotting is one of the best things you can do for your orchids. The chocolate color of some pieces of this fir bark shows that it has begun to break down. Other chunks are still a rusty brown, indicating that the mix still has decent structure. In six months this bark will become mushy and waterlogged, leading to root loss and other problems. The plant should be repotted now, before the mix disintegrates.

Special slotted clay orchid pots are a bit more expensive than standard pots, but the slots greatly increase airflow through the potting medium, lessening the chances of root rot. I used a masonry drill bit to make holes in the sides of the small pot, but they may not be large enough; holes at least as big as the drain hole in the bottom would be more effective.

have been the standard containers for orchids since Victorian times (glaze seals up the pores in the clay, so glazed pots are equivalent to plastic). I prefer terra-cotta pots for several reasons. First, I like the look of the clay; the algae and moss growing on an old clay pot give it a weathered look that is particularly appropriate with orchids. Because earthenware is porous, it absorbs water from the potting mix and wicks it to the outside, where it evaporates. This helps dry the mix more evenly, removing some of the moisture from the center, which otherwise might stay too wet. The clay acts as a moisture meter, too. If the pot is damp to the touch, the mix inside is damp and shouldn't need watering yet. Oxygen, which is so vital for orchid roots, can pass through the clay, as can carbon dioxide and other gases. Thus roots in a clay pot can "breathe" much better than they can in nonporous plastic. Clay also pulls mineral salts out of the mix, leaving a residue on the outer surface of the pot, away from sensitive roots. Finally, clay is heavier than plastic, which you might see as a disadvantage, but the weight helps keep top-heavy orchids from toppling over. I should add that stoneware and porcelain, even if unglazed, are not porous, because they are fired at a much higher temperature than earthenware, effectively turning the clay to glass.

For the above reasons, I use only clay pots for my orchids. However, they are more expensive than plastic, and they do dry out the mix fairly quickly—especially pots less than 4 inches in diameter. Commercial growers prefer plastic because it is cheaper to buy and lighter (and thus less costly) to ship. Plastic, at least in the short run, is less breakable than clay, though it does degrade upon exposure to ultraviolet (UV) light, so its lifespan may be only a year or two. (I have clay pots

Slatted teak and cedar baskets come in a variety of sizes and shapes and develop a wonderful gray patina with age.

that have been in continuous service for forty years!) Avoid the plastic pots with saucers that clip onto the bottom, as these markedly reduce the flow of air into the pot. In general, I think it's best to stick with one type of pot, be it plastic or clay, although you can use their different properties to advantage in a mixed orchid collection. If you are growing mostly slipper orchids that require even moisture, they might do better in plastic, but if you also have a few *Cattleyas* and *Dendrobiums* that like to dry out more between waterings, choose clay for those.

Net pots and cone pots represent a compromise as far as plastic goes. Net pots are made of stiff plastic mesh that allows quite a bit of air and water movement in and out of the mix; they are especially valuable if you grow genera like *Dracula*, whose inflorescences tend to burrow down through the pot. They come in small sizes (1–6 inches in diameter); the plastic mesh is not structurally rigid enough to hold up in larger sizes. I have used net pots quite successfully for *Draculas* and other smaller pendent bloomers, but it can be difficult to wet them thoroughly, as water seeks the easier path out through the sides rather than down through the mix. A cone pot, especially designed for orchids, is merely a standard plastic pot with a slotted or netted cone that juts up into the center from the bottom to help aerate the middle of the mix. While more expensive than regular plastic pots and harder to repot into, cone pots can help if you find that your mix is souring in the middle. You can make a cone pot by inverting a small net pot and placing it on the bottom of a larger pot; then place the orchid and mix carefully in the larger pot so as not to tip over the net pot. Adjust the relative sizes of the net pot and the regular pot for more or less aeration. This combination works very well.

Glazed stoneware or earthenware pots are not porous, so the potting mix dries more slowly than it would in unglazed earthenware. Shallow pots drain less well than taller pots of equal volume. The round pot (upper right) lacks a drainage hole and thus is not suitable for orchids.

Baskets are excellent for specimen-sized orchids, being both large enough to contain the plant and porous enough to keep the large volume of potting medium well aerated. This spectacular *Sophrocattleya* Jin is in a 10-inch cedar basket. The Spanish moss has been added for decorative effect.

Slatted cedar, teak, or redwood baskets are other choices; they have much the same properties as net pots yet come in larger sizes. For simplicity's sake, I usually refer to cedar baskets in the text, but I find all three woods to be very satisfactory. Teak is perhaps my favorite, as it has a smooth grain and develops a lovely driftwood gray patina with age. *Stanhopeas, Gongoras,* and other large, downward-blooming orchids do very well in slatted baskets, and they are very popular with growers of *Vanda*-alliance orchids. In the case of *Vandas, Ascocentrums, Angraecums,* and other fat-rooted monopodials, the basket provides a stable platform for the newly potted orchid to root into and a place for hooking a hanger. As the big roots grow, they can meander easily out through the slats and into the air, which is where they prefer to be. Orchids potted in baskets are difficult to wet properly unless you really drench them with a hose or place them in a bucket of water, so for the windowsill grower, baskets are not too practical.

The other drawback of baskets is that because the slat openings are 1/2 inch wide or more, your choice of potting mixes is limited to materials such as the coarser grades of bark, long-fibered sphagnum or sphagnum blends, lava rock, charcoal chunks, or coconut fiber. I usually put a square of 1/2-inch-mesh hardware cloth over the bottom of the basket, which helps contain the mix. The mesh is large enough that even *Stanhopea*'s flower spikes can usually poke through. I have also used the 8–14-inch circular wire baskets that are popular for displaying nonorchidaceous hanging plants like fuchsias or ferns. The openings between the wire spokes are too large for even the coarsest medium, so the basket must be lined with sheet moss, coconut (husky) fiber, or long-fibered sphagnum before it is filled with bark or another orchid mix. I prefer New Zealand (NZ) sphagnum to sheet moss, though it is a little harder to install, as I think the pendent flower spikes have an easier time pushing through it. Sheet moss does look attractive, though, especially if you can keep it alive once the orchid is in place. In either case, soaking the moss thoroughly will make it much easier to line the basket. The main drawback to wire baskets is that they eventually rust (the ones I have been able to find are painted but not galvanized, so they rust after three or four years).

Pot Size

Orchids like to be underpotted; that is, they prefer a pot that accommodates a year or two of rhizome growth and no more. While putting a little orchid into a big pot might seem like a good idea (more root room, more moisture), the reality is that in a pot that's too big the roots and medium quickly develop a rotten, anaerobic zone in the middle. All orchids, even terrestrials, need lots of oxygen around the roots, and smaller pots have more external surface area, where air can be exchanged, compared to interior space. Trust me—it is far better to have

Time to repot. With its pseudobulbs reaching the rim of the pot, this **Maxillaria hedwigae** will soon be out of room.

are sized in ½-inch increments, and the more options you have, the better. Along with the height of the plant, you should consider its clump size, root mass, and rate of growth. Say you have just divided the *SLC* Jewel Box into two pieces, one having six pseudobulbs and the other ten. Jewel Box is a fairly rapid grower by *Cattleya* standards, putting up several new leads from each rhizome in a year, but the new pseudobulbs grow quite close together. Thus you can safely figure that putting it in a new pot that is 1 inch wider than the base of the plant in all directions would give it room to grow for one to two years before it needs repotting. The six-pseudobulb division, which is about 3 inches in diameter at the base, would therefore fit nicely into a 5-inch pot, while the ten-pseudobulb piece would be better accommodated in a 6-inch one. In discussing plants and pots, I use the pot's diameter to indicate size; thus a 5-inch pot means one with a 5-inch top diameter. Of course, that pot could be 3 inches or 3 feet tall, but pots suitable for orchids are usually about equal in height and width, within a range of one and a half times taller or shorter than the diameter.

Some specialty suppliers carry clay orchid pots that are slit down the sides before being kiln-fired or that have extra drainage holes cut into the bottom, and these do provide better airflow through the pot for species that need it. You can even drill your own extra holes in clay pots using a special masonry drill bit, which you can get at a hardware store. Use a ½-inch or smaller bit, and make sure the pot is good and wet (soak it for ten minutes in a bucket) before starting. That will make the drilling easier and the clay less likely to crack. Don't bear down too hard, or you are likely to chip or crack the pot. Oh, the lengths we orchid growers will go to for our plants!

CROCK

For decades, or perhaps centuries, the accepted way to improve drainage in a pot has been to add crock—traditionally, broken bits of clay pots—to the bottom before potting. The reality is, though, that crock doesn't improve drainage. I won't bore you with the details, which have to do with the capillary action of water, but suffice it to say that with traditional potting soils, adding crock just decreases the effective size of the pot's interior. However, for most orchid mixes, which are extremely coarse to begin with and thus similar to crock in their capillary abilities (or lack thereof), adding crock can improve the aeration of the mix by reducing the dead zone in the core of the pot where decay usually begins. Have I confused you yet? The point is, unless you are using a peat-based mix like Pro-Mix, adding crock reduces the volume of the mix relative to the volume of the pot and provides a crockery channel for air to flow up into the center (much the way a

a plant in a small pot that needs to be watered twice a week than one in a large pot that needs watering every ten days.

As you gain experience, you will be able to judge what size pot to use for a particular plant without even thinking about it, but here are some guidelines for beginners. Generally, pick a pot whose top diameter is roughly a third to a half of the height of the plant. Thus, if you have a 10-inch-tall *SLC* Jewel Box, a 4- or 5-inch pot would be appropriate; and a 2-inch-high *Pleurothallis* can happily inhabit a 1-inch-diameter thumb pot. Tall, canelike orchids such as *Phalaenopsis Dendrobiums* do not really fit this formula, however. Even though they may be 24 inches tall, they can be accommodated in a 4–5-inch pot. It is a good idea to have clean pots in a range of sizes on hand. I have everything from ½-inch clay pinky pots (I had to throw these myself, as no one makes them) to 8- and 10-inch-diameter pots. Under 6 inches, pots

Clay crocking should be oriented so that it doesn't block the drain hole in the bottom of the pot.

Clay crocking placed incorrectly

Finally, a use for those darn Styrofoam peanuts! Here they are arranged so as not to impede drainage.

small net pot can be used to create an "air cone," as I described on p. 58). I have pretty much abandoned crocking pots myself, but I know growers who swear by it, so I will add the following for their sake.

If reducing the relative volume of mix in the pot were your only criterion, any old crock might do. I have used Styrofoam "peanuts" (not the biodegradable kind!) if no pot shards were available. But since airflow is equally important, you can't simply dump a few peanuts or small shards into the empty pot and be done with it, for they can easily settle over and block the drainage holes in the pot, impeding rather than improving airflow and drainage. Take the time to select several shards that are large enough and curved enough to be arranged in the pot to provide a physical channel for air to flow up through the hole or holes and into the center of the mix. I think the illustrations convey this more clearly than words. Styrofoam peanuts are effective for small pots (2½ inches or less) because you can wedge them into the bottom in such a way that they create an airflow channel and do not obscure the drainage holes.

POT CLIPS

Clips are especially useful with loose media like bark and bark mixes, lava rock, and Turface. A newly potted orchid is likely to pitch or tip out of these mixes until its new roots have worked through and attached to the inside of the pot. You can buy pot clips made for all the different pot diameters, or you can construct your own with pliers plus needle-nosed lock-jaw pliers and a few spools of galvanized wire. Pot clips work very well with clay pots but can be adapted for plastic ones, too. The idea is to create a spring-loaded clip that will attach

to the rim and keep the rhizome firmly pressed into the pot. The finished clip should fit snugly around the rim and put enough downward pressure on the rhizome that it keeps the plant from shifting. Galvanized wire comes in different thicknesses, or gauges: 14-gauge wire is suitable for 3-inch and smaller pots, while 10- or 12-gauge (which, counterintuitively, is thicker than 14-gauge) is necessary for larger pots. For very large plants you can use 8-gauge wire, which is very thick and stiff, but I find it hard to bend. Make sure you buy galvanized wire, which is zinc-treated to resist rust. Hot-dipped galvanized wire has an especially heavy coat of zinc, but it tends to chip off when you bend it, so you rarely find it available.

For net pots or slatted baskets, I find it easier to twist a piece of 18-gauge wire around one side of the rim, loop it between the rhizomes of the orchid, then attach it to the other side of the rim so that it pulls the plant down slightly into the container.

To hang pots either from a bar or hook or on a wall covered with wire or hardware cloth, you can buy or make hangers. To hang a pot overhead, use a two-strand wire hanger that clips to the rim (with plastic pots you can drill or melt holes near the rim to run the hangers through). To suspend pots from a wall, one-strand clips are preferable. The easiest way to make one is to run wire up through the drainage hole before potting, then bend it over the rim and also up the outside from the bottom. The only disadvantage of this arrangement is that it's difficult to stand the pot up on a bench for display at your local orchid society meeting!

Mosses, Ferns, Liverworts, and Algae

Live mosses will inevitably colonize the surface of your pots, potting mix, and mounts when you grow orchids in a humid environment. I welcome mosses in my collection for several

Styrofoam can also be used as a potting medium, but it is too loose to anchor this newly potted *Cattleya*. A pot clip is threaded through the pseudobulbs and over the rhizome in the center of the pot.

The clip is forced over the rim, locking the plant in place so its roots can become established.

reasons. First, they serve as the proverbial canary in the coal mine, warning me of salt buildup or stale potting mix before the orchid itself is affected. Healthy, moist moss should be bright green. If it starts to turn brown or tan, it's time to repot or leach fertilizer salts with distilled water or rainwater. In fact, the purer your water and higher your humidity, the more kinds of moss you will foster. A friend who raises orchids in a damp greenhouse and waters with rainwater has an incredible number of mosses growing, many of which probably originated as spores on imported orchids and may be the species that grew with them in the wild. Second, moss provides a natural substrate for the orchid roots to grow through, much as they would in their native setting. This is especially important on a mount, as the cushion of live moss will retain some moisture (and nutrient ions) for the orchid between waterings. As the orchid roots expand, so does this blanket of moss. Third, orchids growing in moss-topped pots just *look* right.

There are about ten thousand species of moss, and identifying them requires years of botanical training and a very good microscope. In other words, I don't know which species of moss are growing in my collection, but I can at least identify the different styles of growth. The most useful for orchids are the low (less than $1/16$ inch high) carpeting species that fan out like tiny groundcovers across a pot or mount. The taller, tufted mosses provide a better root zone, but they can overwhelm a miniature orchid. Mosses reproduce by spores, dustlike particles that float around in the air or cling to clothes or hands. If conditions are to their liking, moss spores will find their way

into a pot and germinate. Once established in your collection, they will produce more spores and thus will quickly colonize a freshly potted or mounted orchid. (Occasionally, if your water is especially pure, sphagnum mosses will begin growing from spores locked in the dead sphagnum fibers.) You can hasten this process by "planting" small pieces of moss on a newly repotted or mounted plant. Rather than bringing in mosses from the woods, I prefer to tear little pieces from older mounts and dab them onto the new medium or tie them on as I am mounting plants. You'll learn which ones will do best in your conditions, so stick with these.

Ferns and liverworts reproduce from spores, too, and in a humid environment you may well find some ferns coming up in the pots. I usually pluck these out because, with a few exceptions, they will eventually get too large and crowd out the orchids. Liverworts are common epiphytes that require very damp conditions like those in a cloud forest; they don't thrive in cultivation unless you use peat-based mixes. Liverworts should be removed, because they form thick mats that can greatly restrict the penetration of water and air into the pot. Hand-picking with a tweezers will remove most of the liverworts, but small pieces can regrow, so you have to watch for their recurrence. Painting on a solution of 1 part vinegar to 4 parts water will kill liverworts (and mosses, for that matter). However, it may damage the orchid roots or leaves, so experiment with it carefully.

Unlike mosses, ferns, and liverworts, which have visible "leaves" and/or stems, land algae are basically colonies of cells that cover surfaces with a thin wash of green. With high humidity, fertilizer, and light, you will inevitably have some algae growing. The sorts that give clay pots a green patina are attractive, I think, and I do little to discourage them. In very wet conditions, though, algae can build up into a dark green, jellylike slime on the potting mix, which—like liverworts—will restrict airflow to the orchid roots. The easiest solution to this problem is to let the surface of the mix dry out between waterings. If this fails, or if you want to remove algae buildup from the leaves of your orchids, washing with a solution—1 tsp/gal—of a disinfectant like Physan 20 or an equivalent will usually take care of it without harming the orchids.

Potting Mixes

Since most tropical orchids are epiphytes, and because even ground-dwelling genera, like the various slipper orchids or cymbidiums, spread their roots through moss and rotting humus rather than mineral soil, standard potting mixes developed for other houseplants and greenhouse plants, like weeping figs or African violets, aren't suitable. Whether they grow naturally on trees or in humus, every orchid I've ever met required a porous, free-draining, well-aerated mix to grow well. A simple but vitally important rule to remember is: *Good drainage or death!*

A number of orchid mix components as well as ready-made mixes are available commercially, and every grower eventually discovers one or more that work well; your choices will depend on the plants you grow, your watering style, the growing environment, and local availability. When you are just starting out with orchids, it is safest to use one of the tried-and-true mixes like fir bark, but as you gain experience, you may want to experiment with others. A word of caution, though. Try out a few plants in a new mix for at least a year before shifting all your plants to it. When New Zealand sphagnum first became available in the late 1980s, many growers, after spectacular early results, started switching over to it completely. But after their orchids began to die they learned that NZ sphagnum accumulates fertilizer residues more efficiently than other mixes, leading to toxic levels of soluble salts unless the medium is flushed regularly with distilled water or rainwater. The story was the same with other "new" media like rock wool and coir. So find a mix that works for you and stick to it unless, after careful experimentation, you discover another that works better. Furthermore, although no single mix works equally well for all orchids, limit yourself to as few different types as possible. This will simplify watering, fertilizing, and repotting immensely.

Don't get consumed by the quest for the *ultimate potting mix*. Some enthusiasts spend what I consider an inordinate amount of time searching for the perfect blend of ingredients guaranteed to produce prize-winning plants. It doesn't exist! One person I know repots his entire collection every year, plunging into the latest fad mix without carefully testing it and learning how he and the plants respond to it. The plants suffer—oh, how they suffer still! Orchids will grow in chopped tires, gravel, coconut-husk fiber, bark chips, peat/perlite-based mixes, New Zealand sphagnum moss, and so on, but each medium retains water, nutrient ions, and salts in very different ways. It takes some experience to learn how much to water and fertilize with each kind.

As I've said, it's a good idea to begin with a potting mix that's known to work, such as fir bark. Observe how it retains water, how quickly it breaks down, and how various plants fare in a fine, medium, or coarse mix. Then experiment with a different medium or a blend of several components. When you divide a particularly robust orchid, pot a couple of divisions in the new mix and the rest in the old and compare their responses over the course of a year or two. Is growth more vigorous in the new mix? Is flowering more exuberant? How are the roots? If there is a marked improvement, try more divisions in the new mix, but *be conservative!* Evaluate the mix for a year or two before repotting your whole collection in it. Remember that what works for a friend or a member of your Internet chat group may not work for you. Also, it often takes a year for problems to become evident.

One of the great mysteries of horticulture is what might be called the you-factor. Two people can take divisions of a single plant potted in the same mix and grow it under ostensibly the same conditions, and one thrives while the other shrivels. Why? No one can say, exactly. Maybe the successful grower was less heavy-handed with the hose. Maybe her fan moved a bit more air, or her windows let in a bit more light. Maybe his water was more suitable. What works for one grower may not work for you; that's the you-factor. I absolutely believe that the best horticulturists are simply very good observers and good experimenters. Some people seem to be born with an ability to look at a plant empathically and tell whether it is thriving or not, but most of us come to that understanding through experience. Any gardener can usually pick the "better" of two plants, meaning a plant that is healthier, thriving more than its companion. Recognizing the difference is the fundamental skill of horticulture; the trick is in figuring out the most likely reason for the weaker plant's failure to thrive. That takes experience, experimentation, and an open mind.

When trying to discover what ails a particular plant or an entire collection, try to eliminate as many variables as possible. If you are providing the recommended amounts of light, water, humidity, and fertilizer; the right day and night temperatures; and sufficient air movement, yet several orchids that thrive for a friend grow poorly for you, either move on to others that are easier to grow or begin to test hypotheses.

Could the plants have a virus or just be genetically weak? As with all organisms, some individuals within the species will have a constitution that is more amenable to cultivation. If you have eliminated most other variables, it may be time to try another potting mix or, even better, try mounting the plants on plaques. Just don't blame the mix for every failure—in the end it may be that certain plants are not right for your conditions. Chalk it up to the you-factor and move on.

Whatever mix you choose, aim for a good balance between water-holding ability and aeration. All roots need both water and air (oxygen) to survive, and the two tend to be mutually exclusive. The more water a mix contains, the less oxygen, and vice versa. In a sense, water and air have to occupy the same spaces, or pores, between soil particles, and where water collects, it will drive out the air. Plants like cattails, which are adapted to the waterlogged soils of swamps and marshes, can tolerate lots of water and very little oxygen around their roots. Epiphytes represent the other extreme, tolerating—even requiring—a lot of air circulating around their roots and relatively little water. In a medium that holds too much water, an orchid's roots can literally suffocate. Also, disease-causing fungi like *Pythium* and *Fusarium* thrive in poorly oxygenated (anaerobic) environments. A waterlogged mix and disease organisms can thus act synergistically to kill the orchid's roots. At the same time, the mix should retain some water, so that the roots can absorb what they need to replace what is lost through the leaves—especially in the lower humidity of a house.

The solution is to make sure that the spaces between particles are large enough to hold less water and allow more air exchange; the coarser the mix, the more aerated it will be. Such a mix will retain very little water within the pores, but if it's composed of a fibrous material like bark or moss, as most orchid mixes are, it will sponge up some of the water passing through. So while the pores remain open and full of air, water is retained. Roots growing in contact with these fibrous materials can draw out water just as a cotton rag will draw water from a kitchen sponge. Again, whatever mix you use, your aim is to provide enough water to meet the plant's needs and enough air to allow the roots to breathe. In the table on p. 70 I compare the various components' ability to retain water, among other criteria.

If you decide to experiment with blending your own mix to fine-tune it to your own plants, conditions, and watering tendencies, go slowly. Start with fir bark and try adding no more than 15%–20% of either an inorganic material (to increase drainage) or an organic material (usually to increase moisture and nutrient-holding capacity). If you are dividing a large plant, pot one or two divisions in the new blend and one in the old for comparison. In the end, you may find that the original mix was better.

ORGANIC COMPONENTS (IN ORDER OF POPULARITY)

FIR BARK: Made from the processed bark of the Douglas fir, this is the most popular orchid medium today for several reasons. It is relatively cheap and, as a byproduct of the logging industry, relatively environmentally friendly. Fir bark produced for orchids is graded or sized. FINE bark pieces have an average diameter of 1/4 inch, MEDIUM about 1/2 inch, and COARSE 1 inch or so. The fine grade, which has smaller pore spaces, retains more water and less air. It works well with semiterrestrial genera like *Paphiopedilum* and *Cymbidium,* as well as some of the fine-rooted miniatures and seedlings. Medium-grade bark is more porous, and most of the popular genera like the *Cattleya* alliance, *Phalaenopsis*, *Oncidium*, and *Dendrobium* thrive in it. The coarse grade, which is less common, works for large-rooted orchids like *Vandas* and the bigger *Angraecums*. It is often used in humid, tropical climates where orchids are grown outdoors year-round.

One advantage of fir bark is its natural decay resistance. When fresh, the chunks of bark contain oils, resins, and tannins that repel water and discourage decay. This works to the grower's advantage, since a newly potted orchid will require less water in the period before its root system recovers and it puts on more top growth. After being subjected to water and fertilizer, the bark begins to break down slowly, and it starts retaining more and more water just as the growing orchid needs more. Eventually, though, the bark begins to decay noticeably and become spongy, at which point the roots become sodden and are at risk of rotting. Ideally, you should repot before this last stage of decay sets in, and through experience you will learn when that time has come. Since the surface chunks rot more slowly than the pieces deep inside the pot, dig down a few inches and pull out a chunk from the middle. Squeeze it. Is it spongy or firm? Crack or cut it in two. Is the center dark brown like the exterior, or does it have a lighter, more crystalline appearance? Spongy bark is past replacing, while firm but uniformly darkened bark will need to be replaced soon. A lighter center means the bark should last another six months or so.

Figuring out when to water a plant in bark is tricky, because the surface dries out quickly but water doesn't wick up from the center as it would with moss, so it is easy to overwater. The best way to gauge dampness with bark or any other organic mix is by weight. Learn how a just-watered pot, a semidry pot, and a dry pot feel, and use the weight as a guide. Weight difference is especially noticeable in plastic pots; unglazed earthenware pots wick moisture from the medium, allowing it to dry more evenly. If the clay is cool and damp to the touch, the mix inside will be damp as well. You can also use a sharpened pencil to determine moisture. Stick the pencil into the center of the pot and leave it there for fifteen minutes. If when you

Fine fir bark   Medium fir bark   Coarse fir bark

withdraw it the wood at the tip is dark and wet, then the bark is wet too.

One quirk of fir bark has to do with the way it breaks down. The microorganisms that decompose the bark—or any organic material, for that matter—are limited in their growth by the availability of carbon and nitrogen, both of which they need for growth. Fresh fir bark contains relatively large amounts of available carbon but little nitrogen. Consequently, the decomposers sequester most of the available nitrogen that is applied in standard fertilizers, causing a deficiency in the orchid, which cannot scavenge it as effectively. To give the orchid enough nitrogen for its needs, you should use a fertilizer that has a very high proportion of nitrogen (say, 30%, as in a 30-10-10 orchid formulation). Or you can alternate the high-nitrogen fertilizer and a standard formulation.

Redwood bark, from the coast redwoods (*Sequoia sempervirens*) of California, is less available and more costly than Douglas fir bark, but it offers more decay resistance. Otherwise, what I have said about fir bark also applies to redwood.

Tree fern: This fiber comes from the chopped-up trunks of Southeast Asian, Central American, and South American tree ferns, which belong to the family Cyatheaceae. Tree-fern trunks consist of bundled conductive tubes that carry water and nutrients to the crown. When the trunk is chopped up, the bundles separate into individual tubes or fibers, each ½–3 inches long, black, and very stiff and wiry. The fibers are very decay-resistant and moderately absorbent. When used as a potting material, the fibers form an interlocking matrix like a pile of pick-up sticks, providing a well-aerated space for roots to travel through. Water is held mostly on the surface of the fibers and in pores created in this matrix.

Tree fern is the second most popular orchid potting medium in the United States, but harvesting the fiber necessarily kills the plants; traditionally, wild ferns have been harvested,

so there are ethical questions regarding its use. Currently, all *Cyatheas* are listed in CITES (Convention on International Trade in Endangered Species), Appendix II. Although only a limited number of species are threatened or endangered, determining the species from chopped trunks is virtually impossible except in a laboratory, so all the tree ferns are on the list, just as all wild orchids are. This makes importation of the fiber more difficult, and the consumer has no way of knowing whether or not a particular batch comes from a threatened species. *Dicksonia selowii* (Brazilian tree fern) has long been one of the most popular materials for orchid plaques in Brazil. It is softer and denser than *Cyathea*-type fibers (more like osmunda, really), so it holds far more water than other tree-fern fibers and is difficult to use if you are used to the coarser types. This species grows in some of the most threatened habitat in Brazil, so it too is threatened with extinction and should not be used.

Tree fern comes in long-, medium-, and short-fibered grades. The grades are a gauge of both length and average fiber diameter, and the grades are equivalent to fine, medium, and coarse fir bark in terms of their use. (The main reason it is graded is that the long fibers are impossible to wedge into a small pot—imagine trying to cook full-length spaghetti in a soup bowl.) I have generally used medium grade, as the fine has quite a bit of dust in it. Tree fern also comes in roughly 1-inch squares for use with *Vandas* and other thick-rooted orchids in slatted baskets or large pots.

Tree fern is very springy, and when you force the fibers into the pot along with the plant, they bow under the tension, holding the orchid in place without any need for pot clips or stakes (unless it is very top-heavy to begin with). Since you have to force the fiber and the roots into the pot all in one motion, it takes some practice to know the right amount of fiber to use for a particular pot. I recommend practicing sans orchid a few times so you feel comfortable with the procedure. Take a ball of fibers that is just a bit larger than the pot's inter-

Fine tree fern   Medium tree fern   New Zealand sphagnum moss

nal diameter. Pack the fibers by rolling your thumbs over the lip of the pot and down inside (sort of a thumbs-up to thumbs-down motion). The mass of tree fern should work into the pot relatively easily. If you find that you really have to jam it in, remove some and start again. When you're done, the fibers should be wedged tightly enough that they don't fall out when you invert the pot. With the orchid the procedure is the same, except that you should work the ball of fibers in and around the roots before wedging it into the pot. Be careful not to press down on the rhizome of the plant, keeping your thumbs toward the rim of the pot. I rarely use tree fern alone, but rather mix it with New Zealand sphagnum and coarse perlite on a 2:1:1 basis by volume. This is my standard mix for miniature orchids. I don't use tree fern in pots over 4 inches in diameter, both because of cost and because in large pots it retains quite a bit of water at its core. Since the fibers make only a subtle color change from black to chocolate brown as they dry, it is difficult to judge when to water a large pot. One reason for mixing the sphagnum in with the fern is that the moss helps distribute moisture and gives a more accurate reading of the dryness of the mix.

Tree fern used as a minor component (less than 30%) of a bark or charcoal mix will settle more easily into the pot, making thumb wedging less necessary.

LONG-FIBERED SPHAGNUM: Sphagnum mosses are widespread cool- and cold-climate mosses that grow especially well in boggy soil. In fact, they are the dominant and most important species in northern peat bogs. (The dense floating mats of sphagnum gradually decay to form peat moss, which is harvested for horticulture and, to some extent, for fuel.) Living sphagnum moss has long, fibrous, leafy stems, which grow close together. When sphagnum is harvested and dried, the strands are usually 2–4 inches long, and they dry to a buff or reddish tan color. The fibers are fairly brittle when dry, so rewet them carefully before potting to avoid breaking them up.

Sphagnum has some wonderful properties that make it valuable as a stand-alone medium or as a constituent in a mix. It is fairly sterile and low in pH (which may contribute to its antiseptic properties), and the cells, even when dead, readily soak up water. Sphagnum fibers distribute moisture much more evenly through a mix than most other ingredients can. When the fibers come in contact with a root, they basically give that root access to all the water in the moss, not just what is directly around it. I think of long-fibered sphagnum as a supplemental root system for this reason, and it is especially valuable when you are trying to rehabilitate an orchid with few living roots. *Live* sphagnum, if you're able to get it, works well for certain orchids. I have raised *Pogonias* in it successfully, and I know one *Disa* grower who swears by it. The danger with live sphagnum, though, is that the moss will start growing and will bury the lower part of the orchid in a hummock of fibers. Live sphagnum is very intolerant of salt, so don't use it unless you use rain or purified water.

NEW ZEALAND SPHAGNUM (NZ SPHAGNUM) is better than domestic sphagnum, which becomes rather flimsy when dried. It's marvelous stuff (Chilean moss is equally good). I use NZ sphagnum alone or with tree fern and perlite, gravel, or bark. Be sure to thoroughly wet the moss before potting by letting it soak up moisture in a pail of water and then wringing it out. It expands when wet, so if you pot with dry sphagnum and then water, it can become too tightly packed within the pot. Like peat moss, totally dry sphagnum is very difficult to rewet, requiring several waterings at five-minute intervals or soaking for an hour in a pail. Try not to let the moss become completely dry between waterings. Even a bit of dampness makes rewetting much easier.

Some people like to pack the wet moss into the pot tightly, while others drape it around the roots very loosely and wire or clip the plant to the pot until it takes hold. I prefer the middle road, draping enough moss around and through the roots to

A blend of equal parts of medium-grade tree fern, NZ sphagnum, and coarse perlite

Pro-Mix BX

Coir

keep the plant firmly seated while allowing the moss to remain spongy and aerated. Hold the plant by the crown and drape and weave the fibers around the roots, adding just enough so the plant will fit snugly without compression. Use your thumbs and/or a bamboo stick to work roots and moss into the pot, keeping the fibers vertical as much as possible. Sphagnum fibers accumulate mineral salts readily, and once the salts reach a critical level, they begin concentrating in the root zone; when this happens, a healthy plant can lose its roots within a month without warning. The fibers also begin to decay rapidly at this point. To prevent this, drench the pots heavily at each watering, and repot every twelve months or so.

PEAT-BASED SOILLESS MIXES: Pro-Mix BX is a trademarked soilless potting mix developed for the greenhouse industry that has been adopted by some orchid growers. It is a blend of chunky peat moss and perlite, adjusted to a pH of about 5.7, with limestone, a wetting agent (detergent), and a bit of soluble fertilizer (a "starter charge") added as well. When dry it is fairly porous and is a bit difficult to wet properly (in part because dry peat repels water and also because the material shrinks as it dries, pulling away from the sides of the pot and allowing irrigation water to flow down the sides and out the bottom). But the high proportion of peat in the mix can sop up large amounts of water, so when it is wet, it is *very* wet. Pro-Mix and other such peat/perlite mixes have become popular with growers producing orchids for mass merchandisers, supermarkets, and home centers, as it is more familiar to both the staff and the consumer than bark. I have seen some impressive *Phalaenopsis* grown in a peat/perlite medium, and because it dries more slowly, it is easier to handle on a windowsill. However, proper watering takes some skill. Wait until the mix begins to dry and lighten in color but before it starts pulling away from the sides of the container. If it does get that dry, you may have to set the pot in an inch or two of water for

an hour so the peat can rewet. For terrestrial orchids I have also used a mix we use for our hardy perennials, 60% southern pine bark (a bit flakier and more decomposed than Douglas fir bark), 25% perlite, and 15% peat moss.

COIR AND HUSKY FIBER: The rough fiber that surrounds a coconut has many uses, and one use is for growing orchids. The fresh fibers are called husky, and it is used like osmunda or long-fibered sphagnum. As with these others, packing it right takes some practice. It also dries out less evenly than NZ sphagnum (because it doesn't wick water the way moss does), so the surface will feel dry while the core is still very wet. Husky fiber also breaks down rapidly. For these reasons, it has never become very popular in the United States, though in tropical regions, where the fiber is easier to obtain, it is certainly common. It can be used to line baskets to prevent finer materials from filtering out. Coir is to husky fiber as peat is to sphagnum—the decomposed remains; it comes in compressed bricks that expand when soaked in water. It can be used as a substitute for peat, but I feel that it is inferior.

OSMUNDA: Until bark mixes became popular in the 1960s, osmunda fiber was the preferred orchid medium. When I first began growing orchids in the early 1980s, I could still buy it in the orchid section of my local garden center. However, osmunda, which is simply the harvested roots and rhizomes of ferns in the genus *Osmunda* (you may know cinnamon fern or royal fern from your local woods and swamps), has several drawbacks. Foremost is that harvesting the fiber means destroying the ferns, which are very slow-growing to begin with. Second, the fiber is difficult to pot with correctly. Typically, it comes in chocolate brown to black chunks or wedges. When completely dry, they are rather brittle, but after soaking and squeezing a few times in water, they become spongy and soft. The idea is to wedge the wet chunks in

Coconut (husky) fiber   Osmunda fiber   Peat moss

around the orchid roots using your fingers or a dibble-like potting stick so that the plant doesn't wobble but still has adequate air space. The problem is that packing the chunks in compresses them, and it is easy to compress them so much that porosity is compromised. Even if potted correctly, the osmunda holds quite a bit of water and is hard to rewet if it dries out completely. This difficulty, along with its high cost and the problem of overharvesting, has greatly reduced osmunda's popularity, though you can still find it occasionally.

PEAT MOSS: Peat is the layer of partially decomposed remains of sphagnum mosses and bog plants that forms underneath the live mat of vegetation in cold bogs. The depths of a bog hold very little oxygen; temperatures are always low, nutrients scarce, and the acidity extremely high, which in effect pickles the peat and prevents it from decaying totally. Peat is the main ingredient of soilless mixes like Pro-Mix, and it can be added to fir bark in limited amounts (10%–20%) to create semiterrestrial media. I do not recommend it for general use with epiphytic orchids. **Chunk peat** is not shredded like typical peat moss, and it is available in different size grades. The chunks hold together rather well over time, acting like water-absorbent chunks of bark, really. The coarse grade, containing chunks 1–2 inches in diameter, is a potential addition to orchid mixes in which you need both free drainage and moisture retention. It can also be used in slatted baskets. One of my friends uses it, but I have not had any experience with it.

CORK PELLETS: The unprocessed bark of the cork oak (*Quercus suber*) makes an excellent material for mounting orchids, and it is a renewable resource. Cork oak orchards are periodically stripped of their outer bark, which is mostly processed into wine corks, then allowed to regrow for several years before being harvested again. As a mount, cork is extremely decay-resistant and durable, but when ground into chunks and used as a potting mix, it is less satisfactory. In the

dark, damp confines of a pot, insects and fungi decompose the cork fairly quickly, and unlike fir bark, which breaks down into a humuslike peat, cork turns into a pasty mush after a time—a disastrous condition for air-loving orchid roots.

SUGAR-CANE BAGASSE: Bagasse is the shredded remains of sugar cane—mostly the seed heads and stalks—after the juice has been extracted. Some growers like to use it as a component of terrestrial and semiterrestrial mixes. It drains freely at first but decomposes quickly.

INORGANIC COMPONENTS

PERLITE: Perlite is a form of volcanic glass that has been rapidly heated to more than 1,600°F, which causes it to pop like popcorn as the internal water vaporizes. The resulting material is white, inert, and lightweight, so it's easy to ship and carry; it never breaks down and is excellent for keeping organic mixes like fir bark and tree fern porous as they age. Also, because perlite does not hold water, adding any size to the mix effectively lowers the water-holding capacity. Medium-grade perlite (usually called supercoarse or coarse) is an excellent nonabsorbent additive. **Sponge rock**, which is large-diameter (large-grade) perlite (1/4–1/2 inch), is a popular additive with some growers who need a very free-draining potting medium. One caution: perlite dust is irritating to the lungs and throat; be sure to pour lots of water through the bag before you use it to keep down the dust. Once the perlite is in the pot, irrigation water quickly flushes any dust out the drainage holes, so it is a concern only when in the bag.

CHARCOAL: Hardwood charcoal is added to highly acidic media such as cork or redwood bark to absorb some of the acids. As its use in purification filters attests, charcoal also absorbs minerals from water, helping to keep harmful salts away from roots. It may also have some antibacterial proper-

Chunk peat moss   Sugar-cane bagasse   Coarse perlite

Fine charcoal   Fine gravel   Aliflor

ties. Many orchid supply companies sell fine- and medium-grade charcoal (the size grades are the same as for bark) for use in mixes, though mesquite charcoal, sold as a barbecue charcoal in season, is fine to use; it comes in rather large chunks that have to be crushed for use in fine- or medium-grade bark mixes. In a pinch, I have also scavenged charcoal from the fireplace, but that is a dirty, dirty job (you can put it in a burlap sack and then club it with a wooden mallet—just don't let the neighbors see you). I have added charcoal to bark mixes for years, though I cannot say I have any proof of its effectiveness. Like any filter, charcoal will become clogged after a time, so timely repotting is still important. The last thing you want is for the saturated charcoal to start leaching minerals back into the mix. Aside from its pH-buffering and mineral-absorbing functions, charcoal is very decay-resistant and coarse-textured and, like sponge rock, does not hold water. Accordingly, I add it to bark mixes more to ensure that they remain open and porous as they age than as a filtering

agent. Match the size of the charcoal to the grade of fir or redwood bark. Charcoal dust makes a decent wound dressing when shaken onto a freshly cut rhizome.

WASHED GRAVEL OR GRIT: Washed fine gravel is a good amendment to bark or bark/tree-fern mixes, providing aeration around the organic component much the way perlite or Turface does. Gravel has one major advantage or disadvantage over perlite, depending on the size of the pot: weight. Pots that are 3 inches or less in diameter can tip over easily with a tall plant in them, and gravel acts as ballast to help keep the plant upright. In larger pots, though, the weight becomes cumbersome. The easiest way to get gravel of the proper grade ($\frac{1}{8}$–$\frac{1}{4}$-inch diameter) in small quantities is to buy aquarium gravel from a pet store. Choose the uncolored, natural brown and gray river gravel with edges worn somewhat smooth. Chicken or turkey grit, which is ground-up rock (usually granite) is okay to use as well, as long as you dump it into a sieve and

Comparison of Various Potting-Mix Components

Component	Cost	Water Retention	pH	Decay Resistance	Weight
Aliflor or LECA (Lightweight expanded clay aggregate)	Moderate to high (mainly shipping costs)	Moderate to low	Neutral	Very high	Fairly heavy
Notes: Must be leached thoroughly, as it can absorb salts. Requires good complete fertilizer alternating with cal-mag type.					
Charcoal	Low	Low	Neutral	High	Fairly light
Notes: Used primarily as additive to bark mixes to decrease water retention, increase decay resistance, and help absorb salts.					
Chunk peat	Low (if you can find a source)	High, though difficult to wet initially	Low	High	Light when dry, fairly heavy when wet
Notes: A coarse grade that does not crumble easily is worth experimenting with in bark mixes.					
Coir	Moderate	High	Low	Moderate	Light (fairly heavy when wet)
Notes: Usually comes in compressed bricks that must be soaked overnight. Getting attention because of concerns about overharvest of peat, but it is inferior to peat.					
Crushed brick	Low	Fairly low	Neutral	Very high	Heavy
Notes: See comments for lava rock.					
Fir bark	Low	Low when fresh, medium when partially decayed	Low	Moderate	Fairly light
Notes: The medium of choice in the U.S. for epiphytic orchids. Readily available, and many orchids thrive in it. Select appropriate grade for plant and container.					
Gravel/grit	Low	Very low	Depends on parent rock	Very high	Heavy
Notes: Inexpensive, useful for adding weight to light mixes. Excellent with fine bark and tree fern for small pots and seedlings. Do not use in pots over 3 in. diameter.					
Husky fiber	Moderate (low if purchased from importer of fragile goods — used as packing material)	Moderate when fresh, high when stale	Fairly low	Fairly low	Light
Notes: Popular where coconuts grow. Falls between tree fern and NZ sphagnum in texture and moisture-holding capacity. Tends to dry unevenly and to break down rapidly.					
Lava rock	Moderate	Very low	Neutral	Very high	Fairly heavy
Notes: Salt absorption a potential problem. Works well in slatted baskets, and where overwatering is a concern.					
Long-fibered (New Zealand) sphagnum	Low to moderate	High	Low	Moderate	Light unless very wet
Notes: Use alone or as component. Very good water absorbency, wicking properties. Some antiseptic qualities when fresh. Acts as supplemental root system for weak plants. Absorbs salts.					
Peat	Low	Very high	Very low	Moderate	Light when dry, fairly heavy when wet
Notes: Holds a lot of water, so is useful to avoid underwatering, especially of terrestrials or plants in dry house. Use no more than 25% in mix.					
Peat-based mixes (like Pro-Mix)	Low	High	Near neutral	Moderate	Light unless very wet
Notes: A good choice for some windowsill growers, though easy to overwater.					
Perlite	Low	Very low	Moderately high	Very high	Very light
Notes: Used as component (usually less than 25% by volume). Adds porosity and lowers water retention.					
Pumice	Moderate to high (mainly shipping costs)	Low	High	High	Fairly heavy
Notes: See comments for LECA.					
Redwood bark	Moderate	Low when fresh, moderate when partially decayed	Very low	Moderate (higher than fir bark)	Fairly light
Notes: Like fir bark. Redder color, more decay-resistant.					
Rock wool	Moderate	Low to high, depending on type	Neutral	Very high	Fairly heavy when wet
Notes: Not attractive. Requires practice to use effectively. Fertilizing is tricky.					
Rubber	Low	Low	Neutral	High	Fairly heavy
Notes: Try it if recycling is important to you and aesthetics are not.					

COMPONENT	COST	WATER RETENTION	pH	DECAY RESISTANCE	WEIGHT
Sugar-cane bagasse	Low (if you can find it)	High	Low	Low	Light
Notes: Suitable for moisture-retentive mix (less than 20% of blend). Interesting silky-rough texture when fresh. Provides more structure than peat or coir, but decomposes quickly so requires annual repotting.					
Tree fern	High	Moderately low	Moderately low	High	Light
Notes: Superb for orchids, but conservation concerns may restrict use in future.					
Turface	High (mainly shipping costs)	Very low	Neutral	Very high	Heavy
Notes: Limited uses; can be used in terrestrial blends.					

Fine fir bark

Medium fir bark

Coarse fir bark

Fine tree fern

Medium tree fern

NZ sphagnum

Sphagnum/tree fern/perlite

Osmunda

Peat moss

Chunk peat moss

Coir

Husky fiber

Sugar-cane bagasse

Pro-Mix

Coarse perlite

Fine charcoal

Aliflor

White pumice

Fine Turface

Fine gravel

Crushed brick

Rock wool

Supercoarse vermiculite

Coarse pumice

Rock wool

Crushed brick chunks

rinse it with water to remove dust and fine particles that could clog the mix. Look for the coarser grade, with diameters as described for washed gravel. I knew one grower who had very good luck raising rupicolous *Laelias* and many other miniature orchids in straight gravel, though I found it hard to water and fertilize correctly myself. Potting is certainly easy, though, as the stones work themselves around roots very quickly with a few taps of the pot.

LAVA ROCK: Lava rock is a very good growing medium for orchids because it does not rot, is well aerated, and retains water. The only problem is that it tends to accumulate mineral salts. Do not use lava rock if your water contains large amounts of dissolved minerals.

LIGHTWEIGHT EXPANDED CLAY AGGREGATE (LECA): These pellets, also known as grow rocks and Aliflor, are made by spinning clay in a revolving or rotary kiln, which yields little ceramic balls of various diameters. Expanded clay got its start in the construction industry as a lightweight aggregate in concrete. The hydroponics industry, especially in Europe, capitalized on it as a medium in soilless culture because of its light weight and absorbency. Since orchid-growing has much in common with hydroponics, it was not long before people started experimenting with it. It absorbs salts, so use it only with pure water. **Pumice** is a volcanic mineral that can be employed much like LECA.

CRUSHED BRICK: You can buy crushed brick from a brick manufacturer, or you can crush a few new red bricks (not concrete bricks) with a sledgehammer, but wear safety glasses! I have seen 1-inch-diameter crushed brick used occasionally in slatted baskets, where it functions much like lava rock, with similar advantages and drawbacks. **Broken clay pots (crock)** can be used as a medium in the same way, though they are best employed for crocking.

ROCK WOOL: This is an insulation material made from lava deposits that are melted, spun, given a water-repellency treatment, then bound together in a wool-like fleece. Like LECA, rock wool has crossed over from industry into the hydroponic and horticultural world. It can be manufactured to either absorb or repel water, and by combining the two kinds, you can achieve different water-holding capacities. I don't find it aesthetically pleasing, and I think it is difficult to pot with properly. In order to stabilize the plant in the pot, you need to pack the rock wool in dangerously tightly.

TURFACE: This calcined clay material is available in grades equivalent to perlite and can be used as a substitute for perlite or other aggregates (materials added to a mix to increase pore space), especially in mixes for terrestrial orchids or seedlings. It does have some water- and nutrient-retaining ability. Because Turface is heavy and very expensive to ship from the few places it is manufactured, I rarely use it.

VERMICULITE: A very lightweight claylike mineral that is used to increase aeration, vermiculite does hold some water. It is used extensively in general horticulture, but less often for orchids. It is suitable for semiterrestrial blends.

GROUND RUBBER: Old automobile tires are definitely an eyesore in the landscape and difficult to recycle. Orchid growers, especially those in humid tropical climates, have experimented with shredded tires as a potting medium. I have seen tire chunks used primarily in slatted baskets with *Vanda*-alliance species, and I don't think you could find more a rot-resistant potting material. I also doubt that you could find anything uglier. Chunks as large as 1½ inches square are used for large-rooted *Vandas*. Rubber does not absorb water or nutrients, though some water does collect temporarily in the cracks between chunks. Its primary function is as a holdfast for roots to twine around.

Fine Turface   Supercoarse vermiculite

Dividing Orchids
DIVIDING SYMPODIALS

By definition, sympodial orchids send up growths one after the next on a creeping horizontal rhizome with several leaves, leafy stems, or pseudobulbs strung along it at intervals, terminating in a lead or dominant growth and bud. A healthy plant usually produces secondary rhizomes originating from side or axillary buds farther back on the rhizome. These will eventually branch as well, resulting in a plant with multiple leads.

In theory, dividing such a plant is simply a matter of severing some of these rhizome connections, separating the pieces, and teasing apart the roots. In reality, it is usually not this straightforward, as many species produce only short sections of rhizome between the growths, and the rhizomes have a way of knitting and weaving through one another. Also, the rhizomes often hide in a nest of intertwined roots, which makes it hard to see the rhizomes and separate the severed pieces. Don't be afraid to *gently* tear the sections apart. Just make sure you are grasping the roots and rhizome, not the more easily damaged leaves.

Small, clumping plants like *Masdevallia*s have such short rhizomes that severing them is difficult. Fortunately, they are easily broken apart. To divide a small plant like this, I remove it from the pot or mount, shake out as much of the old potting medium as possible, gingerly grab the plant with both thumbs and forefingers where the roots meet the leaves, and twist in opposite directions (one hand turning away, the other hand turning toward me). Or I rock the sections back and forth so that the leaves clap together like hands until the sections begin to split apart. Then the roots can be teased asunder. Remember to grasp the plant by the rhizome and roots, not the leaves. Inevitably, you will break off a few leads and leaves, but enough of the intertwined rhizomes will remain in the sections to easily reestablish the new plant. Once you've made the initial division, it becomes easier to

make the rest, splitting the clump into smaller and smaller pieces. As with larger plants, though, you can easily reach a point of diminishing returns; if the sections are too small, they won't recover quickly from the trauma. With miniatures, try to leave at least six healthy leaves and/or pseudobulbs per division.

A variation of this technique is effective for dividing larger species with short sympodial rhizomes. *Stanhopeas,* for example, have large, deflated-beach-ball pseudobulbs set quite close to one another, making it difficult to sever the rhizome hidden in between. If you grasp the three or four newest pseudobulbs and bend the set at right angles to the ones behind them, then tear, they usually come apart clean—it's much like separating bananas. For species with longer rhizomes, a sharp razor blade or pruning shears makes a cleaner job of it.

Once you have divided the plant, whether large or small, remove as much of the old potting mix as you can. If left in place, it will hasten the souring of the new mix. However, orchid roots are very good at gluing themselves to the substrate—a handy skill when growing in trees—so you will find some bits of mix stuck to the roots. Don't try to remove these particles; tearing them off will injure the root, allowing an entry place for disease.

Now examine the roots. Healthy live roots are somewhat stiff and turgid and will snap like a carrot if bent too far. They should be white or translucent white (roots that develop inside the pot do not have the thick coat of velamen present on air roots, so they look less opaque). Roots growing in bark mixes will show some tan or reddish brown tannin staining, but if you snap the root, it should break cleanly and be crisp and turgid inside. Dead roots are usually gray-brown; they are mushy or papery and disintegrate easily. Often the outer part of a dead root pulls away, leaving just the threadlike inner core hanging there. Even with the best of care, roots eventually die and are replaced by new ones, so don't be alarmed by dead ones. After you tease away most of the old potting mix, snip

1. This *Laeliocattleya* has grown out and away from the pot, and the potting medium has decayed badly. The plant should have been repotted a few months ago, when the new roots on the developing growth were just beginning to grow.

2. I have removed the plant from the pot and turned it over to show both the white aerial roots and the subterranean roots stained light brown from tannins in the decayed bark mix. Luckily, most of the roots are still alive.

3. The plant has only one lead. Although most of the old, leafless pseudobulbs are still alive, I decide to sever the rhizome with flame-sterilized pruners in order to accommodate the orchid in a 5-inch clay pot.

4. I consider two healthy, mature pseudobulbs and a nearly mature new growth to be the minimum size for a division of a *Cattleya*-alliance orchid.

5. Because most of the roots on this division are aerial, I have trimmed them back to about 4 inches. If long aerial roots are buried in potting mix, they will usually rot. By trim-

ming them, I leave enough root to keep the plant hydrated while encouraging the cut roots to branch and form a system more appropriate for conditions in the pot.

6. I don't want the sensitive aerial roots to suffocate, so I choose a pot one size smaller than normal for a division this large. By butting the tail end of the rhizome against the side of the pot, I leave room for the next new growth to develop inside the rim of the pot. By the time this plant needs to be repotted again, in a year, a new subterranean root system will have formed. At that time, I will put it in a pot large enough to accommodate two new leads.

7. I attach a rhizome clip after lightly packing medium-grade fir bark in among the roots. Notice that the rhizome is just at the surface.

8. The finished division, ready to go back into the collection. Monitor newly repotted orchids carefully for signs of drought stress, such as shriveling pseudobulbs and wrinkled or yellowing leaves.

or cut the dead roots off—be sure to use sterilized cutting tools—as close to the rhizome as possible. I prefer to leave healthy roots intact when repotting, though if you break some during the division process, cut them back past the injured section. Most orchids can regenerate new root tips from a healthy root if the existing tip is injured. The roots of most slipper orchids and pleurothallids cannot do this, however; once the root tip is damaged, the root can grow no farther. Don't remove such compromised roots—just be extra careful to avoid damaging the growing tip when working with these orchids.

DIVIDING MONOPODIALS

Monopodial orchids produce a vertical stem clothed in alternating leaves. Usually, a single root develops from each older leaf axil along the lower part of the stem. The length of the internodes—the spaces between successive leaves—determines how fast the stem will lengthen. Some monopodial genera, like *Phalaenopsis*, *Aerides*, *Sarcochilus*, and *Ascocentrum*, have very short internodes, and thus the plants stay rather compact. *Ascocentrums* in particular also freely produce offsets along the lower part of the stem; these begin as a few

1. This *Masdevallia* hybrid has grown quite large in the eighteen months since it was last repotted.
2. Pieces of fine fir bark have clogged some of the small drainage holes in the 3-inch square plastic pot. The roots on that side are concentrated near the surface, where the oxygen supply is better, and the interior of the mix has few roots. I will switch to a 2½-inch clay pot, which will give the roots better aeration.
3. By delicately tearing and twisting the clump, I am able to tease apart large sections.
4. I manage to get six small clumps out of this plant. This particular division has eight leaves and three new leads

developing, and its roots are in pretty good shape. I have removed a few dead leaf bases but left the roots untrimmed.
5. Since the *Masdevallia* has new leads on three sides, I center it in a pot just large enough to accommodate it for a year. Cradling the plant in one hand, I bunch a blend of medium tree fern, perlite, and NZ sphagnum moss in around the roots, then gently force the roots and mix into the pot and pack a few more bits of mix around the rhizome.
6. The completed plant is firm in the pot, so no clip is required.

1. Though not large enough to warrant division, this *Paphiopedilum* will benefit from fresh potting medium.
2. Terrestrial rather than epiphytic, *Paphiopedilums* have stiff brown roots covered with hairs that aid uptake of water and nutrients. The roots will not branch if cut, so I must take care to minimize damage during repotting.
3. I have teased apart two mature fans for demonstration. These could be potted separately or left in the same pot. Splitting them apart should induce each to form a new fan, whereas only one would have been produced if they were left connected.
4. The roots are set into a clean pot, and a mix of fine fir bark, sugar-cane bagasse, and perlite is sprinkled in. I tap the pot gently with my palm or rap it lightly on the potting bench to work the mix into the crannies between the roots.
5. The finished plant.

leaves sprouting from an old leaf axil and eventually develop their own stem and roots. Once these offsets have at least five leaves and a few stout roots, they can be carefully severed just above their point of attachment to the main stem with a sharp, sterile blade or snips.

Phalaenopsis and related genera such as *Doritis* are less likely to produce removable offsets, because their internodes are very short and hidden by the leaf bases. Thus division is seldom necessary; instead, the plants are usually repotted to reset the stem lower. For growers who like to have divisions to share with friends, *Phalaenopsis* can be downright uncooperative. However, some produce little plantlets called keikis from buds on their flower stems. Keikis may be a sign of trouble in the mother plant—damage to the growing tip, root problems, or other stresses—or it may be just a natural means of reproduction. Not all orchids produce keikis spontaneously, but researchers have discovered the hormones that convert flower buds into vegetative growths. The hormones are available as a paste, known as keiki paste, which can be applied to a healthy, undeveloped flower bud to trick it into becoming a little plantlet. When the plantlet forms a few leaves and roots, it can then be snipped off. Keiki paste works best on species that tend to produce keikis naturally. (Some sympodial species, particularly certain *Dendrobiums, Pleurothallis,* and the equitant *Oncidiums,* readily form keikis; however, with sympodials you should remove the keiki only after it has formed at least two leaves or pseudobulbs with associated roots and has begun to grow another.)

Monopodials with longer internodes—including many *Vandas* (especially the TERETE-leaved *Papilionanthes*), some *Angraecums,* and *Renantheras*—will quickly climb up and away from their container or mount. In the wild, this is a way to boost the plant higher on its chosen branch, but this habit make these orchids difficult to maintain on a windowsill or under lights. As the plant grows taller, the lower leaves usually begin to die, leaving only shriveled leaf bases, under which

Viruses are the most insidious threat to your orchid collection, because they are invisible to the naked eye and impossible to cure once a plant is infected (see "Viruses" in Chapter 10). Seedlings fresh from the lab are quite reliably virus-free, because virus organisms aren't passed on to the seed. Tissue-cultured clones are likewise mostly virus-free, as long as the lab operators took precautions to isolate uninfected tissue. However, many older cultivars, especially divisions passed around from grower to grower, are likely to be infected. All orchid viruses yet discovered spread through exchange of fluids, so people are one of the two main vectors of these diseases in cultivated situations (sucking insects are the other). The techniques I'm about to describe may seem like overkill, but in the case of orchid viruses the old saw is true: "An ounce of prevention *is* worth a pound of cure." Considering the cost per pound of orchids today (I have paid upward of $50 for a *Lepanthes* weighing half an ounce, putting its value at over $2,000 a pound!) and that the only recourse once a plant has become infected is to discard it or risk infecting others, I think a little precaution is warranted.

The most common way that we spread viruses is on cutting tools. While it's handy to have a trusty pair of pruners bulging out of your back pocket, ready to snip off a yellow leaf here and a spent bloom there, this is a dangerous habit, because viruses can lie in wait on the blade, ready to infect the next plant you groom. *It is vital to disinfect cutting tools between plants.* There are two ways to disinfect: with heat and with chemical sterilants. Viruses are killed at temperatures above 250°F, and "flaming" your tools is a good, albeit somewhat overdramatic, way to sterilize them. (The flame of a candle or cigarette lighter is not hot enough to do a quick and effective job.) I have a propane torch used to solder copper pipes that has a self-igniting trigger. You simply pull the trigger and out shoots a blue flame that will fry anything in sight. Run this flame over all blade surfaces in a slow, rhythmic motion, so that every section is under the flame for a couple of seconds. This works only with all-metal pruners, as the heat can travel down to plastic handles and turn them goopy.

Instead of pausing to flame your instruments every few seconds, you can save a lot of time by using utility razorblades (the kind you get at the paint store for scraping windows). They come in packs of a hundred and are very cheap, so you can use a new one for every plant. Using the blades takes some getting used to if you are accustomed to the scissorslike operation of pruners. Keep an old coffee can nearby to toss the used blades into, and when you have exhausted your supply, spread the pile on a piece of aluminum foil over a cookie sheet and bake them in the oven at 400° for an hour. After they cool, they are ready

for another round. As individual blades become rusty or dull, discard them.

You can sterilize your tools chemically with household bleach (chlorine) or alcohol (use rubbing or isopropyl alcohol rather than the good Scotch—it's more effective and you won't be tempted to have a wee nip now and then). Dilute bleach to 10% by adding 1 part bleach to 9 parts water. Alcohol can be used full strength (usually 70%) right out of the bottle. Use bleach to sterilize used pots and rhizome clips as well. I don't like using bleach to sterilize tools myself, because it has such a powerful smell and because I inevitably fling droplets onto my clothes, which develop into the telltale white dots of sloppy laundry work. Alcohol is easier on the nose and clothes, and you can flame the treated tool to burn off any residue (this may also aid disinfection and is in any case a dramatic flourish to impress your friends with). Tools should soak in either alcohol or bleach for at least ten minutes, meaning you will need either two or three sets of tools or a lot of patience. Only the cutting surfaces of the tool need to be submerged.

One final note. Your hands can also spread viruses, especially when you're dividing plants, and though you can swab them with alcohol between orchids, it is easier to wear latex (or latex-free) disposable gloves.

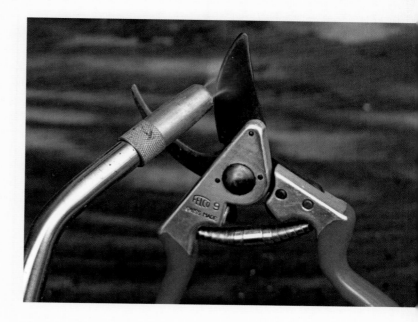

The fastest way to sterilize pruning shears is with a small propane torch. Pass the flame over the blade(s) for three to five seconds to kill viruses and other pathogens that might otherwise be transmitted in sap from an infected plant.

This monopodial was getting very lanky, so the grower simply cut off the top 8 inches of the stem (which had a few small roots already) and potted it in NZ sphagnum. The sphagnum wicks water to the undersized root system, preventing dehydration while the cutting becomes established.

new roots emerge. Hormones in the growing tip suppress the development of lateral shoots as well as roots, but as the stem lengthens and the growing tip gets farther from the base of the plant, side shoots and roots will usually develop along the lower stem, along with a good number of healthy roots farther up. At that point it is simple to sever the main stem just above the side shoots. Just how many roots are necessary to sustain the severed top depends on your conditions. In general, you'll want at least one root for every inch or two of stem, and the roots should be at least as long as the leaves. In a greenhouse with an average relative humidity of 80%, you can get by with fewer roots per division than you need in the drier conditions of a house. If a severed top, once repotted, begins to look desiccated or shriveled, you may have to rehydrate it occasionally until it establishes an adequate root system. The easiest way to do this is to place the plant top in a large clear plastic bag for a few weeks, taking care to look for signs of fungus disease. After the beheading you'll have a more manageable top section, complete with roots, and a bottom section with one or more side shoots that will begin to grow in earnest once the main growing tip has been removed. Of course, once the side shoots have formed enough roots, you can also cut off a few to share with friends.

CHAPTER 9

Mounting Orchids on Plaques and Branches

WE ALL ASSOCIATE plants with the earth, with soil, rock, and humus. So we are amazed at epiphytism, one of the most remarkable and counterintuitive abilities of the majority of members of the orchid tribe. Most small plants growing in forested areas are forced to live beneath the trees, where light is in short supply. Epiphytes—technically, plants and fungi that grow on the aboveground parts of a larger, woody plant without parasitizing it—have overcome that limitation by learning how to live on branches in the forest canopy, where light is more plentiful. With new opportunities come new challenges, and in the case of epiphytism, these include obtaining adequate water and nutrients, as well as finding a trunk or branch that is not likely to die, break off, and fall to the ground. In temperate climates only ferns, club mosses, true mosses, and, especially, lichens are capable of surviving as epiphytes; hardy or temperate-climate orchids are all ground dwellers. In the damp subtropics and tropics, many, many more plants can survive as epiphytes. In cloud and rain

ABOVE: *Schomburgkia* species and bromeliads growing epiphytically along the Napo River in Amazonian Peru

forests, every tree is covered in a coat of ferns, orchids, and mosses, as well as other plants, such as bromeliads, that have adapted to a high-rise life.

I find it truly amazing to be able to cultivate orchids as air plants on a branch or a piece of cork or tree fern. If you are used to raising orchids in pots, growing them on mounts is a liberating experience. The way their roots trail into every crevice in the bark, knitting the plant to its support, the look of a perfectly proportioned little *Pleurothallis* hanging from a mossy branch like a self-styled mobile—well, it's just *right*. Granted, mounted plants require more frequent watering and higher humidity than potted plants, but they are less prone to root disease and require less yearly maintenance. You can even grow mounted plants on a windowsill if you stick with the more drought-tolerant, adaptable genera such as the small *Oncidiums*, *Encyclias*, *Leptotes*, *Laelias*, and *Brassavolas*.

Encyclia citrina 'Yasnita' AM/AOS, a pendent species, is just about impossible to grow in a pot. However, it thrives on a mount, even indoors.

A wall becomes a garden when you grow mounted orchids.

When mounting or potting a particular orchid and placing it in an appropriate growing spot, it is helpful to keep in mind its position on an idealized host tree. Beginning at the base of a tree growing in the rain or cloud forest, we find first a shaded, heavily moss-covered trunk emerging from the ground. In this sheltered, damp, stable environment grow semi-epiphytes, including some *Paphiopedilums*, *Zygopetalums*, and *Angraecums*, which have some roots that travel through the moss and others that wind down into the leaf litter on the forest floor. As we move farther up the trunk, we find conditions that are still relatively stable and shaded, with enough moss to catch and hold water between rains. Here you might find a *Dracula* or a large *Masdevallia*, *Stanhopea*, *Pescatorea*, or *Phalaenopsis*, with roots that creep over the mossy trunk and big flat leaves adapted to the low light conditions. On the upper surfaces of higher, horizontal limbs of larger trees, a thick moss mat will also develop, but here, though there's more light and air movement, there is less available water. These larger horizontal limbs support the densest community of epiphytes, including *Cattleyas*, certain *Oncidiums*, *Lycastes*, and many other larger orchids that are too heavy for smaller branches, as well as smaller *Bulbophyllums*, pleurothallids, and the like, which revel in the brighter light combined with moisture-retentive moss. In general, vertical or diagonal tree branches shed water more quickly than horizontal branches, so less moss develops in these drier conditions. More drought-tolerant orchids, including *Cycnoches,* the mule-ear *Oncidiums, Encyclias,* and some *Dendrobiums* and *Maxillarias,* thrive on these drier branches in wet climates and are also able to survive seasonally dry conditions.

On the smaller branches and twigs, conditions are unpredictable. Small twigs, exposed to more light and wind, are likely to die or be snapped off rather than continue growing for a long time. Even if a twig does survive, an orchid growing on it will find itself farther inside the dimming branch canopy as the tree continues to grow. Twig epiphytes, the group of

Clumps of *Bifrenaria harrisoniae* growing as lithophytes in full sun in Brazil

The rambling little *Epidendrum porpax* is another easy species to try on a mount. All it requires is a good misting every few days and a thorough drenching at the sink once a week.

orchids that are adapted to the uncertain life on the outskirts of the canopy, are typically small (the lighter they are, the less chance that they will hasten the twig's breaking off); fast-maturing, so that they can begin flowering and setting seed before conditions change; and adapted to high levels of air movement. Some examples of twig epiphytes are the equitant *Oncidiums, Trisetellas,* some *Stelis* and *Pleurothallis, Sigmatostalix,* and *Ornithocephalus.*

In general, large or thin-leaved evergreen orchids that prefer the lower trunk need more shade and water than those with more leathery leaves that grow farther up. Twig epiphytes often have swollen, water-storing leaves and nests of thin roots. They require bright light and lots of air movement coupled with adequate humidity to thrive. Plants with finer roots or those that lack fleshy leaves or pseudobulbs need a more water-retentive mount than do plants with thick roots and/or water-storing leaves and stems.

I should mention that certain orchids have adapted to life on rocks rather than on trees. These **lithophytes** (rock-growers), including many of the small, rupicolous *Laelias* and some Australian *Dendrobiums,* grow in places where the soil is too thin or rainfall too sparse to support trees. These orchids require high light levels and can withstand a great deal of heat and drought and still thrive. You can certainly grow them on mounts, however.

Mounting Procedure

EQUIPMENT

- mounts (cork or tree-fern slabs, tree branches)
- wire cutter, needle-nosed pliers, and regular pliers or a locking Vise-Grip
- 14–18-gauge galvanized wire
- 8–12-pound-test monofilament fishing line
- long-fibered sphagnum, osmunda fiber, or natural live sheet moss
- scissors
- for wooden mounts: electric drill with a drill bit about the same diameter as the wire

CHOOSING A MOUNT

Mounting orchids on plaques or sections of tree branch offers several advantages over potting. Foremost is the natural presentation this affords. I often mount several small species on a single branch, creating a miniature orchid garden that is especially lovely on display (try to select species with similar requirements and bloom times when creating a mounted garden). Also, mounted plants are less likely to suffer root and stem rots and need less frequent maintenance—I have one *Laelia pumila* that has been growing happily on the same slab

A section of tree fern. You can use a small saw or a serrated kitchen knife to cut it into smaller slabs.

of cork for seventeen years now! If you suspend the mounts on a vertical rack or section of wire fencing, you'll have room for far more plants than you can accommodate on benches. On the downside, mounted plants require more frequent watering and higher relative humidity, so they are more difficult to care for indoors. Furthermore, while miniatures are easily accommodated on mounts, larger species (over 10 inches tall) can become quite unwieldy when grown this way.

Some orchids, especially certain twig epiphytes growing in a humid greenhouse, can simply be suspended on a string, with their roots splayed out in the air. However, for most epiphytic orchids it is preferable to use sections of bark, trunk, or branch, which simulate their natural condition, retain some water and nutrients, and give you a surface to hang the plants from. And these materials make a beautiful backdrop for the orchids.

The two most popular mounts are sections of cork (bark from the cork oak tree) and slabs of tree-fern trunk. The former is readily available, renewable, lightweight, and very decay-resistant. Unless attacked by boring insects, it will last for years. Cork has very little moisture-holding capacity, so it works well with orchids adapted to drier situations, such as vertical limbs. When constructing a cork mount, orient the slab so the fissures in the bark run vertically rather than horizontally to create channels for water flowing over the plaque and roots. Tree fern is more expensive than cork, but the matrix of water-retentive fibers is perfect for more moisture-sensitive species whose roots can wind through the plaque. Tree fern is always hung with the fibers running vertically, so

Cork oak slabs are lightweight, very long lived, and relatively inexpensive. I boil used slabs in water for thirty minutes to clean and sterilize them. They can be reused several times.

when you water the top of the plaque, water travels down and pools amid the fibers at the bottom, just as it does in the bottom of a pot, providing a ready-made reservoir for the orchid. The downside to tree fern is the difficulty of removing the orchid when it comes time to remount it. The roots weave through the tree fern so thoroughly that the only option may be to cut or tear them away. Also, because tree fern is moderately absorbent, it will retain and build up soluble salts just as potting media do, which can harm the roots unless you thoroughly drench it every time you water. (Cork, on the other hand, does not easily retain salts.)

In search of a more moisture-retentive, environmentally friendly mount (I worry about the effects of harvesting tree fern on the survival of the species), I and other growers have turned to the woods and fields around us. In my area, popular trees and shrubs from which to create mounts include sassafras, white oak, highbush blueberry, dogwood, and hop hornbeam. In other parts of the country, persimmon, various oaks, mesquite, and bald cypress are possibilities. The bark of some trees (notably walnut) is unsuitable because it contains allelopathic chemicals, which inhibit the growth of other plants. And any tree whose bark decays easily is obviously not a good choice. Different orchids have their preferences, too. In the wild you often find particular epiphytes growing only on a specific genus or species of tree. You'll have to experiment to find the most suitable wood. If the roots of the orchid attach willingly to the bark, I consider the mount successful. I have mounted orchids on cut sections of blueberry, oak, cypress, persimmon, and sassafras branch, sections of tree fern, slabs of cork bark, and living trees in a conservatory. I even established a large *Cattleya mossiae* on an oak log with an eyebolt screwed into one end for a hanger. The *Cattleya* eventually encircled the log completely, making a wonderful, though space-hogging, display 2 feet in diameter.

PREPARING THE MOUNT

For wood mounts I usually cut 2–6-inch lengths of 1/2–2-inch-diameter twigs or branches. If you have access to a band saw or table saw, you can slice the bark-covered outer section off a larger limb to create a slab that hangs more easily against the wall. Or use a hatchet to split the branch in half lengthwise as you might for kindling. (The only drawback to using a sliced slab is that the bark may eventually separate from the underlying wood.) Lay the section of branch or the slab on a flat piece of lumber and drill a hole completely through with a small (3/32-inch or so) drill bit. When drilling a crooked twig, think about how you want it to hang and orient the hole accordingly. Push a length of 16- or 18-gauge galvanized wire through the hole, then double up the last inch or so with pliers and pull the wire back through. The doubled-over section will get stuck in the hole, anchoring the wire in place. Bend the

Dendrobium cuthbertsonii growing on a section of blueberry branch. The grower has tied a half dozen seedlings onto one gnarled branch and suspended it from the greenhouse roof like a mobile. Blueberry *(Vaccinium corymbosum)* produces beautifully gnarled branches covered in flaky bark. Removing a branch here and there, especially in winter, will not harm the shrub.

free section of wire into a hook for hanging the mount. Sections of wire fencing or hardware cloth suspended from a rack or wall are perfect for hanging a collection of mounted orchids.

Tree-fern and cork mounts can be wired in a similar fashion, but usually you'll need at least 14-gauge wire (the lower the gauge number, the thicker the wire) to push through the material. With these mounts predrilling isn't necessary; I usually snip off the wire at an angle to create a sharp point, grasp it about 1 inch behind the point with a pair of pliers, and begin pressing the wire through a little at a time. Once through, the hanger will be more stable if, instead of doubling it and running it back through the hole, you bend it in a U-shape like a staple and (using wide-mouthed pliers), push the tip of the wire back into the mount in another place. The wire hanger makes a splendid place to attach a label with a small hole punched through it.

When I grew plants primarily under fluorescent lights, the low headroom they afforded left little room for racks on which to suspend mounts. So instead of hanging the mount, I shoved the base into a small clay pot just big enough for it to snug into. Sections of tree branch, cork, or tree fern can all be handled this way. If the mount is loose in the pot, I jam pieces of Styrofoam packing peanuts down around its base. In this way, a plant can grow happily on the mount and also send roots down into the pot for additional moisture. You can even attach a wire hanger to the mount so that the plant can be removed from the pot for temporary display.

RAFTS (HORIZONTAL MOUNTS)

Water pools more readily on a flat surface, whether it is a slab of tree fern or a large horizontal limb in the canopy of some rain forest giant. Just the small added moisture provided by a horizontal mount or raft may be enough to grow moisture-loving species like *Masdevallias*. I have used twigs, tree-fern slabs, and chunks of cork in this way, and the plants present themselves beautifully. To hang a raft, loop a piece of wire like a basket handle and attach it to both ends of the wood or slab as described above for vertical mounts. You can leave the hanger as a simple loop that can be suspended from a hook or squeeze the apex of the loop into a small hook in the manner of a wire coat hanger. If you bend the loop to one side, you can attach it to a rack just as you would a vertical mount. Alternatively, a flat-bottomed raft can be set on a table or bench alongside potted plants.

Once you start mounting orchids, it is easy to get carried away, because they just look so *right* growing as epiphytes—especially miniatures. However, if you are just beginning, go slowly. Mounted orchids need more day-to-day attention than potted plants, because their roots dry out quickly. On a win-dowsill it may be difficult to provide enough moisture for any but the most drought-adapted species unless you soak them daily.

Attaching the Orchid

Orchid roots growing in a substrate, be it moss or potting mix, are physiologically different from roots that develop in the open, exposed to air and light. Exposed roots have a thicker coating of velamen and, most important, contain chloroplasts that allow them to photosynthesize as leaves and stems do. How much the additional photosynthesis contributes to the plant's overall carbon budget is anyone's guess, but it certainly increases the photosynthetic surface area of a mounted plant relative to a potted one. When you water air roots, they turn green. The water renders the white velamen temporarily translucent, making the underlying chlorophyll visible. Roots growing into a dark, damp mix have less velamen and no chlorophyll, so they appear white and opaque—much like cave insects. The two types of roots are very different, and once formed, they cannot change to the other type. Consequently, if you pot a formerly mounted plant or decide to mount a potted plant, the roots must go through a transition phase, during which new roots will grow that are adapted to their new environment.

To mount a formerly potted orchid or to reestablish a mounted one with a damaged root system, it helps to create a transitional area around the base of the plant. I like to use a piece of live sheet moss, osmunda, or dried long-fibered (preferably New Zealand) sphagnum for this purpose, as these materials wick up moisture when you water. Carefully weave a few strands of moistened moss through the roots, so that the fibers will shield much of the root system from air and light. As new roots grow from the rhizome or from the original roots, they will adapt to their new situation and head out over the moss and the mount. How much moss to use depends on the size of the plant and mount. You don't want to have such a large pad that it bulges out from the mount, but too little will not do the job. As a general rule, use an amount about equal to a quarter of the volume of the pot the plant was in. A plant taken from a 2-inch thumb pot will need only a thimbleful of moss to get it going.

Some growers have had good success with a 1/8-inch-thick slice of Oasis, the florist's foam used for flower arranging, as a transitional support system. Cut the pad to roughly a quarter of the dimensions of the mount. Since Oasis is rather stiff and brittle, it works best with flat mounts. Trying to bend it around a small branch will usually lead to crumbling; in this case, try a longer, narrower section. Oasis has the advantage of consistency and decay resistance, but it does look a bit artificial until moss starts growing on it. Like moss,

1. I removed this small clump of **Dendrobium aggregatum** from a large specimen whose roots were clinging tightly to the cork mount. I cut the roots free with a sterile razorblade, leaving short stubs from which new root tips will sprout.

2. A 5-inch length of white oak will serve as its new support. After cleaving the log in two with a hatchet, I drill a small hole through one end for the hanger wire.

3. I pass a piece of 16-gauge galvanized wire through the hole, then use pliers to double the wire over and squeeze it back into the hole to keep it firmly in place.

4. A small pad of live moss will protect and nurture the roots.

5. While holding the orchid and moss with one hand, I wrap 8-pound-test monofilament fishing line around the pseudobulbs and roots, making six or eight loops before tying it off.

6. I drill or punch a hole in a label and thread it onto the hook, then work the free end down between the loops of fishing line to hold it.

7. The finished plant. The old leaves are permanently fixed in their rather odd positions, but the new leads will emerge properly oriented.

Oasis is difficult to wet when fully dry, so keep it damp.

Removing a plant from an old mount has its own hazards. On a tree-fern plaque the roots will weave through the material, which makes intact removal all but impossible without the aid of a laser surgeon. Even on cork the roots will glue themselves to the mount, and when you pull them away, a strip of root remains attached. These roots are as good as gone once they have been torn. Excise them with a razorblade.

Theoretically, neither cork nor tree fern goes bad quickly; it is usually salt buildup rather than physical degradation that causes problems. If new root tips seem to die when they touch the fern or cork, try leaching the mount a few times and see if the problem clears up. Soak the mount in distilled water (let it float plant side up) for an hour or so, swishing it around occasionally to circulate the water. Distilled water is very good at removing salt residues. Repeat this a week later. If you decide that you have to remove the plant from its mount, try to preserve as many roots as possible. Tease the roots free with your fingers or excise them from the cork or fern with a sterile razorblade, pruners, or a knife, then remount the plant and keep it in a humid place until new roots establish. Another possibility is to hot-glue or tie the whole thing onto a larger piece.

One nice thing about flaky-barked twig mounts such as blueberry, bald cypress, and some oaks is that the outer flecks of bark peel away with the roots, so when you remove a plant from an old mount, the root comes away undamaged. An old twig mount may have disintegrated so much that the plant can be excised, then attached to a new twig with little disturbance.

Whether you are mounting a formerly potted division or remounting a plant whose plaque has deteriorated, first groom the orchid, trimming off dead pseudobulbs, stems, flower stalks, and roots with a sterile tool. Also gingerly remove as much of the old potting mix or decayed mount materials as possible from around the root system. Unless the roots have been badly torn by removal from another mount, I do not like to trim the live root system itself, as I feel that the more roots the plant has, the faster it will recover.

When *remounting* a plant, I like to use some sphagnum or live sheet moss to help the root system get reestablished and cushion it during the mounting procedure, but in this case I lay the moss pad down first, then spread the roots over it and tie them in place, rather than weaving the moss through them. This exposes them to the light and air they're used to while affording them extra moisture underneath until new roots form.

A sphagnum, Oasis, or osmunda pad also provides a place for live sheet moss to germinate and get established. I find that mounted orchids—especially many miniatures that need consistent moisture—look and perform best once a colony of moss has grown in around their roots. The live moss develops along with the orchid's root system and provides just the sort of damp yet well-ventilated conditions the roots experience in the wild. There is also something aesthetically perfect about a little orchid growing happily from a leprechaun green patch of moss coating a twig or section of bark. Live moss also can alert you to cultural problems before the orchid itself is noticeably affected. Mosses are very sensitive to excessive fertilizer salts, poor water quality, fungal pathogens, and low humidity, so a healthy stand of it indicates that conditions for the orchid are

also good. Brown, dying moss may indicate a problem with your water or watering practices. If your growing space is humid enough (say, consistently over 50%–60% RH) to make mounted orchids happy, mosses will undoubtedly begin to grow on their own from airborne spores. Established orchids usually have bits of moss growing amid their surface roots, and these will begin to grow over a mount almost immediately. However, I often tear bits of moss from an established mount and dab them onto a newly mounted orchid's sphagnum pad to give the covering a head start.

I have seen every kind of fastening system, from hot glue to old pantyhose and colored phone wire, used to secure orchids to the mount, but by far the best material is plain old monofilament fishing line. It is cheap, it lasts for years, and (unless you buy one of the fluorescent orange brands) it is nearly invisible. I use 8–12-pound test, preferably clear or light blue. (Fishing line is rated for the amount of pulling force it can handle without breaking. Thus the higher the test, the thicker the line). It takes a bit of practice to coordinate fingers, mount, line, moss, and orchid, but here's my procedure.

Once you've groomed the plant and prepared the mount, cut a length of fishing line long enough to wrap around the plant and mount at least seven to ten times with enough left on the ends to tie a knot. Wad the dampened moss pad and place it against the mount where you want the orchid to attach. Use your thumb and forefinger to hold the moss in place, then sneak 6 inches of the fishing line between your thumb and the mount so it will be ready when you need it. With your other hand, place the plant against the mount so that its roots are even with the moss (remember to work some strands of sphagnum around the roots if they've just been removed from a pot). Adjust the rhizome so that it lies against the upper edge of the moss pad. This way, when new buds grow, they can send roots down into the pad and leaves up and away from it. Then begin to wrap the monofilament around and around the roots and moss, taking care to occasionally weave it up between leaves or pseudobulbs and down over the rhizome. I try not to wrap the leaves themselves, as it is hard to get the line snug, and the wrapping is more obvious than when it is down amid moss and roots. Keep the line taut as you wrap. You want it to be just tight enough to hold the plant firmly in place without cutting into the roots and rhizome. If you wind too tightly, you may compress the moss too much, which makes it difficult to wet. Spiral the line up and down the mount as you wrap to anchor as much of the rhizome and roots as possible. When you are down to about the last 6 inches of line, knot the two ends behind the mount several times, then trim off the excess line with scissors or a wire cutter. You can also use the scissors to trim off any wild strands of sphagnum that are sticking out. Bravo!

CHAPTER 10

Pests and Diseases

OF ALL THE CHAPTERS in this book, this one is the hardest for me to write. Diseases and pests are depressing and even a bit disgusting, and I wish I could avoid the subject entirely. However, I know from experience that the best defense is a good offense. If you know how to recognize problems before they become severe, *and* you address them quickly, you can avoid disasters.

I don't like to use deadly pesticides in the house if I can help it, though I have certainly used my share of them in greenhouses. There is no question that pesticides can cure many problems quickly and effectively, but they do so at some cost in terms of safety. Accordingly, I focus here on safer means of pest and disease control. If you have persistent problems, or if you are operating a greenhouse in which spraying pesticides becomes necessary, I recommend that you purchase the most recent edition of the American Orchid Society's *Orchid Pests and Diseases,* available from the AOS bookstore (see Appendix 2). The book is a font of helpful information and includes pesticides appropriate for use on orchids.

ABOVE: Green aphids on a *Miltonia spectabilis*

All in all, orchids are not as subject to attack by pests and diseases as some other house and landscape plants are. However, a host of insects, mollusks, fungi, bacteria, and viruses can potentially prey on orchids, and it is important to know what they are. In the wild it is rare to see a sick orchid, perhaps because the vulnerable ones succumb early in the struggle to survive; however, I think the more likely reason is that pests and diseases are unable to spread as readily among isolated individuals. Also, pests in the wild are controlled by predators that are not present indoors. Every orchid starts out disease-free from seed, but in a crowded collection they are more vulnerable to infection (just as children are more vulnerable to outbreaks of flu in a crowded school than at home). One sick plant brought in from a friend or a nursery may quickly infect others growing nearby. The more plants you acquire, the harder it is to inspect them all for hidden scale or rot.

Although plant swaps and society meetings are good places to buy cheap orchids, they are also, unfortunately, places to inadvertently acquire a problem plant. Home growers are generally not aware of the range of disease and pests that can afflict orchids, nor are they as likely as a commercial nursery to treat problems prophylactically (as a preventive measure before symptoms are manifest). I don't mean that all commercial nurseries are completely sanitary and all hobbyists Typhoid Marys, just that the more fastidious and knowledgeable the grower, the less chance that the plants will have problems. You should always go over a new plant very carefully. Peel back dried sheaths to look for scale, examine the rhizome, check the leaves for signs of spotting and the pseudobulbs for signs of rot. If possible, pop the plant out of the pot to see how the roots look. If you do use chemical insecticides or fungicides, this might be the time to give the plant a prophylactic spraying or dunk. Putting the new plant in a quarantine area —a separate room in the house or greenhouse—is a great idea, but it's not practical for most folks. Also effective, though not realistic, would be to acquire all one's plants as sterile seedlings or tissue-cultured plantlets still in the flask.

Sanitation is crucial in preventing and controlling problems. Dead leaves, rotten pseudobulbs, spent flowers, decayed potting mixes—even empty pots left around—can provide a breeding ground for pests and diseases. Keep a can of sterile razorblades handy so you can groom as you water. In an enclosed growing area or in the greenhouse, a wet-dry vacuum is great for sucking up detritus from under benches and pots. Don't let the collection get too crowded (easier said than done, I know) because that makes observation and treatment more difficult.

In general, pest problems (insects and mollusks) are easier to treat than diseases (fungi, bacteria, and viruses). If you suspect that a plant has a disease you don't recognize, it may be better to discard it rather than risk infecting others. The same goes for orchids that are weak growers, either because they aren't suited to your conditions or because they have genetic defects. A weak plant may have a hidden disease, but even if it doesn't, it may be susceptible to the first one that comes along.

Orchid Pests

APHIDS: These ubiquitous pests are sort of the mosquitoes of the plant world. They reproduce parthenogenically, meaning that the females give birth to young without having to mate. Consequently, their numbers can build up at an astounding rate. Aphids use their piercing mouthparts to spear into the plant's phloem tissues and extract sugars, proteins, and other nutrients in the sap. Since they are soft and fragile, they can pierce only the softest parts of plants, preferring tender new leaves, stems, and flowers. They are primarily seeking proteins and lipids; much of the sugar in the sap is excreted in the form of honeydew. The honeydew is a magnet for molds (not to mention ants), and often it is the sticky, sooty honeydew on leaves or the table that alerts you to the aphids' presence. Hardy insects, aphids can easily enter a greenhouse or living room during the warmer months. It's a good idea to screen greenhouse vents and intakes with a fine-weave fabric sold for this purpose. Orchids are really not the first choice of most aphids because the plants generally don't grow fast enough to provide the colony with a ready supply of succulent young tissue. It is usually other houseplants, herbs, or even the weeds growing outside the window or the greenhouse that harbor them. When a colony gets too crowded, some of the adults acquire wings and fly off to find new territory—which might include your hapless orchids. The most insidious thing about aphids and other sucking insects, such as thrips, is their ability to transmit viruses (and possibly other diseases) from one plant to another, just as mosquitoes transmit malaria from person to person.

Fortunately, aphids are easy to control. The clusters of green, yellow, or black soft-bodied insects are readily spotted with the naked eye. You'll see them on flowers and flower stems and the undersides of expanding new leaves. If you take the plant outdoors or to the sink and blast it with a jet of water, you'll dislodge the pests. What happens is that their mouthparts are so firmly imbedded that they break off under the pressure of the water, and the dislodged insects have no way to feed. You will have to repeat the hosing off several times, because young or hiding aphids can quickly rebuild the colony. Remember, it takes only one to start a new colony.

Insecticidal soap (made from fatty acids and generally safe for humans, though it will dry out skin), ultrarefined horticultural oils, or rubbing alcohol will also kill aphids on contact.

SCALE: Like aphids, scale insects suck plant sap and may secrete honeydew. Unlike aphids, the adults of most types are protected by a limpetlike shell made of waxy secretions, which makes them immobile or practically so. When the eggs hatch, the immature insects (termed crawlers) set out a short distance to find a suitable spot to settle. After molting, they form a shell, and there they sit, sucking and laying eggs until they die. Three types of scale affect orchids: armored scale, soft scale, and mealybugs (which are often categorized separately). All three can slowly drain the life from your orchids. They tend to hide under dried sheaths or leaf bases where they are not readily apparent, and their waxy coating makes them more difficult to kill than aphids.

ARMORED SCALE. The primary armored scale affecting orchids, and one of the worst orchid pests in general, is Boisduval scale (also called oyster-shell scale). The females are flattened, yellowish white disks about 1/16 inch in circumference. The football-shaped males cluster together in white cottony masses much as mealybugs do. Boisduval scale has a thick detached shell and thus is a bear to get rid of. Even after an infestation is cured, the insects leave yellowed or darkened patches of tissue on the plants that do not go away. It seems to me that the insect is actually injecting some cellular toxin into the plant, because the tissue damage is more extensive than the colony itself. Scraping and rubbing with a cotton swab wetted with alcohol is effective, as are thorough and repeated sprayings of horticultural oil, which is most effective on the crawler stage. The shells of dead scales will remain in place, but they will flake away easily with light pressure from a fingernail; underneath they'll appear dry and dusty. Be sure

Scales often hide under sheaths. I have pulled away the papery sheath on this **Lycaste** to reveal an infestation of soft brown scale.

A **Cattleya** infected with Boisduval scale. The males are massed together in the centerfold of the leaf, while the females are scattered across the surface.

to look under sheaths, around rhizomes, and beneath leaves. Because the creatures are slow-moving, they are not usually found on inflorescences. Severe infestations may require the use of a strong systemic insecticide. Usually this pest comes in on an infected plant and spreads through the collection, so inspect new purchases carefully.

SOFT SCALE has a shell, but it is more pliable and is attached to the back of the insect, which is visible beneath. Brown soft scale is a ubiquitous plant pest, and unfortunately it has become resistant to many insecticides, so it's very commonly brought in on houseplants or purchased orchids. I bought an areca palm with soft brown scale in 1982, and it subsequently spread to other houseplants and then my orchids; I wasn't able to finally eradicate it until 1996! This species is less destructive than Boisduval, as it does not cause severe tissue damage, but the numbers can build up more quickly. However, it does exude honeydew, which adheres to benches, couches, windowsills, and other surfaces and invites sooty mold. Treat soft scale as you would treat Boisduval.

MEALYBUGS coat themselves with a waxy cotton, which is more easily penetrated by insecticidal soap, alcohol, or oil than the shells of other scale insects are. Mealybugs appear as fluffy white colonies that hide away on rhizomes, pseudobulbs, axils, and the undersides of leaves. They can also attack roots and inflorescences. Mealybugs excrete honeydew, so sooty mold or ants are another clue to their presence. A colony can get so thick that affected tissues turn yellow. Root infestations are very difficult to control without resorting to systemic insecticides. Mealybug-destroyer ladybugs are a control option in an enclosed space; if you let them loose in your house, they are likely to fly away.

THRIPS: These tiny, soft-bodied insects feed by rasping away leaf or flower tissues. Flower thrips cause unopened buds to dry out and fail to open, and greenhouse thrips produce sunken, blackened or silvery areas on leaves. With a 10× hand lens, you may be able to see the tiny, aphidlike nymphs, though little dots of black excrement on leaf or flower surfaces are a more obvious sign that thrips are in the area. Like aphids, they can spread viral, fungal, and bacterial infections from plant to plant. Soap and oil sprays as well as predatory mites are effective controls.

FUNGUS GNATS: If you see tiny black flies rising up from the surface of the potting mix when disturbed, you have fungus gnats. The 1/8-inch-long larvae feed on organic potting materials. However, I have often observed the larvae rasping away at the dormant vegetative buds as well as root tips of minia-

The stippling and bleaching on the leaves of this *Epidendrum* are caused by myriad tiny phalaenopsis mites (visible as tiny rust-colored specks) slowly sucking the sap out of the tissues. Unlike the two-spotted spider mite, this species does not form a fine web over the leaf.

ture orchids. They can cause significant damage if not controlled. BT, parasitic nematodes, and predatory mites are all effective controls.

SPIDER MITES AND FALSE SPIDER MITES: These mites are a common pest of houseplants as well as plants growing outdoors, so it is easy for orchids to become infested too. They suck out chlorophyll and sap with piercing mouthparts, and in warm, dry weather they reproduce incredibly quickly. They can be seen with a hand lens and even with the naked eye if you have good eyesight. The two-spotted spider mite spins webbing—especially in particularly bad infestations—that is more easily visible than the pests themselves. False spider mites like the phalaenopsis mite do not spin webs. Damage shows up as silvery pitting on the leaves. Two-spotted spider mites prefer soft-leaved orchids such as *Oncidiums* and some *Dendrobiums*; the phalaenopsis mite is not so particular. Predatory mites are effective against spider mites, as is soap or oil sprayed on the affected tissues.

In the tropics and subtropics, many other insects, including wasps and caterpillars, attack orchids, but these are rarely a problem in the home collection.

SLUGS AND SNAILS: Conditions that are perfect for orchids are unfortunately also perfect for slugs and snails, which seek out the cool, damp recesses of pots. They come out at night to rasp away at root tips, flowers, developing leaves, and even dormant buds. One hungry slug can do tremendous damage,

Though superficially similar to Boisduval scale, mealybugs are easy to brush off, whereas scale insects cling like limpets. Mealybugs turn pink when you wet them with alcohol (just as some people do).

and the tiny garden snails will eat away at miniature plants until the rhizome has no more dormant buds. Fortunately, a new, reputably safe control called Sluggo has become available that replaces the toxic metaldehyde baits of yesteryear. Sluggo lures the critters in to feed, and once they ingest it, they stop feeding immediately and starve. Cruel, maybe, but so is the havoc they can wreak on your orchids.

Orchid Diseases

This term encompasses fungal, bacterial, and viral pathogens. All three types are invisible to the naked eye, so it is the symptoms that we must watch out for. There is no cure for virus infection except through a complicated laboratory procedure called meristemming, combined with antiviral agents. Fungal and bacterial diseases, however, can generally be controlled with both cultural and organic/biological methods.

FUNGAL AND BACTERIAL INFECTIONS: Certain fungi are vitally important to orchids, nurturing the developing seeds and helping mature plants scavenge nutrients (see Chapter 12). However, a host of other fungi cause leaf spots, lesions,

and root, pseudobulb, and rhizome rots. Most disease-causing fungi need humid, stagnant conditions to thrive, so by not watering on cool or cloudy days and by increasing the aeration of potting media and the air movement around the plants, you can avoid or greatly diminish many fungus problems. Bacterial soft rots and leaf spots are also opportunistic, and good cultural practices can eliminate much of their threat. Fungal and bacterial spores require water to germinate, so it is unlikely that you will see leaf diseases on orchids growing on a windowsill, but overwatering and the resultant breakdown and stagnation of the potting medium can foster root and rhizome rots as easily there as in a humid greenhouse. You can spray prophylactically during cool, humid weather or when you've recently had a problem. All of the fungicides/bactericides listed in the table on pp. 94–95 are relatively safe and effective if you follow the directions.

ROOT, STEM, AND PSEUDOBULB ROTS: Black rot, caused by the damping-off fungi *Pythium* and *Phytophthora*, produce slowly spreading black lesions on affected tissues. Overwatering and stagnant, humid conditions allow the disease to erupt. Inoculating the plant with beneficial fungi or

ABOVE LEFT: A momma slug tends to her eggs. Crock in the bottom of a pot provides a perfect place for slugs to hide.

ABOVE RIGHT: Slug damage on *Cattleya* roots; notice the slime trail.

LEFT: Slug damage on *Pleurothallis* flowers

bacteria can dramatically lower the chances of infection, an especially valuable step when unflasking tender seedlings. Bacterial soft rots (*Erwinia* spp.) produce similar symptoms, but they develop much faster, causing watery lesions that seem to pop up overnight and move quickly through the plant. If you catch it fast enough, you can amputate the affected parts and treat the plant with ammonium chloride spray. Bacterial infections enter through wounds—a good reason to always use sterilized pruning equipment. Apply charcoal powder (charcoal ground up with a mortar and pestle) to the wound edges after excising diseased tissue. Again, poor culture is the main cause of these infections.

Rhizoctonia fungi attack roots primarily. Roots that seem to have died from overwatering or stale potting mix are often really killed by these fungi, which thrive under anaerobic conditions. Proper potting and watering as well as inoculation with beneficial fungi are the best preventive measures.

The symptoms of *Fusarium* wilt are similar to those of *Rhizoctonia*. Root loss leads to desiccation and yellowing of the plant, making it look as though it has been severely underwatered. Roots will be dead and papery, and if you cut the rhizome you will see a ring of purplish brown staining produced as the fungus invades the vascular tissues. Prevention is the same as for *Rhizoctonia*.

Though it is clear that this **Cattleya** is severely dehydrated, it is not immediately apparent why.

A close inspection reveals that the roots are completely dead —probably killed by *Rhizoctonia* that became established as the potting medium decayed. Timely repotting would have prevented this problem, but now it is too late.

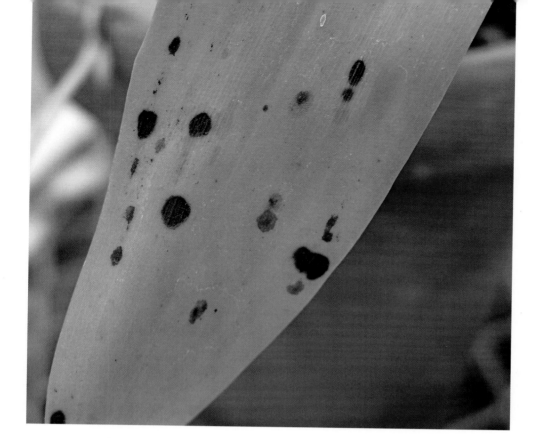

LEAF SPOTS: Although not as potentially deadly as rhizome and root rots, leaf spotting can certainly mar the plant's appearance and weaken it somewhat. Spores of leaf-spot bacteria and fungi germinate on wet surfaces, so avoid watering and misting in the evening or on cool, humid days. Droplets from fog or mist systems can also be a problem for plants located nearby—primarily a problem in the greenhouse. Good air movement greatly reduces symptoms by keeping leaves dry.

Bacterial brown spot (*Pseudomonas* or *Acidovorax*) is the most common leaf spot in my experience. Except among the *Phalaenopsis* alliance, where it can be quite aggressive, brown spot causes round or oval brown or black spots with a watery margin. If possible, prune off infected tissues and apply a prophylactic spray of baking soda and oil or a copper/soap fungicide every two weeks, especially during spells of wet weather.

Anthracnose is a group of widespread fungal pathogens that attack many different species of plants. In orchids the disease produces a line of dead tissue that progresses slowly down the leaf blade and pseudobulb. A line of little tan dots (the fruiting bodies of the fungus) visible on dead tissue where it meets living tissue is a sign that your plant has anthracnose rather than leaf-tip dieback caused by salt injury or *Cercospora* infection. Cut away affected parts well below the line of infection and treat the plant with a copper/soap fungicide.

Cercospora fungi are also widespread and fairly host-specific. At least nine types affect different groups of orchids. Like *Fusarium, Cercospora* infection leads to leaf dieback. It usually begins as little spots of brown tissue surrounded by a yellowish ring (not the watery ring seen in bacterial brown spot). Treat as for *Anthracnose.*

BOTRYTIS FLOWER BLIGHT: *Botrytis* is yet another opportunistic fungus; among orchids it mainly attacks flowers, especially during periods of cool, humid weather. I see it mostly in greenhouses, and other than good sanitation you can use preventive sprays of baking soda, oil, or copper/soap. Try to avoid wetting the flowers as you water, and provide good air movement to dry them quickly if you do get them wet. The disease shows up as little brown spots on flowers, and if left unchecked, it will flare up into a fuzzy gray mold under very humid conditions. Obviously, you want to avoid anything that causes the premature death of flowers—so clean up those dead leaves and spent blooms!

Organic and Biological Pest and Disease Controls

When using any chemical, always apply it in a well-ventilated area and wear protective gloves, a face shield, and a respirator. Even "safe" insecticides can be irritants if you inhale them or get them on your skin. Be sure to buy gloves labeled for pesticide use, such as heavy nitrile gloves. Read and follow all the

Organic and Biological Controls

Control Agent	Treats	Comments
Baking soda (mixed with horticultural oil or soap). One commercial product is Remedy.	Mildews, black spot, leaf spot, *Anthracnose*, *Phytophthora*, *Botrytis*, *Acidovorax*	Baking soda mixed with water at the rate of 4 tsp/gal with 2 tsp/gal refined horticultural oil or insecticidal soap has been shown to have some fungicidal effect, and it is nontoxic. I have had mixed results. Must be reapplied every two weeks.
Beneficial bacteria (*Streptomyces griseoviridis*). Commercial preparations include Mycostop, BioYield, Companion, EcoGuard, and Subtilex.	Root, rhizome, and pseudobulb rots	*Streptomyces*, a soil bacteria that colonizes roots and stems, secretes a natural fungicide. Apply twice a year to prevent diseases from getting established. Most effective in potting mix, but in a humid greenhouse it can survive on the surface of the mix and possibly on mounts.
Beneficial fungi (RootShield, BOTRY-Zen, and similar products)	RootShield: *Pythium*, *Rhizoctonia* and *fusarium* (root, rhizome, and pseudobulb rots); BOTRY-Zen: *Botrytis* (flower blight)	Use of beneficial fungi to control pathogenic fungal infection is new but looks promising. RootShield (*Trichoderma harzianum*, strain T-22) is used against *Pythium*, *Rhizoctonia*, and *fusarium* root and rhizome rots. BOTRY-Zen is labeled for use only on grapes, but it seems highly effective at preventing *Botrytis* infection. Both fungi colonize affected tissues before the pathogen can get established and prevent disease spores from germinating. RootShield (applied once a year) is effective against root rot and damping-off of both seedlings and mature orchids. These products will not cure an infection once it is established.
BT (*Bacillus thuringiensis israelensis*), sold as Gnatrol	Fungus gnats	BT is a widely used biological control for agricultural pests such as corn borers and potato beetles. One specific strain, sold as Gnatrol, attacks fungus gnat larvae. Applied as a root drench, it is extremely effective and is very safe for both beneficial insects and people. As this is a living organism, store the concentrate according to directions and mix only what you need for that day. Treat a greenhouse collection with a Hozon-style proportioner attached to a garden hose.
Copper/soap fungicide (Soap-Shield)	Leaf spots (may also have bactericidal effect)	This product combines insecticidal soap with copper for effective, nontoxic control and prevention of leaf spot diseases, including *Anthracnose* and *Cercospora*.
Dimethyl and ethyl benzyl ammonium chloride (Physan 20, Greenshield)	*Botrytis*, *Erwinia* (bacterial brown rot), and possibly other fungal infections. Also controls algae on leaf and hard surfaces; may have some antibacterial effect.	Physan-20, a bleaching agent sold mostly for disinfection of equipment, is a great cleaning agent for the greenhouse (I have used many gallons of it). Mixed at a third to a half the recommended strength, or 1 tsp/gal, it can be used as a fungicide/algaecide/bactericide on plants. It kills on contact; apply it every 7–10 days or so to prevent disease. Wear protective clothing and equipment.
Insecticidal soap (Safer's Soap)	Aphids, mealybugs, mites, thrips	Insecticidal soaps (made from fatty acids) kill soft-bodied insects by clogging their air passages. Spray all parts of the plant to coat insects thoroughly. They have a strong, soapy chemical odor; if possible, apply outdoors. Mixed solution deteriorates quickly, so mix only what you need. Insects should wither and drop off within a day. Reapply after one week.
Iron phosphate (Sluggo)	Slugs and snails	Sluggo, which is much less toxic than metaldehyde, is in the form of bait pellets that you sprinkle around the plants. When slugs or snails eat it, the iron phosphate causes them to stop eating and eventually die. Unused bait breaks down into fertilizer.
Isopropyl alcohol (rubbing alcohol)	Aphids, scales, mealybugs	Undiluted rubbing alcohol can be used as an aerosol spray against aphids and mealybugs; to kill stubborn colonies of scale or mealybugs inside sheaths or leaf bases, apply with a cotton swab. Alcohol soaks mealybugs' cottony covering, revealing the pink bugs underneath. It is fairly safe for plants and reasonably effective against insects, though controlling an outbreak requires two or three labor-intensive treatments a week apart.
Mealybug destroyer (*Cryptolaemus montrouzieri*)	Mealybugs	Both adults and larvae of this small black, red-headed ladybird beetle feed on mealybugs. They are most effective in an enclosed space, as they fly off in search of new prey once mealybug levels decline.
Parasitic nematodes (*Steinernema feltiae*)	Fungus gnats, scales	Some species of nematodes, tiny worms that are ubiquitous in soils, decompose organic material, some are plant pests (so far not on orchids), but others are insect predators. *Steinernema feltiae* is specific for fungus-gnat larvae and is very effective. In the right conditions it can establish itself and provide longer-term control than Gnatrol. The nematodes come on a sponge that is kept refrigerated until you're ready to use it, then soaked in water. Apply the solution as a root drench, either by dunking the plants or by using a proportioner or watering can. The sponges are viable for only a month or two. You can't really overapply nematodes, so if you need only a few (they are sold by the million), make the solution more concentrated. I have not tried the nematodes used to treat scale, but I have read that results have been mixed. They are best applied on a damp, misty day so that they can get to the scale in a film of water. They invade the body of the scale insect and introduce a bacterium, which in turn kills the host.

Control Agent	Treats	Comments
Predatory mites and midges	Different mite species are used against spider mite adults, nymphs, larvae, and eggs; immature thrips; and fungus gnat eggs and larvae. The supplier can identify the best species for your problem. Aphid midges are effective controls for aphids.	Predatory mites *(Phytoseiulus persimilis)* ruthlessly attack spider mites, often consuming every last one. Mites are shipped in vermiculite and can be used in a greenhouse or indoors. Mist the plants beforehand and shake the vermiculite over the foliage. Don't water the plants right away to avoid washing off the mites. Midges are shipped and applied the same way. For fungus gnats, I prefer BT or nematodes.
Ultrarefined horticultural oil (SunSpray)	Aphids, scales, mealybugs, thrips, mites, some fungal diseases	This highly refined mineral oil mixes with water (shake it thoroughly before applying) and works by smothering soft-bodied insects. Unlike soaps, it also kills eggs. It is the best nontoxic spray to use against the various orchid scales, though it is most effective against the crawler and egg stages. You can also swab it on as described for rubbing alcohol. Though research on orchids is lacking, it also suppresses leaf-spotting fungi, perhaps by preventing spores from attaching and germinating.

directions on the label, and when you're trying out something new, treat just part of a plant and wait a few days for signs of a phytotoxic reaction. Symptoms of phytotoxicity include rapid yellowing or discoloration of leaves, browning root tips, and loss of flower buds. I prefer to mix an untried chemical at half the rate recommended on the label, then see if it works before upping the dosage. To lessen the chances of a phytotoxic reaction, apply the chemical on a cloudy day when temperatures are between 60° and 80° or spray early in the morning so the plants are dry by the time the sun is up. (Many pesticides contain oil-based "carriers" that make them easier to apply, and these oils can refract and concentrate sunlight, leading to "sunburn" on leaves.)

The field of biological control (encouraging or introducing one organism to combat another) has seen remarkable advances in the past ten years, and it certainly offers the best long-term solutions for pest and disease problems. You can find a number of suppliers of biological controls on the Web. Remember that if you use beneficial organisms, you cannot spray pesticides, so you have to learn to live with a certain base level of pest infestation to sustain populations of the predatory species.

Viruses

Orchid viruses are distressing both because they are invisible and because they are incurable unless you have access to a sophisticated tissue-culture lab. The horticulture industry is finally becoming aware of just how widespread and entrenched viruses have become. Some twenty-six different viruses have been found to infect orchids, and there are doubtless many more. Many originate in the wild and are brought into cultivation in infected wild-collected plants, though two of the three most common — cymbidium mosaic virus (CyMV), orchid tobacco mosaic virus (TMV-O), and bean yellow mosaic virus (BYMV) — originated in other crop plants and mutated to become pathogens of orchids. The good news is that virus infection can be prevented through good sanitation and pest control. To become infected, the sap of a healthy orchid needs to come into contact with the sap of an infected plant. The two ways this can happen are through

Botrytis spotting on a *Cattleya* flower. These spots will continue to grow rapidly if conditions are favorable.

Tobacco mosaic virus on a
Cattleya

mechanical transmission (cutting tools, hands coming into contact with wounds) and insect transmission (usually aphids and thrips, the most mobile of the sucking insects that commonly affect orchids). Mechanical transmission can be avoided if you follow the sterile procedures outlined on p. 77. Insect transmission can be minimized by keeping aphids and thrips under control.

Virus symptoms are often difficult to distinguish from certain leaf spots. However, virus damage *looks* more deep-seated in the leaf tissues. Depending on the individual plant's general health and nutrition, the amount of light it receives, and other factors, the symptoms may be nothing more than a slight yellowish or whitish streaking parallel with the leaf veins; in a moderate case, the streaks are more numerous, and some show pitting from tissue collapse or browning from tissue death. A severe case is pretty obvious. The leaf is bleached out in zones, patches, or bands; there is quite a bit of tissue

collapse; and, at least on the underside, much brown or black streaking is evident. Often the bleached areas fade into more heavily pigmented areas, but the damaged areas have a three-dimensional look, because the virus spreads through the inner layers (the mesophyll of the leaf) rather than being concentrated on the surface the way fungus infections usually are.

DETECTING VIRUSES

The most straightforward (though not the cheapest) way to test for viruses is to send a sample of tissue from an infected orchid to a lab for a serological test. You can buy a kit to do your own testing as well, or do what is called a bioassay, in which a test plant (not an orchid) that is especially susceptible to the disease is inoculated with sap obtained from orchids you suspect have a virus. For more on this procedure, refer to the AOS's *Orchid Pests and Diseases*.

CHAPTER 11

Troubleshooting Guide

The puckered lip on this *Paphiopedilum malipoense* may be genetic, but more likely the puckering was caused by some environmental stress when the plant was in bud.

Problem	Possible Cause	Comments
Failure to bloom	Not enough light	This is the most common cause of blooming problems, especially indoors. Move the plant to a brighter location. Put windowsill plants outdoors during summer. If growing under lights, move plant toward the center, where light is brighter. (See p. 25.)
	Too little temperature fluctuation	Many orchids require a 5°–10° drop in night temperature at certain times of year to initiate bloom. Move the orchid closer to a window, where it will be cooler at night, leave the window open in summer, and lower the thermostat at night in winter. Enclose artificial light tables in plastic or an insulating material to trap heat when lights are on and thus lower the temperature more markedly when they are off. (See p. 29.)
	Temperatures too extreme	Cool-growing orchids kept too warm or warm growers kept too cool will often fail to bloom or will bloom late, even if reasonably healthy. Choose species whose needs correspond best to your growing environment. (See p. 29.)
	Artificial lights set at a constant day length	Orchids native to regions more than 10° north or south of the equator may use longer or shorter days as a cue to bloom. If growing under lights, set the timer so that day length gradually decreases from 16 hours during summer to 11 hours for a brief time during winter. (See p. 26.)
	Damaged root system	If roots are compromised, the plant will suffer. Check inside the pot for mushy or spongy roots or sodden mix. Repot into fresh mix and try not to overwater. Recently repotted plants, even if healthy, may not bloom the first year as they adjust to the new container.
	Low humidity	Species that evolved in a humid cloud forest are very susceptible to flower spike abortion if humidity drops or remains below 60% for more than a few hours. The spike can be aborted while still in its sheath or hidden by the leaves, so you won't notice it without searching. (See p. 32.)
	Excessive or insufficient fertilization	Fertilize when orchids are actively growing vegetatively to keep them healthy and give them the reserves needed for flowering. Heavy fertilization, especially as an orchid is initiating flower buds, may cause buds to abort. This can happen when the spike is still sheathed or hidden in the leaf base, so it is not evident.
	Immaturity	Seedlings have to reach maturity before flowering. It may take two to four years for the plant to bloom.
	Genetic problems	Occasionally a plant—especially a seedling with complex ancestry—will refuse to bloom properly. The problem is bad genetics, and there is nothing much you can do about it. Buy plants in bud or bloom or stick to proven awarded clones to avoid this problem.
Bud blast or drop	Immature flower buds turn yellow and fall off as they are developing	Developing flowers may abort for any of the reasons listed above, but the most likely cause is a sudden shock or change. If you buy a plant in spike from a greenhouse and take it home to a drier, dimmer windowsill, the shock of change will often cause the buds to abort, as will shipping a plant in spike during hot or cold weather. Don't remove the spike until it has totally turned brown, as new buds may appear once it has settled in. It is common for a healthy orchid to abort a flower bud, especially the last one or two on a spike. Setting a seedpod will often cause other flowers to drop prematurely. The use of emergency heaters that burn kerosene or propane may produce ethylene gas that will cause rampant bud drop. (When I had to run propane heaters in a greenhouse one winter night I lost just about every spike in the place!) High salt levels and overfertilization are other potential causes. Putting short-day-length bloomers in a room where lights are left on at night can also lead to bud blast.

PROBLEM	POSSIBLE CAUSE	COMMENTS
A spike produces keikis and no flowers	Improper temperature or day length	Some *DENDROBIUMS*, *PLEUROTHALLUS*, and *PHALAENOPSIS* readily produce vegetative shoots or keikis from flower buds. An occasional keiki is normal, but if you get only vegetative buds, the most likely cause is insufficient drop in temperature or change in day length for the flower buds to develop.
	Poor health or genetics	Keikis can also be a sign of root trauma or bad genetics.
Wrinkled or pleated leaves	Leaves get stuck as they emerge, usually because of insufficient water or low humidity	*ONCIDIUMS*, *ODONTOGLOSSUMS*, *MILTONIOPSIS*, and other orchids with thin, strappy leaves are prone to pleating as leaves develop. Insufficient water causes the emerging leaves to stop growing and then start again, so the leaf gets caught in other leaf bases and wrinkles. Also, many orchid leaves produce sugary exudates, and if humidity is low or leaves are kept dry, the sap hardens and binds the developing leaves, which pleat as the plant tries to force them out. Proper watering and humidity and a weekly shower to rinse off accumulated sap will prevent this.
Yellowing leaves	Natural senescence	Except for naturally deciduous species such as the nobile *DENDROBIUMS* and *CATESETUMS*, orchid leaves should live for at least a year and often two to five years before being shed. An occasional yellow leaf on the oldest growths of sympodial orchids or the lowest leaves on monopodials is normal, especially if it turns yellow and falls off gradually. *ONCIDIUMS* and others that produce a fan of new leaves often shed the outermost few as roots grow and break through them. *VANDAS* and *PHALAENOPSIS* also drop leaves when roots split through their bases.
	Insufficient nitrogen	Yellowing leaves, even if they don't fall off, can be a sign of poor nutrition, especially a lack of nitrogen.
	Too dry or too wet	If a plant is losing more leaves than it is replacing with new ones, you should be concerned. The most likely causes are insufficient water or root trauma caused by overwatering. The plant sheds leaves in an attempt to balance water uptake with the loss of water through foliage.
	Rot disease	If a whole pseudobulb or developing growth turns yellow almost overnight, the stem may have a bacterial or fungal infection. Amputate the infected section with a sterile instrument and hope for the best.
Black or brown spots on foliage or psuedobulbs	Fungus infection caused by *Cercospora*, *Colletotrichum*, or other fungi (see Chapter 10)	Leaf-spotting fungi typically form circular lesions on leaves because the spores germinate and grow outward in all directions. The tissue at the outer circumference of the spot will appear watery or yellow, with brown, black, or tan dead tissue toward the center. Strong air movement is your best defense against leaf spots, as the spots need standing water to germinate. Fungicidal sprays, including preventives like horticultural oil, may be needed to control a bad infection.
	Response to strong sunlight	Strong sunlight may cause portions of the leaf to bleach or blacken, especially the surfaces most exposed to the sun. Orchids in the *ONCIDIUM* alliance may respond to strong sun with small black stippling on exposed leaf surfaces; most others will develop blackened lesions. Sun damage can be distinguished from disease by location and the lack of a watery band around the margin.
	Virus infection	A virus infection will initially cause bleached or faded stippling, striations, or "tattoos" on the foliage, which may eventually turn black. The blackened areas remain small and dispersed, and they are evenly spread over the leaf surface.
Dying leaf tips	Salt damage from water	Some genera, notably *COELOGYNE* and *MILTONIA*, exhibit slow but steady leaf-tip dieback. Watering with rainwater or RO water should clear up the problem eventually. Overfertilization, which elevates salt levels much as poor-quality water does, will cause a similar reaction, but it shows up quickly and will not affect subsequent growth if fertilization is reduced.

Most orchid leaves should live for two to four years. Premature leaf drop is most often correlated with lack of water or poor nutrition.

Leaf-tip damage on a *Paphiopedilum* caused by high levels of soluble salts in poor-quality water

Problem	Possible Cause	Comments
Dying leaf tips	Fungus infection	Pathogens may cause tip dieback, especially in a humid greenhouse, and it is difficult to tell this from salt-related injury. First assume that salt is the cause, and if the problem persists, treat for fungus infection.
	Dryness	Drought stress may cause leaf-tip dieback, but you will also see other symptoms, such as shriveled pseudobulbs and poor root growth.
Sticky honeydew on leaves and/or inflorescences	Natural exudates	Developing leaves and inflorescences of many orchids exude sugary sap. Whether the sap attracts potential pollinators or is a way to eliminate wastes is unclear. In a greenhouse, where the plants are routinely drenched, the sap washes off before it's noticeable, but on a windowsill, you may see it, especially on *Phalaenopsis*, *Cymbidiums*, and some of the *Oncidium* alliance. Too much sap buildup can cause flower buds to become distorted. Rinse plants with a jet of warm water from the spray hose in the kitchen sink, then let them sit for ten minutes and wet them again.
	Insect infestation	Sucking insects, especially aphids, exude large quantities of honeydew as they feed, and this builds up as a tacky substance on anything it lands on. If you notice sticky leaves, check the plants and nearby houseplants carefully for aphids and scale.
Root-tip dieback	Dryness	Actively growing root tips lack velamen, so they are whitish to dark green or ruddy red. Root growth typically occurs in flushes that coincide with active top growth; at other times root elongation slows or ceases. Drought or low humidity slows root growth; they will usually begin growing actively once watering is increased.
	Salt injury	Roots should have a small band or dot of green tissue at the tip, with white velamen covering the rest. If actively growing root tips are fertilized with too strong a concentration or come into contact with salt-laden potting mix or pot rims, they will shrivel and die. If you see shriveled or black root tips, you should repot or thoroughly flush roots and pot with distilled water.
Pseudobulbs gnawed or eaten	Rats and mice	In a greenhouse or cellar, rats can be a real problem for some orchids — particularly *Stanhopeas* and *Gongoras* but occasionally other pseudobulbous species. Mice will occasionally gnaw the pseudobulbs of these orchids down to the rhizome but will not eat the leaves. Damage is quick and progressive. A few snap traps with peanut butter bait should catch the culprits.
Orchid does not put out new growth for more than a year	Loss of dormant buds	The rhizomes of sympodial species have numerous dormant growth buds, which age and are lost with time. New growths continually replenish the supply, but if thrips, snails, slugs, or some other stressor destroy all viable buds, the plant will have no means to regrow. If the roots are intact, it may sit for a year or two, then eventually succumb. There is nothing you can do at that point. As a last resort, spray the plant thoroughly with a solution of 1 tsp sugar and a few drops of Superthrive (or other vitamin-B potion) in a quart of water, enclose the plant in a clear plastic bag and keep in bright (sunless) light until new roots and/or leaves are visible, then remove it from the bag and pot it.
Plant seems loose in pot	Root loss	Fungal infection (see Chapter 10) from overwatering or salt damage caused by poor-quality water.
	Roots have not reestablished a good hold after potting	When repotting, clip top-heavy plants in place with a rhizome clip to ensure that roots are not disturbed when the plant is watered or moved (see Chapter 8).

Live and dead roots on a
Phalaenopsis

PART THREE

Orchid Reproduction

CHAPTER 12

Reproduction in the Wild

IF YOU MEASURE SUCCESS by sheer number of species, no other group of plants, save maybe the grass family or the composites (daisy family), comes close to the success of the orchids. The reasons that orchids have become so incredibly diversified can be summed up in one word: insects.

The orchids have taken insect pollination to a level of sophistication rarely matched in the plant kingdom. Many, many orchids have evolved relationships with specific insects, adjusting the size of their flowers, the perfumes and nectars they produce, and even their color to maximize their attractiveness to one or two species of bee, fly, wasp, ant, moth, butterfly, or beetle—or, I should add, hummingbird. This specificity ensures that the plant has the insect's undivided attention, but it also means that orchids are especially threatened by habitat loss and agricultural pesticides, because the loss of the pollinator is catastrophic—it can mean extinction of the species. The diversity of insects is mind-boggling, so orchid species can evolve to host individual insects almost ad infini-

Since orchids rely on the one bug–one flower method rather than temporal or physical barriers to remain genetically isolated, if pollen from one species is deposited on a similar species or even a similar genus, chances are the stigma will accept it as genuine, and hybrid progeny will result. The ability to accept pollen from related species is called promiscuity, and orchids are some of the most promiscuous plants on earth, as a quick scan of *Sander's List of Orchid Hybrids* will demonstrate. Chance hybridization does happen occasionally in the wild, and if some of the progeny are born with flowers suited to a different insect species or another environmental niche, a new orchid species has been born.

Just which family of plants the orchids are descended from is open to conjecture, but we can safely say that they are related to the lilylike monocots. The relationship is evident in the composition of the flower. In a true lily, such as a tiger lily or Easter lily, the flower is arranged in a pattern of threes (in the language of botany, they are trimerous). The three **petals** are surrounded by three **sepals,** which are so similar to the petals in form and color as to be indistinguishable from them. However, if you look at the base of the flower, the sepals are

tum. If an orchid can be pollinated by only one or two insects, it is effectively isolated genetically from all related species growing nearby. If each species attracts and is pollinated by a different insect, there is little chance of accidental cross-pollination and hybridization. That is why you can find a dozen closely related but distinct species of orchids all growing and blooming on one tree branch. Wind-pollinated plants, such as grasses, and those pollinated by a number of insects, like the composites, have to isolate themselves physically or temporally from related species. They may grow on different mountain ranges or in distinct habitats, have pollen proteins that the stigma can detect and either accept or reject, or have nonoverlapping bloom periods. The only reason grasses and composites rival orchids in diversity is that they are much more widely adaptable as far as habitat, growing on dry deserts, alpine summits, and tropical savannas with equal ease.

RIGHT: The orange color and tubular shape of ***Masdevallia mendozae*** flowers have evolved to attract hummingbirds, which pollinate them as they search for nectar within the throat of the bloom. The flower is constructed so that the bird's head and beak are correctly positioned to pick up and deliver pollen.

Orchids are one of the most diverse families of plants on earth. Many species are native to a single valley or mountaintop, where they have coevolved with a specific pollinator, host tree, or mycorrhizal fungus. Habitat and pollinator specificity, as well as a high degree of endemism (being native to only a small area), are warning flags for conservationists concerned about extinction, for these plants are at the greatest risk. I have no doubt whatsoever that loss of habitat through land clearing has already caused orchid species to go extinct. I have seen this process myself in Ecuador, where in visits to the type localities (the places of initial discovery) of certain rare species I found not forest but endless eroded cow pastures and no orchids. While there may be a place for "ex situ" conservation (maintaining cultivated collections of orchids for possible reintroduction to the wild), the reality is that this approach is too expensive and fraught with problems to have much long-term impact on a species' survival. Large-scale habitat protection is really the only answer, and as orchid growers, we should all support organizations like the Nature Conservancy (the Web site is www.nature.org) that are working with landowners and with governments to protect the land and educate people about the need to protect habitats.

You can do your part by caring for your own piece of ground and any orchids that grow there and by not supporting the commercial collection of wild orchids. Buy from reputable nurseries that have a policy of carrying only nursery-propagated material.

attached behind or outside of the petals. The six **stamens**, the male parts of the flower, surround one large **pistil**, the female part, which is tipped with a three-winged or three-lobed **stigma** (the place that pollen attaches to). The pistil is attached at its base to an immature ovary, which is located below or behind the petals and sepals. If the flower is pollinated, the ovary will swell and develop into a three- or six-chambered seedpod.

Orchids, too, are trimerous, and their flowers are really lily flowers that have been highly modified for efficient insect pollination. Orchid flowers are asymmetrical, in that you can divide them into equal parts only vertically. The three sepals often mimic the petals in color but tend to be different in shape. Remember, though, that the sepals are always behind the petals, at least where they attach to the stem above the ovary. The sepals typically form a triangle, with one—the dorsal sepal—at the top, jutting straight up from the flower, and the two lateral sepals slanting down on either side. In some groups of orchids, such as the slipper orchids and the little terrestrial *Corbas*, the dorsal sepal is modified to form a large parasol that arches over the sexual parts of the flower, protecting them from the elements and helping to guide pollinators to the right place. Among the pleurothallids, such as *Dracula* and *Masdevallia*, the petals are very reduced in size, so the sepals are the showy part of the flower. The triangular arrangement of the sepals gives *Masdevallias* a recognizable shape. In fact, the geometrical regularity and balance of the three sepals lends even the most bizarre orchids a refined, ordered appearance.

Orchid petals, on the other hand, cannot be called orderly or refined. In their quest to lure every manner of insect to the blooms, the plants have evolved the most fantastic, magnificent, bizarre, and beautiful petals in the plant kingdom. Like the sepals, the three petals are arranged in a roughly triangular fashion, with two projecting out horizontally or at upward angles from the center and one pointing straight down. The lateral petals may be colored or patterned like the sepals, though just as often they are very different in shape or even hue. The lower petal is the real standout. Lying just below the sexual parts of the flower, it is the advertising sign, the welcome mat, and the grand entrance all rolled into one. Consequently, nothing has been spared in its elaboration. In fact, this lower petal has become so fanciful that we don't even call it a petal anymore, but rather a lip or labellum—really a unique third part of the flower. Whether shaped like a banner, a ruffled petticoat, a dancing doll, or the back of a female bee, this amazing lip is essentially *orchid*. The labellum is what makes the flowers of this fabulous clan so recognizable.

The lip attracts an insect's or hummingbird's attention and guides it in. It may even provide a nectar reward, because nectar pools at the base of the lip, where it attaches to the stem. But in order for the flower to be fertilized, the pollinator must successfully transfer pollen onto the stigma. Orchids have an engineering solution for this as well. As in the lilies, the flower has one pistil (female part), but instead of six stamens there are three. In a lily flower, the pistil juts out on a long stem called a style, and the pollen-filled **anthers** hang from thin filaments. In orchids the style and filaments are fused—forged into a single strong unit called the **column** or gynostemium. As far as evolutionary taxonomists are concerned, it is the column, more than the colorful lip, that sets orchids apart from all other monocots, and it is the reason they are considered the most highly evolved plants on earth! (The Malvaceae, or hibiscus family, also have a column, but only the filaments are fused.) Look at the very center of the orchid flower and notice the thick, hook-shaped column protruding there. It may be short and stubby or long and tapered, but it always has the same basic shape. Most orchid flowers are **resupinate**—that is, they rotate 180° as they develop (that is why the **peduncle** looks twisted) so that the column angles down and the lip is bottommost. Some orchids, like *Calopogon*, are nonresupinate—they do not rotate before they open—so the column curves upward. In any case, just under the hooked or clawlike tip, protected from the elements by the roof of the column, you'll see a sticky, translucent pocket. This is all that remains of the stigma, the female part of the flower. It is linked to the ovary by a series of pollen tubes that snake down the column like fiber-optic cables. The stigma has three lobes, like the lily's, but these have been reduced to wings, two of which often flare out like a hooded cobra from either side of the column, while the other wing forms a sort of flap, called a **rostellum**, above it. This arrangement physically separates the pollen from the stigma. At the very tip of the column (or, in the case of the slipper orchids, on either side of it) is the trap-door anther cap. This cap stays shut as an insect, a beak, or a hybridizer's toothpick enters the flower; then, as it backs out, the cap hinges open, exposing the anthers and pollen.

Now I said that orchids have three stamens—or at least they did originally. In the more primitive slipper orchids (sub-tribe Cypripedioideae), one stamen is enlarged into a sterile **staminode**, which serves the same purpose as the rostellum. (Because they lack a rostellum, some taxonomists feel the Cypripedioideae should be split off as a separate family.) The two anthers sit on either side of the column just below the tip under a rudimentary anther cap. If you pop off this cap, you can pick out the pollen in a gooey, grainy mass. But in all other orchids the staminode has disappeared, and the two stamens have migrated to the tip of the column, where they have fused into a two-chambered structure covered by a single anther cap. Instead of the slipper orchids' gooey, incoherent pollen, most orchids have hard, usually teardrop-shaped packages of pollen called pollinia (singular, **pollinium**). Orchids produce huge quantities of ovules, and thus they need large amounts of pollen to fertilize them. The pollinium assures that if a flower is fertilized, it will receive all the pollen it needs in one package. Typically, from one to three pollinia are attached to a stalk called a viscidium, with a very sticky foot. When the pollinator backs out of the flower and pops the anther cap, the viscidium springs out and the foot sticks to the pollinator's head, thorax, abdomen, or beak. The glue acts like quick-drying

Beguiling *Paphiopedilum rothschildianum* lures insects with bold stripes to the slipperlike lip. After entering the slipper, the insect has no choice but to force its way under one of the pollinia to exit through the rear, where the lip attaches to the back of the flower. When it enters another flower, it will transfer the pollen from this one before receiving another dollop.

With a little imagination (or a whiff of the proper pheromone), the complex hooked lip of *Stanhopea napoensis* is transformed into a female bee waiting for love. As a male bee attempts to copulate, it backs up against the column jutting down from above. As it does, it receives and/or deposits pollinia.

some of the pollinia will be deposited on other orchids of the same species growing in another location. Outcrossing—transferring pollen, and thus genes, to other, less closely related individuals—has obvious advantages. While inbreeding appears less catastrophic among orchids than it does among dogs or people, over generations it will reduce the genetic variability within the population and make the species more vulnerable to variables such as disease or climate change.

Orchids lure pollinators in various ways. Colorful flowers, a lip patterned with guides that act like homing beacons on a runway, fragrance that hints at a nectar treat—all help get an insect's attention. A few pleurothallids and *Bulbophyllums* even have little dangling tassels that I imagine are designed to look like fungal threads or another insect's eggs—just what a gravid female gnat would search for as a place to deposit eggs. As Charles Darwin himself surmised, the remarkable foot-long nectar spurs of *Angraecum sesquipedale* have evolved to serve one species of moth that has the especially long proboscis needed to access the nectar hidden in the base. The most ingenious orchids, however, have discovered that the promise of sex is even more powerful than the lure of food. Sex and sexual deceit: for a culture obsessed with sex, as ours is, flowers that use mimicry and pseudocopulation to effect pollination hold a special, puerile fascination. To pollination biologists, though, mimicry is the most delicate and highly evolved strategy a plant can use. Take, for example, the genus *Arthrochilus*. Plants in this small group of terrestrials from Australia and New Guinea have a lip with hinged parts that so resembles the female of a particular species of wasp that males repeatedly try to mate and fly off with the flower. As the struggling wasp rotates on the lip, to which it is tethered, its backside bumps against the anther cap and is dabbed with pollinia. If this wasp species goes extinct, so will the orchid.

Visual mimicry is not the only way to lure a pollinator. *Stanhopeas* and other orchids pollinated by euglossine bees release a powerful pheromone that the male bees gather frantically in order to lure females. Again, plant and insect have evolved together, and each depends on the other for its survival.

Plants have two basic strategies as far as seeds go. Either they produce a few large seeds or lots of small ones. Large seeds have more food reserves and a better chance of germinating if they find an acceptable place, while small seeds have fewer reserves and thus more difficulty germinating, but their

epoxy, cementing the pollinia to the insect or bird so that it can't easily be groomed off or harvested for food. The column of each orchid species is shaped and sized for the proportions of a particular pollinator. If the wrong insect visits the flower, it may be too large or too small to trip the anther cap, and even if it does, the pollinia are likely to attach in the wrong place. However, when the correct insect (or bird) visits and is daubed as it backs out of the flower, the pollinia will attach at precisely the right place on its body to line up with the stigmatic surface of the next flower the insect enters completely. Since the pollinator picks up pollen only as it leaves the flower, then deposits it on the next one it visits before picking up more pollinia, the orchid has effectively prevented self-pollination. The only way for the flower to pollinate itself would be for the insect to immediately reenter the same flower, and I guess insects are unlikely to do that. Now the insect might go on to another bloom on the same inflorescence, but at least

ORCHIDS AND FUNGI

Very little is known about the orchids' fungal hosts. Even when fungal hyphae are isolated from an orchid seedling, they rarely, if ever, fruit—that is, produce mushrooms or other spore-bearing structures by which they can be identified. Through DNA analysis, dozens of fungi that are new to science are now being identified from orchid cells. Some orchids appear to associate with a single fungus species throughout their range, while others associate with groups of related fungi. Just how common these fungi are, what their ecology is, and whether or not they get anything from the orchid in return are questions that remain largely unanswered. What is clear is that orchids will not germinate in the wild without the fungi. This fact adds a whole extra dimension to the topic of orchid conservation. To protect the orchid, you must protect the fungus, which means protecting what the fungus feeds on, the plants it might associate with, and the habitat it needs to survive.

sheer numbers mean that a few from each capsule have a chance of finding a good place to grow. Oaks and coconuts are examples of the first strategy. A single coconut is very costly for the palm to produce, but it can survive months at sea and still have the resources to germinate should it chance to land on a suitable beach. Orchids are one of the best examples of the latter strategy; each capsule produces thousands, even tens of thousands, of tiny, tiny seeds that fan out on the breeze in hopes of finding a branch or patch of earth to grow on. Orchids can produce so many seeds only because they invest so little in each one. Most seeds, even the smallest, contain an immature plant or embryo that has a bit of stored energy to help it germinate. Orchid seeds, however, are merely a few cells enclosed in a thin, papery skin that helps them remain aloft. The only way they can germinate is through parasitism.

The orchid family, along with a few other groups of plants, has evolved complex relationships with particular species of fungus. When an orchid seed lands in a suitable place, it must be attacked by that fungus, whose hyphae (its "roots") penetrate the seed's cell walls and begin to proliferate inside. The seed digests the hyphae, thus drawing from its host the carbohydrates and enzymes it needs to begin growing. Almost all plants form associations with specific soil fungi, which fuse with the plant's roots, forming new hybrid structures called mycorrhizae. The fungus helps the plant gather specific nutrients more effectively, and in return it gets carbohydrates from the plant. This tit-for-tat relationship is called a symbiosis. Orchid seedlings, on the other hand, appear to enter into a one-way relationship with the fungus, drawing off food without offering anything in return. Technically, then, orchid fungi cannot be said to be mycorrhizal or symbiotic—"unwilling host" would be more apropos. Interestingly, at least some

As fine as dust, the thousands of seeds in this ripe *Epidendrum cinnabarinum* seed capsule will float off in the breeze on the off chance that a few will find the right spot—and the right fungus—that will allow them to germinate and grow.

orchid hosts do form mycorrhizae with other plants. The *Corallorhizas* (coralroots) sponge off fungi associated with forest trees like birch and beech. In a sense, then, these orchids feed off the tree by way of the fungus.

Once an orchid seed is infected with the fungus, it begins to swell and grow. The mass of cells forms a protocorm—basically a rudimentary rhizome that produces the first roots and the vegetative shoot. The developing seedling remains underground (or under moss) for six months to five years, until it has grown enough of a root system to support the emerging shoot. While some epiphytic orchids have green, photosynthetic protocorms, all orchids rely primarily on the fungus until they sprout leaves and begin photosynthesizing in

earnest. Considering that they spring from such tiny seeds, emerging orchid seedlings are surprisingly large, thanks to the fungus. Under cultivation, smaller tropical species can mature and bloom within six to twelve months from the time they send out their first leaf, but large, slow-growing *Paphio-pedilums* and *Cattleyas* may take five to seven years before opening their first bloom.

Phragmipedium caudatum. No one knows how long it takes for slow-growing *Phragmipediums* to mature, but probably five to ten years, judging by their growth rate in cultivation.

CHAPTER 13

Hand Pollination and Care of Seedlings

THOUGH IT TAKES QUITE A LOT of specialized equipment to raise orchids from seed, a number of commercial labs will grow seedlings for you if you provide them with a seedpod. This makes it easy for the dedicated hobbyist to raise his or her own seedlings or make new hybrids.

Hand-Pollinating

Hand-pollinating an orchid is fun once you understand the basics, and it's the only way you're likely to get seed from plants under cultivation. The orchid uses quite a bit of energy to produce a pod filled with thousands of seeds, so it's important to pollinate only healthy, established plants and avoid stressed, diseased, or newly potted ones.

With the exception of orchids like *Sobralias,* whose flowers last for only a day, it usually takes twenty-four to forty-eight hours for the stigma of a newly opened flower to become

ABOVE: ***Paphiopedilum chamberlainianum.*** This flower has been open for two days and shows no sign of fading. Now is a good time to pollinate.

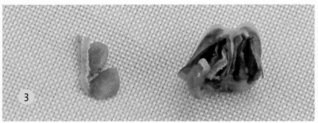

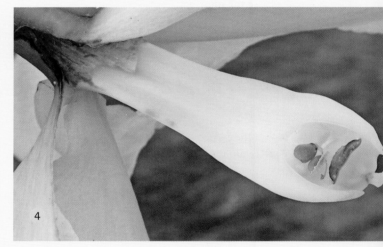

1. A *Cattleya* flower with its lip removed, showing the anther cap sitting at the very tip of the column.

2. The same flower after I have removed the anther cap and the four pollinia by flicking a toothpick upward against the tab on the lower edge of the hinged cap. The stigmatic surface is just visible under the column.

3. The anther cap is on the right, and two of its comma-shaped pollinia are on the left. The long, thin part of each pollinium is the sticky viscidium, designed to adhere to the pollinator. The pollen itself is massed inside the oval section. Notice how the pollinia fit neatly into four slots within the anther cap with the viscidia facing out.

4. From underneath, the stigmatic depression is clearly visible on the lower side of the column. The viscidia adhered easily to the toothpick I used to place the pollinia on the stigma. If the stigma is receptive, it will have more than enough tacky stigmatic fluid to hold on to the pollen sacs as the toothpick is pulled away. Within a few days the edges of the stigma will swell and eventually engulf the pollen.

5. If pollination is successful, the ovary behind the flower will begin to swell within a week or two. Though two seedpods are a lot for this *Encyclia cochleata* to ripen at one time, removing one at this point is tricky and could cause the other to become infected. *E. cochleata* seed ripens fully in about 120 days. These two-month-old capsules are about halfway there. They will be ready for GREEN-POD culture in another three weeks.

receptive. A receptive stigma is spongy and exudes quantities of sticky, viscous fluid designed to catch and hold pollinia. If you dab the stigmatic surface with a toothpick, fluid will adhere to the tip if it is ready to receive pollen.

Pollinia typically ripen a bit ahead of the stigma, so in choosing the male, or **pollen parent**, look for a flower that is about the same age as the one you wish to pollinate. Place the tip of a toothpick or tweezers just under the anther cap, which sits atop the column like the cone of a missile. At the bottom, where the cap curls under the column, there is usually a little tab or hook that snags the insect as it backs out. Flick this tab out and up and the cap will hinge open. If your position is right, the viscidium will stick to the toothpick as you do this, so as you pull it away you'll see the pollinia attached. *Catesetums* are the most fun, because when you trip the trigger mechanism by inserting your finger inside the hooded lip, the pollinia slam down on your finger with surprising force. I imagine it's quite hard on a bee. When you are pollinating miniatures, a magnifying glass or hand lens is a great help. In almost all of the orchids I have ever seen, the pollinia are golden or bright yellow, so they stand out even if tiny. Once you've collected the pollinia on the toothpick, dab them into the stigmatic fluid of the chosen plant. It may take a few tries, but the fluid should retain the pollinia as you pull the toothpick away.

Many plants can recognize pollen of their own or a related species by its protein "fingerprints." If you are hybridizing and are having trouble getting the pollen to "take"—be accepted by the stigma—you can circumvent this problem by actually destroying the fingerprint proteins on the surface of the pollen grains. The easiest place to find protein-destroying enzymes is in your own spit, and it's common knowledge among hybridizers that letting the pollinia soak for five or ten minutes in a gob of spit may help it take. If you find this thought repugnant, you can use a few drops of enzymatic contact lens cleaner (the fluid that wearers of contact lenses use to clean off protein deposits). In either case, let the pollinia soak for up to five minutes, then stir them around and soak for another few minutes. Don't rinse the pollinia before dabbing them onto the stigma.

If the pollination attempt is successful, within a few days the stigma will swell and the lobes on either side will grow and close over the stigma. It's quite fascinating to see the stigma's slow-motion swallowing of the pollinia. It reminds me of films I've seen of carnivorous snails swallowing prey in their mantle. You'll know you've failed if after a few days the stigma turns brown and dries out. After being accepted by the stigma, the pollen sprouts tubes, which grow down through the column over a period of several weeks and find their way to the ovules in the immature ovary. Once fertilized, the ovules develop into seeds. Usually, within days of pollination, you'll see the ovary begin to swell in anticipation. The flower petals and sepals

Ripening Time for Seeds of Selected Genera

Species	Mature (days)	Green Pod (days)
Bulbophyllum	90	60
Calanthe	120	80
Cattleya	300	200
Coelogyne	360	240
Cymbidium	300	200
Cypripedum	100	60
Dendrobium	360	240
Epidendrum	100	65
Laelia	270	175
Masdevallia	100	60
Miltonia	270	175
Odontoglossum	210	135
Paphiopedilum	300	200
Phalaenopsis	180	120
Stanhopea	210	135
Stelis	75	50
Vanda	600	400

often wither but remain clinging to the base of the column as the seed capsule develops. Although you can pollinate a number of flowers on a single plant, unless your plant is especially large and robust you should remove all but one or two of the developing pods within two or three weeks once it is evident that they have been fertilized successfully. The energy required to mature numerous pods can really weaken a plant.

It takes from three to one hundred weeks for the capsule to mature, at which point three seams split open along the sides, allowing the dustlike seeds to shake out into the breeze. However, if you are collecting seeds to sow, it is usually better to harvest them before they are mature; this is called greenpod or green-seed culture. The best time to do this varies from genus to genus but it's usually about two-thirds of the time it takes for the capsule to ripen fully, as the table above shows.

Flasking

Although the ovary may begin to swell soon after pollination, don't start counting your seedlings until a few weeks or even months have passed. It takes that long for the pollen to travel down and successfully unite with the ovules. It's not uncommon for a seed capsule to wither a few weeks after pollination when the process has been unsuccessful because the parents were incompatible. After a month or even three months have passed, you can start to relax. It takes a long time for all those thousands of seeds to mature, however. Seeds of small species tend to ripen more quickly, as do those of temperate-zone orchids that must produce a pod before winter.

In the wild, orchid seeds need the help of specific fungi to begin growing and to get large enough to put up leaves. This complicates the process of germinating your own seed, since you're unlikely to have the right species of tropical fungus just lying around the house. If you have a plant that originated in the wild, it is possible, though unlikely, that you could get some of the seed to germinate if you sprinkle it around the roots of the wild plant. If some of the proper fungus survived on the roots of the parent plant (which is most unlikely, given the barrage of fungicides that orchids are subjected to in cultivation), a few seedlings might be able to get established. Until the 1920s, this symbiotic method of orchid seed germination was the only technique available to growers, so seedlings were rare and orchids in general remained very expensive.

In 1922, Lewis Knudson, working at Cornell University, discovered that it is possible, by artificially providing the seed with the nutrients, carbohydrates, and hormones it would normally get from the fungus, to induce germination and normal maturation. This asymbiotic method of seed germination revolutionized the propagation of orchids and, more than any other factor, led to their explosion in popularity during the twentieth century. Not only could seedlings of species be produced easily, but hybridization could proceed at full speed. Knudson's technique was quite a remarkable innovation. He found that by combining sugar, in the form of sucrose, with various mineral nutrients and agar (a jelling agent obtained from algae), and heating and sterilizing the mixture in a sealed container (sterility is important to prevent opportunistic bacteria and fungi from taking over and killing the seeds), orchid seed that had been sterilized in a bleach solution and sown on a surface would germinate and grow. Subsequent research has shown that some species germinate better if certain plant hormones, especially cytokinins, are added to the mixture.

It is possible to set up a small home laboratory for orchid seed flasking. Laboratory chemical suppliers and some orchid supply specialists sell premixed germination medium, to which you simply add water, fill some sterile jars, and boil them in an autoclave or pressure cooker for thirty minutes. I have germinated seed successfully using a premixed medium, a pressure cooker, clean baby food jars, and a sterile "hood" made from a cardboard box set on its side and lined with aluminum foil (the hood helps exclude mold spores). Sheets of clear plastic draped over the opening allow you to see what you're doing as you work inside the box. If you liberally douse the interior, your hands and arms, and all the equipment with a 10% bleach solution, you can keep it sterile enough to get a reasonable percentage of clean flasks if you work quickly. Commercial operations have what are called laminar flow

A sterile "mother" flask containing about thirty husky *Ascocenda* seedlings growing on agar jelly enriched with sugars and nutrients. Narrow-necked flasks like this have fallen from favor because of the difficulty of removing the seedlings. These seedlings are about ready to come out.

hoods to work under; air is forced through a very fine filter that scrubs out microorganisms, then blows this at the operator and working surface. This setup is a heck of a lot more pleasant to work with than a bleach box (though the bleach did turn my arm hair a pleasant light blond). If you are interested in pursuing this course, I recommend reading *Micropropagation of Orchids* as well as some of the other books on micropropagation that are listed in the bibliography.

Fortunately, if you want to raise your own seedlings and hybrids but do not want to set up a lab, flasking services will do it for you and send you the seedlings when they are ready. Believe me, once you figure in the cost of materials and equipment, the time it takes to flask, and the big learning curve necessary to master orchid seed sowing, these services are a very attractive option. The cost is usually somewhere around a dollar per delivered seedling. Or you can ask some of the nurseries you do business with if they would like any of the seeds you have produced. If they are interested, they might flask them for you and give you a percentage of the resulting seedlings.

Most orchid seeds are now sown when the pod is immature (green pod), whether you do it yourself or send the pods off to be flasked. Seed that is about two-thirds ripe has been found to germinate much more readily than seed that has been allowed to fully ripen, turn brown, and dry out. (See the table on p. 111 for seed-ripening times for selected genera.) If you're using a lab, be sure to ask someone there to tell you the ripening time for the species or hybrid you are sending.

Unflasking and Caring for Seedlings

Seedlings growing in vitro (literally "within glass") in a sterile laboratory vessel must be carefully weaned from this rarefied atmosphere. Once removed, they are vulnerable to pathogens, and the leaves that develop in the saturated atmosphere of the flask have no waxy protective cuticle, so their tissues can quickly dry out and die if not attended to. Also, the seedlings have been on life support in the flask, receiving all the sugars they need from the medium and not having to photosynthesize much at all. When you take them out, they must go through an important and delicate transition period as they adjust to their new environment.

Whether you have received a flask from the lab, purchased one at an orchid show, or raised the seed yourself, the seedlings are ready to remove once they have a decent nest of roots and at least a few leaves. Theoretically, you can leave seedlings in vitro indefinitely, as long as you reflask them when they exhaust the medium they are growing in. In practice, though, it is not really feasible to keep reflasking larger seedlings. The timing depends on the species, but in general you should remove seedlings from the flask when the leaf span is about ³/₄–1 inch. By the time they are ready to come out, the agar is usually stained black by exudates from their roots, and the medium they are in is pretty well exhausted. If the seedlings have been shipped to you by a flasking service or a

If you have more than one seedling of the same type, pot them up in a community pot after removing them from the flask. Six months after removal, these **Dendrobium petiolatum** seedlings are almost large enough to be potted separately.

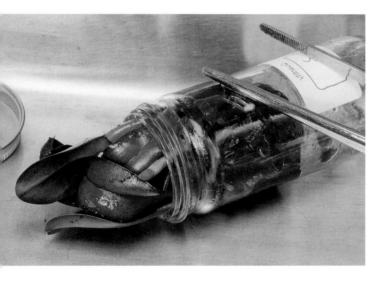

A mini-flask containing a single robust **Phalaenopsis** seedling. A short soak in warm water will loosen the agar, and gently swirling the plant through the water will wash free all the bits of jelly. Seedlings removed from sterile flasks need extra humidity and attention until they can form new leaves and roots better suited to life in an unclean world.

nursery, they are probably all jumbled up anyway, with some roots torn from the agar. However, as long as there is no sign of contamination (patches of white or gray fungal hyphae or discolored circles of bacteria), you can leave seedlings in the flask for a week or two. If you can't get to them right away, keep them in a bright spot out of direct sun.

Find a clean, bright place to unflask your seedlings. I prefer to do it indoors, away from established plants that might transmit pathogens. Wash your hands thoroughly and fill a bowl with distilled water. Seedlings growing in agar can be gently lifted with tweezers. Try to hold them gingerly by the roots instead of by the leaves or crown. Drop the seedlings into the bowl and let them soak for a few minutes. The water will loosen the agar and make it easier to remove. I swish the seedlings around with my fingers and carefully pick off any stubborn patches of agar by hand. If you have received seedlings grown in a liquid medium (medium without agar in which the seedlings float half submerged), it is still a good idea to clean them with distilled water, which washes away exudates and excess salts. I often put a few drops of a systemic fungicide like Subdue, at one-quarter the recommended strength, in the soak water to help them through the transition period. Another option is to inoculate the potting mix with a beneficial fungus like RootShield, which will protect them from damping off (you cannot combine RootShield and a fungicide, however). Since the seedlings are sterile, there is really no point in treating them with a contact fungicide or disinfectant at this point. I also put a few drops of a B-vitamin solution in the water; doing this makes me feel better, though I can't say whether it really helps or not.

The roots produced in vitro are almost like water roots. They often lack velamen and are thinner than roots produced in vivo (outside the flask). I prefer to pot newly unflasked seedlings in New Zealand sphagnum, because its wicking action allows these roots to function until the plant produces new ones. The moss also has some antifungal effects. Since a small seedling will be overwhelmed in a large pot, and watering is difficult to control in tiny pots, orchid seedlings are usually put in a community pot. A square plastic 4-inch pot should be large enough for ten to twenty-five seedlings; an 8-inch round will hold from fifty to one hundred. Space is always an issue, but I prefer to use several smaller pots rather than one big one, because fungal diseases can spread quickly through a pot of seedlings, and if you put all your seedlings in one basket, so to speak, you can lose the lot almost overnight.

A mature *Dendrobium petiolatum*

Start with a wad of moss and wrap it around the first seedling, being careful to work the roots in between the fibers of the moss. Keep the moss and seedling in one hand as you add another seedling and a small clump of moss. In effect you are making a multilayered sandwich. Take care to keep all the seedlings aligned so that the crown, where roots meet leaves, is just at the surface. If you bury them too deeply in the moss, they are more susceptible to damping off; if they're too high, the new roots will have difficulty getting established in the moss. Once you have a bundle that will fit snugly in a 3- or 4-inch pot, carefully work it into the pot and then adjust the height of individual seedlings by teasing them up or adding a bit more moss around one that's too high. Work quickly enough that the seedlings remain wet, and mist them if you have to answer the phone or feed the baby. When a pot is filled, I gently blow off any water droplets, especially those lodged in leaf bases, and loosely stretch a plastic bag over the top, holding it on with a rubber band around the pot. Leave the drainage holes uncovered to allow water out and air into the interior. If you keep your growing environment above 75% humidity, you may not need the bag.

Even if you have a greenhouse, I think it's best to place unflasked seedlings under a fluorescent light fixture set up exclusively for this purpose in order to isolate them from potential insect pests and diseases until they are stronger. Most labs raise flasks of seedlings under fluorescent lights, so the leaves are already conditioned to its intensity, and you won't risk burning them. Watch the seedlings carefully for any sign of disease. Damping-off disease causes darkened, watery areas, usually around the crown of the plant. It's normal for the seedlings to shed a few leaves in the weeks after unflasking, but if you see any that are quickly turning yellow and toppling over, remove them promptly and drench the rest with a 1/4 tsp/gal of Physan 20 (ammonium chloride). Leave the bag off the pot until the seedlings are almost dry. Assuming that the agar wasn't terribly depleted, newly unflasked seedlings should have enough nutrient reserves in their roots to last a week or two. After that, 1/4 tsp/gal of a complete soluble fertilizer will keep them growing well. After the first week, I remove the rubber band (earlier if I see any sign of disease) to let in more air. Keep the moss evenly moist, and gradually remove the bag over the next week or two. By that time the leaves will have hardened off somewhat (adjusted to their new environment) and will be able to withstand drier air. Ideally, though, you want to keep the humidity above 50%.

Continue to give the seedlings weekly doses of dilute fertilizer and watch them for disease. Once they begin to crowd each other, or after nine to twelve months, pot each one separately or repot them in a larger community pot. At this point you can treat them like mature plants and move them to the main growing area.

CHAPTER 14

Hybridization

IN NATURE the physical, anatomical, and genetic barriers that separate species are more fluid than you might think, especially among plants. The high school biology definition of a species—a group of genetically similar organisms that can produce fertile offspring — works if you are talking about the differences between horses and donkeys, but it collapses completely if you include plants, especially orchids. This definition presupposes natural genetic barriers that keep one species separate from the next. A horse and a donkey can mate and produce a mule, but because the parents are too genetically dissimilar, their hybrid offspring is sterile. On the other hand, highly evolved insect-pollinated plants such as orchids rely more on specific pollinators, nonoverlapping blooming times, and geographical isolation than on genetic barriers to prevent interspecific hybridization. If one orchid species is pollinated

ABOVE: By cross-pollinating lovely yellow *Paphiopedilum armeniacum* with the amazing *P. rothschildianum* (p. 117), an intrepid breeder created the striking hybrid *P.* Dolgoldii (p. 118), which, incidentally, graces the cover of this book.

by insect species A and another by insect species B, or one blooms in March and the other in September, most of the time the two will remain genetically separated, as they will if they grow on different mountain ranges. Occasionally, though, a few individuals of the first species may bloom out of season, or one insect may disregard the rules and visit the two species in succession. Then a hybrid between the two may result, and, unlike a mule, more often than not it will be fertile. In fact, chance hybridization is one of the driving forces of plant evolution, so it behooves plants to make it relatively easy. This fact came as a surprise to me, as I had the very anthropocentric idea that we human tinkerers were the only ones making hybrids. We think of hybridization as distinctly artificial, but that is not really the case.

Because the genetic barriers between orchids are so weak, it is very, very easy to produce hybrids in cultivation. In fact, it is even possible to make fertile hybrids between different genera —a feat not easily accomplished with other plants. Now if daylily (Hemerocallis) hybridizers can make 55,000 registered hybrids using only 22 original species, just imagine the possibilities when you start with 25,000–35,000 orchid species! Granted, not every orchid can combine with any other orchid, but even so we are talking about millions of potential recombinations. It's a notion that makes a plant breeder's pulse quicken.

At this point you might reasonably ask, "With more than 25,000 species to choose from, why bother hybridizing at all?" An orchid breeder can come up with rational arguments like improved vigor, larger flowers, and longer bloom time, but in reality people get into breeding because it's fun! There is nothing like the anticipation that builds when you see the first flower buds on your hybrid seedlings and know that you will be the first person to see a new bloom. We are a curious species, and all it takes to get the orchid hybridizers' toothpicks flying is to ask "What if . . . ?"

Scientific plant breeding requires a lot of patience and a lot of room. I had professors in college who spent their careers tweaking a single plant line and did not see their efforts come to fruition until they were ready to retire. You often have to grow thousands of seedlings to find one that's really special. This is hard enough if you work on annual bedding plants, but nigh impossible if you grow orchids, which are slow and costly to produce, especially if most are discarded. Accordingly, commercial orchid breeders tend to be conservative, making crosses they know they can sell, even if only a few seedlings are truly exceptional. Few breeders have enough space to hold on to all of their hybrid seedlings until they bloom so that they can cull out the best. Instead, they sell the unbloomed seedlings to buyers who hope that the plants will turn out to be great. In a sense, it's a sort of lottery, in which for twenty dollars you buy a chance that might turn out to be a total dud or an exceptional beauty.

It's fun to gamble on unbloomed seedlings, but be realistic about your odds. Your chances of getting that one in a thousand are fairly small, but you can do a few things to raise the odds. First, buy from a breeder with a good track record. Once you get interested in a particular genus, it won't be long before you learn which breeders' plants are garnering the most awards. While you are at it, make note of particular parents that seem to consistently yield high-quality hybrids. The AOS Awards Quarterly is a rich source of information about both breeders and prizewinning crosses. Second, many breeders will sell mother flasks (containing fifteen or more seedlings) or mini-flasks (containing three to five seedlings). For the price of one blooming orchid you can buy ten or even one hundred tiny seedlings that you can grow on and compare. If you have the space and some patience, this is a great way to improve your chances of having a winner. Third, if possible, visit breeders in person. Most will be glad to show you what crosses they are excited about and allow you to look through batches of seedlings and select some yourself. It's always best to pick the more vigorous seedlings in a group, and most everyone does that. Avoid buying the last few seedlings from a particular batch, as these are likely to be the runts, lacking both vigor and much chance at greatness. If you happen to be there when a batch of seedlings is coming into bloom for the first time, you may have the opportunity to select a superior flower—but be aware that any breeder worth her salt has already taken the best ones.

Since commercial breeders have to be conservative if they want to stay in business, much of the really oddball breeding is left to small nurseries and hobbyists. Combining two untried species or breeding with the less popular groups can be very interesting if your main concern is curiosity rather than the bottom line. I can't imagine anyone getting rich on Lepanthes hybrids, but I personally think that this incredibly rich and varied genus would be fascinating to work with. Even if you pick a particular species you are fond of and work to improve its flower shape and color, the results can be tremendously rewarding. Called line breeding, this "improvement work" is less risky than experimenting with untried hybrids, as chances are pretty good that you'll get some award-quality offspring after a few generations.

Although you don't need to be a geneticist to try your hand at breeding, knowing a few basics will help immensely. You cannot cross just any orchid genus with any other and expect to get viable seed. The two plants have to have enough in common genetically that their chromosomes "match up," so to speak. Since both the male and the female parent contribute a set of chromosomes to the offspring, and these strings of genes work in concert, if one set is organized very differently from the other, genetic confusion will reign and the seed will never develop. Generally, orchids in the same genus and those

Paphiopedilum rothschildianum 'The Baron' AM/AOS

in closely related genera (the same subtribe) will form viable offspring. You can cross a *Laelia* to a *Laelia* or a *Laelia* to a *Sophronitis,* but you cannot cross a *Laelia* to a *Phalaenopsis*—they're just too different. If the two sets of chromosomes (genes) match up reasonably well—that is, the genes that code for root construction, flower texture, or chloroplast formation find their twin easily—then the seed will probably develop normally. If the two sets of genes not only match up well but complement each other in certain ways, the resulting seedlings may grow more vigorously than either parent. This phenomenon is called hybrid vigor. For example, if one parent is a cool grower and the other a warm grower, the offspring are likely to be comfortable growing at a wider range of temperatures. Hybrid vigor is one of the chief advantages of hybrid plants over the parent species, and it's one of the main reasons breeders are interested in hybridizing. In the right circumstances, you can produce plants that grow faster, bloom more freely, and are generally more fit to handle the vicissitudes of a cultivated life. However, if the genes from the two parents don't complement each other well, the seedlings will be weak. This is called outbreeding depression, and unfortunately it is as common a result as vigor—especially if you are using dis-

tantly related species or trying to produce complex hybrids involving several different genera.

Using pollen from the plant being fertilized (either from another flower on the plant or another division of the same clone) is called selfing. Orchid breeders self plants if they have only one example of a species or if they are trying to breed progeny that exhibit more recessive traits. For example, if you have a yellow form of the typically red *Sophronitis coccinea,* selfing it would probably yield more yellow offspring than you'd obtain by crossing it with a typical form or, possibly, even with another yellow clone. The result would be labeled *Sophronitis coccinea* var. *lutea* × self. If you are attempting to hybridize one species with another, then obviously you would obtain pollen from one species and place it on the other. From a conservation standpoint, it is best to outcross a species—that is, take pollen from one clone and use it on another clone—since the progeny will have a broader gene pool and perhaps more vigor. Finally, without getting bogged down in cellular genetics, when deciding which plant will carry the pod, suffice it to say that the female parent contributes slightly more genetic information than the male (sorry, dads). For this reason it is important to accurately record which plant is the female parent (pod parent) in a particular cross. The female is written first, as in *Laelia anceps* × *L. furfuracea.* The progeny from this cross might be different from those of the reverse, *L. furfuracea* × *L. anceps,* so it's useful information to preserve.

Hybridizing two species or genera is basically reshuffling the deck of genes in hopes you'll be dealt a royal flush. You really don't know what you are going to get until you see the seedlings bloom. In line breeding the goal is slightly different. When you cross two individuals of the same species or backcross a hybrid with itself or one of its parents, you are in effect stacking the deck of genes, so that you are more likely to get a royal flush or at least a straight. If you cross two awarded clones of a species, you are much more likely to get award-quality offspring than if you use run-of-the-mill parents. When you are breeding to produce plants that express a rare trait such as an atypical flower color, you are more likely to get results if you use parents that carry these rare traits genetically, even if they don't demonstrate this fact. Rare traits—be they emerald green eyes and auburn hair in humans or blue flowers among orchids—are typically recessive. In other words, you have to receive a double dose of the gene or genes that code for this trait in order for it to manifest itself. Your parents need to have the proper genes—red hair or blue flowers—in their background, even if they themselves don't express or manifest the trait. You won't get a blue-flowered orchid if the parents don't have those genes, but you might if you repeatedly backcross violet or purple parents. Eventually, if you are lucky, a seedling will inherit just the right combina-

The artificial hybrid **Paphiopedilum** Dolgoldii 'Streeter's Choice' HCC/AOS combines some of the best features of both parents. Such a winning combination is easier to achieve in theory than in practice.

tion of recessive genes and will bloom blue. Of course, if you self a plant, you increase the chances that the offspring will express more recessive traits. Since you are not adding extra genes to the mix, you can be reasonably confident, unless you are selfing a very complex hybrid, that the progeny will approximate the quality of the parent. The same may be said for sibling ("sib") crosses.

The danger with line breeding and selfing or sibbing plants is inbreeding depression, which is sort of the opposite of outbreeding depression. In the case of outbreeding, the genes are too different; in inbreeding, they're too similar. Many recessive genes are deleterious or lethal if they are expressed. Since the chance of any recessive gene manifesting itself increases if you breed closely related plants, you are more likely to see these deleterious genes show up in the offspring of inbred parents.

Table of Hybrid Genera

Taking advantage of orchids' amazing ability to interbreed with not only different species but closely and even distantly related genera, breeders have created some incredibly complex intergeneric hybrids. The first person to cross-pollinate two genera and produce viable offspring has the privilege of naming this new hybrid or artificial genus, as long as they follow the rules of botanical nomenclature. Some names honor a person, as in *Johnkellyara,* but most are recombinations of the original generic names, like *Laeliocattleya.* You will notice in the following table that many hybrid genera involve three, four, or even six natural genera. Of course, you can cross only two at a time, so to produce *Aerasconetia,* say, the breeder first had to cross *Aerides* with *Ascocentrum* to create *Aeridocentrum;* once that bloomed, it was crossed with *Neofinetia* to get the composite hybrid genus *Aerasconetia.* Given that it takes from two to seven years for a seedling to flower, you can appreciate the amount of time that has gone into creating these complex hybrids. The table lists as many of these artificial genera as I could find, based on the information in *Sander's List of Orchid Hybrids.* In the interest of completeness, I include some parental genera here that are not covered in Part Four.

Hybrid Genera

HYBRID GENUS	ABBREVIATION	WILD GENERA
Acinbreea	Acba	Acineta × Embreea
Adacidium	Adcm	Ada × Oncidium
Adaglossum	Adgm	Ada × Odontoglossum
Adioda	Ado	Ada × Cochlioda
Aerasconetia	Aescta	Aerides × Ascocentrum × Neofinetia
Aeridachnis	Aerdns	Aerides × Arachnis
Aeridisia	Aersa	Aerides × Luisia
Aeriditis	Aerdts	Aerides × Doritis
Aeridocentrum	Aerctm	Aerides × Ascocentrum
Aeridochilus	Aerchs	Aerides × Sarcochilus
Aeridofinetia	Aerf	Aerides × Neofinetia
Aeridoglossum	Aergm	Aerides × Ascoglossum
Aeridoglottis	Aegts	Aerides × Trichoglottis
Aeridopsis	Aerps	Aerides × Phalaenopsis
Aeridovanda	Aerdv	Aerides × Vanda
Aeridovanisia	Aervsa	Aerides × Luisia × Vanda
Aitkenara	Aitk	Otostylis × Zygopetalum × Zygosepalum
Alangreatwoodara	Agwa	Colax × Promenaea × Zygopetalum
Alexanderara	Alxra	Brassia × Cochlioda × Odontoglossum × Oncidium
Aliceara	Alcra	Brassia × Miltonia × Oncidium
Allenara	Alna	Cattleya × Diacrium × Epidendrum × Laelia

HYBRID GENUS	ABBREVIATION	WILD GENERA
Alphonsoara	Alph	Arachnis × Ascocentrum × Vanda × Vandopsis
Andrewara	Andw	Arachnis × Renanthera × Trichoglottis × Vanda
Angraecentrum	Angctm	Angraecum × Ascocentrum
Angraecostylis	Angsts	Angraecum × Rhynchostylis
Angraecyrtanthes	Ancyth	Aeranthes × Angraecum × Cyrtorchis
Angraeorchis	Angchs	Angraecum × Cyrtorchis
Angrangis	Angrs	Aerangis × Angraecum
Angranthellea	Angtla	Aeranthes × Angraecum × Jumellea
Angranthes	Angth	Aeranthes × Angraecum
Angreoniella	Angnla	Angraecum × Oeoniella
Angulocaste	Angcst	Anguloa × Lycaste
Anoectomaria	Anctma	Anoectochilus × Haemaria
Ansieium	Asdm	Ansellia × Cymbidium
Aracampe	Arcp	Acampe × Arachnis
Arachnoglossum	Arngm	Arachnis × Ascoglossum
Arachnoglottis	Arngl	Arachnis × Trichoglottis
Arachnopsis	Arnps	Arachnis × Phalaenopsis
Arachnostylis	Arnst	Arachnis × Rhynchostylis
Aranda	Aranda	Arachnis × Vanda
Aranthera	Arnth	Arachnis × Renanthera
Arizara	Ariz	Cattleya × Domingoa × Epidendrum
Ascandopsis	Ascdps	Ascocentrum × Vandopsis

Angulocaste Paul Gripp 'Jamboree Gold' AM/AOS

Hybrid Genera (continued)

Hybrid genus	Abbreviation	Wild genera
Ascocenda	Ascda	Ascocentrum × Vanda
Ascocleinetia	Ascln	Ascocentrum × Cleisocentron × Neofinetia
Ascofinetia	Ascf	Ascocentrum × Neofinetia
Ascogastisia	Agsta	Ascocentrum × Gastrochilus × Luisia
Ascoglottis	Asgts	Ascocentrum × Trichoglottis
Asconopsis	Ascps	Ascocentrum × Phalaenopsis
Ascorachnis	Ascns	Arachnis × Ascocentrum
Ascovandoritis	Asvts	Ascocentrum × Doritis × Vanda
Aspasium	Aspsm	Aspasia × Oncidium
Aspodia	Asid	Aspasia × Cochlioda
Aspodonia	Aspd	Aspasia × Miltonia × Odontoglossum
Aspoglossum	Aspgm	Aspasia × Odontoglossum
Ayubara	Ayb	Aerides × Arachnis × Ascoglossum
Bakerara	Bak	Brassia × Miltonia × Odontoglossum × Oncidium
Baldwinara	Bdwna	Aspasia × Cochlioda × Odontoglossum × Oncidium
Banfieldara	Bnfd	Ada × Brassia × Odontoglossum
Baptirettia	Btta	Baptistonia × Comparettia
Barangis	Brgs	Aerangis × Barombia
Barbosaara	Bbra	Cochlioda × Gomesa × Odontoglossum × Oncidium
Bardendrum	Bard	Barkeria × Epidendrum
Barkonitis	Bknts	Barkeria × Sophronitis
Bateostylis	Btst	Batemannia × Otostylis
Baumannara	Bmnra	Comparettia × Odontoglossum × Oncidium
Beallara	Bllra	Brassia × Cochlioda × Miltonia × Odontoglossum
Beardara	Bdra	Ascocentrum × Doritis × Phalaenopsis
Bifrenidium	Bifdm	Bifrenaria × Zygowarrea
Bifreniella	Bifla	Bifrenaria × Rudolfiella
Bishopara	Bish	Broughtonia × Cattleya × Sophronitis
Blackara	Blkr	Aspasia × Cochlioda × Miltonia × Odontoglossum
Bloomara	Blma	Broughtonia × Laeliopsis × Tetramicra
Bokchoonara	Bkch	Arachnis × Ascocentrum × Phalaenopsis × Vanda
Bollopetalum	Blptm	Bollea × Zygopetalum
Bovornara	Bov	Arachnis × Ascocentrum × Rhynchostylis × Vanda
Bradeara	Brade	Comparettia × Gomesa × Rodriguezia
Brapasia	Brap	Aspasia × Brassia
Brassada	Brsa	Ada × Brassia
Brassidium	Brsdm	Brassia × Oncidium
Brassioda	Broda	Brassia × Cochlioda
Brassocattleya	Bc	Brassavola × Cattleya
Brassochilus	Brchs	Brassia × Leochilus
Brassodiacrium	Bdia	Brassavola × Diacrium
Brassoepidendrum	Bepi	Brassavola × Epidendrum
Brassoepilaelia	Bpl	Brassavola × Epidendrum × Laelia
Brassokeria	Brsk	Barkeria × Brassavola
Brassolaelia	Bl	Brassavola × Laelia
Brassolaeliocattleya	Blc	Brassavola × Cattleya × Laelia
Brassosophronitis	Bnts	Brassavola × Sophronitis
Brassotonia	Bstna	Brassavola × Broughtonia
Brilliandeara	Brlda	Aspasia × Brassia × Cochlioda × Miltonia × Odontoglossum × Oncidium
Brownara	Bwna	Broughtonia × Cattleya × Diacrium
Brummittara	Brum	Comparettia × Odontoglossum × Rodriguezia
Buiara	Bui	Broughtonia × Cattleya × Epidendrum × Laelia × Sophronitis
Burkhardtara	Bktra	Leochilus × Odontoglossum × Oncidium × Rodriguezia
Burkillara	Burk	Aerides × Arachnis × Vanda
Burrageara	Burr	Cochlioda × Miltonia × Odontoglossum × Oncidium
Caloarethusa	Clts	Arethusa × Calopogon
Campbellara	Cmpba	Odontoglossum × Oncidium × Rodriguezia
Carpenterara	Cptra	Baptistonia × Odontoglossum × Oncidium
Carterara	Ctra	Aerides × Renanthera × Vandopsis
Casoara	Csr	Brassavola × Broughtonia × Laeliopsis
Catamodes	Ctmds	Catasetum × Mormodes
Catanoches	Ctnchs	Catasetum × Cycnoches
Catasandra	Ctsda	Catasetum × Galeandra
Cattkeria	Cka	Barkeria × Cattleya
Cattleyopsisgoa	Ctpga	Cattleyopsis × Domingoa
Cattleyopsistonia	Ctpsta	Broughtonia × Cattleyopsis
Cattleytonia	Ctna	Broughtonia × Cattleya
Cattotes	Ctts	Cattleya × Leptotes
Charlesworthara	Cha	Cochlioda × Miltonia × Oncidium
Charlieara	Charl	Rhynchostylis × Vanda × Vandopsis
Chewara	Chew	Aerides × Renanthera × Rhynchostylis
Chilocentrum	Chctm	Ascocentrum × Chiloschista
Chondrobollea	Chdb	Bollea × Chondrorhyncha
Christieara	Chtra	Aerides × Ascocentrum × Vanda
Chuanyenara	Chnya	Arachnis × Renanthera × Rhynchostylis
Cirrhophyllum	Crphm	Bulbophyllum × Cirrhopetalum
Cischostalix	Cstx	Cischweinfia × Sigmatostalix
Cleisocalpa	Clclp	Cleisocentron × Pomatocalpa

HYBRID GENUS	ABBREVIATION	WILD GENERA
Cleisodes	Clsd	Aerides × Cleisocentron
Cleisofinetia	Clfta	Cleisocentron × Neofinetia
Cleisonopsis	Clnps	Cleisocentron × Phalaenopsis
Cleisopera	Clspa	Cleisostoma × Micropera
Cleisoquetia	Clq	Cleisocentron × Robiquetia
Cleisostylis	Clsty	Cleisocentron × Rhynchostylis
Cleisothera	Cltha	Cleisostoma × Pelatantheria
Cochella	Chla	Cochleanthes × Mendoncella
Cochlecaste	Cccst	Cochleanthes × Lycaste
Cochlenia	Cclna	Sarcanthus × Stenia
Cochleottia	Colta	Cochleanthes × Galeottia
Cochlepetalum	Ccptm	Cochleanthes × Zygopetalum
Colaste	Cste	Colax × Lycaste
Colmanara	Colm	Miltonia × Odontoglossum × Oncidium
Conphronitis	Conph	Constantia × Sophronitis
Cookara	Cook	Broughtonia × Cattleya × Diacrium × Laelia
Coryhopea	Crhpa	Coryanthes × Stanhopea
Crawwhayara	Craw	Aspasia × Brassia × Miltonia × Oncidium
Cycnodes	Cycd	Cycnoches × Mormodes
Cymphiella	Cymph	Cymbidium × Eulophiella
Cyrtellia	Cyrtl	Ansellia × Cyrtopodium
Darwinara	Dar	Ascocentrum × Neofinetia × Rhynchostylis × Vanda
Debruyneara	Dbra	Ascocentrum × Luisia × Vanda
Degarmoara	Dgmra	Brassia × Miltonia × Odontoglossum
Dekensara	Dek	Brassavola × Cattleya × Schomburgkia
Dendroberia	Denga	Dendrobium × Flickingeria
Devereuxara	Dvra	Ascocentrum × Phalaenopsis × Vanda
Diabroughtonia	Diab	Broughtonia × Diacrium
Diacattleya	Diaca	Cattleya × Diacrium
Diakeria	Dkra	Barkeria × Diacrium
Dialaelia	Dial	Diacrium × Laelia
Dialaeliocattleya	Dialc	Cattleya × Diacrium × Laelia
Dialaeliopsis	Dialps	Diacrium × Laeliopsis
Diaphanangis	Dpgs	Aerangis × Diaphananthe
Dillonara	Dill	Epidendrum × Laelia × Schomburgkia
Diplonopsis	Dpnps	Diploprora × Phalaenopsis
Domindesmia	Ddma	Domingoa × Hexadesmia
Domintonia	Dmtna	Broughtonia × Domingoa
Dominyara	Dmya	Ascocentrum × Luisia × Neofinetia × Rhynchostylis
Domliopsis	Dmlps	Domingoa × Laeliopsis
Doncollinara	Dclna	Cochlioda × Odontoglossum × Rodriguezia
Dorandopsis	Ddps	Doritis × Vandopsis
Doricentrum	Dctm	Ascocentrum × Doritis
Doriella	Drlla	Doritis × Kingiella
Doriellaopsis	Dllps	Doritis × Kingiella × Phalaenopsis
Dorifinetia	Dfta	Doritis × Neofinetia
Doriglossum	Drgm	Ascoglossum × Doritis
Doristylis	Dst	Doritis × Rhynchostylis
Doritaenopsis	Dtps	Doritis × Phalaenopsis
Dorthera	Dtha	Doritis × Renanthera
Dossinimaria	Dsma	Dossinia × Haemaria
Downsara	Dwsa	Aganisia × Batemannia × Otostylis × Zygosepalum
Dracuvallia	Drvla	Dracula × Masdevallia
Dresslerara	Dres	Ascoglossum × Phalaenopsis × Renanthera
Duggerara	Dugg	Ada × Brassia × Miltonia
Dunnara	Dnna	Broughtonia × Cattleyopsis × Domingoa
Dunningara	Dngra	Aspasia × Miltonia × Oncidium
Durutyara	Dtya	Batemannia × x Zygopetalum × Zygosepalum
Eastonara	Eas	Ascocentrum × Gastrochilus × Vanda
Edeara	Edr	Arachnis × Phalaenopsis × Renanthera × Vandopsis
Epibarkiella	Epbkl	Barkeria × Epidendrum × Nageliella
Epibrassonitis	Epbns	Brassavola × Epidendrum × Sophronitis
Epicatonia	Epctn	Broughtonia × Cattleya × Epidendrum
Epicattleya	Epc	Cattleya × Epidendrum
Epidella	Epdla	Epidendrum × Nageliella
Epidiacrium	Epdcm	Diacrium × Epidendrum
Epigoa	Epg	Domingoa × Epidendrum
Epiglottis	Epgl	Epidendrum × Scaphyglottis
Epilaelia	Epl	Epidendrum × Laelia
Epilaeliocattleya	Eplc	Cattleya × Epidendrum × Laelia
Epilaeliopsis	Eplps	Epidendrum × Laeliopsis
Epiopsis	Eps	Cattleyopsis × Epidendrum
Epiphronitis	Ephs	Epidendrum × Sophronitis
Epistoma	Epstm	Ambostoma × Epidendrum
Epitonia	Eptn	Broughtonia × Epidendrum
Ernestara	Entra	Phalaenopsis × Renanthera × Vandopsis
Eryidium	Erdm	Erycina × Oncidium
Eulocymbidiella	Eucmla	Cymbidiella × Eulophiella
Euryangis	Eugs	Aerangis × Eurychone
Eurygraecum	Eugcm	Angraecum × Eurychone
Eurynopsis	Eunps	Eurychone × Phalaenopsis
Fergusonara	Ferg	Brassavola × Cattleya × Laelia × Schomburgkia × Sophronitis

Hybrid genus	Abbreviation	Wild genera
Fialaara	Fia	Broughtonia × Cattleya × Laelia × Laeliopsis
Forgetara	Fgtra	Aspasia × Brassia × Miltonia
Freedara	Frda	Ascoglossum × Renanthera × Vandopsis
Fujioara	Fjo	Ascocentrum × Trichoglottis × Vanda
Fujiwarara	Fjw	Brassavola × Cattleya × Laeliopsis
Galeansellia	Gslla	Ansellia × Galeandra
Galeopetalum	Gptm	Galeottia × Zygopetalum
Galeosepalum	Glspm	Galeottia × Zygosepalum
Gastisia	Gsta	Gastrochilus × Luisia
Gastisocalpa	Gscpa	Gastrochilus × Luisia × Pomatocalpa
Gastritis	Gtts	Doritis × Gastrochilus
Gastrochiloglottis	Gchgl	Gastrochilus × Trichoglottis
Gastrosarcochilus	Gsarco	Gastrochilus × Sarcochilus
Gastrothera	Gsrth	Gastrochilus × Renanthera
Gauntlettara	Gtra	Broughtonia × Cattleyopsis × Laeliopsis
Georgeblackara	Gbka	Comparettia × Leochilus × Oncidium × Rodriguezia
Goffara	Gfa	Luisia × Rhynchostylis × Vanda
Gohartia	Ghta	Gomesa × Lockhartia
Gomada	Gmda	Ada × Gomesa
Gomettia	Gmtta	Comparettia × Gomesa
Gomochilus	Gmch	Gomesa × Leochilus
Gomoglossum	Gmgm	Gomesa × Odontoglossum
Goodaleara	Gdlra	Brassia × Cochlioda × Miltonia × Odontoglossum × Oncidium
Gottererara	Gott	Ascocentrum × Renanthera × Vandopsis
Grammato-cymbidium	Grcym	Cymbidium × Grammatophyllum
Grammatopodium	Grtp	Cyrtopodium × Grammatophyllum
Graphiella	Grpla	Graphorkis × Cymbidiella
Hagerara	Hgra	Doritis × Phalaenopsis × Vanda
Hanesara	Han	Aerides × Arachnis × Neofinetia
Hartara	Hart	Broughtonia × Laelia × Sophronitis
Hasegawaara	Hasgw	Brassavola × Broughtonia × Cattleya × Laelia × Sophronitis
Hattoriara	Hatt	Brassavola × Broughtonia × Cattleya × Epidendrum × Laelia
Hausermannara	Haus	Doritis × Phalaenopsis × Vandopsis
Hawaiiara	Haw	Renanthera × Vanda × Vandopsis
Hawkesara	Hwkra	Cattleya × Cattleyopsis × Epidendrum
Hawkinsara	Hknsa	Broughtonia × Cattleya × Laelia × Sophronitis
Helpilia	Hpla	Helcia × Trichopilia
Herbertara	Hbtr	Cattleya × Laelia × Schomburgkia × Sophronitis
Higashiara	Hgsh	Cattleya × Diacrium × Laelia × Sophronitis
Hildaara	Hdra	Broughtonia × Laeliopsis × Schomburgkia
Himoriara	Hmra	Ascocentrum × Phalaenopsis × Rhynchostylis × Vanda
Holttumara	Holtt	Arachnis × Renanthera × Vanda
Hookerara	Hook	Brassavola × Cattleya × Diacrium
Howeara	Hwra	Leochilus × Oncidium × Rodriguezia
Hueylihara	Hylra	Neofinetia × Renanthera × Rhynchostylis
Hugofreedara	Hgfda	Ascocentrum × Doritis × Kingiella
Hummelara	Humm	Barkeria × Brassavola × Epidendrum
Huntleanthes	Hnths	Cochleanthes × Huntleya
Ionettia	Intta	Comparettia × Ionopsis
Ionocidium	Incdm	Ionopsis × Oncidium
Irvingara	Irv	Arachnis × Renanthera × Trichoglottis
Isaoara	Isr	Aerides × Ascocentrum × Phalaenopsis × Vanda
Iwanagara	Iwan	Brassavola × Cattleya × Diacrium × Laelia
Izumiara	Izma	Cattleya × Epidendrum × Laelia × Schomburgkia × Sophronitis
Jewellara	Jwa	Broughtonia × Cattleya × Epidendrum × Laelia
Jimenezara	Jmzra	Broughtonia × Laelia × Laeliopsis
Joannara	Jnna	Renanthera × Rhynchostylis × Vanda
Johnkellyara	Jkl	Brassia × Leochilus × Oncidium × Rodriguezia
Johnyeeara	Jya	Brassavola × Cattleya × Epidendrum × Laelia × Schomburgkia × Sophronitis
Jumanthes	Jmth	Aeranthes × Jumellea
Kagawara	Kgw	Ascocentrum × Renanthera × Vanda
Kanzerara	Kza	Chondrorhyncha × Promenaea × Zygopetalum
Kawamotoara	Kwmta	Brassavola × Cattleya × Domingoa × Epidendrum × Laelia
Keferanthes	Kefth	Cochleanthes × Kefersteinia
Kirchara	Kir	Cattleya × Epidendrum × Laelia × Sophronitis
Klehmara	Klma	Diacrium × Laelia × Schomburgkia
Knappara	Knp	Ascocentrum × Rhynchostylis × Vanda × Vandopsis
Knudsonara	Knud	Ascocentrum × Neofinetia × Renanthera × Rhynchostylis × Vanda
Komkrisara	Kom	Ascocentrum × Renanthera × Rhynchostylis
Kraussara	Krsa	Broughtonia × Cattleya × Diacrium × Laeliopsis
Laeliocatonia	Lctna	Broughtonia × Cattleya × Laelia
Laeliocattkeria	Lcka	Barkeria × Cattleya × Laelia
Laeliocattleya	Lc	Cattleya × Laelia

Hybrid genus	Abbreviation	Wild genera
Laeliokeria	Lkra	Barkeria × Laelia
Laeliopleya	Lpya	Cattleya × Laeliopsis
Laelonia	Lna	Broughtonia × Laelia
Lagerara	Lgra	Aspasia × Cochlioda × Odontoglossum
Lancebirkara	Lbka	Bollea × Cochleanthes × Pescatorea
Lauara	Lauara	Ascoglossum × Renanthera × Rhynchostylis
Laycockara	Lay	Arachnis × Phalaenopsis × Vandopsis
Leeara	Leeara	Arachnis × Vanda × Vandopsis
Lemaireara	Lemra	Broughtonia × Cattleyopsis × Epidendrum
Leocidium	Lcdm	Leochilus × Oncidium
Leocidmesa	Lcmsa	Gomesa × Leochilus × Oncidium
Leocidpasia	Lcdpa	Aspasia × Leochilus × Oncidium
Leptodendrum	Lrtdm	Epidendrum × Leptotes
Leptokeria	Lptka	Barkeria × Leptotes
Leptolaelia	Lptl	Laelia × Leptotes
Leptovola	Lptv	Brassavola × Leptotes
Leslieara	Lesl	Broughtonia × Cattleyopsis × Diacrium × Epidendrum
Lewisara	Lwsra	Aerides × Arachnis × Ascocentrum × Vanda
Liaopsis	Liaps	Laelia × Laeliopsis
Lichtara	Licht	Doritis × Gastrochilus × Phalaenopsis
Liebmanara	Lieb	Aspasia × Cochlioda × Oncidium
Limara	Lim	Arachnis × Renanthera × Vandopsis
Lioponia	Lpna	Broughtonia × Laeliopsis
Lockcidium	Lkcdm	Lockhartia × Oncidium
Lockochilettia	Lkctta	Comparettia × Leochilus × Lockhartia
Lockochilus	Lkchs	Leochilus × Lockhartia
Lockogochilus	Lkgch	Gomesa × Leochilus × Lockhartia
Lockopilia	Lckp	Lockhartia × Trichopilia
Lockostalix	Lkstx	Lockhartia × Sigmatostalix
Lowara	Low	Brassavola × Laelia × Sophronitis
Lowsonara	Lwnra	Aerides × Ascocentrum × Rhynchostylis
Luascotia	Lscta	Ascocentrum × Luisia × Neofinetia
Luicentrum	Lctm	Ascocentrum × Luisia
Luichilus	Luic	Luisia × Sarcochilus
Luinetia	Lnta	Luisia × Neofinetia
Luinopsis	Lnps	Luisia × Phalaenopsis
Luisanda	Lsnd	Luisia × Vanda
Luistylis	Lst	Luisia × Rhynchostylis
Luivanetia	Lvta	Luisia × Neofinetia × Vanda
Lutherara	Luth	Phalaenopsis × Renanthera × Rhynchostylis
Lycasteria	Lystr	Bifrenaria × Lycaste
Lymanara	Lynra	Aerides × Arachnis × Renanthera
Lyonara	Lyon	Cattleya × Laelia × Sophronitis
Maccoyara	Mcyra	Aerides × Vanda × Vandopsis
Macekara	Maka	Arachnis × Phalaenopsis × Renanthera × Vanda × Vandopsis
Maclellanara	Mclna	Brassia × Odontoglossum × Oncidium
Maclemoreara	Mclmra	Brassavola × Laelia × Schomburgkia
Macomaria	Mcmr	Haemaria × Macodes
Macradesa	Mcdsa	Gomesa × Macradenia
Mailamaiara	Mai	Cattleya × Diacrium × Laelia × Schomburgkia
Masonara	Msna	Aganisia × Batemannia × Colax × Otostylis × Promenaea × Zygosepalum
Matsudaara	Msda	Barkeria × Cattleya × Laelia × Sophronitis
Maxillacaste	Mxcst	Lycaste × Maxillaria
Maxilobium	Mxlb	Maxillaria × Xylobium
Maymoirara	Mymra	Cattleya × Epidendrum × Laeliopsis
Mendosepalum	Mdspl	Mendoncella × Zygosepalum
Micholitzara	Mchza	Aerides × Ascocentrum × Neofinetia × Vanda
Milpasia	Mpsa	Aspasia × Miltonia
Milpilia	Mpla	Miltonia × Trichopilia
Miltada	Mtad	Ada × Miltonia
Miltadium	Mtadm	Ada × Miltonia × Oncidium
Miltassia	Mtssa	Brassia × Miltonia
Miltistonia	Mtst	Baptistonia × Miltonia
Miltonidium	Mtdm	Miltonia × Oncidium
Miltonioda	Mtda	Cochlioda × Miltonia
Mizutara	Miz	Cattleya × Diacrium × Schomburgkia
Moirara	Moir	Phalaenopsis × Renanthera × Vanda
Mokara	Mkra	Arachnis × Ascocentrum × Vanda
Monnierara	Monn	Catasetum × Cycnoches × Mormodes
Moonara	Mnra	Aerides × Ascocentrum × Neofinetia × Rhynchostylis
Moscosoara	Mscra	Broughtonia × Epidendrum × Laeliopsis
Nakagawaara	Nkgwa	Aerides × Doritis × Phalaenopsis
Nakamotoara	Nak	Ascocentrum × Neofinetia × Vanda
Nashara	Nash	Broughtonia × Cattleyopsis × Diacrium
Naugleara	Naug	Ascocentrum × Ascoglossum × Renanthera
Neobatopus	Nbps	Cryptopus × Neobathiea
Neoglossum	Neogm	Ascoglossum × Neofinetia
Neograecum	Ngrcm	Neofinetia × Angraecum
Neostylis	Neost	Neofinetia × Rhynchostylis
Ngara	Ngara	Arachnis × Ascoglossum × Renanthera

Hybrid Genera (continued)

HYBRID GENUS	ABBREVIATION	WILD GENERA
Nobleara	Nlra	Aerides × Renanthera × Vanda
Nonaara	Non	Aerides × Ascoglossum × Renanthera
Nornahamamo-toara	Nhmta	Aerides × Rhynchostylis × Vandopsis
Northenara	Nrna	Cattleya × Epidendrum × Laelia × Schomburgkia
Norwoodara	Nwda	Brassia × Miltonia × Oncidium × Rodriguezia
Notylettia	Ntlta	Comparettia × Notylia
Notylidium	Ntldm	Notylia × Oncidium
Notylopsis	Ntlps	Ionopsis × Notylia
Odontioda	Oda	Cochlioda × Odontoglossum
Odontobrassia	Odbrs	Brassia × Odontoglossum
Odontocidium	Odcdm	Odontoglossum × Oncidium
Odontonia	Odtna	Miltonia × Odontoglossum
Odontopilia	Odpla	Odontoglossum × Trichopilia
Odontorettia	Odrta	Comparettia × Odontoglossum
Okaara	Okr	Ascocentrum × Renanthera × Rhynchostylis × Vanda
Oncidenia	Oncna	Macradenia × Oncidium
Oncidesa	Oncsa	Gomesa × Oncidium
Oncidettia	Onctta	Comparettia × Oncidium
Oncidiella	Onclla	Oncidium × Rodrigueziella
Oncidioda	Oncda	Cochlioda × Oncidium

HYBRID GENUS	ABBREVIATION	WILD GENERA
Oncidpilia	Oncpa	Oncidium × Trichopilia
Onoara	Onra	Ascocentrum × Renanthera × Vanda × Vandopsis
Opsisanda	Opsis	Vanda × Vandopsis
Opsiscattleya	Opsct	Cattleya × Cattleyopsis
Opsistylis	Opst	Rhynchostylis × Vandopsis
Orchiserapias	Orsps	Orchis × Serapias
Ornithocidium	Orncm	Oncidium × Ornithophora
Osmentara	Osmt	Broughtonia × Cattleya × Laeliopsis
Otaara	Otr	Brassavola × Broughtonia × Cattleya × Laelia
Otocolax	Otcx	Colax × Otostylis
Otonisia	Otnsa	Aganisia × Otostylis
Otosepalum	Otspm	Otostylis × Zygosepalum
Owensara	Owsr	Doritis × Phalaenopsis × Renanthera
Pageara	Pga	Ascocentrum × Luisia × Rhynchostylis × Vanda
Palmerara	Plmra	Batemannia × Otostylis × Zygosepalum
Pantapaara	Pntp	Ascoglossum × Renanthera × Vanda
Parachilus	Prcls	Parasarcochilus × Sarcochilus
Parnataara	Parn	Aerides × Arachnis × Phalaenopsis
Paulara	Plra	Ascocentrum × Doritis × Phalaenopsis × Renanthera × Vanda

Neopabstopetalum Adelaide 'Jade Dragon' HCC/AOS. New hybrid genus names are always being coined because of taxonomic name changes as well as new intergeneric combinations. *Neopabstopetalum (Pabstia [Colax] × Neogardneria × Zygopetalum)* used to be called *Woodwardara*. Are you confused yet?

Hybrid genus	Abbreviation	Wild genera
Paulsenara	Plsra	Aerides × Arachnis × Trichoglottis
Pehara	Peh	Aerides × Arachnis × Vanda × Vandopsis
Pelacentrum	Plctm	Ascocentrum × Pelatantheria
Pelachilus	Pelcs	Gastrochilus × Pelatantheria
Pelastylis	Pelst	Pelatantheria × Rhynchostylis
Pelatoritis	Pltrs	Doritis × Pelatantheria
Perreiraara	Prra	Aerides × Rhynchostylis × Vanda
Pescatobollea	Psbol	Bollea × Pescatorea
Pescawarrea	Psw	Pescatorea × Warrea
Pescoranthes	Psnth	Cochleanthes × Pescatorea
Pettitara	Pett	Ada × Brassia × Oncidium
Phaiocalanthe	Phcal	Calanthe × Phaius
Phaiocymbidium	Phcym	Cymbidium × Phaius
Phalaerianda	Phda	Aerides × Phalaenopsis × Vanda
Phalandopsis	Phdps	Phalaenopsis × Vandopsis
Phalanetia	Phnta	Neofinetia × Phalaenopsis
Phaliella	Phlla	Kingiella × Phalaenopsis
Phillipsara	Phill	Cochleanthes × Stenia × Zygopetalum
Phragmipaphium	Phrphm	Paphiopedilum × Phragmipedium
Plectochilus	Plchs	Plectorrhiza × Sarcochilus
Plectrelgraecum	Plgcm	Angraecum × Plectrelminthus
Pomacentrum	Pmctm	Ascocentrum × Pomatocalpa
Pomatisia	Pmtsa	Luisia × Pomatocalpa
Potinara	Pot	Brassavola × Cattleya × Laelia × Sophronitis
Prolax	Prx	Colax × Promenaea
Propetalum	Pptm	Promenaea × Zygopetalum
Raganara	Rgn	Renanthera × Trichoglottis × Vanda
Ramasamyara	Rmsya	Arachnis × Rhynchostylis × Vanda
Recchara	Recc	Brassavola × Cattleya × Laelia × Schomburgkia
Renades	Rnds	Aerides × Renanthera
Renafinanda	Rfnda	Neofinetia × Renanthera × Vanda
Renaglottis	Rngl	Renanthera × Trichoglottis
Renancentrum	Rnctm	Ascocentrum × Renanthera
Renanda	Rnnd	Arachnis × Renanthera × Vanda
Renanetia	Rnet	Neofinetia × Renanthera
Renanopsis	Rnps	Renanthera × Vandopsis
Renanstylis	Rnst	Renanthera × Rhynchostylis
Renantanda	Rntda	Renanthera × Vanda
Renanthoglossum	Rngm	Ascoglossum × Renanthera
Renanthopsis	Rnthps	Phalaenopsis × Renanthera
Rhinochilus	Rhincs	Rhinerrhiza × Sarcochilus
Rhynchocentrum	Rhctm	Ascocentrum × Rhynchostylis
Rhynchonopsis	Rhnps	Phalaenopsis × Rhynchostylis
Rhynchorides	Rhrds	Aerides × Rhynchostylis
Rhynchovanda	Rhv	Rhynchostylis × Vanda

Hybrid genus	Abbreviation	Wild genera
Rhyndoropsis	Rhdps	Doritis × Phalaenopsis × Rhynchostylis
Richardmizutaara	Rcmza	Ascocentrum × Phalaenopsis × Vandopsis
Richardsonara	Rchna	Aspasia × Odontoglossum × Oncidium
Ridleyara	Ridl	Arachnis × Trichoglottis × Vanda
Robifinetia	Rbf	Neofinetia × Robiquetia
Robinara	Rbnra	Aerides × Ascocentrum × Renanthera × Vanda
Rodrassia	Rdssa	Brassia × Rodriguezia
Rodrettia	Rdtta	Comparettia × Rodriguezia
Rodrettiopsis	Rdtps	Comparettia × Ionopsis ×

Potinara Baghdad's Magic 'Winchester' AM/AOS

HYBRID GENUS	ABBREVIATION	WILD GENERA
		Rodriguezia
Rodrichilus	Rdchs	Leochilus × Rodriguezia
Rodricidium	Rdcm	Oncidium × Rodriguezia
Rodridenia	Rden	Macradenia × Rodriguezia
Rodriglossum	Rdgm	Odontoglossum × Rodriguezia
Rodriopsis	Rodps	Ionopsis × Rodriguezia
Rodritonia	Rdtna	Miltonia × Rodriguezia
Rolfeara	Rolf	Brassavola × Cattleya × Sophronitis
Ronnyara	Rnya	Aerides × Ascocentrum × Rhynchostylis × Vanda
Rosakirschara	Rskra	Ascocentrum × Neofinetia × Renanthera
Roseara	Rsra	Doritis × Kingiella × Phalaenopsis × Renanthera
Rothara	Roth	Brassavola × Cattleya × Epidendrum × Laelia × Sophronitis
Rotorara	Rtra	Bollea × Cochleanthes × Kefersteinia
Rumrillara	Rlla	Ascocentrum × Neofinetia × Rhynchostylis
Sagarikara	Sgka	Aerides × Arachnis × Rhynchostylis
Sanderara	Sand	Brassia × Cochlioda × Odontoglossum
Sanjumeara	Sjma	Aerides × Neofinetia × Rhynchostylis × Vanda
Sappanara	Sapp	Arachnis × Phalaenopsis × Renanthera
Sarcocentrum	Srctm	Ascocentrum × Sarcochilus
Sarcomoanthus	Sran	Sarcochilus × Drymoanthus
Sarconopsis	Srnps	Phalaenopsis × Sarcochilus
Sarcorhiza	Srza	Rhinerrhiza × Sarcochilus
Sarcothera	Srth	Renanthera × Sarcochilus
Sarcovanda	Srv	Sarcochilus × Vanda
Saridestylis	Srdts	Sarcochilus × Rhynchostylis × Sarcanthus
Sartylis	Srts	Rhynchostylis × Sarcochilus
Sauledaara	Sdra	Aspasia × Brassia × Miltonia × Oncidium × Rodriguezia
Schafferara	Schfa	Aspasia × Brassia × Cochlioda × Miltonia × Odontoglossum
Schombavola	Smbv	Brassavola × Schomburgkia
Schombocatonia	Smbcna	Broughtonia × Cattleya × Schomburgkia
Schombocattleya	Smbc	Cattleya × Schomburgkia
Schombodiacrium	Smbdcm	Diacrium × Schomburgkia
Schomboepidenrum	Smbep	Epidendrum × Schomburgkia
Schombolaelia	Smbl	Laelia × Schomburgkia
Schombonia	Smbna	Broughtonia × Schomburgkia
Schombonitis	Smbts	Schomburgkia × Sophronitis
Scottara	Sctt	Aerides × Arachnis × Luisia
Scullyara	Scu	Cattleya × Epidendrum × Schomburgkia

HYBRID GENUS	ABBREVIATION	WILD GENERA
Seahexa	Sxa	Hexadesmia × Hexisea
Severinara	Sev	Diacrium × Laelia × Sophronitis
Shigeuraara	Shgra	Ascocentrum × Ascoglossum × Renanthera × Vanda
Shipmanara	Shipm	Broughtonia × Diacrium × Schomburgkia
Shiveara	Shva	Aspasia × Brassia × Odontoglossum × Oncidium
Sidranara	Sidr	Ascocentrum × Phalaenopsis × Renanthera
Silpaprasertara	Silpa	Aerides × Ascocentrum × Sarcanthus
Sladeara	Slad	Doritis × Phalaenopsis × Sarcochilus
Sobennigraecum	Sbgcm	Angraecum × Sobennikoffia
Sophrocattleya	Sc	Cattleya × Sophronitis
Sophrolaelia	Sl	Laelia × Sophronitis
Sophrolaeliocattleya	Slc	Cattleya × Laelia × Sophronitis
Staalara	Staal	Barkeria × Laelia × Sophronitis
Stacyara	Stac	Cattleya × Epidendrum × Sophronitis
Stamariaara	Stmra	Ascocentrum × Phalaenopsis × Renanthera × Vanda
Stanfieldara	Sfdra	Epidendrum × Laelia × Sophronitis
Stangora	Stga	Gongora × Stanhopea
Stanhocycnis	Stncn	Polycycnis × Stanhopea
Stellamizutaara	Stlma	Broughtonia × Broughtonia × Cattleya
Stewartara	Stwt	Ada × Cochlioda × Odontoglossum
Sutingara	Sut	Arachnis × Ascocentrum × Phalaenopsis × Vanda × Vandopsis
Teohara	Thra	Arachnis × Renanthera × Vanda × Vandopsis
Tetracattleya	Ttct	Cattleya × Tetramicra
Tetradiacrium	Ttdm	Diacrium × Tetramicra
Tetrakeria	Ttka	Barkeria × Tetramicra
Tetraliopsis	Ttps	Laeliopsis × Tetramicra
Tetratonia	Tttna	Broughtonia × Tetramicra
Thesaera	Thsra	Aerangis × Aeranthes
Trautara	Trta	Doritis × Luisia × Phalaenopsis
Trevorara	Trev	Arachnis × Phalaenopsis × Vanda
Trichocidium	Trcdm	Oncidium × Trichocentrum
Trichonopsis	Trnps	Phalaenopsis × Trichoglottis
Trichopsis	Trcps	Trichoglottis × Vandopsis
Trichostylis	Trst	Rhynchostylis × Trichoglottis
Trichovanda	Trcv	Trichoglottis × Vanda
Trigolyca	Trgca	Mormolyca × Trigonidium
Tubaecum	Tbcm	Angraecum × Tuberolabium
Tuckerara	Tuck	Cattleya × Diacrium × Epidendrum
Turnbowara	Tbwa	Barkeria × Broughtonia × Cattleya
Uptonara	Upta	Phalaenopsis × Rhynchostylis × Sarcochilus
Vanalstyneara	Vnsta	Miltonia × Odontoglossum × Oncidium × Rodriguezia

Hybrid Genus	Abbreviation	Wild Genera
Vancampe	Vcp	Acampe × Vanda
Vandachnis	Vchns	Arachnis × Vandopsis
Vandaenopsis	Vdnps	Phalaenopsis × Vanda
Vandaeranthes	Vths	Aeranthes × Vanda
Vandewegheara	Vwga	Ascocentrum × Doritis × Phalaenopsis × Vanda
Vandofinetia	Vf	Neofinetia × Vanda
Vandofinides	Vfds	Aerides × Neofinetia × Vanda
Vandopsides	Vdpsd	Aerides × Vandopsis
Vandoritis	Vdts	Doritis × Vanda
Vanglossum	Vgm	Ascoglossum × Vanda
Vascostylis	Vasco	Ascocentrum × Rhynchostylis × Vanda
Vaughnara	Vnra	Brassavola × Cattleya × Epidendrum
Vejvarutara	Vja	Broughtonia × Cattleya × Cattleyopsis
Vuylstekeara	Vuyl	Cochlioda × Miltonia × Odontoglossum
Warneara	Wnra	Comparettia × Oncidium × Rodriguezia
Westara	Wsta	Brassavola × Broughtonia × Cattleya × Laelia × Schomburgkia
Wilburchangara	Wbchg	Broughtonia × Cattleya × Epidendrum × Schomburgkia
Wilkinsara	Wknsra	Ascocentrum × Vanda × Vandopsis
Wilsonara	Wils	Cochlioda × Odontoglossum × Oncidium
Wingfieldara	Wgfa	Aspasia × Brassia × Odontoglossum
Withnerara	With	Aspasia × Miltonia × Odontoglossum × Oncidium
Wooara	Woo	Brassavola × Broughtonia × Epidendrum
Yahiroara	Yhra	Brassavola × Cattleya × Epidendrum × Laelia × Schomburgkia
Yamadara	Yam	Brassavola × Cattleya × Epidendrum × Laelia
Yapara	Yap	Phalaenopsis × Rhynchostylis × Vanda
Yoneoara	Ynra	Renanthera × Rhynchostylis × Vandopsis
Yonezawaara	Yzwr	Neofinetia × Rhynchostylis × Vanda
Yusofara	Ysfra	Arachnis × Ascocentrum × Renanthera × Vanda
Zygobatemannia	Zbm	Batemannia × Zygopetalum
Zygocaste	Zcst	Lycaste × Zygopetalum
Zygocella	Zcla	Mendoncella × Zygopetalum
Zygocolax	Zcx	Colax × Zygopetalum
Zygodisanthus	Zdsnth	Paradisanthus × Zygopetalum
Zygolum	Zglm	Zygopetalum × Zygosepalum
Zygoneria	Zga	Neogardneria × Zygopetalum
Zygonisia	Zns	Aganisia × Zygopetalum

Hybrid Genus	Abbreviation	Wild Genera
Zygorhyncha	Zcha	Chondrorhyncha × Zygopetalum
Zygostylis	Zsts	Otostylis × Zygopetalum
Zygotorea	Zgt	Pescatorea × Zygopetalum
Zygowarrea	Zwr	Warrea × Zygopetalum

Laeliocattleya 'Mari's Magic'. "Splash-petal" hybrids sport petals colored like the lip. Though very rare in the wild, this sort of recessive trait can be developed easily if you understand the genetics of the orchids you are breeding with. Whether you want to do so is a question of taste.

PART FOUR

Common
Orchid
Genera
from
A to Z

Introduction

This section looks in detail at the most popular genera, spelling out their individual requirements, habits, and charms. If the orchid you're interested in is not on this list, it may be a hybrid. (See the table of hybrid genera in Chapter 13.) When you know the species or genera that were the plant's parents, look them up in the alphabetical listing that follows. Culture for a hybrid is similar to that for its parents.

To help you decide what orchids you may want to grow, each entry contains important points that will guide you toward—or away from—that particular plant.

The icons at the top of the entry will tell you where the plant can be grown:

At a window   Under lights   In a greenhouse

If you see an entry with a greenhouse and you don't have one, simply look for a more suitable plant. If a plant can be grown in more than one place, the entry includes the appropriate icons.

Another clue to help you decide to try a particular plant is the level of skill it requires. Look for these words at the beginning of the entry:

Beginner
Experienced
Expert

BEGINNER: A novice orchid grower (with the information in this book) should have no trouble cultivating these orchids.

EXPERIENCED: These orchids are a bit more complicated to grow, usually because they need more specialized conditions such as very bright light, high humidity, or careful watering.

EXPERT: These orchids are challenging for even experienced growers, often because their needs are so exacting that they need careful attention or cultural conditions that are difficult for most of us to provide. Pay careful attention to the cultural parameters I spell out, and if you feel you cannot provide them, try another genus instead.

The individual entries include the Latin name and the abbreviation registered with the Royal Horticultural Society, if there is one, followed by the pronunciation. Next I list the subtribe that genus is placed in. The orchid family is so large that taxonomists have subdivided it into tribes and subtribes, and knowing the subtribe will give you a frame of reference — a genealogy, really (see Appendix 1 for more on taxonomy). For example, if you know that *Sophronitis* and *Leptotes* are both in the Laeliinae, along with *Cattleya,* you'll have some clues to their needs. I have also included the number of known species in the genus, which is always a best guess, as new orchids are continually being discovered. Following this is the native range of the genus, which can provide a helpful context.

Under Good Introductory Species, I list a few that should be satisfactory first plants in that genus. I chose them either because they are more readily available than others or because in my own and others' experience, they are among the showiest and most easily grown.

The introductory information is followed by an overview of the genus—the shape of the plants, the characteristics of the flowers, and other information. The Culture section gives specifics on watering, light, potting, and other requirements. Note that in this book "indoors" means either on a windowsill or under artificial lights in the house as opposed to a greenhouse or outdoors. As to fertilizing, a light dose is $1/4$ tsp/gal of a complete, balanced fertilizer applied once a week or $1/2$ tsp/gal every other week. A moderate dose is $1/2$ tsp every week or 1 tsp every other week, and a heavy dose is $1 1/2$ tsp every week or 1 tbsp every other week. (For more information on fertilizing, see Chapter 7.)

Angraecum (Angcm) 🔆 🏴

(AN-GRAY-EH-COME)
SUBTRIBE: Angraecinae
NUMBER OF KNOWN SPECIES: 210
NATIVE RANGE: Africa and Madagascar
SKILL LEVEL: Experienced
GOOD INTRODUCTORY SPECIES: *Angraecum leonis,* *A. sesquipedale*

Angraecums are marvels of coevolution. The oft-repeated story of Charles Darwin hypothesizing that the foot-long nectar spur of the Madagascaran *A. sesquipedale* had evolved along with a specific moth having a proboscis of similar length—and the subsequent discovery of just such a moth—is certainly one of the most impressive accounts in the annals of evolutionary biology. Like almost all moth-pollinated flowers, *Angraecums* are glistening white to be clearly visible in moonlight, and to make sure no moth can pass them by, they become intensely and sweetly fragrant after sunset. Most have a long spur that curves and twists like a horn or tail behind the flowers. The moth's sugary nectar reward is produced toward the bottom of this long spur. From our point of view, the spur adds enormously to the beauty of the flowers, which are star-shaped and fronted by a big lip that poufs out like a kerchief caught in a breeze. They have a certain kinetic balance to them, like a well-constructed mobile. *Angraecums* are monopodial orchids, with leaves zigzagging up stems that may be short and stout or thin and vinelike. Fat, slow-growing roots push out from the lower section of the stem and head into the air or across whatever substrate they happen to contact.

Angraecum scottianum

Aerangis rhodosticta

Several related genera are also worth seeking out. *Aerangis* (AIR-ANG-ISS) and *Aeranthes* (AIR-ANT-THEEZ) are very similar to *Angraecum* in both culture and appearance.

CULTURE

To succeed with this genus, remember two things. First, they relish warm, very humid conditions during spring and summer, with a slightly cooler and drier rest period in winter. Second, they are rather slow to reestablish after root loss caused by careless repotting or some other trauma. The first two plants I received were compromised from the start and very slow to recover, which — unjustly — gave me a bad taste for the genus until I tried again a few years later with healthy plants. You may have to pay a bit more for a well-established *Angraecum*, but you will not be disappointed. Many species are rather small, and they do very well in the humidity of a light box or enclosed room as well as a greenhouse; their need for humidity makes them a poor choice for a windowsill.

TEMPERATURE: Warm to intermediate (with an intermediate to cool rest in winter)

LIGHT: Somewhat bright (1,500–2,500 fc)

HUMIDITY, WATER, AND FERTILIZATION: Humidity should range from 70% to 90%. Since the roots prefer to run free on a mount or through the slats of a basket, *Angraecums* should be watered or misted almost daily. Give them moderate applications of fertilizer during the warmer months.

POTTING AND MEDIA: Though the large species, such as *A. sesquipedale* and *A. magdalenae*, are best potted in a coarse, loose mix (coarse bark or bark mixed with charcoal), many of the smaller species as well as the pendent or vining types are happiest mounted on a piece of cork or tree fern. Offsets can be removed and potted separately once they have at least three or four roots. Try to choose a mount that will allow for some growing room, as you should not disturb an established plant any more than necessary.

Arpophyllum (no abbr.)

(AR-PO-FILL-UM)

SUBTRIBE: Laeliinae

NUMBER OF KNOWN SPECIES: 5

NATIVE RANGE: West Indies through Mexico into northern South America

SKILL LEVEL: Experienced

GOOD INTRODUCTORY SPECIES: *Arpophyllum giganteum*

At first glance, *Arpophyllums* appear to be orchids designed by committee. Vegetatively they resemble some of the larger *Laelias,* with tall, slightly swollen pseudobulbs and long, stiff, sickle-shaped leaves grooved slightly down the middle. The dense foxtail spike of very small, bright pink flowers looks as if it belongs on some hardy terrestrial like *Dactylorhiza* or *Platanthera;* it's a bit strange to see it sprouting from what appears to be a *Laelia purpurata* in all other respects. The spike grows out of a large, *Laelia*-esque sheath, but it is obviously no *Laelia.* The individual blooms are less than $\frac{1}{2}$ inch across, but they are thickly massed on the top third of the 6–10-inch inflorescence. I have to admit, though, that despite a slight incongruity between flowers and plant, I do like *Arpophyllums*

and wonder why they are not more widely cultivated. They are fairly easy to grow if you have sufficient space, and the thick, brightly colored spikes appear just in time for the winter and spring orchid shows. The growths cluster tightly together, though the leaves arch out from the plant, so it is possible to raise a spectacular specimen plant with a dozen or more spikes in an 8-inch clay pot.

CULTURE

A big *Arpophyllum* can be more than 2 feet high with a greater spread, so they are not windowsill plants. If you have a greenhouse, though, they will grow perfectly well with *Cattleyas.*

TEMPERATURE: Intermediate

LIGHT: Bright (2,000–3,000 fc)

HUMIDITY, WATER, AND FERTILIZATION: Humidity should range between 60% and 80%, and the plants should never be allowed to dry out completely. Moderate year-round fertilization will bring the plants to specimen size quickly.

POTTING AND MEDIA: A 6–8-inch clay pot is about right. Because the growths can get rather top-heavy, I do not recommend plastic pots. On the advice of the friend who gave me my first division of *A. giganteum,* I used the mix of tree fern, NZ sphagnum, and perlite that I pot pleurothallids in, and this has worked very well. I think the plants enjoy the moisture retained by this finer mix.

Arpophyllum alpinum

Ascocentrum (Asctm)

(AS-CO-SEN-TRUM)

SUBTRIBE: Sarcanthinae

NUMBER OF KNOWN SPECIES: About 10

NATIVE RANGE: Asian tropics and Indonesia

SKILL LEVEL: Experienced

GOOD INTRODUCTORY SPECIES: *Ascocentrum ampullaceum, A. curvifolium* (the parent of most *Ascocenda* hybrids), *A. miniatum*

Ascocentrums are simply delightful orchids. These small plants produce drumstick clusters of some of the most brilliantly colored flowers imaginable. Orange, vermilion, magenta, cerise, or red, they practically shout "Look at me, look at me" and are sure to attract attention on display. They are related to *Vandas,* and hybridizers have taken full advantage of their intense colors and diminutive proportions to scale down the bodacious *Vandas* to a size that even windowsill growers can accommodate. In fact, the *Ascocenda* hybrids have almost single-handedly brought *Vandas* to the frozen masses, allowing growers in the north and those without the space for a 4-foot-tall plant the pleasure of raising these fabulous monopodials.

Like *Vandas* and *Renantheras, Ascocentrums* produce one stiff, strap-shaped leaf at a time, alternating left and right in a ladderlike way that lifts the stems gradually higher. Chubby velamen-covered roots erupt from the lower reaches of the stem and snake off into the air or glue themselves to any substrate they encounter. Flower spikes appear from the middle leaf axils in late winter or spring (watch for them just above the point where last year's spikes emerged) and grow to 6–8 inches. The individual flowers are small (less than 1 inch wide), but they are packed so densely on the spike that the individual flowers merge into a larger conglomerate bloom. Another notable feature of *Ascocentrum* flowers, and one which is often passed on to hybrid offspring, is their uniform coloration. With the exception of the area around the column and the column itself, all the segments have the same luminous color.

Culture

Although much smaller than *Vandas, Ascocentrums* still require the bright light, airy root run, and frequent watering demanded by their larger cousins. I certainly would suggest either the species or their hybrids to beginners wishing to try their hand at the *Vanda* tribe, but they require a bit more

Ascocenda (Vanda Saha × Ascocenda Yip Sum Wah)

attention than a *Phalaenopsis* or mini-*Cattleya* indoors. The large fleshy roots need ample air, so pot them in slatted baskets. Many roots simply head off into the ether, so daily misting or dunking is necessary to keep the plant hydrated. Ample light is also important. Look for some red spotting on the exposed foliage, which indicates they are receiving adequate radiation. For growers north of 40° latitude, it may be difficult to provide enough light indoors during winter, even on a south-facing windowsill. A greenhouse, sunroom, or HID light fixture should do the trick, though. *Ascocentrums* and *Ascocendas* relish spending the summer outdoors if the humidity remains high enough. Even though these are small plants, they can *eventually* get quite large. Recently, RF Orchids received a Certificate of Cultural Merit from the American Orchid Society for their clone *Ascocentrum curvifolium* 'Crownfox', which sported 3,840 flowers and 480 buds on 160 inflorescences; the plant was more than 5 feet tall and 3½ feet wide! Granted, it has been growing in near perfect conditions for thirty-eight years.

TEMPERATURE: Warm to intermediate

LIGHT: Very bright (3,000–4,000 fc)

HUMIDITY, WATER, AND FERTILIZATION: Roots will fail to grow adequately if the humidity remains below 60% or so, and levels of 70% or more are ideal during the warmer months. I like to grow *Ascocentrums* wired into slatted baskets with no medium save a few chunks of charcoal to give the roots a foothold, and I water them liberally. As

Ascocentrum curvifolium

long as you take care not to let water sit in the leaf axils during cool, cloudy weather, daily watering or misting will keep the plants turgid and the leaves growing steadily. The fleshy roots can absorb quite a bit of water, so if you have them in a greenhouse, make a pass with the hose, then return in a few minutes and wet them down again. The old leaves should remain on the plant for years, so if you find two- or three-year-old leaves dropping off, it's probably a sign of insufficient or poor-quality water or, possibly, inadequate nutrition. *Ascocentrums* and their hybrids are heavy feeders; weekly fertilization during active growth is important. About once every other month in spring and summer I like to soak the roots in a slightly stronger fertilizer solution for ten minutes to ensure that they have absorbed what they need.

POTTING AND MEDIA: Slatted baskets or cork mounts are best. You can use medium-grade or coarse fir bark, charcoal, or lava rock in the baskets. You could even raise them in 4–6-inch clay pots as long as you are careful to let the medium dry almost completely between waterings.

Aspasia (Asp)

(AS-PAYS-EE-AH)

SUBTRIBE: Oncidiinae

NUMBER OF KNOWN SPECIES: 8

NATIVE RANGE: Central and South America

SKILL LEVEL: Beginner

GOOD INTRODUCTORY SPECIES: *Aspasia lunata, A. principissa*

Aspasias are very satisfying little epiphytes with a zest for life that translates into fast growth and copious bloom, recommending them to beginner and expert alike. They look like many others in the *Oncidium* alliance: the oval pseudobulbs are topped with a pair of leaves and wrapped by a few more, the creeping rhizome sprouts thick nests of wiry roots, and the inflorescences spring from the base of the pseudobulbs and work their way through the leaves. Scapes of three to eight 1½–3-inch-wide, long-lasting flowers cluster toward the end of each spike. The flowers boast big, crinkled, and colorfully patterned lips backed by contrasting petals and sepals. The lip is typically white around the edges with red, purple, or violet patches around the central yellow crest, or keel. The petals and sepals are green, mahogany, or brown with darker spots or striations.

These 6–10-inch-tall plants seem to grow incessantly for about two-thirds of the year, quickly filling out a mount or small pot but saving all their flowers for one big display in spring or early summer. Their modest size and free-blooming nature make them good choices for indoor growing on an east or south windowsill or under lights.

Aspasia lunata 'The Orchid Man' CCM/AOS

CULTURE

Aspasias are among the easiest members of the *Oncidium* alliance to cultivate. They take well to mounts as long as they receive daily watering/misting during the warmer months, and they do well in baskets or pots. The pseudobulbs rise from the rhizome on ½–1-inch stalks, effectively lifting the plant up and way from a horizontal substrate but helping the clump more quickly colonize a vertical mount.

TEMPERATURE: Intermediate to warm

LIGHT: Somewhat bright (1,500–2,000 fc)

HUMIDITY, WATER, AND FERTILIZATION: Average orchid humidity in the range of 50%–70% will suffice. Mounted plants appreciate daily watering or misting during spring and summer, as well as fertilization every two weeks. My plants rest for a few months during the winter, with growth and flowering recommencing as the sun gets higher in the sky during late winter.

POTTING AND MEDIA: Because they have a wandering growth habit, I find slab mounts of cork or tree fern ideal for *Aspasias*. Cedar baskets 6–8 inches in diameter work wonderfully for larger specimens. The plants are fairly easy to divide and repot after flowering, and they freely branch and multiply, so you will soon have some to share.

Barbosella (Bar) 🌡 🏠

(BAR-BO-SELL-AH)

SUBTRIBE: Pleurothallidinae

NUMBER OF KNOWN SPECIES: About 22

NATIVE RANGE: Central and South America

SKILL LEVEL: Experienced

GOOD INTRODUCTORY SPECIES: Barbosella cucullata

Barbosellas are among the most widespread and common of the pleurothallids (a subtribe of some 8,000 species of mostly miniature orchids from the cloud forests of the American tropics), and their curious little flowers are produced in one or two flushes during the year. New leaves grow almost nonstop throughout the year, and the rhizomes readily branch, so the little plants clump up very quickly. Barbosella cucullata, one of the larger species, has leaves that are fleshy, long, and narrow; others, like the creeping, 1/8-inch-tall B. miersii, have oval leaves spaced along a rapidly advancing rhizome (of course, for a tiny plant, "rapid" is a relative term). Even the apparently clumping B. cucullata spaces out its leaves so that the plants

quickly rise from the pot like dough left too long on the counter. This is not a problem, however, as the plants are easy to divide and repot. The flowers have a stiff, upright stance and dance above the foliage on hair-thin stems originating from the point where the leaf meets the RAMICAUL (a modified stem that replaces the pseudobulb in pleurothallids). I find Barbosellas among the easiest of the pleurothallids to grow, in part because they hail from moderate elevations (3,000–6,500 feet) and they store some extra water in their leaves—in case you forget to water them for a few days. Their small stature (the largest is less than 3 inches high) and year-round growth make them ideal for growing under artificial lights.

CULTURE

A breezy, humid environment suits these miniatures just fine. Grow them as you would Pleurothallis.

TEMPERATURE: Intermediate to cool

LIGHT: Somewhat bright (1,500–2,000 fc)

HUMIDITY, WATER, AND FERTILIZATION: Maintain humidity above 70%, especially if you're growing them on mounts. Steady moisture and light fertilization throughout the year are important, because growth is continuous.

POTTING AND MEDIA: The creeping species have to be mounted, and cork, tree fern, and tree branches work equally well. Place a small pad of NZ sphagnum under the roots before mounting to help the plant get established. Barbosellas do not produce many roots—often just one per growth—but the growths keep coming, so they reestablish quickly. The taller species grow well in 1–2-inch plastic or clay thumb pots filled with NZ sphagnum or a tree fern–moss blend.

Barkeria (Bark) 🏠

(BAR-CARE-EE-AH)

SUBTRIBE: Laeliinae

NUMBER OF KNOWN SPECIES: 15

NATIVE RANGE: Mexico and Central America

SKILL LEVEL: Experienced

GOOD INTRODUCTORY SPECIES: Barkeria elegans,
B. spectabilis, B. lindleyana

Barkerias are easy to grow but a tad awkward in habit, so they have not gained the popularity of so many other members of the Cattleya alliance. They produce thin, canelike or spindle-shaped pseudobulbs more or less like those of Epidendrums, with tough, thickened, 3–4-inch-long lance-shaped leaves clustered along the top third of each cane. From the top of the newest canes come wiry spikes 6–16 inches long with flowers clustered toward the tip. The pretty pink, white, or lavender blooms have ace of spades–shaped lips spotted or barred in

Barbosella species

Barkeria scandens

purple, rose, or yellow, and narrow, uniformly colored petals and sepals that may reflex backward, suggesting birds in flight.

CULTURE

Barkerias grow as epiphytes in fairly exposed situations, so they prefer bright light. The roots, large in proportion to the overall size of the 6–12-inch plants, have a thick white velamen and are fond of air and light. A mounted position suits them, and the lean life on a slab of cork keeps their growth compact and presentable. If they are receiving enough light, the leaves will assume a maroon tinge, with purple spots or freckles often evident, too. Winters in their native habitats are cool and dry, so curtail watering by 30%–50% and keep them where the night temperatures dip into the 50s for the best bloom later, in the warm season. Many species naturally drop some or all of their leaves during this cool, dry rest period, so don't be alarmed.

TEMPERATURE: Intermediate (cool in winter)

LIGHT: Bright to very bright (2,500–4,000 fc)

HUMIDITY, WATER, AND FERTILIZATION: Humidity should be 50% or higher during the growing season; ample water

and misting and regular light fertilization will produce strong new growths. Curtail fertilizer and watering during the 4–6-week midwinter winter rest.

POTTING AND MEDIA: *Barkerias* do not multiply quickly, so division is rarely necessary. The pseudobulbs cluster together but have the exasperating habit of producing the new lead partway up the previous cane, so the plants "walk" up and away from the pot. This epiphytic adaptation, which allows them to climb up a tree toward the light, and their intolerance of stale potting mix make mounting the best solution. Attach the plants toward the bottom of the plaque or branch to give them room to climb if they so desire. You could use a 2$\frac{1}{2}$–3-inch clay pot with a loose mix like bark, charcoal, or lava rock, repotting when the new leads climb too far above the rim for their roots to find the potting mix.

Bifrenaria (Bif)

(BY-FREN-AIR-ee-AH)

SUBTRIBE: Bifrenariinae

NUMBER OF KNOWN SPECIES: 24

NATIVE RANGE: Brazil

SKILL LEVEL: Experienced

GOOD INTRODUCTORY SPECIES: *Bifrenaria harrisoniae*, *B. tyrianthina*

I imported my first *Bifrenaria tyrianthina* fifteen years ago along with a bevy of other wonderful plants from Brazil. After going through the import procedures and getting my permits, it was quite a thrill to finally receive my box of plants by airmail on a warm August day in 1988. The plants were all a bit dry but in good shape, though for shipping they had been knocked out of their pots and sent bare-root. I had read about *Bifrenaria* in Rebecca Northen's *Home Orchid Growing*, and it seemed like a good genus to try. Although after its harsh air journey the plant took a bit longer to reestablish than the others in the box, it erected its first blooms the second spring, and I have loved them ever since. *Bifrenarias* are distantly related to *Lycastes*, and they can be cultured like the evergreen South American members of that genus. The first things you notice about *Bifrenarias* are the 2-inch-long, leathery, ridged, oval pseudobulbs, which cluster together like eggs in an overcrowded nest. The growths emerge wrapped in protective sheaths, which disintegrate with time, leaving a ragged fringe around the base of each pseudobulb. The younger ones sport a thin, pleated leaf, 12–16 inches long by 3 inches wide, with prominent veins. Healthy growths will often produce two leads instead of one, so the plants can grow to specimen size fairly quickly.

Flowers arise in spring or summer, either singly or in twos and threes from the base of lead growths, with healthy leads

Bifrenaria harrisoniae forma alba 'Marcella Dayan' HCC/AOS

producing two separate spikes. At 2–3 inches, the spikes are short—really just tall enough to loft the flowers up over the rim of the pot. This, combined with the up-curving shape of the blooms, reminds me of a little kitten or a child pulling herself up to see out a window. Some species, including *B. tyrianthina,* have down-curving lips covered in purple fur, which adds to the kittenlike quality of the bloom. The long-lasting, waxy flowers are either rose or green suffused with red or brown.

CULTURE

In the wild, *Bifrenarias* grow in fairly exposed situations on rocks or tree limbs (see photo, p. 81). Therefore, despite the rather thin and fragile-looking leaves, bright light is necessary for bloom. Some people report difficulty flowering this genus, and I think too little light is probably the culprit. They will grow well on a windowsill, but they will take up quite a bit of space after a while, and it is not advisable to divide the plants very often. In a greenhouse, they are very satisfactory, doing well suspended from the purlins, where their leaves can shade the less-light-loving plants below.

TEMPERATURE: Warm-intermediate

LIGHT: Bright to very bright (2,500–3,500 fc)

HUMIDITY, WATER, AND FERTILIZATION: *Bifrenarias* are not too fussy about humidity; 50%–60% should suffice. They should never dry out completely, so water when the surface of the mix begins to look dry. They will bulk up more quickly with moderate fertilization during spring and summer and one heavier dose after flowering or when new vegetative growths are evident.

POTTING AND MEDIA: To avoid disturbing the plants too often, I like to pot them in a slatted basket using medium-grade fir bark or an equivalent. In this way, they can be watered frequently, and the excellent air movement will keep the mix from degrading so quickly. When dividing the plants, time your work to coincide with a flush of new growths, and leave the divisions large (at least 6 mature pseudobulbs).

Bollea (Bol)

(BOWL-EE-AH)

SUBTRIBE: Zygopetalinae

NUMBER OF KNOWN SPECIES: 11

NATIVE RANGE: South American Andes

SKILL LEVEL: Expert

GOOD INTRODUCTORY SPECIES: Though not a beginner orchid, *Bollea coelestis* is the most widely available

Bollea coelestis and *B. violacea* are known as two of the "blue" orchids, for they produce musky-sweet-smelling flowers that are blends of cerulean blue, violet, and lavender. While not the illusive true blue, the smoky, velvety violet purple of a particularly dark clone is striking, to say the least. *Bollea lawrenceana* has flowers that are more lavender purple, while

Bollea violacea 'Willow Pond' AM/AOS

B. hirtzii and *B. patini* bloom pinkish violet. From plant to plant within a species, the flowers can vary quite a bit, some having lighter segment tips, others having darker ones, with overall pigments washed out or very concentrated and intense. When shopping for plants, look for awarded clones or seedlings produced from good forms. The *Bolleas*, like their close relatives the *Chondrorhynchas*, grow in cool, shaded, very wet cloud forests. To capture dim light, they have lost their pseudobulbs and developed large, thin, pleated leaves. They demand high humidity and year-round watering when the surface of the mix is dry, so they are best accommodated in an intermediate to cool greenhouse; their size is difficult to accommodate in an enclosed light box. Each growth consists of a fan of six to twelve overlapping leaves, with the longest toward the center. Thick, unbranched roots spill from the base of the fan and burrow down into moss and duff. The large, waxy flowers arise singly from the base as well, and each new growth may produce several blooms from the lower leaf axils. The flowers are up to 4 inches across. The petals and sepals are cupped forward somewhat, and the small lip looks vaguely tonguelike as it sticks out of the hood formed by the column wings.

CULTURE

A richly colored *Bollea coelestis* is among the most beautiful orchids I've ever seen, with a luminous intensity that is impossible to describe. However, as with most Andean cloud forest species, they need specialized care and conditions to thrive. Moderate temperatures, high humidity, and a medium that never dries completely are important for success. I have little experience with the genus myself, as my cloud forest orchids must fit comfortably into an HID grow room with limited space. I have raised seedlings of *B. coelestis* alongside *Masdevallias* and *Draculas*, but I think the nighttime temperatures in my cellar were too cold for their liking during winter.

TEMPERATURE: Intermediate to cool

LIGHT: Low light (1,000–1,800 fc)

HUMIDITY, WATER, AND FERTILIZATION: If humidity levels drop much below 70%, growth will be interrupted and the leaves may pleat as they try to emerge. Ideally, humidity levels should be in the 80%–100% range, with good air circulation. Because the plants have lush foliage and no pseudobulbs, the mix should never be allowed to dry. With adequate humidity, a good drenching every two to three days should suffice. The plants grow all through the year, so regular, light to moderate fertilization is also important.

POTTING AND MEDIA: Tree fern and/or NZ sphagnum in 4–6-inch clay pots should provide enough growing space for the roots.

Brassavola (B) 🏵 💡 🏴

(BRASS-AH-VOLE-AH)

SUBTRIBE: Laeliinae

NUMBER OF KNOWN SPECIES: 17

NATIVE RANGE: American tropics, usually at low elevations

SKILL LEVEL: Beginner

GOOD INTRODUCTORY SPECIES: *Brassavola nodosa*

These graceful, night-fragrant orchids are among the most easily accommodated indoors of any, so I recommend them, especially the very widespread *Brassavola nodosa*, to beginners wishing to try their first mounted orchid. *Brassavolas* have 6–16-inch-long, pencil-thin leaves that have rolled up and fused to become water storage tanks to help the plants weather droughts. These pendent cylindrical leaves also minimize surface area exposed to drying winds and sun, so *Brassavolas* can grow in situations that are too open for most others in the tribe. Because the leaves have taken on the water storage function, the pseudobulbs are reduced to a narrow sticklike structure between the leaf and the rhizome. If you have a sunny

Brassavola David Sander

window or an airy spot outdoors when the weather is mild, you can grow and flower these orchids. *Brassavolas* are moth-pollinated, and since most moths are active at night, the flowers are white or greenish or yellowish white and penetratingly fragrant after sunset. *B. nodosa*—called the lady or queen of the night—has a rich, sweet perfume reminiscent of jasmine and lily that will scent a room or greenhouse for the month or more that it is in bloom. The most prominent feature of the single or clustered flowers is the large, spoon-shaped, ruffled or lobed lip. The other segments are long and thin, often drooping or hanging down in ringlets.

Two Central American species have been removed from the genus because of anatomical differences, but culturally they are similar. *Brassavola digbyana* and *B. glauca*—now *Rhyncholaelia digbyana* and *R. glauca*—differ from the *Brassavolas* most noticeably in the shape of the leaf and

Brassavola culcullata hybrid

pseudobulb—in this case a strap-shaped, thickened leaf, much like a rather bloated *Cattleya* leaf, attached to a spindle-shaped pseudobulb. Their petals and sepals are also fuller, more like *Cattleyas* or *Laelias,* and they have an even more exaggerated lip. *R. digbyana* adds an incredible feather boa frill or fimbriation to its lip, and hybridizers early on figured out that if you cross it with a *Cattleya,* the offspring inherit this ruffle but take on the more intense coloration of the other parent. Almost every *Brassocattleya, Brassolaeliocattleya,* or any of the other thirty-five complex hybrid genera involving *Brassavola* use this one species. Since it would cause endless confusion to change all these genera to *Rhynchocattleyas,* and so on, the old name has been retained in the hybrid registry.

CULTURE

The most important cultural requirement is adequate light. With the proper exposure, *Brassavola* leaves develop red freckles that can be seen over the green background. If your plants don't have freckles, move them to a brighter location. You can raise them in pots or slatted baskets, but excellent drainage is also important, which is why I prefer mounts. Their drought tolerance makes mounted *Brassavolas* easier to handle indoors than most other orchids. The thick white roots will soak up enough water to keep the leaves turgid if you soak the plants for fifteen minutes once or twice a week. The plants will readily produce more than one flush of growth per season, and the rhizomes branch freely, so it does not take too long to grow specimen-sized *Brassavolas.* The *Rhyncholaelias* are somewhat slower.

TEMPERATURE: Warm to intermediate

LIGHT: Very bright (2,500–4,000 fc). It is possible to bloom *Brassavolas* under HID lights, but a south-facing window coupled with a summer outdoors or a bright location in the greenhouse or sunroom will suit them better.

HUMIDITY, WATER, AND FERTILIZATION: One of the nice things about *Brassavolas* is their tolerance of lower humidity than most orchids feel comfortable with. The roots of mounted plants will continue to grow at 30%–50% relative humidity, though ideally it should be toward the upper end of this range. Water just enough to keep root tips green and leaves turgid (plump and unwrinkled). As I mentioned above, if you are growing them mounted indoors, soak the mount and roots for fifteen minutes in a bucket of water once a week and mist every day or two. Allow potted specimens to dry completely between waterings. If the leaves lose turgor, soak twice a week. Apply a light dose of a balanced fertilizer all year, with a few stronger applications in spring.

POTTING AND MEDIA: Cork or tree-branch mounts work well. The plants will grow on tree fern, but the thick roots will get badly damaged if you have to remount them.

Brassia verrucosa

Brassavolas can easily be divided like *Cattleyas* in spring or when a new flush of roots just becomes visible. If you pot them, use a 3-inch pot for an average-sized division with a well-drained mix like medium-grade fir bark, lava, or pumice. I have had good results potting both *Brassavolas* and *Rhyncholaelias* in 6–8-inch slatted baskets using medium-grade fir bark or bark and charcoal.

Brassia (Brs) 🏵 🏴

(BRASS-ee-ah)

SUBTRIBE: Oncidiinae

NUMBER OF KNOWN SPECIES: 29

NATIVE RANGE: American tropics

SKILL LEVEL: Beginner

GOOD INTRODUCTORY SPECIES: *Brassia caudata, B. arcuigera (longissima), B. verrucosa*

A well-grown *Brassia* or spider orchid in full bloom is guaranteed to stop even those who aren't orchid lovers in their tracks. I have watched people at the Greater New York Orchid Show clustered in awe around a specimen-sized *Brassia rex* (the stunning hybrid of *Brassia verrucosa* × *gireoudiana*), even when glorious *Phalaenopsis*, resplendent *Cattleyas*, and evocative *Phragmipediums* failed to gain their rapt attention. *Brassia* flowers are certainly graceful, with 2–10-inch-long, remarkably thin segments that narrow to a hair-thin point, but I think it is the inflorescence as a whole and not the individual

flowers that makes such an impact. The long green, yellow, or tan petals of each flower form the points of a triangle, and the flowers are arranged in two back-to-back ranks on arching spikes. The arrangement has a herringbone-esque, three-dimensional visual complexity and sculptural quality that make it mesmerizing to all.

Anatomically, *Brassias* resemble their cousins the *Oncidiums*, with their 1–3-inch, oval, flattened pseudobulbs, which emerge from several persistent sheathing leaves and are topped by a long, fairly thin, strap-shaped leaf or pair of leaves. The flat pseudobulbs cluster tightly one after the other on very short rhizomes that branch once in a while to enlarge the colony. The flower spikes emerge from the lowest sheathing leaves, usually in spring or early summer, and the flowers are effective for a couple of weeks. They readily interbreed with each other and with other members of the *Oncidium* alliance, such as *Adas, Miltonias, Odontoglossums*, and of course *Oncidiums*, contributing their dramatic flower shape and arrangement to the brilliantly colored and spotted hybrid offspring. In size and cultural needs they are very similar to *Cattleyas*.

CULTURE

I find *Brassias* easy to grow, even on a south-facing windowsill, though their size (16–30 inches) precludes them from most fluorescent light setups. Because the sheathing leaves wrap the pseudobulbs so tightly, rot can set in easily in a humid greenhouse if there is not enough air movement around the plants.

TEMPERATURE: Intermediate to warm

Brassada (Ada aurantiaca 'Cora' × Brassia keiliana)

LIGHT: Bright (2,000–3,000 fc). Despite the rather thin appearance of their leaves, *Brassias* can take, and in fact relish, fairly bright light. For maximum flowering, the upper surface of the leaves should be yellow-green, and the exposed parts of the pseudobulbs should have a ruddy complexion.

HUMIDITY, WATER, AND FERTILIZATION: *Brassias* grow in rain forests and wet cloud forests, but they adapt to humidity in the 50%–70% range. They require quite a bit of water and regular moderate fertilization after blooming, when the new leads are developing. To keep the pseudobulbs from cupping and wrinkling, water when the surface of the medium dries. During the winter, reduce water and fertilizer by a third. In the greenhouse, place or hang them in a spot with good airflow to reduce the chance of rhizome rot.

POTTING AND MEDIA: *Brassias* are fairly big plants, so I pot them in 6–8-inch clay or plastic pots. Both medium-grade fir bark and tree fern–NZ sphagnum mixes have worked well. A 12-inch cedar basket can house a large specimen quite comfortably. They produce large, branching root systems that will nourish many blooms. Divide and repot in spring after flowering ends.

Broughtonia (Bro) 🏳️

(*BROE-TONE-EE-AH*)

SUBTRIBE: Laeliinae

NUMBER OF KNOWN SPECIES: 5

NATIVE RANGE: West Indies

SKILL LEVEL: Experienced

GOOD INTRODUCTORY SPECIES: *Broughtonia sanguinea*

Broughtonias have a lovely proportion—flattened pseudobulbs about as big as a jumbo olive run over by a shopping cart, topped by two stiff 3–6-inch leaves held to the right and left to form a V. They grow at sea level in the West Indies, favoring the light shade of brushy undergrowth in the low scrub forest. Each mature growth sends out a long, wiry inflorescence that begins as a spear-point bud emerging from between the leaf bases. When the spike has reached one or two feet in length, a cluster of buds forms, then opens to reveal pink or purple, 1½-inch flowers with rounded segments and a big puffy lip. *B. sanguinea*, the most commonly cultivated, sports flowers that are a uniform neon pink to red-pink with just a hint of yellow along the crest of the lip. The clusters of five to fifteen bright flowers dancing on a thin stem above the little plant in fall or winter are positively charming. *Broughtonias* have very short rhizomes, so the pseudobulbs overlap or crowd together, with the stiff, strap-shaped leaves arching out above. Each new growth produces a thick nest of bright white roots as it matures.

Broughtonia sanguinea

Cattleyopsis (*CAT-LEE-OP-SIS*) is a small genus of tough little epiphytes very closely related to *Broughtonia*, both in appearance and cultural needs.

CULTURE

Because they grow in exposed sea-level habitats, *Broughtonias* demand extremely high light and warm temperatures all year to grow and bloom effectively. They are very difficult to satisfy indoors unless they can be positioned within a foot of an HID fixture. I have grown and bloomed them reasonably well in an intermediate greenhouse, hanging them high up on the south-facing gable where the sun is bright and the air warmest. However, growers in subtropical and tropical latitudes have far better results. Because they are less suited to northern latitudes, *Broughtonias* have fallen out of favor with many orchidists. They have been crossed with other members of the *Cattleya* alliance to produce some attractive hybrids. *Cattleytonias, Laelonias, Epitonias,* and others usually inherit the long thin spikes and sun-loving nature of the *Broughtonia* parent.

TEMPERATURE: Warm

LIGHT: Intense (4,000–5,000 fc).

HUMIDITY, WATER, AND FERTILIZATION: Humidity above 50% will suffice. Water enough to keep pseudobulbs plump during active growth, and taper off by 25% as growth matures in autumn. Since *Broughtonias* are usually grown under very bright light, daily watering (for mounted plants) or twice weekly (for plants in baskets) may be necessary. Fertilize moderately throughout the year, except when flower spikes are developing in winter.

POTTING AND MEDIA: *Broughtonias* need excellent drainage and do quite well mounted on cork slabs or 6-inch-long sections of 2-inch-diameter tree branches suspended vertically or potted in cedar or plastic mesh baskets. I prefer to mount them, as they do not take well to being disturbed, but be sure to mount the plant when new root growth starts and look for signs of desiccation until new roots get established.

Bulbophyllum (Bulb) 🏵 🔘 🚩

(*BULB-OH-FILL-UM*)

SUBTRIBE: Bulbophyllinae

NUMBER OF KNOWN SPECIES: More than 1,200

NATIVE RANGE: Africa, Southeast Asia and New Guinea, plus a few in the American tropics

SKILL LEVEL: Beginner

GOOD INTRODUCTORY SPECIES: Many, including *Bulbophyllum lobbii, B. grandiflorum, B. barbigerum*

The genus *Bulbophyllum* contains one of the most remarkable assemblages of flower forms and shapes found in nature, though vegetatively they are fairly similar and easy to recognize. They produce garbanzo bean–shaped pseudobulbs that squat on cablelike rhizomes that may be very short, so that the pseudobulbs are clustered together, or very long, so that the plants appear strung like beads on a string. Leaves are usually thick, medium green, and cupped slightly, with a rounded tip

Bulbophyllum orthoglossum

and a stiff petiole attaching the leaf or pair of leaves to the pseudobulb. The flowers or flower spikes originate from buds in a groove at the base of the pseudobulb. *Bulbophyllum* flowers range from sublime through fantastic, bizarre, and ridiculous. Some look respectably orchidlike; *B. lobbii*, which produces single yellow flowers with down-curved petals and lip, resembles some of the *Dendrobiums* in overall appearance. *B. spiesii* is fantastic, with 10–16-inch-long *Phalaenopsis*-like leaves and 4-inch clusters of hairy, dark red, hooded flowers that look like a passel of dead mousies ready for the flies. *B. scaberulum* and its ilk are downright ridiculous. Their inflorescences, composed of flattened scales from which peek tiny flowers, look like flattened caterpillars studded with small earrings at each joint. The sublime *B. blumei* looks for all the world like a purple *Masdevallia*, while *B. intersitum* looks like a little *Pleurothallis*. I guess the similarities between the *Bulbophyllums* and the pleurothallids are not surprising, as both groups have evolved primarily for fly pollination, and flies seem to have more refined sensibilities than bees or hummingbirds. You could say they prefer interesting to pretty. In a sense, the *Bulbophyllums* are the PALEOTROPICAL equivalent

Cattleytonia Capri 'Lea' AM/AOS

of the NEOTROPICAL pleurothallids, and they provide almost unlimited variations on a theme to delight, mesmerize, and occasionally disgust the collector.

Interesting from a plant geography point of view is the fact that a few species of this overwhelmingly Old World genus are found in the American tropics as far north as the Caribbean and Florida. Although these species are the flattened-worm type and not very desirable horticulturally, it is fascinating to me that a few errant seeds once made it across the Pacific and started life anew in the brave new world of the Andes or the Amazon.

CULTURE

As a whole, *Bulbophyllums* are easy to grow and very resilient in cultivation. As might be expected of such a large, aggregate genus, there are plants for just about every situation. Many are warm to intermediate growers, but a number are from high cloud forests or monsoon climates where the winters are cool and dry. I think *Bulbophyllums* are more adaptable than many orchids. I have grown about fifty intermediate and warm-growing species—a small fraction of the tribe—and have kept them all together in one section of the greenhouse with excellent results. The plants are in active growth for about seven months of the year here in New England, resting during the colder months. If you acquire enough species, you will have a few in bloom all year long. The biggest challenge is containing the plants. Because they grow quickly, even the types with short rhizomes quickly fill a pot and head over the sides; indoors, yearly repotting may be necessary. Mounts or baskets

are better if your situation permits. Fortunately, if you make reasonable divisions (at least five growths) and repot in spring as new growth commences, *Bulbophyllums* rebound quickly from the ordeal. If you do grow them on mounts, it is easy to raise large specimens. I have had *B. lobbii* and the like cover a 1 × 2-foot cork slab in three years.

TEMPERATURE: Mostly warm to intermediate, occasionally cool. The intermediate species I have raised tolerate winter lows in the high 50s without a problem.

LIGHT: Somewhat bright (1,200–2,000 fc). Because of their small to moderate stature, most *Bulbophyllums* adapt readily to windowsills or artificial lights if you can accommodate their rambling ways.

HUMIDITY, WATER, AND FERTILIZATION: Humidity in the 50%–70% range will suffice for most. Higher humidity levels and daily watering/misting during the summer will keep mounted specimens plump. Reduce watering somewhat during the winter. *Bulbophyllums* have a long season of active growth and therefore appreciate moderate fertilization year-round.

POTTING AND MEDIA: I have had the best results mounting plants on cork, tree fern, or a branch, though a slatted basket filled with medium-grade fir bark works well. The root systems of these plants are not extensive. Each maturing growth will flush out a tuft of wiry 1–3-inch-long roots that attach to the mount surface or burrow shallowly into the pot or basket. Accordingly, you should not pot even large species in deep containers. Pans or baskets will provide ample root run and lessen the chance of disease. The short roots and visible rhizomes make division a snap (or snip, as the case may be). While a division of even one mature pseudobulb will often reestablish, it is best to take four to six pseudobulbs and coil them around the pot if necessary.

Calanthe (Cal) 🉐 🚩

(*KAL-ANTH-EE*)

SUBTRIBE: Bletiinae

NUMBER OF KNOWN SPECIES: About 150

NATIVE RANGE: Africa, Asian tropics and subtropics, and Australia

SKILL LEVEL: Beginner

GOOD INTRODUCTORY SPECIES: *Calanthe vestita, C. rosea, C. discolor*

Living in a temperate climate that is too cold for plants to grow for a good portion of the year, I can understand why orchids go dormant as the air turns cold. I only wish I could do the same. It is cheering to see blooming plants in the dead of winter, but I also like to see the surge of growth arising from a leafless houseplant in spring, much like the hardy perennials

Bulbophyllum spiesii 'Paul's Fragrance' AM/AOS

Calanthe rosea 'Cardinal's Roost' AM/AOS

with the large, often three-lobed lip balancing the flower visually from below. The blooms are displayed on 1–2-foot spikes, with the flowers clustered along the top third and the lowest ones sometimes SUBTENDED by a thin, leafy bract. They bloom sequentially, so the display continues for a month or more. The deciduous species flower with the resumption of growth in spring, while the evergreens bloom in summer, fall, or winter.

CULTURE

I find *Calanthes* easy and satisfying to grow. Because they do well in a well-drained houseplant "soil," such as Pro-Mix, watering is more straightforward than it is with epiphytes. They were extremely popular in Europe during the nineteenth century, and in fact the first artificial orchid hybrid, *Calanthe* × *dominyi* (registered in 1856), was a cross of *C. masuca* and *C. furcata.* Japan has a number of subtropical and warm-temperate species, and in the land of the rising sun, the genus—especially the native species—is much loved. The winter-dormant, deciduous types are very easy to accommodate indoors, provided you have a windowsill or a lightly shaded spot for them outdoors during the summer and a cool place to keep them during the winter. Evergreen types grow well with *Phalaenopsis. Calanthes* are fairly tall plants when in flower and leaf (10–60 inches, depending on the species), so they are difficult to accommodate under lights.

TEMPERATURE: Intermediate to warm (store deciduous species at 50°–60° during winter dormancy)

LIGHT: Low (1,000–1,500 fc). *Calanthes* are forest species with thin leaves that burn easily in sunlight. They do well outdoors under trees in summer or on an east-facing windowsill when growing and blooming.

HUMIDITY, WATER, AND FERTILIZATION: For the deciduous species, once growth commences, the plants need constant moisture, 50% humidity, and regular applications of moderate to large amounts of fertilizer. The plants bloom at this time, but the fertilizer does not seem to bring flowering to a premature end. Some growers mix some aged horse manure into their *Calanthe* compost with excellent results. Starting in autumn, let the surface of the medium dry between waterings. In combination with cooler night temperatures, this will trigger leaf drop, at which point watering should be curtailed completely. You can store dormant *Calanthes* in the cellar next to the amaryllis and freesia bulbs. No water is necessary during the winter unless the air in your house is very dry. If it is, once you are sure the plants have dried completely, partially surround the pots with plastic wrap, leaving the area just around the pseudobulbs open. In late winter to early spring, repot and begin watering sparingly until flowers and/or new growth begin.

outdoors. The genus *Calanthe* includes a large group of species that lose their leaves in response to cold or, more commonly, the onset of the dry season. Because leaf drop coincides nicely with our autumn, these deciduous plants are easily accommodated indoors, and because they are terrestrials, they do very well in a standard peat-based potting mix. The deciduous types produce egg-sized pseudobulbs topped with a tuft of large, thin, pleated leaves. The pseudobulbs are often pinched around the waist as if they are wearing a particularly tight corset. A large group of evergreen *Calanthes* have similar pleated leaves but nonexistent or at most vestigial pseudobulbs. These require watering throughout the year. *Calanthe* flowers are often richly colored or bicolored, in shades ranging from orange and yellow through pink, violet, and purple to nearly blue and finally white. The sepals and petals are oriented on the upper side of the flower like the tail of a peacock,

The evergreen species prefer at least 50% humidity, light fertilization, and even watering year-round. Water thoroughly when the soil surface begins to dry.

POTTING AND MEDIA: I pot the deciduous *Calanthes* in 5–6-inch standard clay pots, using Pro-Mix or an equivalent. Annual or biennial repotting will keep the plants vigorous. Try to leave at least two pseudobulbs per division. Back bulbs severed from the newer growths will often produce new leads; this is the fastest way to increase your stocks. Divide and repot only in late winter, just before new growth commences. Most of the root system will be lost during the winter, but a big nest of fat, fuzzy roots will quickly fill the pot as the plants resume growth in spring. I have seen some beautiful specimens created by potting several divisions in 8- or 10-inch pots. The evergreen species can be handled in a similar fashion, though I add about 25% medium-grade fir bark to the Pro-Mix for aeration since they will be watered year-round.

Capanemia (no abbr.)

(*CAP-AN-EE-ME-AH*)

SUBTRIBE: Oncidiinae

NUMBER OF KNOWN SPECIES: 15

NATIVE RANGE: Southern South America

SKILL LEVEL: Experienced

GOOD INTRODUCTORY SPECIES: *Capanemia australis, C. micromera, C. superflua*

I purchased my first *Capanemia micromera* from a Brazilian nursery displaying plants at a large orchid show. I was attracted by the little quill-like leaves on tiny round pseudobulbs, and I figured that this 2½-inch miniature would fit nicely under my cramped fluorescent light. I'm happy to report I was right. The Lilliputian orchid soon erupted in a froth of fragrant, crystalline white flowers in arching, 2-inch racemes. I have found them to be equally happy in a 1-inch thumb pot and on a tree branch mount.

CULTURE

Moderate light, frequent watering when in growth and a well-ventilated spot suit this genus fine. I have not tried them on a windowsill, but I suspect they would be amenable to this type of culture.

TEMPERATURE: Intermediate

LIGHT: Somewhat bright (1,500–2,000 fc)

HUMIDITY, WATER, AND FERTILIZATION: Average orchid humidity (50%–60%) seems fine. Water once the pot or mount dries when in active growth and flowering, but taper off slightly during cool or cloudy weather. Fertilize lightly.

POTTING AND MEDIA: Overall, I think mounting is best for

Capanemia uliginosa

Capanemias if your setup allows it, though 1–2-inch clay thumb pots filled with tree fern, lava, or Turface will also work.

Catasetum (Ctsm)

(*CAT-AH-SEA-TUM*)

SUBTRIBE: Catasetinae

NUMBER OF KNOWN SPECIES: About 70

NATIVE RANGE: American tropics

SKILL LEVEL: Beginner

GOOD INTRODUCTORY SPECIES: *Catasetum macrocarpum, C. pileatum*

If you think plants are just passive supplicants, you've never poked your finger into a *Catasetum*'s male flower. These hermaphroditic orchids (bearing separate male and female inflorescences at different times on the same plant) have evolved a clever snare to guarantee that their pollinia are attached to a visiting bee. A trigger extends down the back of the lip, and as a finger or insect head presses against it, *snap*, the pollinia spring down with a significant force and are glued to the body part very effectively. It feels like a tapping pressure on the fingertip, but it must really knock the poor insect senseless.

Catasetums, which hail from seasonally dry habitats, grow in spring and summer, then drop their leaves and go dormant in autumn and winter. I think this group of orchids is an excellent choice for indoor growers who can put plants outdoors in summer. They will flourish in the bright light and rainfall outdoors and require only an occasional watering during the winter to keep the pseudobulbs from becoming too severely desiccated.

Catasetums have large (3–10-inch) spindle-shaped pseudobulbs marked with ridged scars. When watering is increased in spring, leafy new shoots appear suddenly from the base of the past year's growths. They expand into new pseudobulbs adorned with several 1–2-foot-long, 3-inch-wide pleated leaves. In most species, the flowers appear either after the plants shed their leaves in fall or as new growth commences in spring. Flowering in this genus is controlled by the availabili-

ty of water as much as by temperature and day length. The blooms themselves are tightly or loosely clustered on arching or pendent racemes that spring from dormant buds hidden along the abscission scars (scars that form where leaves or sheaths were attached). It is rare for female flowers to be produced in cultivation, probably because the plants do not receive adequate sunlight. Consequently, it is the male flowers that are pictured in books. These range from white, yellow, and green through red and maroon, most with a hunched or hooded shape to help get the pollinator into proper position.

Clowesia (CLOE-EASE-EE-AH) does not appear in older orchid books, as the genus has only recently been split off from *Catasetum*. The main difference is that *Clowesias* have perfect flowers (functional male and female parts in the same flower), while *Catasetums* do not. Culture is identical. Because the flowers are perfect, they are more easily bred than *Catasetums*, whose male and female inflorescences often don't overlap. Colors range from the feather boa–pink *C. rosea* to the white and yellow *C. warscewiczii* and green and purple *C. russelliana*. In general, the individual blooms last longer than those of *Catasetums*.

Catasetum species

Clowesia rosea 'Dorothy Stah' CCM/AOS

Common Orchid Genera from A to Z   145

As you may have surmised, these plants are easy to cultivate. In some respects I think they are actually easier to raise when summered outdoors and wintered indoors than when kept in a greenhouse all the time. The keys to success are bright light (be careful not to move the plants to a brighter location once in leaf, though, as burning may result), copious fertilizer during active growth, and a dry rest coupled with a drop in temperature.

TEMPERATURE: Warm to intermediate. During the summer, daytime temperatures in the 80°–90° range are preferred, with a drop to 58°–62° during winter dormancy.

LIGHT: Very bright (3,000–4,000 fc—possibly higher to produce female flowers). In the wild, *Catasetums* and *Clowesias* grow in full sun and exposed situations, but they do well in a lightly shaded greenhouse, lath house, or south-facing window. Leaves should be light green or yellow-green.

HUMIDITY, WATER, AND FERTILIZATION: Fairly high humidity (50%–70%) is ideal during active growth. Lower humidity is tolerated but not necessary during dormancy. The plants should be watered heavily during spring and summer, but as autumn approaches, watering should gradually tail off. The leaves will yellow and drop when water is curtailed, and the leafless pseudobulbs need only an occasional drenching to keep them from shriveling entirely and losing roots. I water them about once every ten to fourteen days during dormancy, but the timing will vary depending on where you keep them. Just don't let the pseudobulbs lose more than half their original volume. In spring I like to soak the pots for a few hours in a bucket of water to which I've added 1 tbsp/gal of soluble fertilizer. Continue regular, fairly heavy applications of fertilizer (about 1 tsp/gal) every 7–14 days during summer and withhold fertilizer completely when the plants are dormant.

POTTING AND MEDIA: The only time to divide and repot *Catasetums* is just as new growth begins. For species that bloom at this time, wait until the blooms are past before proceeding. I use straight medium-grade fir bark for these plants, though a more moisture-retentive mix, like NZ moss, tree fern, or coconut fiber, would work, too. The plants should be repotted every year or two, with no fewer than two or three pseudobulbs per division. I prefer 4-inch clay pots, which are small for the size of the plants, but I can water them more liberally without fear of root rot—which can be a problem especially when the plants are dormant. Because the big pseudobulbs and leaves can make the plants very top-heavy in small pots, it's best to hang them from the rafters, where the air movement, sun, and heat are greater and they can't tip over.

Cattleya (C)

(CAT-LEE-AH OR CAT-LEE-AH)

SUBTRIBE: Laeliinae

NUMBER OF KNOWN SPECIES: 48

NATIVE RANGE: Central and South America

SKILL LEVEL: Beginner to experienced

GOOD INTRODUCTORY SPECIES: *Cattleya aurantiaca,*
   C. intermedia, C. mossiae, C. skinneri, and the many, many hybrids available

Cattleyas and their relatives have held a place of preeminence among orchid fanciers since Victorian times. Though many are rather large plants that require more light and space than an average windowsill can provide, the species have been hybridized with smaller relatives such as *Sophronitis* to make them better suited to indoor life. For some reason I am drawn to the sympodial orchids, and the *Cattleyas* are the classic sympodial, with thick creeping rhizomes sending up stems that swell to pseudobulbs, then narrow again at the point where a thick leaf (or leaves) attaches. In most *Cattleyas,* the immature flower buds are protected in a mittenlike sheath

Cattleya intermedia, a Brazilian bifoliate

that juts out at that point of attachment. I will never forget my excitement when I held a *Cattleya* up to the light for the first time and saw two swelling flower buds inside the backlit sheaths, like tiny embryos growing in an emerald womb. The flowers expand until they burst out of the sheath, unfurling their segments to reveal the quintessential orchid flower, with a large ruffled lip, flag-proud petals, and a triangle of sepals. In the years following World War II, the breeding of *Cattleyas* for corsages reached its zenith, with breeders aiming to produce bigger and bigger blossoms. Inevitably, these giants lost all of the proportion and balance of the wild types. *Cattleyas* are not grown for corsages much anymore, and as fashions have changed, so has the size of the plants and flowers. Today's "mini-cat" hybrids (crosses involving smaller related genera like *Sophronitis* and *Laelia* that have brought plant height down to the 6–12-inch range) are better suited for indoor culture, and their flowers are proportionate to their modest size. Still, I find the big species beautiful in their own right, with flowers that are showy but not ostentatious.

The genus has two major groups, the unifoliates (also called the *labiata* group, after the first species discovered) and the bifoliates. Unifoliate species (we can call them one-leafers) are widespread in the Americas. They produce one flattened banana-sized leaf per pseudobulb, tilted at a slight angle so it faces the light. Most of the unifoliates are 12–16 inches in height. Their violet, lavender, or white flowers have that classic corsage look, with a large frilly lip and wide petals, and many are intoxicatingly fragrant to boot. The bifoliates usually produce a pair of smaller leaves on longer, thinner pseudobulbs. They come in a greater range of sizes than the unifoliates. A large *C. guttata* can be close to 3 feet tall, while *C. aclandiae* stands 4–6 inches. The flowers have a heavy, waxy appearance, with sepals and petals much the same in size and color. The lip and indeed the entire flower are smaller than in the *labiáta* group, but the flowers usually make up in number what they lack in size. A well-grown bifoliate may have fifteen or more 1½–3-inch blooms on a short spike, ranging in color from mahogany through purple, green, yellow, and even orange, with a contrasting color in the lip. Brazil and its neighbors have a number of bifoliate species, and to confuse things, a group in Central America (*C. skinneri, C. aurantiaca, C. bowringiana,* and *C. pattini*) has now been split off into the separate genus *Guarianthe*. Whether you call them *Cattleya* or *Guarianthe*, these four species are among the easiest, most floriferous, and satisfying of the lot.

I cannot discuss *Cattleyas* without mentioning their complex hybrids with related genera, as these are more common in cultivation than the species themselves. *Cattleyas* cross with *Laelias* to form *Laeliocattleyas*, with *Sophronitis* to form *Sophrocattleyas*, with *Brassavolas* to form *Brassocattleyas*, *Broughtonias* to form *Cattleytonias*, and *Epidendrums* to form

Cattleya skinneri 'JJ' FCC/AOS

Epicattleyas. Further, these hybrids can be recombined in every possible way to create even more complicated crosses (see the table of hybrid genera, p. 119). With so many genes in the mix, these complex hybrids are available in almost every shade of the rainbow save true blue. Many are very vigorous, blooming more than once a year and thriving under cultivation. However, just as many are so jumbled that they are what growers call mules—nonflowering, weak-growing genetic dead ends. When shopping for hybrids, look for awarded clones, which are likely to perform well.

CULTURE

Culturally, the two groups of *Cattleyas* and most of the hybrids are pretty much the same. Most species have one period of active growth and one flush of blooming per year; in

Sophrolaeliocattleya **Patricia Taafe 'Smerle'** HCC/AOS

some this occurs just as new growth matures in summer or fall, while others wait until the shorter days of winter or the warming nights of spring. It is thus possible to have some plants, whether species or hybrids, in bloom throughout the year. Hybrids often bloom more than once a year. The only hybrids I have had trouble with are those involving *Broughtonia,* which is rather exacting in its requirements and passes this characteristic on to its offspring. I think the main reason that *Cattleyas* and their hybrids are losing ground to *Phalaenopsis* and *Paphiopedilums* among hobbyists is their need for fairly bright light. Unless you have a south- or southeast-facing window, HID lights, or a greenhouse, many of the plants will not receive enough light to bloom well. The hybrids involving *Sophronitis* are a little more adaptable and so are better choices for fluorescents or a windowsill. You can tell the plants are getting enough light when the leaves are thick and light green, perhaps with a flush of red along exposed parts of the pseudobulbs. *Cattleyas* have one main advantage over *Phalaenopsis* from a cultural point of view: because they have pseudobulbs, they are thus more forgiving of underwatering.

As with most sympodial orchids, newly repotted specimens take a season to recover, but established plants should produce new pseudobulbs that are as large as or larger than the preceding ones. Old leaves are eventually shed, but they should last for at least two to three years. Even leafless pseudobulbs will continue to function as water and food storage tanks for the plant, and the more backbulbs the plant has, the better. Divisions should have a minimum of three to four pseudo-

bulbs, and at least two should have leaves. A healthy plant will produce two new leads occasionally, and over time a nice specimen will develop.

TEMPERATURE: Intermediate

LIGHT: Bright to very bright (2,000–4,000 fc). Many orchids are said to need *Cattleya* light, which has become a standard.

HUMIDITY, WATER, AND FERTILIZATION: *Cattleyas* are not as demanding as some other genera regarding humidity. Levels in the 40%–70% range are fine. The plants have rather fat, vigorous roots that branch and ramble through the mix. Water frequently enough to keep at least the lead pseudobulbs plump, but let the mix dry almost completely between waterings to discourage root problems. Many species rest somewhat in winter, at which time watering can be modestly curtailed. *Cattleyas* need moderate levels of fertilizer, especially during active growth.

POTTING AND MEDIA: Even very large *Cattleyas* can be accommodated in 6–8-inch pots. Mini-cats are fine in 3–4-inch pots. Choose a size that will allow space for two or three new growths before the rhizome reaches the edge of the pot. Position the division with the oldest backbulb against the edge, orienting the lead buds toward the middle. Most new growth comes from the

Laeliocattleya **Tropical Sunset 'Cheer Girl'**

leading edge of the rhizome, so this positioning gives the plants some room to grow. The best time to repot *Cattleyas* is just as new roots are evident—usually in spring, though some species and hybrids don't initiate new roots until the current crop of pseudobulbs has hardened. Medium-grade fir bark—with perhaps about 20% charcoal or charcoal plus perlite—is the standard medium for *Cattleyas,* and I recommend it, though I have tried pumice and tree fern. If you wish to grow a specimen-sized plant, consider potting it in a large cedar basket, which will give the plant room to stretch while preventing the center of the root zone from getting sodden and stagnant. I have grown a few plants mounted on vertical fireplace logs with an eyehook in the top, and they do exceedingly well this way if you can afford the space. If you choose a rot-resistant wood like white oak or locust, the plants can grow this way for years and years. You can grow mini-cats mounted on cork, though almost all of the species and hybrids are potted.

Chondrorhyncha (Chdrh) 🏳

(CON-DROE-RINE-KA)
SUBTRIBE: Zygopetalinae
NUMBER OF KNOWN SPECIES: About 30
NATIVE RANGE: Wet cloud forests from Mexico to Bolivia
SKILL LEVEL: Expert
GOOD INTRODUCTORY SPECIES: *Chondrorhyncha andreae,*
    C. chestertonii

Chondrorhynchas are very similar to *Cochleanthes* in overall appearance, flower carriage, and culture, though you can easily tell them apart because *Chondrorhynchas* lack pseudobulbs; their leaves grow in a tight, flattened fan with a nest of white roots spilling from its base. Single-flowered scapes grow out from between the outer leaf bases and stretch out just far enough to hold the flowers away from the leaves. The blooms look like a grain scoop, with a large ruffled or frilly lip capped by the two petals and the sepals bending backward out of the way. The flowers are typically white or yellowish, with the lip marked with brown, red, or pink blotches or spots. They favor wet cloud forests, so high humidity, even moisture, and moderate temperatures are necessary to keep them happy. Many are short enough to fit comfortably under fluorescent lights, and they thrive in enclosed artificial light setups with elevated humidity and a breezy atmosphere. Under such conditions the plants will grow on and off all year, sending out flowers in several flushes as new fans mature. Flower size is much the same throughout this genus, so the smaller species, like *C. ledyana, C. hirtzii,* and *C. velastiguii,* are the most desirable, as their 2–3-inch flowers are disproportionately large. The flowers look dwarfed on the 1-foot-tall (or taller) *C. ecuadorensis.*

Chondrorhyncha discolor 'Mountain Snow', a white form of a blue-violet species now usually listed as *Cochleanthes*

Some closely related, primarily Andean, genera have very similar cultural requirements.

Chaubardia (SHOW-BARD-EE-AH) contains only five or six species at the time of this writing, all vegetatively similar to *Cochleanthes.* They are notable among the subtribe for their generous flower production. One fan may carry up to ten one-flowered inflorescences among its leaves. The flowers are white, red-brown, or yellow. My favorite is *C. kluggii,* with its pure white blooms and blue-violet keel.

Chaubardiella (SHOW-BARD-EE-EL-AH) is a remarkable group of about ten species that produce small fans of 3–8-inch-long leaves and fascinating flowers on prostrate or pendent spikes. The flowers are thick and have a meaty red color with intricate barring and striping. Most inflorescences will rise above the rim of the pot, but a small basket will ensure that none gets caught inside the rim. *C. tigrina* is the easiest species to locate.

The genus *Huntleya* (HUNT-LEE-AH) includes about ten species that also have fan-shaped leaves and no pseudobulb.

The most commonly cultivated, and a spectacular orchid by any standard, is *H. wallisii*, with glistening, waxy, red, yellow, and white flowers almost 8 inches across. I came across one in a very wet low-elevation cloud forest in Ecuador, and it stood out like a large plastic starfish poised amid the overwhelming greenery. As on *Chondrorhynchas*, the flowers arise from between the leaves on short spikes.

Kefersteinia (KEF-ER-STINE-EE-AH) are also most abundant in the wet cloud forests of the Andes. Their fanlike leaves produce very attractive flowers in shades of white, green, yellow, and pink, often with darker stippling on the petals or a ruffled, keeled, or feathery lip. The blooms grow from the leaves on short, lax stems, clustering near the base in a nested display. On the whole, I think they are among the easiest of this group to cultivate.

CULTURE

Like most cloud forest species, *Chondrorhynchas* and their relatives prefer high humidity, moderate light, and strong air movement.

TEMPERATURE: Intermediate

LIGHT: Low (1,200–1,800 fc)

HUMIDITY, WATER, AND FERTILIZATION: Maintain humidity above 70% and water enough to keep the medium from ever drying out completely. Dilute fertilizer applied weekly (or very dilute fertilizer at every watering) will keep the plants growing evenly.

Kefersteinia mysticina

POTTING AND MEDIA: Use 2–4-inch pots filled with tree fern, NZ sphagnum, or another fine mix. I have also seen them growing well in Turface watered almost daily.

Chysis (Chy) ⚑

(KYE-SIS)

SUBTRIBE: Bletiinae

NUMBER OF KNOWN SPECIES: 5

NATIVE RANGE: Seasonally wet forests from Mexico to Venezuela and Peru

SKILL LEVEL: Beginner

GOOD INTRODUCTORY SPECIES: *Chysis bractescens*

Chysis species are an interesting lot. They appear cobbled together from spare parts obtained from several unrelated orchids. Their carrot-thick pseudobulbs are reminiscent of *Catasetums* in the way the leaf scars ring the swollen bulbs and in the way they summarily drop their leaves in autumn as the dry season approaches. Their flowers, however, have the blocky, squared-off shape and wraparound lip of some *Dendrobiums*. This incongruous union makes for plants that are a bit gawky and disproportionate, like adolescents after a growth spurt, but their ease of cultivation and big, waxy, very fragrant flowers earn them a place in many collections.

In the wild, these orchids grow on larger tree trunks in the humid shade of seasonally wet forests. The big, clublike pseudobulbs narrow to a thin base too weak to support the weight of the chubby cane, so they hang pendently or rest horizontally on a pot rim or potting mix. During the growing season, the new growths surge forth with a fan of large, pleated, light green leaves arrayed along the developing pseudobulb. When fully expanded, these bulbs can be over a foot long, with leaves a bit longer, so they do take up quite a bit of real estate at this time. The new growths tend to emerge partway up the older bulbs. Arching spikes of 2–3-inch-wide, white, green, or red-brown flowers spring from the previous year's pseudobulbs with the emerging leaves. The flowers are heavy in substance, long-lasting, and so redolent with citrus and musk that they perfume the room.

CULTURE

Like *Catasetums* (to which they are not related), these winter-dormant, deciduous plants can make good houseplants provided they can spend the summer outdoors in a warm, shaded spot. In the greenhouse they are best grown in hanging baskets in a fairly shaded location; the increased air movement will help discourage disease during the dormant season. Since the flowers are held upright, though, you will have to bring the blooming plants down onto a bench to enjoy them.

TEMPERATURE: Intermediate-warm. They grow at low eleva-

Chysis bractescens 'Longview' CCM/AOS

tions, so night temperatures should be above 65° during the growing season (if you are summering the plants outdoors, wait until the nights have warmed above 65° to leave them out). When dormant, they should tolerate night temperatures in the lower part of the intermediate range (58°–60°).

LIGHT: Low (1,000–1,800 fc)

HUMIDITY, WATER, AND FERTILIZATION: *Chysis* need fairly high humidity (more than 60%) once growth and bloom begin in spring, but they tolerate lower levels during the dormant season. It is important to provide copious water and regular doses of fertilizer when the plants are in active growth. I find that an hour-long soak in a 250-ppm N fertilizer solution (about 1 tsp/gal of liquid fertilizer) as new buds are swelling gets growth off to a good start, and it doesn't seem to affect flowering adversely in this genus. One of the nice things about raising these orchids in slatted baskets is that you can water them almost daily in summer without ill effect. As temperatures cool in fall, cut back on watering by half, letting the mix dry before wetting again. You should see the leaves quickly begin to turn yellow. As the leaves are shed, cut back on watering even further; watering once every seven

to fourteen days will keep the pseudobulbs from shriveling. Slowly increase watering again in the spring as the light gets stronger.

POTTING AND MEDIA: An 8–12-inch slatted basket is ideal. I use straight medium-grade fir bark, though some authors recommend adding moss to hold water during summer.

Cirrhaea (no abbr.)

(SUH-REE-AH)

SUBTRIBE: Stanhopeinae
NUMBER OF KNOWN SPECIES: 6
NATIVE RANGE: Brazil
SKILL LEVEL: Experienced
GOOD INTRODUCTORY SPECIES: *Cirrhaea dependens*

If you like bright green flowers, you might consider growing a *Cirrhaea* or two. Like their close relatives the *Gongoras*, these interesting plants produce long dangling chains of complex, upside-down flowers that look rather like a bunch of origami figures falling through space. A *Cirrhaea* invariably elicits comments along the lines of "wow!" or "coooool" at an orchid show or society meeting. They grow like miniature *Stanhopeas*, with pleated, oval pseudobulbs wrapped in a loose jacket of dry, frayed sheaths clustered tightly together. The younger growths sport a rather large, thin, pleated or veined leaf. The flowers are apple green and white, yellow-green, or some shade of reddish brown and are effective for about seven to ten days. The flower color is highly variable, especially among different clones of *C. dependens,* which may be bright green, yellow, or brown barred with white, among other colors.

CULTURE

Overall this is an easygoing genus, its main requirement being a perch that will allow the foot-long chains of flowers to hang unimpeded. This rules out all but greenhouses and larger indoor grow rooms as suitable places to raise them. When the inflorescence is developing in spring, take care not to shock the plant by moving it, shouting at it, or changing its environment drastically, as the spike may shrivel up and depart from this cruel world.

TEMPERATURE: Intermediate

LIGHT: Somewhat bright (1,200–2,000 fc)

HUMIDITY, WATER, AND FERTILIZATION: Humidity should remain high when the plants are in active growth or bloom. *Cirrhaeas* should receive ample water when in active growth, and less during winter, to give the plants a rest before flowering; water just enough to keep the pseudobulbs from shriveling noticeably. They are sensitive to overfertilization, especially when flowering; fertilize lightly during periods of active vegetative growth and

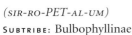

Cirrhaea saccata

Cirrhopetalum **Elizabeth Ann 'Buckleberry'** AM & CCM/AOS

discontinue fertilizer altogether from late winter until blooms have finished.

- **POTTING AND MEDIA:** Slatted baskets are the ideal containers, as they are less likely to obstruct the pendent racemes. NZ sphagnum or a mix of sphagnum and fine fir bark is a suitable medium.

Cirrhopetalum (Cirr)

(SIR-RO-PET-AL-UM)

SUBTRIBE: Bulbophyllinae

NUMBER OF KNOWN SPECIES: About 140

NATIVE RANGE: Southeast Asia

SKILL LEVEL: Experienced

GOOD INTRODUCTORY SPECIES: *Cirrhopetalum auratum, C. makoyanum, C. umbellatum*

While some authorities lump this genus in with the already overwhelmingly large *Bulbophyllum,* I am treating it separately because I think the plants are distinctive enough in floral appearance and culture to be handled as a different genus. *Cirrhopetalums* look just like any other *Bulbophyllum* when out of flower; the intertwining rhizomes are punctuated at intervals by round, oval, or four-sided pseudobulbs carrying a

single thick oval or oblong leaf. Their flowers are instantly recognizable because the blooms are arranged in a circle or semicircle at the tip of a thin stem. The flowers are quite fantastic, thanks mostly to the lateral sepals, which grow out of all proportion to the other segments. The two sepals are like long, tapered wings held together as one to form an imitation lip striped with red, yellow, and/or white. They enfold the small lip, petals, and dorsal sepal, any of which may be decorated with tiny feather boas of delicate hairs. I imagine these hairs are meant to imitate fungal threads or insect antennae, as these baroque blooms are pollinated by small flies or gnats. The fused lateral sepals jut out horizontally, but their tips are more or less drawn out into dangling, threadlike tails. The semicircular arrangement of the flowers has a charming resemblance to a daisy or pinwheel hung from a thread.

CULTURE

I have raised several *Cirrhopetalums* variously on a windowsill, under lights, and in a greenhouse, and I think they are equally easy to grow (though not necessarily to flower) in all three places. Most of the species produce wandering rhizomes with pseudobulbs spaced 1–2 inches apart, so they cannot be contained in a pot for long. Slatted baskets, which allow the roots to burrow in from the sides, are the best choice indoors. In a greenhouse or grow room, they are easily accommodated on cork or tree-fern slabs as well as in baskets. My main difficulty is getting the darn things to flower—a big problem, since they are not raised for their foliage! My first foray into this genus was *C. sikkimense*, which grew well in a pot and then in a 4-inch basket on my windowsill, but after three years it still hadn't produced a flower. At the time, I was managing an orchid greenhouse, so off went the little plant to a favored life under glass. The following autumn my plant erupted with a dozen spikes of pinwheeling red and white flowers! I have had similar experiences with its relatives, and I suspect that to flower well, *Cirrhopetalums* require a large diurnal temperature change (more than 10°F) and/or a cool rest in autumn. These conditions are easier to provide in a greenhouse, but on a sill you might try placing the plant very close to the window, where the temperature variation is more extreme.

TEMPERATURE: Warm to intermediate-cool, depending on the species

LIGHT: Somewhat bright (1,800–2,800 fc)

HUMIDITY, WATER, AND FERTILIZATION: They aren't too particular about humidity as long as it stays above 40%. Water enough to keep the pseudobulbs from shriveling. Use more water during the summer, when most growth occurs, and apply a weak solution of fertilizer regularly.

POTTING AND MEDIA: If you don't mind repotting and dividing the plants every eighteen to twenty-four months, most *Cirrhopetalums* can be maintained in 2–4-inch clay pots. For specimens, you'll need 4–6-inch slatted baskets or a 4 × 6-inch or larger slab. Pot in a fine medium such as tree fern or fine-grade bark.

Cochleanthes (Cnths)

(*KOCK-LEE-AN-THESE*)

SUBTRIBE: Zygopetalinae

NUMBER OF KNOWN SPECIES: 15

NATIVE RANGE: West Indies, Central and South America

SKILL LEVEL: Experienced

GOOD INTRODUCTORY SPECIES: *Cochleanthes amazonica*

Big flowers on small plants are always cute, and this genus is certainly cute. *Cochleanthes* look like many other leafy sympodial orchids when out of flower—one or two long, medium green leaves of thin substance sit on little oval or rounded, flattened pseudobulbs nested in tight clumps. Additional sheathing leaves persist in two ranks on either side of the newer pseudobulbs, lending them a fan-shaped appearance. *Cochleanthes* are small to miniature plants that grow on and off all through the year, and as each new growth matures, it produces one enormous flower with a large, frilly lip backed by smaller petals and sepals of the same or a lighter hue. The

size of the flowers and the way they hang from the plants on short stems have a very endearing puppy dog quality.

CULTURE

I don't consider these beginner orchids, but they are not too difficult once you have some experience. They hail from low- to moderate-elevation cloud forests, so the main challenge is to provide reasonably high humidity and a damp but well-aerated substrate throughout the year. Their small stature and habit of growing and blooming throughout the year make them excellent subjects for enclosed artificial light cases or grow rooms.

TEMPERATURE: Warm to intermediate (probably best at intermediate temperatures)

LIGHT: Low (1,500–1,800 fc)

HUMIDITY, WATER, AND FERTILIZATION: Maintain humidity above 70% if possible, and water just as the surface of the medium has begun to dry. In small pots, water two to three times a week. Mounted plants should be watered daily. I find that this genus is sensitive to poor water quality (which shows up as leaf-tip dieback and root loss). Another danger is water standing in the sheathing leaf bases, which will quickly cause the pseudobulbs to rot.

Cochleanthes amazonica 'Full Moon' HCC/AOS

Plenty of air movement is the best preventive measure, along with adequate humidity. Apply weak fertilizer twice a month throughout the year.

POTTING AND MEDIA: Because *Cochleanthes* produce their large flowers on short stems, choose a fairly small pot so that the inflorescences can dangle free of the rim. Small pots also provide better airflow around the leaf bases where water accumulates and are harder to overwater. You can accommodate the plants on a moisture-retentive mount such as a tree-fern plaque or a twig with a liberal moss pad. Mounting them displays their flowers to great effect but does require that you water almost daily.

Cochlioda (Cda)

(KOCK-LEE-OH-DA)

SUBTRIBE: Oncidiinae

NUMBER OF KNOWN SPECIES: 5

NATIVE RANGE: High-elevation cloud forests in the Andes of Ecuador, Peru, and Bolivia

SKILL LEVEL: Expert

GOOD INTRODUCTORY SPECIES: *Cochlioda rosea*

This small genus related to *Odontoglossum* is known for intensely colored red, pink, or orange flowers designed to lure

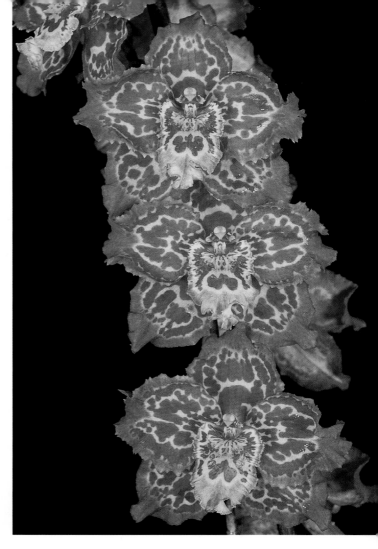

Odontioda Mem. Kendrick Williams 'Mardigras'
HCC/AOS

Cochlioda rosea

warm-blooded hummingbirds, which are better able than insects to fly in the cool to cold temperatures found at the high elevations where *Cochliodas* grow. From this sentence you can glean the two most salient points regarding these orchids: bold, beautiful flowers and a preference for consistently cool, misty conditions that are difficult for many growers to provide. More common than the true species in cultivation are hybrids between them and *Oncidium, Miltonia*, and *Odontoglossum*. However, *Cochlioda*'s intolerance for heat carries through into most of the complex hybrids, so even if you grow only hybrids, you'll want some understanding of the species' needs. The various *Odontiodas* (*Odontoglossum* × *Cochlioda*) are especially colorful, with big, frilly blooms patterned in just about every color save blue, black, and green.

Cochliodas are small to medium-sized plants, with oval, flattened pseudobulbs set in a tight row one after the next. The plants do not branch as freely as *Oncidiums* and some

Odontoglossums, but with good culture, a nice clump will eventually develop. The flower spike arises from inside one of the sheathing leaves that remain around the pseudobulb for the first year. The flowers are heavy for the wiry stem, so they tend to arch out and down, arranging themselves in two ranks, as *Phalaenopsis* flowers do. The blooms are thick in substance, with pointed petals and sepals and a larger, somewhat frilled or keeled lip with a contrasting spot of gold or orange in its center. The blooms last for quite a long time if kept cool, so even though they bloom sequentially, eventually all of the flowers on the spike may be open at the same time. Like most of this subtribe, *Cochliodas* produce lots of thin, wiry, white roots. The roots appear as the new growths are maturing.

CULTURE

If you can provide consistently cool, humid conditions, this genus is reasonably easy to grow. I suppose that's like saying "If you have four arms, cooking is easy." Some of the best plants are raised in the San Francisco Bay area and the Pacific Northwest, as well as in the United Kingdom, where summers remain cool. For the rest of us, it's a challenge to get *Cochliodas* through the summer with their spirit intact. I have been able to grow them in an enclosed light chamber, though by the end of summer they drop leaves and look to be at their wit's end. The complex hybrids—especially *Oncidioda* (*Oncidium* × *Cochlioda*) and *Miltonioda* (*Miltonia* × *Cochlioda*) are easier to grow. Allow only well-established, healthy plants to bloom, clipping off the developing inflorescences of weaker plants.

TEMPERATURE: Cool

LIGHT: Somewhat bright (1,500–2,000 fc)

HUMIDITY, WATER, AND FERTILIZATION: They need high humidity (70%–100%), consistent watering all year, and moderate fertilization during active growth.

POTTING AND MEDIA: Underpot *Cochliodas* in 2–4-inch clay or plastic pots, using a fairly fine medium like tree fern, NZ sphagnum, perlite, and/or bark. Water just enough to keep the two leading pseudobulbs plump. I have never tried the plants on a mount, though tree-fern plaques seem appropriate.

Coelogyne (no abbr.)

(*SEE-LODGE-IN-EE*)

SUBTRIBE: Coelogyninae

NUMBER OF KNOWN SPECIES: More than 100

NATIVE RANGE: Asian tropics, Indonesia, and Pacific islands

SKILL LEVEL: Beginner

GOOD INTRODUCTORY SPECIES: *Coelogyne cristata, C. fimbriata, C. flaccida, C. lawrenceana*

The fourth or fifth orchid I ever bought was a *Coelogyne ochracea.* I purchased it in the spring of 1986 on the recommendation of a local orchid nursery owner, Jim Rice. I liked the way the plant looked, with clustered pseudobulbs that resembled translucent green dates, topped by two long, pleated, rather thin-textured ³/₄-inch-thick leaves. Jim had quite a few of the plants in his greenhouses, which meant that they were either very popular or very unpopular. I kept the plant on the windowsill in my bedroom, and after a month or so, pointed spears began appearing from the bases of the lead pseudobulbs, often two per growth. When they were 3 inches tall, the spears started to unroll like paper tubes, revealing themselves to be new pairs of leaves surrounded by several sheathing bracts. I was beside myself when I noticed that from within each tube was emerging an inflorescence of a half-dozen buds coated in sticky sap. The flowers quickly outstripped the expanding leaves, opening up crystalline white with a complex orange and yellow pattern on the lip. The clump was literally buried in these flowers, which emitted a wonderfully sweet, musky fragrance during the day. This got me hooked on the genus, and I have grown about a dozen species, though I have to say that *C. ochracea* is still my favorite.

Coelogyne cristata

Coelogynes are sympodial, with round or oval pseudobulbs topped by one or two long, thin leaves with prominent parallel veins. One group, which includes *C. ochracea, C. mooreana, C. odoratissima,* and the most famous, *C. cristata,* has crystalline white flowers and orange or yellow keels on the lip. Others, like *C. dayana* and *C. massangeana,* have greenish yellow to brown flowers that hang in long, dramatic chains; *C. pandurata, C. mayeriana,* and *C. parishii* are among a group of "black orchids," with leprechaun green flowers and lips marked with purple so dark as to appear almost black.

CULTURE

Over their wide range, *Coelogynes* grow in a number of different habitats. In general they produce flushes of new growth followed by periods of relative inactivity. In all the species I have raised, the flowers appear out of the unrolling new leaves,

which may begin growing in winter, spring, summer, or fall, depending on the species. Most *Coelogynes* have a strong fragrance, and some, like *C. cristata,* are among the most intoxicatingly fragrant orchids. The species with pendent flowers and those that produce long, adventuresome rhizomes are difficult to accommodate on a windowsill, but the plants are generally easy to cultivate if you select the ones best adapted to your temperature range. Warm-growing species will grow almost continually, though not all new growths will produce flowers. The cool-growing plants from the Himalayas need a somewhat dry, cool winter rest to initiate flower buds, while the intermediate growers fall somewhere in between.

TEMPERATURE: Warm to cool, depending on the species. The cool-growing species require chilling mainly during winter to initiate flowers, and they are reasonably tolerant of high temperatures during the summer as long as you can chill them sufficiently during winter.

LIGHT: Somewhat bright (1,500–2,500 fc)

HUMIDITY, WATER, AND FERTILIZATION: Humidity in the range of 50%–70% is sufficient, though the cool growers tolerate lower levels when winter-dormant. Water quality is a real issue with this genus. Poor-quality water will cause the leaf tips to slowly but persistently die back, and many a *Coelogyne* appears on the show table with leaf tips clipped back like the ears of a Doberman puppy. It is not fatal, but it is unsightly. I am not sure whether the dieback stems from high levels of salt, chlorine, or fluoride, but I have found it more severe in some places than others as I have moved around. Rainwater or RO water does cure the problem effectively. The fuzzy roots of *Coelogynes* want to be kept evenly moist but not sodden, and the plants will bloom luxuriantly if given moderate fertilizer regularly when in active vegetative growth. The sticky sap that covers expanding leaves and flowers can bind them if it is not washed away eventually. A trip to the sink will suffice.

POTTING AND MEDIA: Most species are best accommodated in either plastic or clay pots filled with a fairly fine medium like tree fern, NZ sphagnum, and/or fine fir bark. I prefer plastic, as I can water the plants thoroughly, then let them soak it up for three days to a week before the next watering. The "walking" *Coelogynes* such as *C. cristata* are difficult to keep in pots, so slatted or moss-lined baskets are a better choice. Be sure to hang or raise the pendent-flowered species up on a pedestal as the first buds appear. This genus is notoriously difficult to divide and transplant, but as with many aspects of orchid culture, you'll do best if your timing is right. I prefer not to repot them every year, but they grow quickly and are very intolerant of a stale mix, so you must repot every two to three years. Try to do it when you see a new flush of

Coelogyne **Linda Buckley** (*mooreana* × *cristata*)

growth spears elongating, and leave at least six to ten pseudobulbs in a clump. Smaller divisions will be set back badly and take years to regain their former exuberance. Although it is necessary to pick or shake out some of the old mix, do this gingerly and don't feel that you have to pick out every last piece, because the thin, hairy roots cling heartily and can easily be damaged when torn from the old medium.

Comparettia (Comp) 🔦 🚩

(*COM-PAR-ET-TIA*)

SUBTRIBE: Oncidiinae

NUMBER OF KNOWN SPECIES: 10

NATIVE RANGE: Primarily the Andes of South America, but *C. falcata* is widespread throughout the American tropics.

SKILL LEVEL: Experienced

GOOD INTRODUCTORY SPECIES: *Comparettia falcata*

Comparettias are flamboyant cousins of the *Oncidiums*, boasting flowers in intense shades of pink, orange, or red suspended on thin stems. They are small-twig epiphytes found commonly in tropical fruit orchards as well as forests. From a thick nest of fine roots grow thick, straplike or oblong leaves attached to small, almost vestigial pseudobulbs. Wiry inflorescences arise from the papery sheaths that clothe the pseudobulb and grow to a foot or more in length before sprouting small clusters of colorful dancing-doll flowers with a big two-lobed lip. The base of the lip forms a long nectar spur that is wrapped by the lateral sepals, making the spur a prominent feature in profile. Much like equitant *Oncidiums*, the brilliantly colored flowers appear to hang in space like tiny mobiles by Alexander Calder. Like many twig epiphytes, they are flowering fools, for life on a twig is precarious, and they never know if the next breeze will be their last. This devil-may-care attitude means that you must prevent them from literally blooming themselves to death. A healthy plant with more than two leaves and a good nest of white roots can support multiple inflorescences, but a smaller plant may need to have some buds or the whole spike removed to preserve its food reserves.

Ionopsis (*EYE-ON-OP-SIS*) is a closely related genus of five species with the same cultural requirements and overall appearance as *Comparettia*. *Ionopsis utricularioides* is a common and widespread twig epiphyte that ranges throughout the American tropics. It favors orchards and garden hedges, so it may well be one of the first epiphytic orchids most people encounter on a visit to the New World tropics. The leaves that subtend the pseudobulb remain active, and no leaves are produced from the top of the pseudobulb, unlike *Comparettia*. The ³/₄-inch flowers are similar in shape to *Comparettia*'s and pink with deeper pink veins, concentrating to a rose-red

Comparettia speciosa

Rodrettia **Pretty in Pink**

toward the center. It blooms for a long period during the warmer months, and like *Comparettia* sometimes blooms itself to death in its exuberance. Overall it is easy to cultivate —easier, I think, than its sister genus.

Rodriguezia (ROD-REH-GEEZ-EE-AH) is another related genus that is widespread in the American tropics. The plants produce a few more flowers per pendent spike, the blooms ranging from white to pink and carmine. The petals and sepals are more developed than *Comparettia*'s, so the blooms are larger and fuller. They require similar conditions.

CULTURE

Comparettias require a damp, airy atmosphere that is difficult to achieve on a windowsill. In an enclosed light box or a greenhouse, they grow very well if mounted and misted daily. If you can keep them healthy, they should live for years, but they easily suffer setbacks (desiccation, root loss, excessive flowering) that are difficult to recover from. They are quick to mature from seed, however.

TEMPERATURE: Intermediate

LIGHT: Bright (2,000–3,000 fc)

HUMIDITY, WATER, AND FERTILIZATION: High humidity (above 70%), strong air movement, and daily watering or misting are necessary to keep mounted plants from desiccating. Plants in containers should be watered thoroughly, then the medium allowed to dry almost completely before watering again. Fertilize lightly when in active growth.

POTTING AND MEDIA: I have raised *Comparettias* in 2–3-inch clay pots using a mixture of tree fern and NZ sphagnum plus perlite, though they really prefer to be mounted on a small branch or slab of tree fern. Since their pseudobulbs are so small in relation to the leaves, they should never be allowed to dry out completely; however, a sodden mix quickly leads to root loss. Even in a pot, many roots will simply set out into the air, and these should be misted. A pad of moss at the base of a newly mounted plant will help the roots establish. Division is difficult but rarely necessary, as bigger plants are more resilient and bloom more robustly.

Constantia (Const) 🔔 🏴

(CON-STANT-EE-AH)

SUBTRIBE: Laeliinae

NUMBER OF KNOWN SPECIES: 4

NATIVE RANGE: Brazil

SKILL LEVEL: Expert

GOOD INTRODUCTORY SPECIES: *Constantia cipoensis*

Constantia is a small genus of specialized miniature epiphytes that grow in fire-prone mountainous regions of Brazil. They

Constantia cipoensis 'Greentree' CBM/AOS

grow only on the trunks of *Vellozia*, a yucca-like, fire-adapted shrub or tree with fibrous, spongy bark and beautiful flowers reminiscent of amaryllis. It is a mystery why the *Constantias* are so particular, but it is very difficult to cultivate them on anything but slabs or sections of *Vellozia* bark. Occasionally these charming little plants are available from Brazilian nurseries, but as far as I can tell, only as wild-collected plants still attached to the section of *Vellozia* they were found growing on. The plants form flattened mats of densely packed, pea-sized pseudobulbs that creep over the surface of the wood. The youngest few pseudobulbs are topped by one or two thick, gray-green leaves with a strong central crease. The whole plant may be only $3/4$ inch high, and one to three new leads are produced each season. A single, dainty white flower emerges from the small sheath where the leaf bases meet. The pseudobulbs produced in the wild are generally tougher and more congested than those that grow under cultivation (that makes wild-collected plants—even after a year in a nursery—easy to spot). A few fat roots cling tightly to the *Vellozia* bark or work underneath its outer layers.

CULTURE

Constantia is one of those challenging genera that attract the expert grower of miniatures, but I worry that wild collection is putting pressure on these uncommon plants; I fear that most of the plants wither after a year or two under cultivation. Perhaps intrepid orchidists in their home country have now figured out the secret to successful cultivation.

TEMPERATURE: Intermediate to warm

LIGHT: Very bright (3,000–4,000 fc). Very bright light is necessary to keep the growth tight and leaves thick. I was able to accommodate them under HID lamps (notice the past tense), as long as I hung them within 16 inches of the fixture. The shorter days of autumn initiate flowering.

HUMIDITY, WATER, AND FERTILIZATION: Fairly high humidity (70%–80%) coupled with strong air movement is ideal. Water enough to thoroughly dampen the mount, then let it dry completely. The plants are not heavy feeders.

POTTING AND MEDIA: The plants must be grown mounted, preferably on *Vellozia* wood, which is not commonly available outside of Brazil. I have been able to grow and bloom *C. cipoensis,* the most commonly available species, but after a few years the mount begins to decay, and the real dilemma is what to do next. Since the roots are so entwined in the fibrous bark, it is very difficult to remove the plant without damaging most of them. If you have to move the plant, do so just as new roots are evident on the newest pseudobulbs; if possible, use a small saw to slice off the outer section of *Vellozia* to which the plant is attached. I have not succeeded in reestablishing one, but a friend tied a carefully excised clump onto a blueberry slab with so-so results. If the plant begins to grow away from the *Vellozia,* it may be possible to train it to a new mount before removing it from the old.

Coryanthes (Crths) 🏳

(COR-EE-AN-THEES)

SUBTRIBE: Stanhopeinae
NUMBER OF KNOWN SPECIES: About 28
NATIVE RANGE: American tropics
SKILL LEVEL: Expert
GOOD INTRODUCTORY SPECIES: *Coryanthes speciosa*

The bucket orchids, as *Coryanthes* are called, are implausible plants seemingly dreamed up by a science fiction writer with a love of the bizarre. They are imposing epiphytes resembling *Stanhopeas* in form, with large, pleated leaves perched atop ridged, rounded, 2-inch-wide pseudobulbs. The pseudobulbs cluster tightly together and are practically obscured by a dense nest of roots that sprout from the plant in all directions. In the wild, the roots provide a haven for certain species of ants, which build large nests in the tangle; in return they protect the orchid from would-be browsers and deposit their nutritious wastes where the roots can easily sop them up. The ants also produce quantities of formic acid, which lowers the pH of the root zone quite markedly. *Coryanthes* produce few-flowered, pendent inflorescences that meander down through the roots before poking out and unfolding below. The flowers look like origami swans, doves, bats, and butterflies. When you look at a flower, it is at first difficult to tell what is lip, petal, or column. On close inspection, it is evident that the spotted yellow, white, red, or orange flowers have petals shaped like wings or ears that sweep backward with the sepals. The lip resembles a big ladle, with a handle attaching it to the column and a large basin or bucket suspended below. Two spigots on the column drip-drop-drip a watery stew rich in chemical attractants into the basin, quickly filling it up after the flower opens. The pheromones are needed by male euglossine bees (big tropical bees resembling bumblebees). The bees, which land on the flower and frantically try to gather pheromones to attract a mate, often slip from the waxy folds and fall into the pool. Unable to fly when wet, they have to pass the pollinia as they climb out along a specified path; in the process, the pollinia are glued to their backs to be ready for their next dunking.

CULTURE

Success with this genus requires duplicating the unusual combination of high fertility (from ant wastes) and a very acidic substrate rich in formic acid. Slatted or wire baskets are necessary to permit the pendent inflorescences to develop properly. NZ sphagnum is acidic enough and works well, but if you have hard water, you should water the plant once a month with white vinegar diluted 3:1 with water to lower the pH. Many liquid fertilizers also help lower pH. Because of their size and need for basket culture, *Coryanthes* are difficult to handle indoors; I recommend them only to greenhouse or outdoor growers.

TEMPERATURE: Intermediate to warm
LIGHT: Somewhat bright (1,800–2,200 fc)
HUMIDITY, WATER, AND FERTILIZATION: Maintain humidity in the 60%–80% range, water when the mix begins to dry, and fertilize regularly with a balanced liquid; *Coryanthes* are heavy feeders.
POTTING AND MEDIA: See comments under Culture.

Coryanthes macrantha

Cycnoches (Cyc) ❀ 🏳

(SIC-NO-CHEESE)

SUBTRIBE: Catasetinae

NUMBER OF KNOWN SPECIES: 22

NATIVE RANGE: American tropics

SKILL LEVEL: Beginner

GOOD INTRODUCTORY SPECIES: *Cycnoches loddigesii, C. chlo-rochilon,* and *C. warscewiczii* in section *Eu-cycnoches,* and *C. egertonianum* in section *Heteranthae*

This small genus has evolved for pollination by euglossine bees, and, as with the unrelated *Coryanthes,* the flowers have assumed fanciful shapes that seem to have more in common with abstract sculpture than with the archetypal orchid bloom. They are called swan orchids, and indeed the lip and column in species such as *Cycnoches ventricosum* and *C. loddigesii* resemble a miniature swan with wings folded and long neck curved backward as if to groom itself. The lip is quite remarkable, looking as if it has been carved from a small piece of ivory. The color of the flowers ranges from deep red and bronze through green and white. I find that the subdued hues add to the attractiveness of the flowers, because they don't distract the eye from the elegant form of the swept-back tepals, the curving column, and the sculptural lip.

As with their relatives the *Catesetums,* these deciduous orchids bear dimorphic male and female flowers on separate spikes. In vegetative habit, they look nearly identical to *Catasetums,* with spindle-shaped, 4–12-inch-tall pseudobulbs, the youngest lined with large, pleated leaves. A plant may produce male and female flowers in different years; it rarely produces them at the same time. There are two sections within the genus. Plants in the first, section *Eu-cycnoches,* produce a few large male flowers and, rarely, female flowers that are similar in overall size and arrangement. The male flowers are usu-

***Cycnodes* Jumbo Jewel 'Sunset Valley Orchids'**
AM/AOS, a *Cycnoches* hybrid

ally 3–5 inches across and gathered in arching spikes that appear at the upper end of the newly matured pseudobulb. The sight of six to twelve of these large and intricate blooms is not one you will quickly forget. The plants in section *Heteranthae* send out long, pendent spikes of smaller (1–2-inch) male flowers and, rarely, a few larger female flowers. The interesting taxonomic problem—especially in section *Heteranthae*—is that the male flowers of different species are very similar in appearance. The female flowers are distinctive, but since they are rarely seen, it is often very difficult to determine which species you are growing.

Among *Cycnoches* growers, there has been much speculation regarding the best way to trigger the production of female flowers. Getting your plant to bloom female is an achievement and also helps confirm its identity. Furthermore, you may be able to produce seed if you have pollen available. It makes sense that male flowers are more common, both in the wild and in cultivation, as they are much less costly to produce than a seed capsule. These conservative orchids must be particularly robust and growing under ideal conditions before they will squander their resources on seed production. Accordingly, the best way to produce female flowers is to grow your plants in very bright light (3,000–4,000 fc), fertilize them heavily when active root growth begins, and don't divide plants that have fewer than four pseudobulbs.

CULTURE

As long as you can avoid overwatering your plants during winter dormancy, *Cycnoches* will prove to be rewarding and

Cycnoches haagii

easy to grow. They are not really ideal for under-lights culture because of their size and light requirements, but you can raise them on a windowsill and summer them outdoors. In a greenhouse, hang them from the purlins to put them up in the warmth and light and to allow the pendent inflorescences to develop unimpeded. Watch for spider mites, which love the thin foliage.

TEMPERATURE: Warm during active growth and intermediate during winter dormancy

LIGHT: Intense (3,000–5,000 fc)

HUMIDITY, WATER, AND FERTILIZATION: *Cycnoches* begin growth as the weather warms in spring. Mist the plants every day or two once you see new buds swelling, but do not begin watering in earnest until the growths are 1–2 inches tall and the new roots have sprouted out. It is very easy to overwater dormant plants, resulting in rot. Once the new leads get started, they require ample water and fertilizer to fuel their rapid expansion. As the last leaves expand and the new pseudobulb swells, you will see small nubs swelling about midway up. These are the developing spikes, which will usually open when the plants are still in leaf or just after leaf drop. In early fall, usually after the long-lasting, heavy-sweet-smelling flowers have faded, start reducing water; cease completely when all the leaves have dropped. Average orchid humidity is adequate year-round.

POTTING AND MEDIA: The roots are deciduous, so you can repot yearly just as new growth begins in spring. For all but the largest specimens, 4-inch clay pots are ideal. I prefer a fine medium like fine fir bark, NZ sphagnum, or tree fern, because the plants need quite a bit of water during the growing season.

Cymbidium (Cym) 🎴 🏳

(*SIM-BID-EE-UM*)

SUBTRIBE: Cyrtopodiinae

NUMBER OF KNOWN SPECIES: 44

NATIVE RANGE: Tropics of Asia, Indonesia, Australia, and India

SKILL LEVEL: Beginner

GOOD INTRODUCTORY SPECIES: The legion of large- and small-flowered hybrids are the best starting point.

Most growers do not have room for a large collection of standard *Cymbidiums* anymore, but they grow very well indoors and bloom spectacularly in the depths of winter, so I urge you to try one or two if space permits. The large-flowered species and hybrids are also large plants. These **SEMITERRESTRIAL** orchids produce 3–5-inch-long, egg-shaped pseudobulbs wrapped by the bases of two ranks of long, grasslike leaves. The largest leaves grow to 3 feet or so, and this is typically the height of the potted plants as well. After a chilling period in fall and winter, sticky, pointed shoots become evident at the base of the lead pseudobulbs, and these quickly stretch up and out, soon unfurling sprays of 4-inch, slightly cupped flowers in shades of white, pink, red, yellow, or green. The **SCAPES** are long-lasting—even indoors if the temperatures are below 70° —and they look beautiful surrounded by the grasslike leaves. Standard species and hybrids reached their zenith of popularity after World War II, both as a florist crop and as a favorite among hobbyists. As heating costs have risen and greenhouses have shrunk, breeders have crossed the big boys with smaller species, creating a whole line of compact (some people call

Cymbidium elegans

them miniature, but I consider that term misleading) hybrids that are about half the size of the standards. Many of the smaller hybrids have "blood" from warm-growing parents coursing through their veins, and this circumvents the other problem with the standards—the need to provide adequate chilling to initiate bloom. The smaller hybrids have renewed interest in the genus and allowed a new generation of growers access to these elegant orchids. *Cymbidium insigne* and *C. tracyanum* are robust, showy plants and parents of many of the larger hybrids. *C. devonianum* and *C. tigrinum* are smaller, spring-blooming species needing intermediate temperatures. *C. finlaysonianum* is a pendent-flowered warm grower that is on the smaller side.

Culture

A nice feature of *Cymbidiums* from a beginner's point of view is that they are usually grown as semiterrestrials whether or not they grow this way in the wild. In other words, you can water and pot them more like a typical houseplant. A south- or southeast-facing window is perfect for *Cymbidiums,* and the smallest species and hybrids can be raised under lights. If

Cymbidium **England's Rose 'Green Light'**

you live in a climate suitable for summering orchids outdoors, by all means move your *Cymbidiums* out once the weather moderates and the danger of frost has passed. Pick a spot that receives morning sun and is lightly shaded for the rest of the day. New growths are produced very rapidly during warm weather. Each lead pseudobulb will spawn one or two new growths that will bloom with one or two spikes in season. Standard as well as many compact hybrids require a period of chilling in fall and early winter for successful bloom. Leave your plants outdoors in fall until temperatures fall below 45° or there is a danger of frost, then move them inside to a cool spot such as an unheated sunroom, where temperatures stay below 60°. Reduce watering by half and stop fertilization entirely during this rest period. Many of the newer compact hybrids do not need as severe a rest period; the normal drops in winter temperature combined with a reduction in the frequency of watering should trigger bloom.

Because *Cymbidiums* have been an important florist's crop for so many years, much of the early research into orchid nutrition and disease was carried out on this genus. The first orchid virus to be widely recognized was Cymbidium Mosaic Virus (CMV), and although this and subsequently identified viruses have been found to infect most orchids, the early notoriety has left the impression in many people's minds that *Cymbidiums* are particularly susceptible to virus. That is not true, but I have seen many *Cymbidiums,* especially older clones that have been passed around for decades, exhibiting the telltale streaking and necrosis associated with CMV. Often the plants are so vigorous that they grow well even with a large virus load, but you don't want to have infected plants that could spread the disease to others in your collection. If you

Cymbidium **Street Hawk 'Dark Night'**

notice light-colored or brown streaks on leaves, have the plant tested by a lab or take a sample to someone who can make an accurate assessment. Infected plants should be discarded—pot and all.

TEMPERATURE: Warm to cool. Most prefer intermediate temperatures during the growing season and cool to cool-intermediate temperatures during winter.

LIGHT: Bright to very bright (2,000–4,000 fc)

HUMIDITY, WATER, AND FERTILIZATION: Provide average orchid humidity (50%–70%), water when the mix has dried to a depth of 1–2 inches, and apply a moderate amount of liquid fertilizer throughout the growing season. *Cymbidiums* and *Phaius* were the two genera that responded well to my experiments with controlled-release fertilizers (CRFs) as a substitute for liquid feeding. I sprinkled 1 tsp over the surface of a 6-inch pot and 2 tsp in a 12-inch pot once a year and had excellent growth and flowering. CRFs work well because they stop releasing in cool to cold weather, when the orchids are dormant, but they are too strong for most orchids, especially epiphytes.

POTTING AND MEDIA: In the wild, most *Cymbidium* species send their big, fleshy roots into duffy humus or over moss-covered rocks and tree limbs. The presence of large pseudobulbs is a further clue that these are not true terrestrials, and the pseudobulbs allow the plants to weather occasional dry spells without problems. Choose a potting mix that retains moisture but is still porous. I usually mix 1 part medium-grade fir bark with 2 parts Pro-Mix, though most media designed for *Paphiopedilums* should work fine. The standards need large pots for their huge root systems. A three-bulb division needs at least an 8-inch pot, and large specimens are often potted in 14-inch pots or 3-gallon (or larger) tubs. Compact species and hybrids are satisfied with 6–8-inch pots. The summer-blooming, pendent-flowered types like *C. devonianum* can be grown in pots as well, because the inflorescences grow up for a time, clearing the edge of the pot before arching down. However, when potting the pendent species and hybrids, make sure to set the crown at or above the rim of the container and slope the mix down toward the sides. This will provide a gentler pad for the spike base to rest on.

Dividing *Cymbidiums* is relatively simple. Unpot the plant, tease out the old mix, then use a sharp sterile knife or pruners to cut the short rhizome so that you come away with two- to three-bulb lead divisions. Backbulbs will often regrow, especially if they still have active roots. I prefer to divide and repot in early spring, just as new growth is evident but flowering has finished. Set the bulbs so that their bases are at or just below soil level.

Cyrtopodium (Cyrt) 🏳

(SIR-TOW-POH-DEE-UM)

SUBTRIBE: Cyrtopodiinae

NUMBER OF KNOWN SPECIES: 32

NATIVE RANGE: American tropics

SKILL LEVEL: Experienced

GOOD INTRODUCTORY SPECIES: *Cyrtopodium punctatum*

Although allied to *Cymbidium*, the New World *Cyrtopodiums* look more like *Catasetums* on steroids to me. They range from Florida and the Caribbean through Mexico to Central and South America, preferring warm, seasonally dry, and even fire-prone habitats. These are generally big plants. A well-grown *C. punctatum* can top 5 feet and produce a glorious branched, upright inflorescence of equal height. Others, like *C. belizensis*, are about half that size, and still others, like the terrestrial *C. paludicolum*, produce spikes more than 7 feet tall! The flowers are 1–2 inches across, with a heavy, waxy substance

Cyrtopodium andersonii

and colors ranging from green and burgundy to bright yellow. The beautiful South American *C. hatschbachii* sends up tall sprays of soft pink flowers. The segments resemble those of some of the *Oncidiums* in shape, with rounded ends and smooth or wavy margins. The prominent and often sharply contrasting lip has two wings that reach up around the column like arms raised in a cheer. Out of flower, the first things you notice about these orchids are the impressive spindle-shaped pseudobulbs. Ranging between 8 and 48 inches in height, these water tanks are wrapped in papery sheaths that are the remains of the first leaves produced on the new growth. Only the larger leaves, toward the top of the pseudobulb, remain through the season. Although they are very thin and palmlike, they can tolerate nearly the full intensity of the tropical sun, and in such situations they develop rather stiffly into a two-ranked herringbone pattern.

At the end of the rainy season in the wild, and typically at the end of summer in cultivation, the leaves become completely and quickly deciduous, leaving only the tawny, tightly clustered pseudobulbs. In shape and color, these give the impression of bunched cigars standing on end, hence the common name "cigar orchids."

CULTURE

Though their size and light requirements limit them to outdoor and greenhouse culture, these spectacular orchids are well worth the space. Under those conditions they are quite easy to grow, and a specimen-sized cigar orchid bedecked with hundreds of waxy flowers on 3–5-foot spikes is guaranteed to draw attention.

TEMPERATURE: Intermediate to warm

LIGHT: Very bright to intense (3,000–5,000 fc)

HUMIDITY, WATER, AND FERTILIZATION: *Cyrtopodiums* are not fussy about humidity so long as ample water is available during the growing season. Water when the mix dries just below the surface. Moderately heavy doses of fertilizer applied from the time flowering ceases until leaf drop will yield enormous plants. In late summer, begin reducing water and stop it completely once the leaves are shed. Keep the plants dry until the new growth buds begin to swell at the base of last year's canes. The species you are likely to grow will bloom in winter or spring, and you can gradually increase watering as the spikes and new leaves start expanding, with ample water again by the time blooms fade and new bulbs are maturing.

POTTING AND MEDIA: Choose 6–10-inch clay pots and fill with a fine mix as described for *Cymbidiums* or *Paphiopedilums*, even though not all *Cyrtopodiums* are terrestrial in the wild. These orchids have large root systems, but you can restrain them somewhat by limiting the size of the container. The clunky pseudobulbs are eas-

ily divided at the end of dormancy, just as new growth is evident. For best flowering, leave each division with at least five backbulbs; the growths cluster tightly together, so you can keep the divisions even larger.

Dendrobium (Den)

(*DEN-DRO-bee-um*)

SUBTRIBE: Dendrobiinae

NUMBER OF KNOWN SPECIES: More than 1,000

NATIVE RANGE: India, tropical Asia, Indonesia, New Guinea, Australia, and New Zealand

SKILL LEVEL: Beginner to expert, depending on species

GOOD INTRODUCTORY SPECIES: *Dendrobium kingianum*, *D. phalaenopsis* and its hybrids, *D. nobile*, *D. thyrsiflorum*, *D. loddigesii*

Dendrobium thyrsiflorum

This vast and complex genus offers something for everyone—from massive warm-growing plants with 5-foot canes to 2-inch cool-growing miniatures at home on a twig. *Dendrobiums* have always been among my favorites, with flowers that range from weird to spectacular, always produced in colorful abundance. My first, which I bought when I was a sophomore in college, was a *Dendrobium thyrsiflorum;* I still remember being thunderstruck when it opened its large, pendent, butter-and-egg spikes as the sun warmed my windowsill the following spring.

It is hard to generalize about such a vast genus (and one likely to be splintered into more manageable genera soon), but aside from the "cucumber" types, with their picklelike, swollen leaves, *Dendrobiums* are characterized by canelike pseudobulbs ranging from 2 inches to 6 feet in length, bearing alternate, usually two-ranked, leaves along all or part of their span. The pseudobulbs can be upright, arching, or pendent, and the leaves may be evergreen or deciduous. Fortunately, most of the species fall into four cultural groups (which often have little to do with their taxonomic affinities). The first group, the winter-deciduous or *nobile* type, includes the long cane–forming Asian species such as *D. parishii, D. pierardii,* and *D. loddigesii.* The intermediate to cool evergreen group includes *D. thyrsiflorum* and *D. densiflorum,* as well as unrelated species like *D. victoriae-reginae, D. sanderae, D. forbesii, D. kingianum, D. cucumerinum,* and *D. moniliforme.* The third group consists of species of the cool, high-elevation cloud forest, primarily from New Guinea, in sections *Pedilonium* and *Oxyglossum,* and last but not least, the lowland, warm-growing evergreen *Phalaenanthes,* antelope, and *Latouria* species. When buying or trading a species you are unfamiliar with, be sure to ask whether it is warm-, intermediate-, or cool-growing and whether it is deciduous or evergreen.

Dendrobium wardianum 'Orchid Land' CHM/AOS in section *Dendrobium*

CULTURE

Winter-deciduous *Dendrobiums* (section *Dendrobium*)

I find the plants in this group easy and satisfying to grow as long as I can provide a place for them in winter that stays below 60° at night (with oil prices these days, that means my entire house!). Water and fertilize the plants generously during the summer growth period. Many within this group produce remarkably long, pendent canes, and even the more restrained have canes that arch or bend over under their own weight. (The "neck" of the pseudobulb that attaches to the rhizome is very narrow, so it is unable to support the mature weight of the canes.) Hanging the pots or mounting the plants on slabs is the best way to deal with this habit, although you can stake the canes. If you do stake, be sure to do so as they are developing, for once the leaves mature, they become fixed at whatever angle they find themselves, and repositioned canes look off-kilter. The flowers appear in ones to threes along the most of the stem, and to me they look more natural on canes that have been allowed to develop without staking. As temperatures cool in autumn, begin to restrict water. The leaves of either the current or the previous year's canes will quickly yellow and drop. At this point, an occasional misting and night temperatures between 50° and 55° for two to three months will spur flower bud development. If by spring you have keikis instead of flower buds coming from the stem, chances are the temperatures were not cool enough. No matter—remove the keikis and pot them up to share with friends once they have produced at least one mature pseudobulb. Even perfectly grown plants will usually produce a few keikis for you. Once you see flower buds forming in the nodes along the upper two-thirds of the most recently deciduous canes, increase misting but do not resume regular watering or fertilization until flowering is complete and new growth has begun.

Intermediate to cool evergreen species (including section Callista)

Though this cultural group encompasses many unrelated species, they all have in common a need for a cool but not especially dry rest in winter to harden growths and trigger flowering. Grow them in warm to intermediate temperatures during spring, summer, and early fall, then place them in a spot where night temperatures dip into the mid to low 50s at night during the winter. Many within this group, especially the delightful *D. kingianum,* will grow on a windowsill or under lights set up in a cellar or cool room. On a windowsill, place the plants between the curtain and the window to provide a 5°–10° winter temperature drop. In winter, water enough to keep the canes from shriveling. Blooms will appear in late winter or spring, with new growth evident soon afterward. Water as the medium begins to dry during the growing season and fertilize regularly.

Cloud forest species (primarily sections *Pedilonium* and *Oxyglossum*)

As with all cloud forest orchids, these remarkable *Dendrobiums* require high humidity, good water quality, good air movement, and cool to moderate temperatures year-round. Though they are among the most difficult to grow, I have to admit they are my favorites, producing vivid red, orange, hot pink, purple, or even blue flowers of heavy substance and often of a size and quantity such that they envelop the diminutive canes. I have had excellent results with growing the likes of the exquisite *D. cuthbertsonii, D. lawesii, D. massarangense,* and even the fabulous, ½-inch-tall, blue-flowered *D. delicatulum* in an enclosed light box alongside pleurothallids. I prefer to mount them on tree fern or horizontal slabs or to pot them in NZ sphagnum or tree fern–sphagnum in 1–2-inch thumb pots. Keep humidity above 70%, temperatures between 50° and 75° F as much as possible, and water or mist

Dendrobium chrysotoxum, an intermediate- to cool-growing evergreen species

Dendrobium cutherbertsonii 'Christopher John' AM/AOS in section *Oxyglossum*

Dendrobiums. As a whole, this group needs very bright light, especially in summer, as the canes are produced. Water frequently at this time, and provide regular doses of fertilizer. A modest rest, achieved through a slight drop in night temperatures and a 20%–30% reduction in water and fertilizer, will aid blooming.

The *Latouria* section includes plants that are both beautiful and frightening in flower. Most have a gaping or prominently ridged lip; hairy, contorted petals and sepals; and club-shaped pseudobulbs topped with several oval to lance-shaped leaves. Pay close attention to temperature requirements when buying plants in this section, as it includes some higher-elevation species like *D. engae* that require cool temperatures.

Antelope *Dendrobiums* (section *Spatulata*) are spectacular in flower. Like the *Latouria* and *Phalaenopsis* types, they are from New Guinea and the surrounding islands as well as northern Australia. They are robust growers, with canes that can reach 10 feet or more in height and that erupt in branched

Dendrobium pseudoglomeratum

daily. Frequent applications of dilute fertilizer are better than heavier, less frequent doses, lessening the chance of salt damage to the roots. Section *Oxyglossum* are real miniatures, with ½–3-inch growths clustered on abbreviated rhizomes. Those in section *Pedilonium* are mostly pendent, cane-forming plants that should be hung up or mounted for best presentation.

Lowland, warm-growing, evergreen species (sections *Phalaenanthes*, *Spatulata*, *Latouria*)

These are big, showy, even grotesque-flowered, erect-growing orchids that come mainly from lowland New Guinea. They want water, bright light, and night temperatures above 65° year-round. I envy growers in Hawaii or Taiwan who can provide these impressive *Dendrobiums* the conditions they crave. In dim-wintered New England, I have trouble getting many of this type to grow and bloom well. The exceptions are *D. phalaenopsis* and *D. bigibbum* and their hybrids. The *Phalaenopsis Dendrobiums*, as the species in section *Phalaenanthes* are called, are a popular florist crop, and quantities are imported to the mainland from Hawaii, Taiwan, and elsewhere and sold in nurseries and discount stores at modest prices. Although these are not the ideal windowsill plants that they are sometimes marketed as, they are more forgiving than many other

Dendrobium (Theodore Takiguchi × Aisaki White), a hybrid in section *Phalaenanthes*

Common Orchid Genera from A to Z   167

inflorescences from their upper nodes. Antelope *Dendrobiums* get their name from the curiously twisted petals, which are held upright and angled slightly forward or outward, much like the horns of some exotic ungulate from the Serengeti. Their size and need for heat and light keep me from growing them, unfortunately, though they are popular garden plants in Hawaii.

The recommendations that follow apply to the genus in general.

TEMPERATURE: Cool to warm

LIGHT: Low to very bright (1,500–5,000 fc); all but the antelope species should do well between 2,000 and 4,000 fc.

HUMIDITY, WATER, AND FERTILIZATION: With the exception of the cloud forest species, which require saturated air, humidity in the 50%–80% range is adequate. Appropriate watering and fertilization regimens are discussed above for the individual groups.

POTTING AND MEDIA: Generally *Dendrobiums* prefer to be underpotted, so I recommend 1–6-inch clay or plastic pots, with the 4-inch size being the standard. Many mixes work well, including bark, tree fern, lava, or Turface, and even NZ sphagnum for the cloud forest species. I find *Dendrobiums* neither the easiest nor the hardest orchids to divide. The pseudobulbs/canes are usually tightly clustered, meaning that division is not necessary at every repotting. Many of the species freely produce plantlets, or keikis, instead of blooms from some flower buds, and these can be easily snipped or snapped off once they have at least one mature pseudobulb and some roots, then potted up separately. Most keikis will begin blooming in a year or two. Commercially available keiki paste (hormone) will induce their formation if none are naturally forthcoming. In the wild, keikis are a handy form of vegetative reproduction that supplements sexual reproduction, especially when times are tough.

Dendrochilum (no abbr.)

(DEN-DRO-KIE-LUM)

SUBTRIBE: Coelogyninae

NUMBER OF KNOWN SPECIES: About 130

NATIVE RANGE: Indonesia, Southeast Asia, and New Guinea

SKILL LEVEL: Beginner

GOOD INTRODUCTORY SPECIES: *Dendrochilum cobbianum, D. glumaceum, D. wenzelii*

A well-grown *Dendrochilum* in bloom is as elegant and perfectly proportioned as the finest flower arrangement, and fortunately this genus is very easy to grow well. Several qualities make them ideal in this regard, notably their habit of growth and the quantity and arrangement of their sweetly fragrant

Dendrochilum glumaceum

Dendrochilum wenzelii

blooms. Long, lance-shaped, grasslike, or even terete leaves are held on small, narrow pseudobulbs or merely swollen petioles that cluster very tightly together. Each pseudobulb produces two or even three new leads in a large flush of growth each spring and often again in fall, so a small division will quickly become a dense specimen in two to three years. The 8–14-inch leaves arch out in all directions from the clustered pseudobulbs for a tufted effect that is quite pleasing when the plant is out of flower and especially lovely with the blooms. As the rolled new leaves emerge from spear-tip sheaths, they are quickly overtaken by slender racemes that grow from their centers. When the new leaves are reaching maturity, so too do the delicate, arching or pendent chains of small blooms. Each flower is less than 1/2 inch across, ranging from the soft yellow of *Dendrochilum cobbianum* or yellow-green of *D. latifolium* to the white, orange-lipped *D. glumaceum* or brick red *D. wenzelii*. This last is a particular favorite of mine, as I find its clustered 1/8-inch-thick, terete leaves especially charming. It is not only the arched or pendent carriage of the abundant sprays, but the way they are carefully spread through the foliage that lends them a flower arranger's touch. The flowers are usually arranged in two ranks, giving the raceme a bristly, bottlebrush appearance.

CULTURE

I find *Dendrochilums* to be very amenable to cultivation and reasonably tolerant of treatment that might prove disastrous to plants with a more delicate constitution. Give them moderate light and a smallish (3–6-inch) pot containing a moisture-retentive mix that is changed yearly, and they should grow splendidly.

TEMPERATURE: Intermediate to warm

LIGHT: Somewhat bright (1,500–2,500 fc)

HUMIDITY, WATER, AND FERTILIZATION: Average orchid humidity. Water *Dendrochilums* throughout the year when the mix begins to dry, and apply light but frequent doses of fertilizer.

POTTING AND MEDIA: These plants have a reputation for being fussy about stale potting mix and about root disturbance during repotting, but that doesn't correspond with my own experience. I do think divisions should be fairly large (more than ten growths), and old mix should be carefully teased from the wiry roots to damage them as little as possible, but they rebound pretty quickly. Choose a pot about 1–1 1/2 inches larger than the base of the division. This will allow the fast-growing plants about 3/4 inch all around before hitting the rim. Small pots allow for more frequent watering, with less chance of anaerobic conditions developing in the center of the container. I prefer a fine mix—either fine fir bark or tree fern–NZ sphagnum.

Dichaea (no abbr.) 🔦 🎴

(*DIE-KEY-AH*)

SUBTRIBE: Dichaeinae

NUMBER OF KNOWN SPECIES: About 120

NATIVE RANGE: American tropics

SKILL LEVEL: Experienced

GOOD INTRODUCTORY SPECIES: *Dichaea squarrosa, D. glauca, D. muricata*

Dichaeas are instantly recognizable, for they grow in a unique two-ranked fashion (they do have imitators—most notably the charming little *Dendrobium dichaeoides*). These monopodials produce trailing, pendent, or arching stems clothed in small, alternating, flattened leaves all oriented in one direction so that they appear pressed. Leaves range from 1/2 to 1 1/2 inches in length and are continually produced, so stems can reach several feet in length eventually. In shape, the leaves range from the mouse-eared *D. muricata* to the willowy *D. laxa*. Older or damaged stems send out side branches, and these too set off and branch, so large specimens have a crazy, criss-

Dichaea glauca 'Teabell' CHM/AOS

crossed, matted, or tangled appearance. Some species retain their leaves for several years, while others drop them rather quickly. Semideciduous species like *D. brachypoda* are to my mind the least attractive in the genus. *Dichaeas* are not heavily rooted. A single wiry root will appear here and there along the stem or more numerously from the base of the plant. If a root finds a purchase on a bit of moss or bark, it will continue to lengthen for a time; if not, it will cease growing fairly quickly. Farther up (or down) the stem, single flowers ½–1 inch across pop out from other leaf bases and face out toward the light like the leaves. They are cute little fellas, with an overall rounded and slightly cupped shape and a background color ranging from yellow to green and white, more or less stippled with red or purple spots. Some, like *D. muricata,* have an intensely blue-violet lip. The flowers, like the leaves, are produced year-round, though the plants are almost never covered in flowers.

CULTURE

Dichaeas are cloud forest orchids that need high humidity and frequent misting to keep them plump. The rambling habit of the more commonly available species makes mounting necessary, so regular watering and misting are especially critical. I should note, however, that some *Dichaea* species produce stiffer stems that are erect or arching, and in these the new growth comes strictly from the base of the plant, so potting is more practical. I find both types excellent companions for my other cloud forest miniatures, so long as the temperatures do not get too cool. They are more interesting than captivating, but I find this quality endearing.

TEMPERATURE: Intermediate

LIGHT: Somewhat bright (1,500–2,500 fc)

HUMIDITY, WATER, AND FERTILIZATION: Maintain a saturated atmosphere with humidity above 70% and water or mist daily. The evergreen *Dichaeas* and, for that matter, the semideciduous ones grow almost continually, and I apply a dilute liquid fertilizer weekly.

POTTING AND MEDIA: Many growers prefer tree-fern slabs, which provide ample surface area for the roots to take hold. Pot the stiffer species in small thumb pots, 1–2½ inches in diameter, using NZ sphagnum or a similar moisture-retentive medium.

Diplocaulobium (no abbr.) 🏳

(*DIP-LOW-CALL-OH-BEE-UM*)

SUBTRIBE: Dendrobiinae

NUMBER OF KNOWN SPECIES: About 100

NATIVE RANGE: Southeast Asia to New Guinea and Australia

SKILL LEVEL: Expert

GOOD INTRODUCTORY SPECIES: *Diplocaulobium regale*

When I ordered several flasks of *Dendrobium* seedlings from a nursery specializing in orchids from Papua New Guinea, the description for *Diplocaulobium regale* caught my eye, and I ordered a flask of it as well. I could not find much information

Diplocaulobium regale

about the species (this was during the dark ages before the Age of Internet-enlightenment), but gathered that it hailed from cloud forests on the island. As the seedlings matured, they began to resemble large *Pleurothallis*, with 7–9-inch-long slender stems, sheathed in papery bracts, that supported one large, long, round-tipped leaf. The form I purchased produced rich pink flowers, though red and white forms are also common. In shape the 2-inch flowers resemble *Phalaenanthes*-section *Dendrobiums*, and they come in succession one after the next from the point where leaf meets stem. Each flower lasts only a day or two (three if it is especially cool and humid), but a large plant always has a few in blossom over several months in late winter and spring. The rounded shape of this species' flower is unusual for the genus; most of its hundred-odd members produce elegant flowers with thin, spidery segments reminiscent of some *Maxillarias* or *Dendrobiums*, and all are smaller than *D. regale*. Some of the mat-forming species qualify as miniatures.

CULTURE

Diplocaulobiums are not the easiest of orchids to cultivate. High humidity, good air movement, very bright light, and moderate temperatures, combined with a damp but well-aerated potting mix or mount, are necessary for good blooming and long life.

TEMPERATURE: Warm to intermediate-cool

LIGHT: Bright to very bright (2,500–3,500 fc)

HUMIDITY, WATER, AND FERTILIZATION: Give *Diplocaulobiums* high humidity (above 70%), even watering throughout the year once the surface of the medium dries, and moderate fertilizer. Mounted specimens should be misted or watered daily.

POTTING AND MEDIA: For the larger species, use 4–6-inch clay or plastic pots and a porous but somewhat moisture-retentive potting mix. The smaller ones can be mounted on tree fern or cork plaques.

Disa (Disa)

(DEE-sah OR DIE-sah)

SUBTRIBE: Disinae

NUMBER OF KNOWN SPECIES: 130

NATIVE RANGE: Africa

SKILL LEVEL: Expert

GOOD INTRODUCTORY SPECIES: The intraspecific hybrids, including *Disa* Veitchii, *Disa* Diores, and *Disa* Kewensis, are probably the best ones to start with. For species, try *Disa uniflora* or *D. cardinalis*.

Few orchids can rival *Disas* for sheer eye-shuddering color saturation. Although this terrestrial genus ranges throughout the African continent, only the South African streamside species,

Disa Foam 'Pui' AM/AOS

Disa cardinalis, D. caulescens, D. racemosa, D. tripetaloides, D. uniflora, and D. venosa, are cultivated. *Disas* were very popular during Victorian times, and because the seed will germinate if sprinkled around an adult plant or even a pot of sphagnum moss, many hybrids were produced before the in vitro method came along in the 1920s. These primary hybrids (between two species) as well as secondary hybrids (having at least one hybrid parent) are still very popular among aficionados today.

The aforementioned species grow in marsh or streamside habitats in the hills and mountains of South Africa. Cold, fast-moving rainwater keeps their roots wet and well-aerated, and surrounding vegetation shields them from the hottest rays of the sun. The rosettes of 2–6-inch leaves grow from fleshy tubers. Roots formed from the tuber will in turn produce more tubers a short distance away from the parent, and these will give rise to new plants in turn. A stout, leafy spike arises from the center of each new rosette and lengthens to 3 feet, lifting the blooms developing toward its tip above grasses and low shrubs. *Disa* flowers have a distinct triangular shape; like New World *Draculas* and *Masdevallias*, they are defined mostly by their three sepals. The dorsal sepal forms a prominent bonnet over the small column, while the colorful, bannerlike laterals turn out and down. The small petals and lip wrap the column itself.

Disa Kewensis

CULTURE

Disas can be grown in a mixed collection of orchids, but they require a different sort of culture than most of the commonly grown genera save *Phragmipediums*. This may explain why many *Disa* growers become specialists in the genus. A hydroponic or partly hydroponic system that keeps the plants from ever drying out has proven most effective. They are very sensitive to even moderate levels of soluble salts, so rain or RO water should be used on them at all times. With pure water, you can safely apply a dilute fertilizer, such as Dyna-Gro, designed for hydroponic culture. I think inexpensive water purification systems and higher-quality liquid fertilizers have greatly simplified *Disa* culture. They are also intolerant of heat, so only growers in the north and on the West Coast of the United States can meet their needs without air conditioning. Some of the best *Disas* are grown in the San Francisco Bay area, where conditions are almost perfect. They can be raised successfully under lights, but I would not recommend them for windowsills.

TEMPERATURE: Intermediate to cool (for the species and hybrids mentioned above)

LIGHT: Somewhat bright (1,800–2,500 fc)

HUMIDITY, WATER, AND FERTILIZATION: Again, pure water is essential for good *Disa* culture. If you have a small number of plants, distilled or rainwater will suffice, though many growers install RO systems. Very dilute (50 ppm N)

fertilizer should be added to the irrigation water when new rosettes are forming. After flowering, the plants become semidormant, and though they need to be kept damp, stop fertilizing them. Maintain humidity in the 50%–70% range.

POTTING AND MEDIA: *Disa*'s difficult reputation has attracted some creative growers, who have devised complicated ebb-and-flow water troughs that periodically flood the potted plants, then allow them to drain. I have had little experience with *Disas* myself, but some friends have raised beautiful plants in 6-inch plastic pots filled with a mix of NZ sphagnum and coarse sand; that mix or Turface or lava rock should do the trick, provided you place the pots in a saucer of water. Be sure to flush the pots thoroughly so that water floods over the lip of the tray at every watering. Repot yearly just as new rosettes begin to grow. At that time you can carefully snap or cut off smaller tubers and pot them separately.

Doritis (Dor)

(DOOR-EYE-TIS)

SUBTRIBE: Sarcanthinae

NUMBER OF KNOWN SPECIES: 1–3, depending on the authority

NATIVE RANGE: Southeast Asia

SKILL LEVEL: Beginner

GOOD INTRODUCTORY SPECIES: *Doritis pulcherrima*

This tiny genus is familiar to just about every *Phalaenopsis* grower, even though few people cultivate the species, for it has been crossed with *Phalaenopsis* to create the wildly successful *Doritaenopsis* hybrids. The primary species, *Doritis pulcherrima,* is a terrestrial that looks much like a small, rather stiff *Phalaenopsis*. It produces arching, branched, 1–3-foot inflorescences in summer and autumn that showcase up to twenty small, brightly colored flowers that range from pink to cerise, white, and violet-purple. *Doritis* brings to the hybrids summer flowering; compact foliage, flowers, and inflorescences; and bright pink and purple colors. I think their terrestrial affinities also carry through to the hybrids, making them more tolerant of overwatering and suitable for Pro-Mix–type potting mixes. Basically, *Doritaenopsis* are perfect windowsill and underlights orchids, giving us long-blooming, easy-care orchids that even a beginner should do well with.

CULTURE

The species can be grown like the hybrids, though it is a little less forgiving.

TEMPERATURE: Intermediate-warm

LIGHT: Bright (2,000–3,000 fc)

HUMIDITY, WATER, AND FERTILIZATION: As for *Phalaenopsis*.

Doritis pulcherrima 'Bloomfield's Pink'

POTTING AND MEDIA: A 5–6-inch clay or plastic pot filled with a peat/perlite mix such as Pro-Mix is a good choice, as is a medium suitable for *Paphiopedilums*.

Dracula (Drac)

(*DRAK-YOU-LA*)

SUBTRIBE: Pleurothallidinae

NUMBER OF KNOWN SPECIES: About 100

NATIVE RANGE: Central America and northern South America

SKILL LEVEL: Expert

GOOD INTRODUCTORY SPECIES: *Dracula erythrochaete, D. lotax, D. velutina*

I cannot think of any genus name that suits a group's overall character better than *Dracula*. In Latin, *draco* means "dragon," and, even more apropos, Dracula is the moniker of the mythical bloodsucking count from Transylvania. These small cloud forest orchids with their often huge, warty, hairy, fungus-lipped flowers have a sinister, carnivorous quality, especially if you meet one poking out of the moss in a dark, wet forest. I

find them simply fantastic. *Draculas* are not prissy flowers, not the sort of bloom you'd pin on your chest for a prom or wedding, but they have something else I can describe only as an animistic quality, an animal aliveness that is palpable and bewitching. Like others in their tribe, they are clumping plants, with 6–12-inch-long leaves of rather thin substance that are grooved down the middle. They grow continuously, sending up new leaves year-round and thus quickly bulking up. They also bloom nearly continuously, especially once they reach a critical size that can support this extravagance. The inflorescences begin as wire-thin spear points that lance through the sheath at the base of a leaf, then set off along the surface of the pot or, more likely, turn south into the compost only to emerge again down below. After breaching the pot, the spike continues to lengthen, to a foot or so, before producing the first flower. If the environment is suitably damp, the blooms will expand one at a time, each spike producing up to a half dozen or more sequentially over the course of several months, by which time new spikes will have formed to replace it. The flowers have a distinctly triangular shape, for, like *Disas* and *Masdevallias*, it is the sepals, not the petals, that dominate the red, white, burgundy, and/or chocolate bloom. The three sepals are more or

Dracula tubeana

Dracula gorgona

less fused at their bases to create a cupped, gaping, or flat triangle, and each tip narrows into a long, thin tail that can be as long as 6 inches. Measured from tail to tail, some of the larger-flowered species, like *Dracula hirtzii, D. chimaera,* and *D. vampira,* are thus more than a foot across—larger than the plant itself! The other remarkable thing about these flowers is the lip, which on many species has the cupped and gilled appearance of a mushroom when seen from below. Certainly more than a happy accident, the shape most likely has evolved to lure the small flies or fungus gnats that pollinate the flowers.

CULTURE

I have been to prime *Dracula* country, and it's as cold, wet, and miserable a habitat as you are likely to find in the tropics. Living as they do in saturated cloud forests, *Draculas* are the amphibians of the orchid world, requiring, with a few exceptions, very humid, shaded, cool conditions to thrive. You rarely see *Draculas* at orchid shows, even in the closed display cases that are increasingly popular with growers of miniatures,

because the flowers go limp and spikes wither as soon as the humidity drops below 70%–80%. This being said, I find they take readily to life in an enclosed light box or grow room, so long as you can make provisions for their downward-growing spikes. I either hang them on a wall, put them on an overturned pot, or place then in baskets suspended from the rafters in a greenhouse.

TEMPERATURE: Intermediate to cool

LIGHT: Low to somewhat bright (1,200–2,000 fc)

HUMIDITY, WATER, AND FERTILIZATION: To repeat, high humidity is essential for *Draculas*. A saturated atmosphere, in the 80%–100% range, is ideal, but it must be combined with enough air movement to keep the leaves moving slightly. A constantly damp medium is also important, as *Draculas* lack fleshy leaves to weather an occasional drought. Since they are constantly growing, apply dilute fertilizer either constantly or once every seven to fourteen days. Be sure to adequately flush the medium with rain or RO water, as the plants are very sensitive to salt buildup and stale compost.

POTTING AND MEDIA: Obviously, *Dracula*'s downward-growing inflorescences require a slatted basket or net pot. A 4–8-inch basket or 3–6-inch net pot is about right. Some of the smaller species, such as *Dracula lotax,* do well mounted if you can keep them damp enough. I prefer to pot them in straight NZ sphagnum, repotting once a year and taking care to thoroughly flush or soak the plants in pure water to prevent salt buildup. (Salt injury shows up as leaf-tip dieback.) Divisions should be fairly large, with a minimum of eight leaves, and the roots should be disturbed as little as possible. Smaller divisions take a while to recover and begin blooming again. The best time to divide and repot is mid- to late winter, when temperatures are cool and the plants have had a chance to recover from summer heat stress.

Encyclia (Encycl)

(EN-SIC-lee-ah)

SUBTRIBE: Laeliinae

NUMBER OF KNOWN SPECIES: 240

NATIVE RANGE: American subtropics and tropics

SKILL LEVEL: Beginner

GOOD INTRODUCTORY SPECIES: Many, including *Encyclia (Prosthechea) chocleata, E. fragrans, E. nemorale, E. tampense*

Until the 1970s, many references lumped *Encyclias* in with *Epidendrums,* causing more than a little name confusion among hobbyists. Though the flowers of the two genera are similar in overall appearance—most notably in the prominent, ruffled, lobed, or spoonlike lip and more or less narrow

Encyclia adenocaule 'Leone' HCC/AOS

segments—*Encyclias* all have oval or rounded pseudobulbs topped by several leaves, whereas *Epidendrums* have canelike pseudobulbs and two-ranked, alternating leaves.

Encyclias possess big, plump pseudobulbs and straplike, usually succulent foliage because they prefer seasonally dry habitats—a characteristic that makes them especially good candidates for windowsill and sunroom as well as greenhouse and outdoor culture, provided you can give them bright light. The clamshell orchids, including *Encyclia* (now *Prosthechea*) *chocleata* and *fragrans*, are among the easiest of all orchids to grow and a bit more shade-tolerant than most in the group. The genus as a whole is not as fussy about humidity and watering as, say, *Paphiopedilum* or *Phalaenopsis*, though admittedly, their apple green, brown, maroon, and white flowers don't have the impact of an "art shade" *Phalaenopsis*. The 1–2-inch flowers are borne on branched, often very long spikes that develop from the top of the pseudobulb where the leaves all attach. Usually the spike is very sturdy and stiff, but the sheer weight of a dozen to three dozen flowers all open at once will cause even the most stalwart to droop unless staked.

CULTURE

Often it is overabundance rather than lack of water that threatens the life of *Encyclias*. This is not to say they are cacti, but they do appreciate a well-aerated mix, bright light, and good ventilation to keep water from settling around the crown and pseudobulbs. They produce one or sometimes two flushes of new growth during the warmer part of the year, at which time I increase fertilization and watering somewhat. During winter, curtail watering just enough that the older pseudobulbs pucker a little—a sure sign that the mix has dried thor-

oughly and it's safe to water again. Different species bloom at specific times of the year, timed to day length, temperature, and availability of water. Some flower as the new pseudobulbs mature in summer or fall, others after a winter rest.

TEMPERATURE: Intermediate to warm; a few, such as the striking red *E. vitellina*, need cool conditions.

LIGHT: Bright to very bright (2,000–4,000 fc)

HUMIDITY, WATER, AND FERTILIZATION: Humidity levels above 40% in winter (higher in summer) are adequate. Water when the mix has all but dried, and apply fertilizer moderately when they are in active vegetative growth.

POTTING AND MEDIA: All *Encyclias*, and especially the smaller species, are good candidates for mounts. I had several, including *E. citrina*, *E. bractescens*, and *E. nemorale*, thriving and blooming on tree-fern mounts in a south-facing window. If you choose pots, I recommend clay, and it's best to underpot them so the medium dries out quickly. I have raised specimens on slabs of cork and oak logs as well as in 8–12-inch slatted baskets filled with medium-grade fir bark. Divide the plants just as a flush of new roots is evident from the lead growth. Keep at least three pseudobulbs per division.

Encyclia cordigera

Epidendrum (Epi) 🌸 🏳️

(EH-PEE-DEN-DRUM)

SUBTRIBE: Laeliinae

NUMBER OF KNOWN SPECIES: 1,000 plus

NATIVE RANGE: American tropics

SKILL LEVEL: Beginner

GOOD INTRODUCTORY SPECIES: *Epidendrum pseudoepidendrum, E. cinnabarinum, E. ibaguense* (all large reed-stem species), *E. cilare* (medium-sized), *E. porpax* (small— suitable under lights)

Epidendrum is a huge genus containing something for everyone's tastes and growing situations. They are found at every elevation in the Andes and the mountains of Central America, with some growing terrestrially above the tree line in cold cloud forests and others scampering around the tree trunks in lowland swamp forests. The species range from 6-foot-tall reed-stem types such as *Epidendrum pfavii*, which are almost always in bloom, to true miniatures like *E. porpax* and *E. sophronitoides*, which are at home on a mossy mount. Although you can find one in almost any color save black or cobalt, among hobbyists the most popular are bright reds, oranges, and magentas, as well as kelly greens. *Epidendrum conopseum*, the green fly orchid, the hardiest epiphytic orchid native to the United States, can be found as far north as south coastal North Carolina, where it experiences and survives occasional freezes.

Epidendrums are usually easy to recognize in or out of flower. The plants produce clustered, canelike pseudobulbs that are typically rather thin and of even circumference throughout their length. Leaves are arranged one after the other in two ranks either up the whole cane or just toward the top. The reed-stem species, a group of tall, good-natured, brilliantly colored epis that include *E. ibaguense, E. radicans,* and *E. cinnabarinum*, regularly produce keikis on their flower spikes, and these will eventually break off or simply continue growing until they find a purchase somewhere. In nature the plants walk or climb to new locations quite effectively, and in cultivation this habit makes it easy to pass them along to friends. Many other canelike, scandent, and creeping types produce new canes partway up the main stem, and these branch in turn, eventually forming a shrubby or congested specimen. In the genus as a whole, flowers are borne on branched or unbranched terminal spikes that develop from maturing growths. While a few produce solitary blooms, the majority loft tall racemes topped with clustered blooms that open sequentially, so the plants stay in flower for one month or more, some blooming almost continuously. Each flower has fairly narrow petals and sepals surrounding a spoon-shaped, lobed, or complexly frilled lip in a contrasting or similar color. Some of the most dramatic species send out arched or pendent chains of interlocking flowers. A flowering *Epidendrum ilense* possesses a lyrical grace seemingly at odds with its basketball-star lankiness out of bloom.

CULTURE

For the majority of *Epidendrums*, life in a pot is quite agreeable, though many are a bit tall and gangly for growing under lights (or even in a greenhouse), especially in flower. The reed-stem species will thrive in a sunny window or solarium, and quite a number of smaller ones will fit in cramped spaces. These include cool growers like *E. gastropodium* and miniatures such as *E. moronense* and *E. nanum*. All the species I have grown require bright light (similar to that for *Cattleyas*). In tropical climes, they are popular garden plants appreciated for their long bloom time and bright colors.

TEMPERATURE: Warm to cool, depending on the species

LIGHT: Bright (2,000–4,000 fc)

HUMIDITY, WATER, AND FERTILIZATION: *Epidendrums* are at home in relative humidity of 50%–80%. Most grow nearly continuously through the year, so water them when the medium begins to dry, and apply moderate to heavy doses of fertilizer regularly to keep them growing and blooming well.

POTTING AND MEDIA: I prefer to underpot the plants, which allows more frequent watering with less danger of root rot. This being said, however, many *Epidendrums* can grow epiphytically or semiterrestrially, and they seem less

Epidendrum 'Kayais Lady' AM/AOS

Epidendrum embreei

Galeandra greenwoodiana 'Orchid Art' CHM/AOS

fussy about having stale medium at the roots than other orchids do. The taller ones may require staking to keep the canes from toppling over. I prefer to start the reed-stems anew from keikis every once in a while when the parent gets too large and cumbersome. Medium-grade fir bark or lava is suitable. The smaller creeping or pendent species are best mounted on tree fern or bark slabs.

Galeandra (Gal)

(GAL-ee-AN-dra)

Subtribe: Cyrtopodiinae

Number of known species: 26

Native range: Mexico south to Bolivia and Brazil

Skill level: Beginner

Good introductory species: *Galeandra batemanii, G. baueri, G. dives*

I picked up my first *Galeandra* at a bargain sale held each year by a local nursery. The leafless, lifeless plant seemed a bit of a

risk, even for $3, but after a few weeks under lights, it showed a new bit of green emerging from the base of the newest spindle-shaped pseudobulb. This quickly expanded into a leafy new lead. The thin, narrow leaves appear one after the other along the elongating cane. The first are small and quickly turn yellow and drop, leaving their corn-husk-tan bases to wrap the cane. Toward the top the foliage is longer, each thin leaf set with prominent veins, as in *Lycaste* or *Catasetum*. On my $3 plant, as the uppermost leaves were emerging on the now 6-inch-tall pseudobulb, I noticed an inflorescence poking out from their folds. As it lengthened, five knobby buds arranged themselves in a circle hung just above the leaves.

The flowers are very distinctive, with the narrow sepals and petals forming a five-fingered fan or crown that serves as a fitting backdrop for the large, scooplike lip. The fan is uniformly coppery brown among the different species, and the 2-inch-long lip blushes pink, white, or a deep, vibrant rose shading to pollen yellow deep in the throat. Most of the plants I have seen are certainly pretty in flower, but the deep pink-and-white picoteed cultivar *Galeandra greenwoodiana* 'Orchid Art'— awarded the Nax botanical trophy by the AOS several years ago—is truly knock-your-lava-rocks-off beautiful!

Galeandra is a lovely, easy-to-grow genus that is underappreciated by orchidists outside Brazil. Something about deciduous species appeals to me—the sense of rebirth and starting fresh each spring without the shopworn foliage of summers past. Conveniently, their dormancy and growth cycles make them good candidates for a windowsill, especially if they are allowed to summer outdoors.

CULTURE

The species of *Galeandra* I am familiar with all follow the same seasonal rhythm. New growth begins in late spring and proceeds through midsummer, with flowering commencing as the new lead nears completion. The blooms are very long-lasting, and the plants often rebloom on secondary stems. Thus flowering may carry on into early fall, when cooling temperatures and decreased watering cause the leaves to quickly and unceremoniously yellow and fall.

TEMPERATURE: Intermediate to warm

LIGHT: Bright (2,000–2,500 fc)

HUMIDITY, WATER, AND FERTILIZATION: *Galeandras* are not too demanding about humidity. They are in active growth in the summer, when our humidity is naturally higher anyway, and the lower humidity of the dormant winter months actually helps prevent rotting. They need ample water during the growing and blooming season. If you let them dry out, they will curtail flowering and go dormant early. Begin limiting water in the fall, and cut way back once the leaves are shed, though don't stop watering them completely. Give enough water to keep the lead cane plump, and increase watering again as growth recommences. Take care to prevent water from pooling in the fan of developing leaves, as this may cause the whole growth to damp off. Like other deciduous orchids, *Galeandras* relish frequent and rather heavy fertilization when new leads and roots are expanding, but fertilizer should be withheld completely during dormancy. With adequate water and fertilizer, they can produce canes up to a foot or more long.

POTTING AND MEDIA: Although the genus includes epiphytes, terrestrials, and lithophytes, it's best to grow them as semiterrestrials in a moisture-retentive medium. I use about 1 part tree fern to 1 part NZ sphagnum, but they are not too fussy. Use a fairly small pot (less than 4 inches); I recommend a heavy clay container because the plants get rather top-heavy and are prone to tipping over. They don't form multiple leads very readily, so division is rarely necessary. If you want to multiply your plants, leave at least two or three canes on the lead. Backbulbs will often form new leads once severed from the main bulb. Division and potting are best done just before new growth commences in spring.

Gastrochilus (Gchls) 🔑 🏠

(GAS-TRO-*KYE*-LUSS)

SUBTRIBE: Sarcanthinae

NUMBER OF KNOWN SPECIES: 22

NATIVE RANGE: India, Southeast Asia, and China to the Philippines and Japan

SKILL LEVEL: Experienced

GOOD INTRODUCTORY SPECIES: *Gastrochilus bellinus*, *G. calceolaris*

Gastrochilus is a fairly small genus of monopodial orchids that has danced in and out of the related genus *Aerides* in botanical classifications. The current view is that they are separate, but future DNA analysis may stand this on end. If you enjoy *Phalaenopsis* and have dallied with other monopodials like *Angraecum* or *Aerides*, by all means give this group a try. Out of flower, the plants resemble many other *Sarcanthinae*: thick strap- or tongue-shaped leaves alternate on an ever-lengthening stem propped up as if on stilts by fat, silvery roots. The 1-inch flowers are shaped like a miniature *Phalaenopsis* species. The five petals and sepals are of roughly equal size and color and spread out like five stubby fingers behind the contrasting

Gastrochilus bellinus

Aerides lawrenceae

lip. The outer edge of this labellum (a $10 word for "lip") is fringed in a delicate beard, and its pink, red, or rose and white spotting is set off by the more drab copper, ocher, or yellow of the other segments. Curiously, the flowers are arranged in a circle like spokes on a wheel, so that from just about any perspective some sit upright, others upside down, and still others hang sideways. The spikes are short and grow down from the younger leaf axils, so the blooms develop underneath the leaves. The plants are often raised in baskets hung high up so that the flowers can be easily seen.

CULTURE

Gastrochilus (and *Aerides*) are not well suited to windowsill culture, as they prefer fairly high humidity, an open compost, and rather frequent misting and watering to keep the leaves plump. Their typically small size (many can be kept under 8 inches) and moderate light requirements lend them to under-

lights culture, and they do very well in an intermediate greenhouse as well. They grow most actively in summer and usually bloom in late summer and fall as temperatures cool.

TEMPERATURE: Intermediate to warm, though higher-elevation Himalayan species prefer intermediate to cool.

LIGHT: Somewhat bright (1,200–2,200 fc)

HUMIDITY, WATER, AND FERTILIZATION: Maintain humidity above 60% as much as possible, and never let the medium go completely dry. Plants grown on mounts or in open baskets with no medium should be watered or misted daily, at least during the summer. Many *Gastrochilus* hail from monsoon climates, so a slightly cooler, slightly drier rest is beneficial in winter. Fertilize lightly throughout the year.

POTTING AND MEDIA: Slatted baskets or mounts allow the flowers to be seen more readily, and the big roots appreciate the abundant air and light. If the plants are confined in a pot, use a coarse medium. The lax stems tend to lengthen out beyond the rim of the container quickly, so many of the roots do not find a purchase and become aerial instead. Use caution when repotting, as the aerial roots will sulk if sunk into potting mix. Offsets will eventually develop from older stems, and these can be carefully severed once they have several roots over 2 inches long.

Gongora (Gga)

(GON-GORE-AH)

SUBTRIBE: Stanhopeinae

NUMBER OF KNOWN SPECIES: 52

NATIVE RANGE: American tropics from Mexico south to Bolivia

SKILL LEVEL: Experienced

GOOD INTRODUCTORY SPECIES: *Gongora armeniaca, G. horichiana, G. quinquenervis, G. truncata*

I'll warn you from the outset that although *Gongoras* are quite amenable to cultivation, their long, pendent racemes make hanging-basket or mounted culture mandatory, so they need to be grown in a greenhouse or outdoors (when temperatures permit). In vegetative form and habit they clearly resemble a scaled-down *Stanhopea*; the angled, clumping pseudobulbs are widest below the middle and narrow where they join a pair of thin but starched-stiff, corduroyed leaves. The leaves are broadly lance-shaped and fan out at angles from the plant to create a leafy canopy under which the flowers may hang. Each pseudobulb is wrapped by several papery sheaths that remain attached but slowly get more ragged and torn, and the thin, wiry inflorescences spring from between these.

After the lead growths have fully expanded, flower spikes begin to develop, at first curving out, then burrowing through,

Gongora horichiana

and finally hanging straight down below the nest of roots. If you are growing your plants on a tabletop, watch for these spikes (typically in summer) and elevate or hang the plant until blooming has finished. Some twelve to twenty flower buds whorl around the pendent stem, the first waiting until the last is fully formed before opening so that the whole spike blooms at once. To fully appreciate the marvelous shape of these flowers, it helps to know that they have evolved to mimic the body of a female euglossine bee, though truth be told, their designer has been granted quite a bit of poetic license. A hapless male bee, blind drunk with the flower's overpowering pheromones, might well mistake a toadstool for a suitable mate, but the flower has made at least a modest attempt at creating a beelike gestalt. The lip suggests a thorax, the petals swoop out like wings, and the column curves down like an abdomen to plunk pollen indiscreetly on the nether regions of the suitor's body. To my mind the dangling, 1–2-foot inflorescence has the grace of a paper mobile, with yellow, white, red, and brown spotted flowers hung like swans circling a tether. The flowers are not especially long-lived, but they do last about ten days—certainly longer than *Stanhopeas*.

This is a rapidly coevolving genus. Most species tailor their flower's shape and odor to a particular species of bee, but to the human eye the differences are subtle, so taxonomic confusion runs rampant. Within the widespread *Gongora quinquenervis* species complex, flower color and overall stature can vary quite markedly, so the plant you bloom may not match the description in your orchid encyclopedia. Fortunately, you can't really go wrong with *Gongoras* if you can accommodate them.

CULTURE

Like *Coryanthes*, *Gongoras* inhabit ant nests in the wild, gaining nutrients and protection in exchange for roomy apartments within their dense tangle of roots. Unlike *Coryanthes*, they do not require an intensely acidic medium to thrive. I have raised them in NZ sphagnum–filled baskets or mounted them on cork or tree-fern plaques with a generous pad of moss to get the roots started. They are used to a fairly rich diet of nutrients, however, and liberal fertilization will produce multiple growths and inflorescences.

TEMPERATURE: Intermediate to warm

LIGHT: Somewhat bright (1,800–2,500 fc)

HUMIDITY, WATER, AND FERTILIZATION: Maintain humidity above 60% and provide enough water to keep the mix or root mass from ever drying completely. Fertilize generously when the plants are in active growth.

POTTING AND MEDIA: As mentioned, basket or mounted culture is advisable to prevent misshapen inflorescences. If you do use standard pots, keep an eye out for the emerging inflorescences and help them up and over the rim. NZ sphagnum or sphagnum plus tree fern make suitable composts. Repot in spring before new growth commences. You can divide the tightly nested pseudobulbs by gently prying them apart from above and carefully severing the rhizomes, but division is seldom necessary, and larger specimens make for a more symmetrical display.

Holcoglossum (Hlcgl) 🍶 🏳

(HOLE-CO-GLOSS-UM)

SUBTRIBE: Sarcanthinae

NUMBER OF KNOWN SPECIES: 9

NATIVE RANGE: Indochina, southwestern China, and Taiwan

SKILL LEVEL: Experienced

GOOD INTRODUCTORY SPECIES: *Holcoglossum amesianum, H. kimballianum, H. flavescens*

For many years this small but very attractive genus was lumped in with *Vanda*, and some orchid texts refer to them as a single genus. However, *Holcoglossums* are very distinct and well worth seeking out. They are all terete-leaved (the leaves rolled up like straws), rather small plants with succulent herringbone foliage carried on short or climbing stems. The little needled leaves are pretty in themselves when the plant is not in flower. As in *Vandas*, older stems give rise to offsets toward the base once they reach a critical mass, so eventually the plants can become fine specimens. Most have thick, waxy flowers about 1 inch wide carried in dense spikes that arise between the leaves during the cooler months. The typical flower has a "flying squirrel" look that is common within the tribe—five outstretched, rounded segments and a curved, colorful lip. The whole is slightly cupped, suggesting a rodent falling with arms and legs outstretched. A few, such as *Holcoglossum kimballianum* and *H. subulifolium*, have more lyrical blooms, with thinner segments and proportionally large, bannerlike lips. The former is white overall with a cerise lip, the latter bears 1½-inch, pure white flowers with slightly twisted and ruffled petals that remind me of an antelope *Dendrobium* with a bowl-shaped, delicately fringed lip.

CULTURE

Hailing from mid- to high elevations, most *Holcoglossums* are content in an intermediate or even a cool house, especially in winter. Terete leaves usually evolve as a way for plants to endure exposed, sunny situations. Light is diffused as it passes through the thickened leaves, lessening the damage to chlorophyll caused by intense sunlight. The trade-off is that terete leaves are not effective in dim light. You can safely assume that to prosper, terete-leaved orchids such as the *Holcoglossums* need bright light, which is difficult to provide on a windowsill or even under lights. In a greenhouse, hang them up high where the light is bright and there's good air movement, and they should thrive. Their climbing or scandent habit and numerous large roots suggest basket or mounted culture. I have seen some lovely specimens of *H. kimballianum* and *H. subulifolium* trained to a vertical branch of oak or sassafras.

TEMPERATURE: Ideally, warm in the summer and a bit cooler in the winter, but overall within the intermediate range

LIGHT: Very bright to intense (3,000–5,000 fc)

HUMIDITY, WATER, AND FERTILIZATION: If you grow the plants mounted as I suggest, almost daily misting and watering will keep them hydrated. Properly watered specimens should hold on to their leaves for several years. Bare stems with a few leaves on top indicate water stress. Average orchid humidity and fertilization are sufficient for this genus.

POTTING AND MEDIA: Slatted baskets filled with large charcoal, fir bark, or lava chunks are suitable, as is bare mounting on a log or plaque. The large, fleshy roots demand very good air movement to thrive. Offsets can be removed and potted separately once they have developed roots of their own.

Holcoglossum flavescens

Holcoglossum wangii

Homalopetalum (no abbr.)

(HOME-AL-OH-PET-AL-UM)

SUBTRIBE: Laeliinae

NUMBER OF KNOWN SPECIES: 4

NATIVE RANGE: Caribbean, Mexico, and Central America

SKILL LEVEL: Experienced

GOOD INTRODUCTORY SPECIES: Homalopetalum pumilio

For a lover of miniatures like myself, Homalopetalums have a delicate charm that is irresistible. They stand less than an inch or so tall, with pea-shaped pseudobulbs regularly spaced along a thin creeping rhizome. On top of each one rides a swollen, lance-shaped leaf held slightly off the vertical, as is typical of the subtribe. The species are difficult to come by, and I have grown only Homalopetalum pumilio, but it has lived happily for about ten years now. Each summer it adds a few more growths to its unbranched chain, so the pseudobulbs look like a string of green pearls on a thin brown cord. The last growth to form in summer sports a tiny sheath containing an incipient flower where leaf meets pea, and this waits until temperatures warm in late spring to begin growing. A hair-thin spike rises to 2 inches before lofting a diaphanous, greenish white bloom with narrow segments and a large, diamond-shaped lip. The spidery flower of H. pumilio looks somewhat like a miniature Brassavola, but at slightly more than 1 inch in diameter, it seems pleasantly out of scale with the plant itself. I can't help but think of a struggling toddler trying to keep an immense kite aloft. Other species have flowers that are more squat in appearance and that nestle down among the leathery little leaves.

The related genus **Domingoa** (DO-MING-OH-AH) has two species, *D. nodosa* and *D. hymenodes*, both from the Caribbean and both requiring similar cultural treatment. They are larger than *Homalopetalum* and look much like a thick-leaved *Pleurothallis* in form, with thin, 2-inch pseudobulbs and a leaf twice again as long. The spikes arch out from the leaf, dangling flowers that are translucent green and overall similar in shape to the *Homalopetalums,* but they come successively over the course of a month or so from the same spike.

CULTURE

Much like the smaller *Bulbophyllums,* this wandering genus won't stay put in a pot for very long. *Homalopetalums* are happiest in a bright, humid spot where they receive regular misting and their few thin roots dry between waterings. I have mine mounted on a cork raft with just a sprig of moss applied to the roots.

TEMPERATURE: Intermediate

LIGHT: Bright to very bright (2,000–4,000 fc)

HUMIDITY, WATER, AND FERTILIZATION: Though they can endure periods of lower humidity, 60%–80% is preferred, as is frequent misting and light but constant fertilization. Although they look rather succulent, *Homalopetalums* will suffer if water is either withheld for too long or applied so copiously that their roots become sodden.

POTTING AND MEDIA: Horizontal rafts of tree fern, cork, or wood large enough (2–3 inches) to allow a few years' growth suit them well. Since they rarely branch, division is not often possible; I simply cut away dead pseudobulbs at the end of the chain before retying the plant to a new mount. Remount when new growths are evident, as roots will come from these once they have expanded.

Homalopetalum pumilio

Isabelia (no abbr.)

(IS-AH-BELL-EE-AH)

SUBTRIBE: Laeliinae

NUMBER OF KNOWN SPECIES: 1

NATIVE RANGE: Brazil

SKILL LEVEL: Experienced

GOOD INTRODUCTORY SPECIES: Isabelia virginalis

If you think only people can weave, then you have never seen the miniature *Isabelia virginalis* up close. This monotypic genus knits the most intricate little baskets imaginable to shield its pseudobulbs from the strong Brazilian sun. The pseudobulbs are squatly teardrop-shaped and measure about ³/₈ inch in height. They alternate left and right on an abbreviated, creeping rhizome attached by a few short roots to a twig or branch. Each new growth expands out of a netted sheath of raffia-brown fibers that surround the expanded pseudobulb like a fishnet stocking all frayed at the top where the needlelike

Isabelia virginalis 'Fox Den' CBM/AOS

leaf protrudes. The fibers remain in good shape for several years before withering away to expose the older pseudobulbs to the sun, which turns them a ruddy red. The vegetative habit of these 2-inch plants is so interesting and satisfying that the $1/2$-inch white flowers with a ruby interior are an unexpected bonus. Each new lead produces one flower on a short petiole that barely clears the tousle of fibers. The flowers never expand fully, but their color stands out nicely against the raffia backdrop.

Neolauchea pulchella (*NE-OH-LOCK-EE-AH*) is a closely related Brazilian species that some authors include in *Isabelia*. Its growth habit and requirements are identical to *Isabelia*'s, but it lacks the netted sheaths, and its slightly larger flowers are rosy purple, not white. It is a very worthy addition to any collection of miniatures.

CULTURE

Isabelias require a humid environment with the moisture in the air, not on the roots. They are at their best clinging to a section of wood large and decay-resistant enough to let them creep undisturbed over its surface for years. I find they respond very well to enclosed under-lights culture if I put them up near the lights so the new leaves don't become thin and wane.

TEMPERATURE: Intermediate; a moderate temperature drop in fall spurs flowering during winter.

LIGHT: Bright to very bright (2,000–4,000 fc)

HUMIDITY, WATER, AND FERTILIZATION: Try to maintain humidity in the 60%–90% range, with good air movement and daily misting timed so that the mount dries by nightfall. Regular light fertilization through the year is beneficial, as the plants never seem to rest completely.

POTTING AND MEDIA: I prefer tree-branch mounts, because the short roots seem to appreciate the chance to burrow underneath flaky bark. Cork will work, as will tree fern, but I recommend that you remove plants from Brazilian tree fern *(Dicksonia selowii)*. Some Brazilian nurseries grow *Isabelia* on it, and I find that the roots rot easily. Slice the fern with a clean razorblade to remove the orchid and some of its roots, and attach this to a new mount. The rhizomes grow in tight chains of pseudobulbs that occasionally branch, and these branches can be gently removed and attached to a new mount in spring. Try not to disturb the plants, though, as their meager root systems do not take insult lightly.

Isochilus (no abbr.)

(*EYE-SO-KYE-LUS*)

SUBTRIBE: Laeliinae

NUMBER OF KNOWN SPECIES: 3–7

NATIVE RANGE: Mexico and Central America to Bolivia

SKILL LEVEL: Experienced

GOOD INTRODUCTORY SPECIES: *Isochilus aurantiacus, I. linearis, I. major*

If you are searching for something different among the orchids, consider an *Isochilus* or two, which are distantly related to *Epidendrums*. There is some debate about the number of species, but most people agree there are at least three. Relatively common in wet forests, they tend to grow low on trees, where they are noticeable. When these delicate plants are

Isochilus aurantiacus

out of bloom, you might mistake them for a clump of slender reeds perched on a tree trunk or large limb. Their pseudobulbs have been reduced to thin, reedlike canes lined with two-ranked, flattened leaves suggesting quill feathers. The 8–18-inch-long canes grow up and out from a dense, many-stemmed clump riddled with the withered remains of old, leafless canes that are probably nonfunctional aside from trapping falling debris for the roots to feed on. Fat roots anchor the clump and scavenge the water necessary to keep the leaves from shriveling. In dry conditions, the plant will shed many of its leaves until the rains return. As each stem matures, a tight cluster of brightly colored flowers emerges from its tip. The flowers are somewhat tubular and either bright pink-purple (*I. linearis* and *I. major*) or glowing orange (*I. aurantiacus*). They face up and out, creating a tasseled effect. Because the plants are nearly always in growth, blooms appear on and off throughout most of the year and the plants quickly bulk up to specimen size.

CULTURE

While requiring more humidity than most windowsills can provide, *Isochilus* do exceptionally well under lights, where their nearly constant blooms make them a valuable addition. Since they lack pseudobulbs, you'll need to pay careful attention to watering to prevent leaf drop and to keep the new growths coming.

TEMPERATURE: Intermediate to warm

LIGHT: Somewhat bright (1,800–2,800 fc)

HUMIDITY, WATER, AND FERTILIZATION: Provide high humidity (above 70%) and water regularly so that the roots never fully dry yet do not remain sodden. Fertilize lightly but frequently through the year.

POTTING AND MEDIA: I prefer smallish 2–3-inch clay pots filled with tree fern and/or NZ sphagnum. Clumps are fairly easy to divide if you take care to leave at least six stems and a good number of roots with each division. The roots are startlingly large for the delicate nature of the plant as a whole.

Laelia (L) 🌸 💡 🚩

(*LAY-lee-ah*)

SUBTRIBE: Laeliinae

NUMBER OF KNOWN SPECIES: 58

NATIVE RANGE: Mexico and the West Indies to Brazil (where the genus first evolved)

SKILL LEVEL: Beginner

GOOD INTRODUCTORY SPECIES: *see under group entries below*

This lovely genus contains more than its share of charming, easy-to-grow species perfectly suited to a life on the windowsill or under lights. If you are beginning with orchids, you owe it to yourself to try a few, be it the Lilliputian rock *Laelias*, demure *L. pumila* types, the elegant Mexican group, or the flashy *L. purpurata* clan. Their large, brightly colored *Cattleya*-shaped blooms and their resiliency in the face of less than perfect culture make them excellent additions to anyone's collection. The large, imposing *L. purpurata* is a parent of many, many early *Cattleya* hybrids, and the smaller species are used extensively these days to create the colorful mini-cats, which are better suited to smaller growing spaces. Because this is such a popular genus, containing three or four distinct subgroups, I have decided to consider the subgroups separately.

Mexican *Laelias*

GOOD INTRODUCTORY SPECIES: *Laelia albida, L. anceps, L. autumnalis, L. rubescens*. Among the Brazilian species, *L. pumila* is a good choice.

This group of six species from Mexico and Central America is distinctive in several ways. They usually produce two stiff, tapered leaves on each spindle-shaped or flattened pseudobulb. Flowers are borne on long, arching, sugar-sticky stems that shoot out from between the leaf bases as temperatures cool and days shorten in fall; the stems lengthen for some time before finally revealing the exquisite flowers in late fall and winter. Blooms are roughly *Cattleya*-shaped, though the seg-

Laelia anceps var. *alba* 'Sterling Dickinson' AM/AOS

Laelia jongheana 'Paris' AM/AOS

ments have a starry pointiness that is easily recognizable, and they range in width from 2 to 4 inches. *Laelia anceps* and *L. autumnalis* have long been popular in their home country and elsewhere, and color forms ranging from white to rose, purple, and blue-violet are common in cultivation. The tall spikes are quite elegant, and the flowers come during the darkest days of the year. They are very easy to cultivate on the windowsill or in a greenhouse, though the length of the spikes precludes them from a life under lights (they can reach 4 feet on robust individuals, though 16–24 inches is more common). *L. furfuracea* and *L. albida* are more demure, and probably better choices for HID setups.

Though not closely related, a small group of Brazilian *Laelias* that I call the *L. pumila* types are similar culturally to the Mexican species. The *L. pumila* I purchased in 1987 is still mounted on the same piece of cork it arrived on. The little plant has bloomed reliably every autumn, sending out 4-inch-wide, flat, rounded violet-purple flowers that are large for the size of the vegetative parts. Though much smaller than most of the Mexican species (and consequently much easier to handle under lights), *L. perrinii, L. jongheana,* and *L. pumila* have relatively widely spaced pseudobulbs and are best suited to mounts. The flowers appear with the new growths, which begin in fall, and are borne on short, weak spikes that allow the flower to rest on the leaves.

CULTURE

In nature this group experiences warm, rainy summers and cool, drier winters. They are true epiphytes, producing numerous large, adventurous roots that cling tightly to a section of cork or a small log. You can accommodate them in free-draining pots, but most tend to "walk" quickly upward and away from the potting medium (the pseudobulbs are spaced an inch or so apart along the rhizome), making mounted culture easier in the long run.

TEMPERATURE: Intermediate (to cool in winter)

LIGHT: Bright to very bright (2,000–4,000 fc)

HUMIDITY, WATER, AND FERTILIZATION: I don't find the Mexican *Laelias* too fussy about humidity, and I have had excellent results summering them outdoors, then bringing them in to a cool windowsill for the winter. Mounted and even potted plants should receive enough water in spring and summer to keep roots growing actively and pseudobulbs plump, with a decrease in winter after blooms have passed. Water only enough to keep the lead pseudobulbs from shriveling more than halfway. Too much water during winter dormancy can quickly lead to root rot. Fertilize frequently when the plants are in active growth and discontinue once the bloom spikes begin to lengthen in autumn.

POTTING AND MEDIA: As mentioned, mounting is preferable. A 2–3-inch-diameter, 8–10-inch-long log hung vertically from an eyehook will allow a few years' upward growth for even the largest *Laelia anceps* or *L. autumnalis*. If you grow them in clay pots or slatted baskets, medium-grade fir bark is excellent.

Rupicolous *Laelias*

GOOD INTRODUCTORY SPECIES: *Laelia briegeri, L. lucasiana, L. milleri, L. sincorana*

Many of my first orchids were rupicolous, or rock, *Laelias* (so called because they prefer to grow on rock outcrops in fairly dry but humid regions of coastal Brazil). They range in size from 2 to 6 inches tall and are perfectly at home in a small clay thumb pot. I found I could maintain quite a collection of them on the south-facing window ledge above the kitchen sink. In the wild they, like the Mexican *Laelias,* experience a decidedly cool, dry rest in winter, a condition easily duplicated indoors. They grow in the meager shade of scrub and cacti and so can tolerate very bright sunlight; the squat bead- or spindle-shaped pseudobulbs huddle tightly together beneath short, swollen leaves. The congested nature of the pseudobulbs means you can raise a good-sized specimen in a small container. They grow well enough with less sunlight, but the leaves are thinner and the plants may not bloom as plentifully. When I moved to a darker apartment, I summered the collection outdoors in morning sun; all the plants produced nice

Laelia milleri 'Dr. Koopowitz' HCC/AOS

LIGHT: Bright to very bright (2,000–4,000 fc)

HUMIDITY, WATER, AND FERTILIZATION: Rupicolous species do not need high humidity to thrive, and in fact it can lead to overly soft growths and rhizome rot. This is one group of orchids that consistently performs better on the windowsill than in the orchid greenhouse. If rot is a problem, try a better-ventilated spot, perhaps near a fan. Water the plants once the mix has dried when they are in active growth during the spring and summer, but water less in fall and winter. During the darkest days of January here, I water the plants about once every ten days, and though the pseudobulbs and leaves get a bit shriveled, they plump up again when I increase watering as the light gets brighter in spring. These are not heavy feeders. A moderate shot of fertilizer every few weeks during spring and summer is all that's required.

POTTING AND MEDIA: Small (1–3-inch) clay pots are ideal for these miniatures. I have used tree fern and NZ sphagnum as well as a 1:1 mix of fine fir bark and aquarium gravel quite successfully.

Laelia purpurata group

GOOD INTRODUCTORY SPECIES: *Laelia purpurata*

This group comprises *Laelia purpurata*, *L. tenebrosa*, *L. lobata*, and a few others. Some taxonomists consider them to be distinct enough from the rest of the genus to be split out on their own. These are imposing plants, with growths topping 20 inches on a robust individual. They consist of long, flattened pseudobulbs (they remind me of the razor clams we have here on coastal beaches) topped by an even longer leaf. Unlike the other *Laelias*, they produce a large sheath to cradle the developing flower buds, which appear from the lead growths in late spring and summer. The flowers, with a 6-inch spread, large ruffled lip, and colors that range from white to pink, purple, and bronze, are spectacular. *L. purpurata* is one of the most popular orchids in orchid-rich Brazil, and whole societies are devoted to its culture. Consequently, many named color forms and clones exist, of which a fair number are available from tissue culture. Though large, they are very rewarding plants and the parents of countless *Cattleya*-alliance hybrids.

Schomburgkias (SCHOM-BURK-EE-AH) were still lumped in with *Laelias* when I began growing orchids, though they are quite distinctive. These are large, robust plants with long, hollow, tapered pseudobulbs that are designed as ant condominiums. The ants tunnel into the hollow pseudobulbs and in return provide fertilizer and protection to the plants. They are not indoor orchids; their size and need for very bright light (4,000–5,000 fc) relegate them to the greenhouse or outdoors in tropical climes. If you have the room, however, they are quite spectacular, to say the least. Several thickened leaves are attached near the top of the long, ribbed pseudo-

squat growths and managed to accumulate enough reserves to bloom once they came back indoors for the winter. Usually one to three flowers are produced from each lead growth, with different species blooming during different seasons. The spikes are short (2–14 inches), at least compared to those of the Mexican species. The blooms themselves are easily recognized because the narrow, blunted sepals and petals are of uniform size, and the tubular, ruffled lip curves down like an elephant's trunk. Colors range from sulfur yellow (*L. briegeri* and *flava*) through violets and pinks (*L. lucasiana* and L. *sincorana*) to vermilion (*L. milleri*).

CULTURE

See description above.

TEMPERATURE: Intermediate (to cool in winter)

bulb, and from between the upper two leaves a rodlike flower stem arches out, growing to 2, 3, or even 5 feet above the plants before finally unfurling a tight cluster of 2- to 3-inch-wide flowers that might best be described as *Laelias* that were washed but not ironed. Colors range from browns and tans to pinks and purples. *S. superbiens* is as deep and glowing a rose-purple as the best *Laelia autumnalis*. Grow them in 8-inch pots or larger baskets; water and fertilize copiously in spring and summer, tapering off by two-thirds during winter.

CULTURE

Laelia purpurata and its close relatives require conditions similar to those for *Cattleyas*.

TEMPERATURE: Warm to intermediate

LIGHT: Bright (2,000–3,000 fc)

HUMIDITY, WATER, AND FERTILIZATION: Like the other types of *Laelias*, this group is not overly demanding about humidity; 50%–60% on average will suffice. They are heavier feeders than the other types, though, so water more frequently during their active growth period and fertilize every seven to ten days at this time as well.

POTTING AND MEDIA: Clay or plastic pots and slatted baskets are all used, though I prefer the baskets because the plants can be allowed to reach specimen size, which I think encourages blooming. Use medium-grade fir bark, lava rock, or another free-draining, coarse medium.

Lemboglossum (no abbr.)

(*LEM-BOW-GLOSS-UM*)

SUBTRIBE: Oncidiinae

NUMBER OF KNOWN SPECIES: 12

NATIVE RANGE: Mexico to northern South America

SKILL LEVEL: Expert

GOOD INTRODUCTORY SPECIES: *Lemboglossum bictoniense*

Long part of the large genus *Odontoglossum*, this small group of mainly Mexican and Central American cloud forest species now resides in its own. The small size of many of the species, coupled with floriferous displays of spade-lipped pink, chocolate, white, and/or green flowers, makes them possible candidates for an enclosed light box or a cooler greenhouse. I have to admit I have struggled with the likes of *Lemboglossum cer-*

Laeliocattleya **Aloha Case 'Kevin'** HCC/AOS

Lemboglossum uro-skinneri **'Big Daddy'** HCC/AOS

vantesii and *L. rossii*, for although they like it rather cool and humid, they also demand good air circulation so that water doesn't settle too long in the leaf sheaths, leading to pseudobulb rot. I think my light room may run a bit too cool in winter for them; they do better in the greenhouse, where days are 5°–10° warmer, even though the nighttime temperatures dip just as low. When they thrive, their tight clumps of nickel-sized, flattened pseudobulbs and thin, pale green leaves make for neat and attractive plants even out of flower. The current season's growths produce semipendent inflorescences with from one to three flowers from among the leaf sheaths, mostly in winter. The unusually large and impressive *L. bictoniense* grows at high elevations in Mexico, and it passes some of the burgundy and green spotting and barring of its petals and sepals (along with a light pink lip) on to hybrids with warmer-growing *Oncidiums*. It lofts stiff, 3-foot-tall racemes lined with 2-inch flowers along the upper half, and this spectacular display is inherited by its hybrid offspring. It is as a parent of *Odontocidium* hybrids that this species has attained true horticultural fame.

Mexicoa ghiesbrechtiana, a related species endemic to Mexico, bears arching sprays of purple-brown, white-edged flowers set off by a light yellow dancing-doll lip. It thrives under the same conditions as the smaller *Lemboglossums* and is well worth growing should you come across it.

***Lemboglossum rossii* 'Uschi' AM/AOS**

A fairly cool, breezy, and humid atmosphere plus regular watering through the year are the main ingredients for success with *Lemboglossums*.

TEMPERATURE: Intermediate to cool

LIGHT: Moderately bright (1,800–2,500 fc)

HUMIDITY, WATER, AND FERTILIZATION: Humidity ranging in the 60%–80% range will suffice. Growth continues on and off through all but the coolest parts of the year, so regular watering and light but regular fertilization are necessary. Water when the medium has begun to dry.

POTTING AND MEDIA: Mounting the smaller species on tree-fern rafts helps prevent the pseudobulb rot that can set in with potted culture. If you do choose pots, use small (2–3-inch) clay or plastic pots with all but the largest species. Under my conditions, NZ sphagnum or a tree fern–sphagnum blend gives the best results.

Lepanthes (Lths)

(*LEP-AN-THEESE*)

SUBTRIBE: Pleurothallidinae

NUMBER OF KNOWN SPECIES: 800 and growing

NATIVE RANGE: American tropics

SKILL LEVEL: Expert

GOOD INTRODUCTORY SPECIES: *Lepanthes calodictyon*

Scale is everything. If we were the size of spiders, the utterly fantastic flowers within the genus *Lepanthes* would surely have us transfixed. Unfortunately for humans, one needs a good hand lens or dissecting microscope and reasonably good eyesight to fully appreciate these remarkable creatures and their otherworldly blooms. *Lepanthes* are almost exclusively miniature cloud forest orchids that hold their oval or rounded leaves on thread-thin stems (RAMICAULS) set with a rank of cone-shaped sheaths that give the whole a jointed appearance. Under the proper conditions, they grow and bloom ceaselessly, putting up new stems from a congested rhizome and new flowers from thin zigzag stems that either lie flat against the upper or lower leaf surfaces or arch out and above the plant itself. An individual flower spike seems to go on indefinitely, producing a new flower once the last has faded and continuing this for up to a year or more. For a person with a penchant for miniatures, *Lepanthes* are addictive. The number of species is seemingly inexhaustible, though only a small portion are in cultivation. On just one branch of one tree in the Ecuadorian cloud forest I observed seven different species growing side by side. Like most of the pleurothallids, *Lepanthes* seem to be rapidly evolving and speciating along with their pollinators (presumably small flies and gnats). The three sepals form the bulk of each flower. Though sometimes fused into a disk or boat shape, they retain a basically triangular orientation. The

Lepanthes delhierroi

small petals, lip, and column are often highly modified to suit the whims of whatever small insect a specific *Lepanthes* is trying to attract. I have seen birds, butterflies, fangs, tarantulas, plucked turkeys, and pairs of velvet cushions in the various constellations of petal, column, and lip. Maybe it's a relief that the flowers are so small, or I'd be having some pretty disturbing nightmares after an evening in Lepantheland.

Lepanthopsis (*LEP-AN-THOP-SIS*) is another charming genus of pleurothallids that vegetatively resemble *Lepanthes.* The flowers are very different, though. The blooms arrange themselves in two ranks like little bristly brushes or clothespins strung along a slender line. They need the same culture as their cousins, but I find them a bit easier to grow because they bulk up more quickly and become 2–4-inch-high specimens within a year or two.

CULTURE

Almost without exception, these delicate plants require a fairly cool, very humid, but well-ventilated atmosphere and daily misting/watering. They are challenging but not impossible to grow if you can provide the specialized conditions that most in this subtribe favor. They respond beautifully to under-lights culture in an enclosed box or room and do equally well in a damp greenhouse. My biggest enemies have been small snails and fungus gnat larvae, both of which chew off the ramicauls

as they begin to develop. If left unchecked, they can destroy all of a clump's dormant buds. If that happens, many species will produce keikis from the point where the flower spikes emerge, giving you another chance. Some produce keikis liberally even under the best culture, and enthusiasts enjoy sharing them with their friends.

TEMPERATURE: Intermediate to cool

LIGHT: Low (1,200–1,800 fc)

HUMIDITY, WATER, AND FERTILIZATION: Humidity in the 70%–100% range is perhaps the most important aspect of *Lepanthes* culture; the plants wither and drop leaves quickly when the atmosphere is too dry. Water enough that the plants never dry out completely, and mist them on the days you do not water. Very light but regular fertilization is important, since they grow unceasingly.

POTTING AND MEDIA: Larger clumps can be divided, though some species seem to lose growths as fast as they add them and so never get to be big specimens. Keikis are the easiest means of increase. As with *Restrepias,* a healthy leaf will sometimes yield a keiki even on species that don't normally produce them. Carefully cut off a rather new leaf with a bit of ramicaul and stick the ramicaul in damp NZ sphagnum up to the leaf base. If you keep the moss damp and the cutting humid, a new plant will often begin to grow within a month. For established plants, I use straight NZ sphagnum in tiny thumb pots, or I place the roots in a pad of sphagnum tied to a small chunk of tree fern or an oak or sassafras twig. Mounted plants will do beautifully provided you can mist them daily.

Leptotes (Lpt) 🏵 🔦 🏴

(*LEP-TOE-TEES*)

SUBTRIBE: Laeliinae

NUMBER OF KNOWN SPECIES: 3

NATIVE RANGE: South America

SKILL LEVEL: Beginner

GOOD INTRODUCTORY SPECIES: *Leptotes bicolor, L. unicolor*

Though you would hardly think it from looking at them, *Leptotes* are closely related to *Epidendrums* and *Laelias.* Out of bloom the plants look more like some of the miniature Australian *Dendrobiums,* with their little swollen leaves arranged in snaggletooth clumps on a small piece of cork. The flowers are about 1¹/₂ inches long, which in the case of the smaller *L. unicolor* is about the size of the plant itself (the largest, *L. bicolor,* is about twice that size). The blooms never fully expand; instead, they droop in small clusters just beyond the leaves. The plants have an endearing look that is more charming than beautiful. The succulence of the terete leaves suggests that these are plants of dry, exposed places, but in cultivation they do exceedingly well under lights or on a win-

Leptotes unicolor

Lockhartia (Lhta)

(LOCK-HART-EE-AH)

SUBTRIBE: Oncidiinae

NUMBER OF KNOWN SPECIES: 24

NATIVE RANGE: American tropics

SKILL LEVEL: Experienced

GOOD INTRODUCTORY SPECIES: *Lockhartia micrantha,*
L. elegans

Perhaps more of a curiosity than anything else, these cousins of *Oncidiums* are instantly recognizable in or out of bloom by their flattened herringbone stems, which look to me like braided palm fronds pressed in a book. On close inspection you'll see that *Lockhartia* stems are composed of alternating leaves compressed and folded along the midvein to resemble scales. The stems begin growing vertically but soon arch over as the narrow stem base succumbs to its increasing load. Mature plants have a ribbonlike quality, with meandering 8–14-inch stems weaving hither and yon or sweeping down and up again. Flowers burst out from between the uppermost few leaves, either singly on short stems or in branched panicles. They are uniformly yellow or white barred or spotted with brown and have the dancing-doll shape familiar to students of the Oncidiinae. Blooming is seasonal (typically in summer), but they bloom for a month or more, and the small flowers are pretty against a background of braided green.

CULTURE

The pendulous habit of *Lockhartias* is best accommodated on a mount, though they will do perfectly well in fairly small, freely draining pots. Since they require even moisture through the year, I recommend potting them unless you have a green-

dowsill. They bloom well if given moderate light, and the leaves help buffer them against occasional vacation-induced droughts. Interestingly, the seed capsules contain vanillin, and in Brazil they are harvested for flavoring ice cream and the like.

CULTURE

While I have grown *Leptotes* in 1¹⁄₂-inch thumb pots, they really do better if mounted, and the flowers are displayed more naturally on a perch. Being rather forgiving plants, they are good ones to try if you're just getting your feet (I was tempted to say floor) wet with mounts. Division is straightforward though seldom necessary.

TEMPERATURE: Intermediate

LIGHT: Somewhat bright (1,500–2,500 fc)

HUMIDITY, WATER, AND FERTILIZATION: *Leptotes* are not demanding about humidity, especially in winter — 50%–60% will suffice. Mist or water once the medium becomes dry. They do not have a pronounced rest period, so I prefer year-round light fertilization.

POTTING AND MEDIA: Cork or hardwood twigs make suitable mounts, and if potting *Leptotes,* use small clay pots filled with medium-grade bark, Turface, or lava rock.

Lockhartia bennettii

house or enclosed light room. They are not really difficult plants to care for in a greenhouse; they are more difficult indoors.

TEMPERATURE: Intermediate to warm

LIGHT: Somewhat bright (1,500–2,500 fc)

HUMIDITY, WATER, AND FERTILIZATION: Humidity in the 60%–70% range is appropriate. Water *Lockhartias* once the medium begins to dry, taking care not to let the plants begin to desiccate and lose stems. They grow almost continually, so regular light fertilization is better than more occasional heavy doses.

POTTING AND MEDIA: The plants are top-heavy and will topple over in plastic, so use 2–3-inch clay pots filled with NZ sphagnum or a sphagnum blend. Or mount *Lockhartias* on a tree-fern slab with a moss pad. Divide them in spring, taking care that each division retains at least five or six healthy stems.

Lycaste (Lyc) 🏵 🏠

(*LYE-CAST-EE*)

SUBTRIBE: Lycastinae

NUMBER OF KNOWN SPECIES: 45

NATIVE RANGE: Mexico and the Caribbean to South American Andes

SKILL LEVEL: Beginner to experienced

GOOD INTRODUCTORY SPECIES: *Lycaste aromatica, L. cochleata, L. deppei*

Lycastes are simply wonderful orchids, and many are easily grown, even on a windowsill, especially if they summer out-doors. The ones to start with are undoubtedly the smaller-flowered Mexican and Central American species typified by *Lycaste aromatica.* The large-flowered *L. skinneri,* as well as most of the Andean representatives, which are usually big plants when in leaf, require cool temperatures and high humidity. For all these reasons they are better left in the green-house. *L. skinneri* and its hybrids have long been popular in England, and in my mind the plants carry a certain Victorian formality compared to the carefree disposition and approach-ability of the smaller species.

All *Lycastes* produce large, oval, often ribbed, and somewhat flattened pseudobulbs that nest tightly together like eggs in a basket. During the growing season, new leads arise from the base of the previous year's bulbs and quickly unfold large pleated leaves, as well as a few smaller ones that sheath the new pseudobulb and are summarily shed once it has expanded. The remaining two to three leaves may span 2 feet or more; given that *Lycastes* are often grown to specimen size, they do demand considerable real estate during the warmer months. Fortunately, the Mexican/Central American species and many of the Andean ones as well shed their leaves with the arrival of

Lycaste aromatica

Lycaste skinneri 'Heat Wave'

Lycaste portella CHM/AOS

autumn's cooler nights, quickly reducing the size of the plant to something more manageable indoors during the winter. Depending on the species, flower spikes begin to grow from the base of the newest pseudobulbs either in fall or winter after leaves are shed or in spring as new vegetative growth commences. Most *Lycaste* flowers are notably triangular when viewed face-on, because the three sepals are the dominant feature; the lip and petals cup forward around the column. Some species bear flowers with larger, more outspread petals and curved or drooping sepals, while a few, such as *L. candida*, have reflexed sepals, so the petals and lip become the dominant elements in the design. Flower color ranges from butter yellow and egg yolk orange to kelly green and white, smoky rose, burnt umber, pale pink, bronze, or chocolate. Usually the lip and petals stand in striking contrast to the sepals. Each flower stem bears from one to occasionally three blossoms, but a robust pseudobulb may sport up to a half dozen inflorescences. As a result, *Lycastes*—especially the smaller ones—simply cover themselves in bouquets of flowers that are as well composed as any floral arrangement. Without leaves the flowers are even more effective, though even the species and hybrids with evergreen foliage are striking in flower.

CULTURE

The smaller-flowered, Mexican/Central American *Lycastes* are easily grown indoors in a moisture-retentive medium. Since they are dormant during winter, their water and humidity requirements are easily met on a windowsill, and they love spending the summer outdoors in a shaded spot. The large species and hybrids can be grown indoors, but because they are cloud forest plants, they need higher humidity and controlled temperatures to grow and bloom successfully. In general, I would grow them in a greenhouse or, if you live in the cool tropics, a lath house.

TEMPERATURE: Intermediate to cool (most need a cool rest in winter, even the evergreen types)

LIGHT: Somewhat bright (1,500–2,500 fc)

HUMIDITY, WATER, AND FERTILIZATION: Humidity should be 50%–80% during the growing season and year-round for the evergreen species. Water heavily during the period of active growth and taper off gradually during the fall. Once the deciduous *Lycastes* shed their leaves, water only every other week or so, just enough to keep the roots alive and the pseudobulbs at least half hydrated (see photo, p. 45). Apply fertilizer fairly heavily in spring (after flowering) and through the summer, then curtail it and finally stop during the winter rest.

POTTING AND MEDIA: *Lycastes* grow on trees and rocks and even semiterrestrially. Though they will grow in a variety of orchid media, most expert growers lean toward a semiterrestrial mix of the kind appropriate for *Paphiopedilums*. I have used both fine fir bark and treefern–NZ sphagnum combinations with success. The clumps are easily divided before new vegetative growth begins in late winter; be sure to leave at least two pseudobulbs with every division. Often two leads are produced from each of the previous year's bulbs, so within three years even a small division will be pretty large. Since *Lycastes* make such impressive specimens, I prefer to use 10- or 12-inch slatted baskets that will keep the medium fresher and allow for suitable expansion of the clump. Clay or plastic pots will work, but avoid using standard-depth pots larger than 8 inches, as the center of the mix will sour.

Masdevallia (Masd)

(MASS-DE-VAL-EE-AH)

SUBTRIBE: Pleurothallidinae

NUMBER OF KNOWN SPECIES: 360 and counting

NATIVE RANGE: Primarily South American Andes, with outliers from Mexico to Brazil

SKILL LEVEL: Experienced to expert

GOOD INTRODUCTORY SPECIES: *Masdevallia floribunda*, *M. infracta*, *M. nidifica*

During the 1990s, after new roads were cut into the cloud forests of Ecuador, Colombia, and Peru, a dread disease was unleashed on innocent orchid growers like myself, a disease known simply as acute masdevalloid complex, or AMC. The disease starts out innocently enough with the purchase of a *Masdevallia* or two. With their successful culture come the

Masdevallia prodigiosa

Masdevallia (decumana × deformis)

first symptoms—quickened pulse, sweating palms, and nervousness at the sight of some newly discovered *Masdevallia* on a show table, nursery bench, or in the pages of an orchid magazine. In the late stages of AMC, sufferers reach destitution after spending lavishly on climate-controlled greenhouses, trips to the Andes, and spending sprees at specialty nurseries. I know—it happened to me. Something about *Masdevallias* is intangibly alluring—maybe their reputation for being difficult or the great number of small but extremely colorful and showy species or the fact that plants new to science were being discovered almost weekly during the 1980s and 1990s.

The plants are small—typically in the 2–5-inch range with a few over a foot and still others under an inch. Narrow or spoon-shaped leaves are produced from a clumping rhizome nearly continuously through the year, so plants can bulk up very quickly. The flower spikes emerge from a small sheath that wraps the base of the leaf where it joins the short ramicaul, and these elongate upward or outward to just beyond the foliage before revealing one to sometimes six or more triangular flowers. The showy parts of the flowers are the sepals, which may be almost any shade of the rainbow except true blue. The tip of each sepal narrows to a slender point, which is often drawn out into a long, delicate tail. The petals and lip are tiny in comparison and huddle around the column as if pro-

Masdevallia Kimballiana

Masdevallia veitchiana 'Prince de Gaulle' AM/AOS

Dryadella albicans

tecting it from the rain. Though the plants grow continuously, flowering is seasonal, usually beginning with the advent of cooler nights in autumn.

Dryadellas (DRY-A-DELL-AH) are close relatives of *Masdevallias*, bearing small, triangular flowers down among the slender, thickened leaves. They come from lower altitudes and thus are more easily accommodated indoors. They will even succeed on a windowsill if the air is not too dry.

CULTURE

With few exceptions, *Masdevallias* require a relatively cool, humid environment to thrive. They are the perfect size for enclosed light cases or indoor grow rooms, and I have had wonderful results growing them in the cellar, where the coolness of winter lingers long into the summer and temperatures rarely exceed 80°. They are not beginner plants, but once you have some proficiency, I think you'll find them most rewarding. (But please, beware of AMC and ask your spouse or partner to hide your checkbook if the early symptoms start to appear.) *Masdevallias* have no water storage organ save the fleshy leaves, so they need a mix that never completely dries.

Hot weather—especially when the night temperatures remain above 70°—can do them in quickly, so don't try them if you live in an area where summer nighttime temperatures are generally above that mark. Sudden leaf drop is a sure sign of heat stress. Growing them has taught me the importance of the plant's native elevation to my chances of success. Since elevation or altitude is related directly to temperature, species originating from higher than 3,000 meters above sea level are very difficult to accommodate unless you live in a chilly climate like that of coastal Alaska, San Francisco, or northern Scotland. If you have ever been in a high, cold forest, you'll know why. Species that grow in the lower-elevation cloud forests around 1,500 meters are much more forgiving of occasional heat and are thus a better choice for most of us.

TEMPERATURE: Intermediate to cool, depending on the species

LIGHT: Low (1,200–2,000 fc)

HUMIDITY, WATER, AND FERTILIZATION: As long as you have excellent air circulation, *Masdevallias* will grow in a nearly saturated atmosphere—75%–90% humidity. Water when the medium begins to dry and never allow them to go long without water. Water quality is important for all orchids, but it seems especially so for *Masdevallias* and other pleurothallids. I have found that very dilute fertilizer (50–75 ppm N, or about ¼ tsp/gal of a formula like Miracle-Gro) applied once a week will produce lavish growth and bloom.

POTTING AND MEDIA: Moisture-retentive media such as NZ sphagnum or sphagnum plus tree fern are excellent, as is lava rock or one of the other inert materials such as pumice or Turface if you water frequently. If you can achieve a saturated atmosphere, many *Masdevallias* do marvelously when mounted on slabs or twigs with a moss pad applied around the roots. Yearly repotting, preferably in autumn when the weather cools, is important to keep the compost fresh and the roots healthy. The plants multiply rapidly, so you'll need to repot just to maintain space within your collection. Clumps are easily divided, but take care to leave at least six leaves on each division. Use 1- to 4-inch clay or plastic pots or mesh baskets.

Maxillaria (Max)

(*MAX-ILL-AIR-EE-AH*)

SUBTRIBE: Maxillariinae

NUMBER OF KNOWN SPECIES: 700 plus

NATIVE RANGE: American tropics

SKILL LEVEL: Beginner to experienced

GOOD INTRODUCTORY SPECIES: *Maxillaria cucullata, M. uncata*

Like the *Dendrobiums, Bulbophyllums,* and other very large genera within the Orchidaceae, *Maxillarias* are certainly due for some taxonomic revision to organize and consolidate their clan. That being said, a *Maxillaria* flower is immediately recognizable, giving this group a certain sense of cohesion. Though the foliage may be fanlike, straplike, swollen, or thin, and the pseudobulbs may be as large as a pecan shell or smaller than a match head, the flowers follow a consistent pattern dictated mainly by the prominent triangular sepals. Inside the isosceles of the calyx jut two fanglike or mustachioed petals and a tongue-shaped lip. The sepals usually point slightly forward, so from the side the flower looks as if it's not quite open. Most *Maxillarias* carry the flowers on short stems, so the blooms seem to huddle within a thick nest of leaves and pseudobulbs like frightened chicks. This makes for less than perfect viewing, but, hey, that's their way. Each flower is presented on its own stem, which arises from the base of a recent pseudobulb. Some, like *M. densa* and *M. coccinea,* produce small flowers massed together in a little pompom, while others, including the arachnoid *M. lepidota,* dole theirs out a few at a time on longer stems.

As you might suspect, the wants and tastes of 700 or more species are not easily summarized, but I'll attempt it anyway. In general, I find *Maxillarias* to be easily cultured, though those that hail from higher-elevation and misty cloud forests would scarcely be at home on your living room windowsill. The Mexican and Central American species in the *Maxillaria cucullata* complex are a good starting point, for they will prosper on a windowsill or under lights. Reserve the showy Andean species like *M. sanderiana* and *M. striata* for a greenhouse or enclosed growing space where moderate temperatures and high humidity can be maintained. Most of the species grow quickly, sending up new leads almost continuously through the year and blooming in one or two flushes.

TEMPERATURE: Warm to cool, depending on the species

LIGHT: Somewhat bright (1,800–2,800 fc)

HUMIDITY, WATER, AND FERTILIZATION: Humidity in the 50%–80% range (higher for cool and cloud forest species) is about right. *Maxillarias* generally grow almost continuously, so water evenly throughout the year when the medium has just begun to dry. Regular moderate doses of fertilizer will quickly produce large specimens.

Maxillaria longissima

Maxillaria species

POTTING AND MEDIA: *Maxillarias* seem happiest as large clumps, and they tend to recover slowly from overly aggressive division. I will often mount them or place them in slatted baskets, which keep the potting mix fresher longer, so I can limit the disturbance of repotting to once every two or three years. Bark or tree fern is acceptable, and their numerous short, thin copious roots will cling happily to slabs or branches.

Miltonia (Milt) 🏵️ 🔳

(*MILL-TONE-EE-AH*)
SUBTRIBE: Oncidiinae
NUMBER OF KNOWN SPECIES: 10
NATIVE RANGE: Primarily Brazil
SKILL LEVEL: Beginner
GOOD INTRODUCTORY SPECIES: *Miltonia spectabilis*

Nigh onto a generation ago, taxonomists divided the genus *Miltonia*, moving the bunny rabbit–cute pansy orchids from the mountains of Central and northern South America into *Miltoniopsis* and leaving the Brazilian species in the original genus. With pointy petals and sepals and an often oversized lip, species like *Miltonia spectabilis* look more like friendly bearded trolls than bunnies—and they are certainly a more rough-and-ready group than *Miltoniopsis*. They are blood relatives of *Oncidium* and *Odontoglossum*, and as such can readily be reshuffled with a hybridizer's toothpick to create *Odontonia*, *Miltonidium*, *Miltassia*, and even the unpronounceable four-way composite *Vanalstyneara*, with a bit of *Rodriguezia* thrown in for good measure. Well, that last sentence contains enough Latin to last me all morning, so let's get to some specifics about the plants.

Miltonias are leafy, medium-sized orchids that ramble around on what are regrettably long rhizomes if you intend to confine them to a pot. They retain the two or three leaves that flank the developing pseudobulb as well as the pair produced at its apex. The foliage is fairly thin in substance by orchid standards, with a crease in the middle and a blunted tip. Leaves range in length from 6 to 18 inches, and the oval or cupped pseudobulb stands around 2 or perhaps 4 inches from tip to toe. I haven't grown all the *Miltonias*, but those I have tried, including pink and white *M. spectabilis* and the lovely grape purple *M. spectabilis* var. *moreliana*, pale yellow *M. flavescens*, and brown-and-yellow *M. clowesii*, easily produce several flushes of new growth annually. Only one of these flushes is accompanied by flowers. Blooms are large—up to 3 inches long and almost as wide—and present themselves well on spikes of one to twelve flowers that spring out of the sheathing leaves.

CULTURE

Miltonias are fairly adaptable plants; the main impediment to their culture is their rambling nature rather than recalcitrance or failure to thrive. You can contain them in pots for a time, in baskets a bit longer, and on large plaques almost indefinitely.

Miltassia **Royal Robe 'Jerry's Pick'** HCC/AOS

In fact, I mounted a piece of *M. spectabilis* var. *moreliana* on a 2-foot length of firewood hung vertically from the greenhouse purlins, and it developed into a solid colony that was really something to see, though it was too large to move from its perch for the show table.

TEMPERATURE: Intermediate to warm

LIGHT: Bright (2,000–3,000 fc)

HUMIDITY, WATER, AND FERTILIZATION: Aim for a relative humidity of 60%—about average for orchids. The plants grow quickly, at least during the warmer months, so frequent watering/misting and relatively heavy fertilization are warranted then, with a decrease during the winter.

POTTING AND MEDIA: Though short, their roots are as plentiful as spaghetti in an Italian restaurant, sprouting out along the rhizome as the new growth matures. Shallow pots or baskets filled with medium-grade fir bark have worked well for me. When mounting *Miltonias*, I prefer a large slab of cork or a section of log, and I'm careful to mist the newly mounted plant frequently until it rambles over itself and forms a nest of growths through which the roots can weave.

Miltoniopsis (Mltnps)

(*MILL-TONE-EE-OP-SIS*)

SUBTRIBE: Oncidiinae

NUMBER OF KNOWN SPECIES: 6

NATIVE RANGE: Central America south to the Peruvian Andes

SKILL LEVEL: Experienced to expert

GOOD INTRODUCTORY SPECIES: I recommend trying one of the many hybrids first, either the *Miltoniopsis* hybrids or intergenerics like *Miltonidium*.

Thin-skinned aristocrats with immense flowers possessing a naïve beauty, *Miltoniopsis* are irresistible prizes at orchid sales, but few indoor growers can provide the necessary cloud forest conditions they demand. Beware the Ides of March, for summer's heat is around the corner and with it the potential decline of the pansy orchid. That's the conventional wisdom, anyway. Many hobbyists and nurseries raise *Miltoniopsis* to perfection, and hybridizers have interbred the handful of species to create some remarkable hybrids with flowers nearly 6 inches in circumference, flat as a dinner plate, and sporting lips decorated with waterfalls or inkblots so suggestive they could stand in for Rorschach cards at the psychologist's office. As in *Miltonia*, the sheathing leaves that fan out on either side of the developing pseudobulb are retained once the growth matures, so plants get quite leafy. The rhizomes are short compared to *Miltonia*'s, so the pansy orchids are more easily housed in pots. Less than a foot high, they are small enough to grow comfortably under lights, and in fact they thrive in an

Miltoniopsis endresii

enclosed light box or a grow room set up in a basement. Flowers appear on spikes growing from between the sheaths and pseudobulb; the spikes grow about as tall as the leaves and so present the flowers among or just above the foliage. The species' flowers are about half the size of those on some of the more outrageous hybrids; as far as I'm concerned, the 2–3-inch pansylike blooms are more in scale with the thin, light green foliage. Whether species or hybrid, the fragrant flowers are produced once or twice a year, and the blooms last up to a month in the greenhouse.

CULTURE

Cloud forest conditions—especially buoyant, very humid air and pure water—are important for success with *Miltoniopsis*. Like other "cool" orchids, they are especially popular in chill maritime climates such as the Pacific Northwest and western

Miltoniopsis Rainbow Falls 'Terry' HCC/AOS

Europe. It's interesting, though, that only one—the Central American *M. warscewiczii*—is technically a cool grower in the wild. The other species—*M. phalaenopsis, M. roezlii, M. vexillaria, M. bismarckii,* and *M. santanaei*—grow at intermediate elevations and intermediate to warm temperatures. It's more important to prevent excess heat and dryness than to provide cold.

TEMPERATURE: Intermediate to cool

LIGHT: Bright (2,000–3,000 fc). Leaves develop a slight reddish or pinkish tinge when they are receiving adequate light.

HUMIDITY, WATER, AND FERTILIZATION: Shirt-soaking humidity, around 80%, is ideal if coupled with strong air movement. *Miltoniopsis* are salt-sensitive plants, so weak but regular fertilization is best, with enough watering and misting to prevent the medium from drying completely. Leaf-tip dieback, a sign of salt or fertilizer burn, is common with this genus; and if the problem develops, leach the plants with distilled water and repot as soon as possible. If the new leaves emerge with accordionlike folding, it is a sign of not enough water or humidity, or possibly root rot if the mix has degraded.

POTTING AND MEDIA: NZ moss and moss blends provide the constantly damp but not saturated root zone these orchids relish. Repot in autumn, taking care to leave three to five growths per division and to minimize root disturbance as much as possible. A 3–6-inch clay or plastic pot is small enough to discourage staleness in the center of the mix. I have never tried, nor have I seen, a mounted *Miltoniopsis*.

Neocogniauxia (no abbr.)

(KNEE-OH-COG-NO-EE-AH)

SUBTRIBE: Laeliinae

NUMBER OF KNOWN SPECIES: 2

NATIVE RANGE: Jamaica and Hispaniola

SKILL LEVEL: Expert

GOOD INTRODUCTORY SPECIES: *Neocogniauxia hexaptera*

Though they are known as "difficult" orchids, I include these two lovely species from the Caribbean because I think they are ideal subjects for a basement light box or grow room or a cool greenhouse. With 2–4-inch-high canelike pseudobulbs and proportionately large, bright orange flowers, these charming miniatures resemble a cross between an *Epidendrum* and a *Sophronitis*. Cloud forest dwellers, they are slow to recover from less than ideal conditions such as excessive heat and poor-quality water. Healthy plants stay in bloom for a month or more, and the sight of the luminous, 1½-inch flowers floating above the narrow, dark green leaves and dainty canes is not one you'll quickly forget.

CULTURE

Cloud forest conditions are requisite. *Neocogniauxia hexaptera* grows well for me among the pleurothallids, provided I repot it carefully each fall and take care not to let it suffer any setbacks. Root rot caused by salt buildup, decomposed media, or overwatering will surely kill them.

Neocogniauxia hexaptera

Neofinetia falcata 'Hannah's Lavender' CHM/AOS

TEMPERATURE: Cool to intermediate

LIGHT: Somewhat bright (1,800–2,200 fc)

HUMIDITY, WATER, AND FERTILIZATION: *Neocogniauxias* need very high humidity—70%–100%—and excellent air movement. Never allow them to dry completely, and fertilize very lightly throughout the year, as growth occurs on and off through the seasons.

POTTING AND MEDIA: Clay thumb pots in the 1½–2½-inch range work well when filled with NZ sphagnum or a sphagnum blend. Repot annually in autumn, but try not to divide the plants, for they will sulk for a year or two.

Neofinetia (Neof) 🔆 🚩

(*NEO-FIN-ET-EE-AH*)

SUBTRIBE: Sarcanthinae

NUMBER OF KNOWN SPECIES: 1

NATIVE RANGE: Japan, Korea, and China

SKILL LEVEL: Experienced

GOOD INTRODUCTORY SPECIES: *Neofinetia falcata*

Neofinetia falcata has been revered in its native Japan for centuries, and hobbyists have named and preserved numerous forms that command astronomical prices at specialty nurseries. It is a small monopodial plant with a herringbone leaf arrangement like *Vanda* and *Ascocentrum* and a tendency to sucker freely, sending up new stems alongside older ones and rather quickly becoming a compact, densely leafy specimen. In

fact, new vegetative stems are often produced at the expense of flowers, especially if the plant does not receive an adequate cool winter rest. The flowers are a study in curves. They are borne on long, curved pedicels from a short spike that originates between one of the newer leaves and the stem. The petals and sepals arch backward and/or sideways from a narrow lip bedecked with two fanglike lobes. An elaborately long nectar spur arcs out and down from the back of the bloom. The whole reminds me of a piece of elaborately crafted wrought-iron furniture painted a pure, flat white.

CULTURE

Mist or water daily, but be aware that the species is subject to rot initiated when water stands too long in the leaf bases or within the growing tip of the plant (more a problem in the greenhouse than in the house). If possible, avoid watering the leaves and invert the plant to dislodge water during cool, cloudy weather. Placing the plant near a fan will also lessen this problem.

TEMPERATURE: Intermediate to cool. In the wild, especially in Korea, *Neofinetias* can experience some freezing without damage, making them a good subject for garden culture in subtropical climes such as southern Florida.

LIGHT: Bright (2,000–3,000 fc)

HUMIDITY, WATER, AND FERTILIZATION: Aim for 60%–70% humidity. Fertilize moderately during the warmer months and discontinue in winter. See comments on watering under Culture.

Ascofinetia Petit Bouquet CCM-AM/AOS

POTTING AND MEDIA: Slatted baskets are the containers of choice in the United States because they allow the thick, pearly roots to slither out into the air and sun. In Japan the plants are often displayed in traditional glazed ceramic containers. Wrap a few lengths of NZ sphagnum around the roots when repotting, or work in some pieces of fir bark or chunks of charcoal to provide a little extra water retention for the plant indoors. Since the stems multiply freely, it is a simple matter to sever a rooted piece with a sterile blade (avoid cutting into the main stem itself) and pot it separately to begin a new specimen. Leave the main clump as is to develop into an even larger mass of leaf, root, and flower.

Notylia (Ntl) ❦ ▤

(*NO-TILL-EE-AH*)

SUBTRIBE: Oncidiinae

NUMBER OF KNOWN SPECIES: 55

NATIVE RANGE: Mexico to Brazil

SKILL LEVEL: Experienced

GOOD INTRODUCTORY SPECIES: *Notylia barkeri*

Notylia albida

Notylia is a genus of small to miniature twig epiphytes that produce oblong leaves of medium substance atop rudimentary pseudobulbs nested in a tousle of thin, wiry white roots. They are at their best perched on a little branch of persimmon or sassafras, where their foxtail inflorescences can hang down unimpeded by pot or bench top. Like the equitant *Oncidiums*, they are a good choice for windowsill growers who want to branch out into mounted culture, as they are reasonably forgiving as long as you can soak them in a bucket for five minutes every three days or so. The species are fairly similar, and I suspect that the most widely available—*Notylia barkeri*—represents several distinct but look-alike species, as it is variable in size, length of inflorescence, and other characteristics. At any rate, the small white-and-green or pale pink flowers are very intricate up close. Their narrow, pointed petals and sepals hunch forward around a long column with a knob for a tip. The blooms are crowded on dangling spikes that arch out and down below the tangle of roots and 4-inch leaves.

CULTURE

As mentioned, this is a good genus to try if you are dabbling with mounted culture. Just watch the condition of the leathery leaves. If they become wrinkled, soak the plant for up to a half hour in water. When they receive adequate misting and water, the thin roots have $1/2$-inch green tips—a sign of active growth.

TEMPERATURE: Warm to intermediate

LIGHT: Somewhat bright (1,800–2,200 fc)

HUMIDITY, WATER, AND FERTILIZATION: Humidity around 50%–60% is suitable if bolstered with daily misting. Water enough to keep the leaves turgid, and fertilize lightly once or twice a month.

POTTING AND MEDIA: Once established on a mount, the plants rarely need dividing and should be remounted only if the slab or twig they are on has degraded. A few strands of NZ sphagnum threaded around the roots will help keep the plants better hydrated indoors.

Odontoglossum (Odm) ▤

(*OH-DONT-OH-GLOSS-um*)

SUBTRIBE: Oncidiinae

NUMBER OF KNOWN SPECIES: 181

NATIVE RANGE: Andean South America

SKILL LEVEL: Expert

GOOD INTRODUCTORY SPECIES: Try the intergeneric hybrids, such as the countless *Odontocidiums, Wilsonaras,* or *Maclellanaras,* before the species or hybrids within the genus. Hybrid vigor and warmth tolerance make these intergenerics much easier to grow and flower.

Odontoglossums are some of the largest and most vibrant

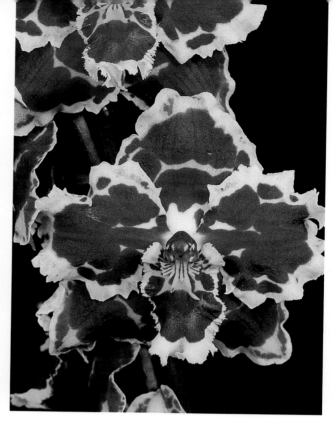

Odontoglossum cirrhosum 'Super Sunset' AM/AOS

Odontioda Castle de Ux 'Blackberry' HCC/AOS

Odontoglossum wyattianum

orchids of the high Andean cloud forests. It is an unforgettable experience to see trees bedecked in 6-foot bouquets of yellow, white, purple, and brown flowers arching out from robust leafy clumps that grip tightly to trunks and larger limbs. The flowers are variously star-shaped, ruffled, or spiderlike in appearance, and most sport full-body tattoos, stripes, spots, or bars of a contrasting color. The species grow at elevations above 4,000 feet (1,200 meters), where temperatures are moderate to cold and rain and mist are almost constant. Fat oval or round pseudobulbs topped by two or three long leaves may stand 8–16 inches high when out of bloom. Flower spikes that begin at the base of the bulb sneak out from between the sheathing leaves and arch up and out from 1 to 4 feet, often branching once or twice before the first flowers open. The plants are almost always in growth, and in a large collection some are in flower at any time of the year.

Since *Odontoglossums* demand cool, very humid conditions as well as considerable elbow room, they are most popular as greenhouse plants in cooler climates like the United Kingdom and northern California, as well as in their native Colombia and Ecuador. Elsewhere, intergeneric hybrids involving *Odontoglossums* are far and away more common in cultivation. Many of these complex hybrids have warmth-tolerant *Oncidiums*, *Brassias*, and *Miltonias* in their background and are thus much easier to grow. In fact, it is difficult to find true

Osmoglossum
pulchellum

Odontoglossum species except in breeders' collections. They have been mostly supplanted by hybrids, and a quick scan of grower catalogs on the Internet tells why — so many colors, so many patterns, so many shapes. The monumental genetic reshuffling within the *Oncidium/Odontoglossum* alliance has produced hybrids with just about every conceivable color combination and patterning. Some are positively psychedelic, others simply ostentatious, and still others as sublime as a Hawaiian sunset. Indoors, I suggest trying the *Odontocidiums, Wilsonaras,* and *Maclellanaras* first, as they are likely to be more warmth-tolerant.

Osmoglossum (OZ-MOE-GLOSS-UM) is a small genus recently split off from *Odontoglossum,* and one species in particular — *Osmoglossum pulchellum* — is justifiably popular among orchidists for its easy culture and vibrant white, highly fragrant flowers. It is a native of Mexico and Central America, and in the wild it grows in seasonally dry forest, so it adapts well to a life outdoors in the summer and indoors during the winter. The grassy, 12–16-inch leaves are a perfect backdrop for the flowers, which hang from thin stems for a month or more in winter. A cool, somewhat dry rest should follow blooming.

CULTURE

Cloud forest conditions are necessary for the species and for hybrids involving other primarily cool-growing genera like *Odontioda* (with *Cochlioda*) and *Vuylstekeara* (with *Cochlioda* and *Miltoniopsis*). By cloud forest conditions I mean temperatures of 50°–80°, humidity of 70% and higher, and strong air movement — the sort of place where moss grows on your shirt cuffs if you linger too long. *Odontocidiums, Wilsonaras,* and *Maclellanaras,* as well as the battery of other more warmth-tolerant hybrids, need proportionally less cloud as the per-

centage of cool-growing ancestry decreases, and many will adapt to life on the windowsill if you can add some humidity to the air. The height of the spikes makes under-lights culture a challenge; the spikes are often underengineered for the large size and quantity of flowers, so staking is advisable. Just be sure to stake the inflorescence before the buds become resupinate (twist upside down). You can tell they have twisted by the spiraled creasing in the flower's pedicel. At that point their position and orientation become fixed, so staking later than that will lead to a helter-skelter floral arrangement as they try to readjust.

TEMPERATURE: Cool for the species and cool-growing hybrids; intermediate for warmer-growing hybrids

LIGHT: Somewhat bright (1,500–2,500 fc). *Odontoglossums* are fairly shade-tolerant.

HUMIDITY, WATER, AND FERTILIZATION: Humidity is very important to good "Odont" culture. Levels consistently below 60% lead to accordioning or pleating of the emerging leaves, and crinkled leaves never recover, instead standing in mute testimony to your atmospheric transgressions for the rest of their life. Ideally, humidity should approach 80% for the species, and the potting mix should be barely dry when you water. *Odontoglossums* are sensitive to root rot, so it is better to underpot them and water a bit more frequently. Underpotted plants also seem to bloom more willingly. Since they have no defined rest period, they need light but regular fertilization throughout the year for good flowering.

POTTING AND MEDIA: For all but the largest species, 4–6-inch pots are adequate. *Odontoglossums* will quickly decline in a stale mix, so it's important to divide and repot annually in fall or winter, even for the hybrids. Preferred mixes include NZ moss blends and medium-grade fir bark.

Oerstedella (Orstdl)

(OAR-STED-EL-AH)

SUBTRIBE: Laeliinae

NUMBER OF KNOWN SPECIES: 6

NATIVE RANGE: Central America to northern South America

SKILL LEVEL: Beginner to expert

GOOD INTRODUCTORY SPECIES: Oerstedella centradenia

Oerstedella is a bit of an enigma to me. How can a small genus contain some species that are so easy to cultivate and others that are frustratingly slow and difficult? The first species I grew was O. centradenia, a very easy, vigorous, almost ever-blooming little orchid with thin, narrow, alternating leaves along the upper third of each thin stem. New stems are produced from the rhizome, which also sends out stubby, dispro-portionately fat, fleshy roots, but keikis are also freely made from the stem tips, so very soon you have a somewhat jumbled mass of bamboolike stems and roots with short clusters of ³/₄-inch, bright pinky purple, star-shaped flowers sporting paper-doll lips marked with a white spot. Since the keikis are easy to remove and give to a friend, this is one of those pass-along orchids like *Dendrobium kingianum* that everyone seems to acquire sooner or later. The roots are happiest with-out any medium, and I find it grows well even on a windowsill when plunked into a 3-inch clay pot filled with a few pieces of crock for extra surface area. *O. wallisii* is a bit larger, with chrome yellow flowers and a contrasting lip of white with purple spots. It does better in a coarse potting mix. My favorite is certainly *O. endresii*, a cloud forest species that is more demanding of humidity and moderate temperatures, which seems to grow at a painfully slow pace compared to its warm-growing relatives. Its 8-inch stems are topped with absolutely charming white and deep violet-blue flowers that last for quite a while in cool weather. It does not produce keiki very often, so seedlings and patience are your best bet for acquiring *O. endresii*.

CULTURE

See description above.

TEMPERATURE: Warm to cool, depending on species

LIGHT: Somewhat bright (1,500–2,500 fc)

HUMIDITY, WATER, AND FERTILIZATION: Humidity around 50%–60% (higher for *O. endresii*) is adequate. Leaf drop from the stems is a common response to drought in these orchids, which lack real water storage capacity. So be sure to water often enough to prevent that. Fertilize moder-ately throughout the year.

POTTING AND MEDIA: To reiterate, small clay pots filled with crock, charcoal, or Styrofoam are best for *O. centradenia*. The others prefer a more moisture-retentive mix. Keikis can be removed once they have at least two stems and a few roots. Division of the main clump is difficult but possible at any time of the year.

Oerstedella (**H. Phillips Jesup** × *centradenia*)

Oncidium (Onc)

(ON-SID-EE-UM)

SUBTRIBE: Oncidiinae

NUMBER OF KNOWN SPECIES: 620 plus

NATIVE RANGE: American tropics

SKILL LEVEL: Beginner

GOOD INTRODUCTORY SPECIES: Many, including *Oncidium leucochilum, O. longipes, O. ornithorhynchum, O. pul-chellum* and its hybrids, *O. sphacelatum* and its relatives

If you like yellow—sprays of yellow and brown arranged like hoop-skirted dancing dolls, birds in flight, or flying squirrels with arms outstretched—then you will love the *Oncidiums*. These easy-to-grow orchids come in other colors, too, but I associate them with primrose, gold, canary, and butter yellow. Their adaptability, floriferousness, and airy aesthetic have made *Oncidiums* popular florist plants, and it is likely that one of your first orchids was a dancing doll purchased for a modest sum from a nursery, grocery store, or home center. They have an advantage over *Phalaenopsis* and *Paphiopedilums* in that their often exaggerated pseudobulb helps them weather the vicissitudes of indoor culture with grace. The most common in the cut-flower and houseplant market are the *O. sphacelatum* types, which send up branched, arching sprays hung with dozens of 1–1½-inch flowers above leafy, clumping pseudobulbs. They are robust plants with enormous nests of thin white roots springing from the lime-sized pseudobulbs. Hybridization with *Lemboglossum* and *Odontoglossum* introduces other colors into the mix, but the floral effect is similar.

There are many other types of *Oncidiums,* and all but the high-elevation cool growers should do well on a windowsill or in a grow room if the flowers can clear the lights, and they are certainly valuable additions to a greenhouse collection. Some of my favorites are the so-called mule-ear *Oncidiums* like *O. splendidum,* which grow in drier locales in Central America. They have decent-sized pseudobulbs, but as insurance against drought they have evolved long, swollen leaves that are as plump as any desert succulent's. They will be happy where cacti thrive, albeit with a bit more frequent watering.

Oncidium Pokie 'Leuticke's Choice'

The **EQUITANT** *Oncidiums* are equally charming and readily adapt to indoor culture. These miniature twig epiphytes from the Caribbean have vestigial pseudobulbs and so rely entirely on their swollen leaves to weather dry spells. The leaves are curved and triangular in cross-section, like a sickle with an exaggerated taper to its edge. Preferring a mount to a pot, they will festoon a windowsill or light box with delicate sprays of multicolored flowers in every color save blue and green.

Psychopsis (sigh-COP-sis) are singularly spectacular Central and South American orchids long classified under *Oncidium.* These are the fabled butterfly orchids, whose exotic beauty so bewitched the Victorian aristocracy that they are rumored to have started the European orchid fever of the nineteenth century. I had much better luck cultivating these incredible plants in a south-facing window than I have had in the greenhouse, as they very quickly develop pseudobulb rot when water lingers between the big, flat bulbs and the tight-fitting bases of the leaves—especially in the higher humidity of the greenhouse. The flat leaves are thick, almost plastic in texture, and with good light they develop very pretty maroon and dark green leopard spots. During the summer, newly mature growths send up tall, stiff spikes that climb up a few feet then flatten out as if rolled with a pin before revealing the first of many successive blooms. With a span of 6 inches from petal tip to petal tip, the flowers are showstoppers. The lip and petals are heavily ruffled, spotted, or barred in orange and yellow. The sepals, similarly patterned, are long and thin, splaying out above the petals like strange antennae. The swept-back, winglike petals, skirted lip, and thin sepals do give the flowers an unmistakable insectlike appearance, an effect heightened by the two whitish eyespots of the column wings. Provide them with bright light, warmth, and regular watering during the growing season, taking care to keep water off the leaves as much as possible and making sure the plants are surface-dry by nightfall.

Sigmatostalix (sig-MAT-oh-STAL-ix) are little twig epiphytes that grow freely and easily on a mount or in a small pot or basket. The flowers are small but abundant, and on close inspection they possess a long, beaklike column that projects out from a very complex lip and splayed-back petals and sepals.

Ornithophora (formerly *Sigmatostalix*) *radicans* is my favorite, as its apple green, white, and brown flowers keep coming and coming over the course of the warmer months and the plants rapidly reach specimen size.

CULTURE

All of the *Oncidiums* and their relatives that I am familiar with like a freely draining potting mix. I let the pot dry before watering again, checking the condition of the lead pseudobulb or fleshy leaves for signs of hydro-insufficiencies. The lead

Oncidium **Angel Cake 'Ramona',** an equitant

bulb and the two behind it should be plump, and mule-ear and equitant leaves should look reasonably plump and unwrinkled. In most species the new growths produce numerous wiry roots as they mature, so divisions recover quickly if you time repotting correctly. Pleated foliage is less common among *Oncidiums* than among *Odontoglossums* or *Miltonias*, but if you see pleating, it could be the result of low humidity or a buildup of sticky exudates that some plants secrete from developing leaves. If an exudate is the problem, put the plant outdoors during summer rains or let it have a lukewarm ten-minute shower once every few weeks during its vegetative growth spurts (avoid dandruff shampoos and conditioners, as they will wreak havoc on your *Oncidium*'s delicate skin — just kidding).

Equitant species are very susceptible to crown rot when water lingers too long between the leaf bases. Also, the nest of thin roots is easily lost to a decomposed potting mix. They are safest on mounts, and I think they often perform better on a windowsill than in a greenhouse, as the drier air decreases the chance of crown rot.

Though staking is not needed with many species, it may be necessary with those that send out weak or extra-long spikes.

TEMPERATURE: Typically intermediate to warm, though a few species are cool growers, and many others can tolerate cool temperatures during winter dormancy.

LIGHT: Bright to very bright (2,000–4,000 fc). The mule-ear and equitant types as well as *Psychopsis* prefer the brightest light.

HUMIDITY, WATER, AND FERTILIZATION: It is tough to generalize about such a large genus, but for most species, humidity in the 40%–80% range (lowest for mule-ears and highest for the cloud forest species) should suffice, along with frequent watering and fertilization during the warmer months, when plants are most active. The larger *Oncidiums* are fairly heavy feeders in active growth, but the equitants and other twig epiphytes, like *O. crista-galli* and *O. globuliferum,* may burn themselves out on a rich diet of nitrogen.

POTTING AND MEDIA: Underpot *Oncidiums* to encourage rapid drying of the potting mix. A 6- to 8-inch pot will suit the robust *O. sphacelatum* types, while the miniatures will get by in a 2-inch thumb pot. I have had excellent results with the mule-ear *Oncidiums* in 6–10-inch slatted baskets. I have found mounting less satisfactory, except for the equitants and other twig epiphytes. Most common orchid media will work well with *Oncidiums.*

Ornithocephalus (no abbr)

(*OR-NITH-OH-CEPH-AL-ISS*)

SUBTRIBE: Ornithocephalinae
NUMBER OF KNOWN SPECIES: 35
NATIVE RANGE: Mexico and the Caribbean to Brazil
SKILL LEVEL: Beginner
GOOD INTRODUCTORY SPECIES: *Ornithocephalus inflexus,* though most are equally easy

If you always dive into your orchid collection with a hand lens, then this genus is tailor-made for you. *Ornithocephalus* are dainty miniatures with flattened, pointed leaves produced in a distinctive fan shape much like the tail of a bird. They are technically monopodials, and the fan of leaves can grow on indefinitely, losing old leaves at about the same rate that new ones are born and once in a while sprouting a new fan toward the base. One plant has been in my collection for fifteen years and is still growing, though with attrition and division it is not much bigger now than when I bought it. Small fuzzy roots grow out from the base of the leaves both above and below the fan and work their way quickly into whatever moss or duff is available. Once or twice a year, translucent spikes appear from between the leaves formed since the last bloom, and these arch out to just beyond the tips of the 1–3-inch-long leaves. Small but intricate flowers tinted crystalline white, yellow, or green cluster tightly along the upper two-thirds of each raceme. The

Ornithocephalus bryostachys

Latin name comes from the resemblance of the column and lip to a little birdie perched in the cup of petals and sepals. It is really quite an exquisite likeness.

CULTURE

These are perfect subjects for artificial light setups, though I did bloom them successfully for a few years on a windowsill. In the greenhouse, a well-ventilated spot will prevent the rot that is a potential problem when water works up inside the leaf sheaths. The plants grow continuously, and any interruption because of poor culture will remain evident as a stunted section of fan leaves until they are eventually shed.

   TEMPERATURE: Intermediate to warm
   LIGHT: Somewhat bright (1,500–2,500 fc)
   HUMIDITY, WATER, AND FERTILIZATION: Because *Ornitho-cephalus* have little water storage capacity, keep humidity above 60% if possible and mist or water daily. Light fertilization once or twice a month is suitable year-round.
   POTTING AND MEDIA: It is possible to grow these little plants

in pots, but they look more natural on mounts, where the fans can hang down as they would in nature. Tree-fern blocks, cork, and twigs are all suitable; I always place a small pad of NZ sphagnum on the mount, then carefully tie on the fan with the base centered on the moss. The root system is not too extensive, so try not to strangle it with the monofilament or wire, and weave a few strands between a few of the lower leaves for good measure.

Paphiopedilum (Paph)

(*PAPH-EE-OH-PED-ILL-UM*)
SUBTRIBE: Cypripedioideae
NUMBER OF KNOWN SPECIES: 60
NATIVE RANGE: Asian tropics
SKILL LEVEL: Beginner to experienced
GOOD INTRODUCTORY SPECIES: *Paphiopedilum callosum,*
   P. hirsutissimum, P. sukhakulii, and their hybrids

All orchid blooms stand out from the crowd of flowering plants. Among the orchids, though, it is *Paphiopedilum* flowers that are to me the most otherworldly. They look as if they have been assembled by someone with an eccentric bent and a good eye for proportion and balance. The result is a flower that transcends that term and becomes almost animal in spirit. Personality? These plants have it in spades. As a whole, "Paphs" are easy to grow where African violets flourish, but I think it is their animism and oddness as much as their agreeable nature that has made them so popular among orchidists. They differ from most of the plants covered in this book in that they are ground dwellers, sending brown, fuzzy roots

Paphiopedilum sukhakulii 'Sorrento'

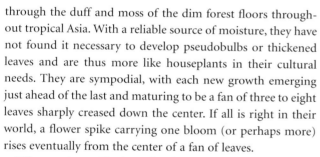

Paphiopedilum callosum 'New Wave'

Paphiopedilum micranthum 'Pink Cloud' AM/AOS

through the duff and moss of the dim forest floors throughout tropical Asia. With a reliable source of moisture, they have not found it necessary to develop pseudobulbs or thickened leaves and are thus more like houseplants in their cultural needs. They are sympodial, with each new growth emerging just ahead of the last and maturing to be a fan of three to eight leaves sharply creased down the center. If all is right in their world, a flower spike carrying one bloom (or perhaps more) rises eventually from the center of a fan of leaves.

What you immediately notice about a *Paphiopedilum* flower is the lip. Among these and the other related "slipper" orchids, such as *Phragmipedium, Selenipedium,* and *Cypripedium,* the lip has been modified into a bucket or pouch designed to snare an unsuspecting bee. The insect is attracted to the glistening pouch, thinking it has found a source of nectar. However, the rim is either waxy and slick or rolled inward, so that once the bee falls or climbs in, it cannot fly out but instead must crawl, humiliated, out the rear of the flower, picking up and/or depositing pollen as it squeezes past the column that blocks the way. To prevent the pouch from filling up with rainwater and thus drowning the bee, the dorsal sepal has evolved to become a roof or umbrella that redirects moisture away from the opening. The other two sepals fuse together behind the pouch like arms held behind its back. The two

petals, on the other hand, thrust out at a downward angle from the lip like colorful flags or ribbons advertising adventure to any passing bee. In some species the petals are equal to the dorsal sepal in size and color. In others they widen a bit toward the ends like flippers or fins. Still others curve and taper like a handlebar mustache. The most exotic, like the fabled *Paphiopedilum rothschildianum,* are long and thin or spiraled like the old-fashioned metal icicles we used to hang from the Christmas tree.

The purpose of the petals and sepals is to direct the pollinator safely into the pouch, and they accomplish this with bars and patterns of spots that serve as visual trail guides. To us, though, the lines, dots, and tessellations are extremely elegant. The often fantastic and always evocative patterns include colors ranging from apple green to piglet pink, cabernet, butter yellow, ivory, and umber.

Unlike most orchids, those in the slipper family resist tissue-culture cloning, and thus superior cultivars command very high prices. However, Paph growers have perfected seedling culture, and species as well as hybrids are widely available. This is fortunate because, as ground dwellers, these often uncommon plants are especially vulnerable to overcollection in the wild (it is a lot harder to collect epiphytes unless you cut down their tree).

Paphiopedilum 'Western Thunder', a "toad"

CULTURE

Paphs are popular orchids, and much has been written about their culture. Some of the species and many of the hybrids are very easy to grow, while others demand more exacting care. The easiest for the house are the spotted-leaved species, which tolerate a fair amount of shade and prefer warm to intermediate temperatures. This group includes *P. urbanianum, P. barbatum, P. wardii, P. sukhakulii, P. lawrenceanum,* and the vigorous *P. callosum.* They grow well on an east windowsill and thrive under fluorescent lights. A bit more challenging are the so-called Chinese Paphs, such as *P. armeniacum, P. malipoense,* and *P. micranthum,* which made quite a splash in the 1980s when they were introduced into horticulture in the West. They are slow-growing, heavily mottled plants bearing enormous, crepe-paper-balloon blooms of yellow, pink, or green on stiff stems a foot or more above the low-slung leaves. They prefer a mix that retains more moisture, but they tolerate cool temperatures well, an advantage if your house is cold during winter. The green-leaved, single-flowered group includes the likes of *P. insigne, P. hirsutissimum,* and *P. exul.* These and related species are the parents of the much-loved and ridiculed "toad" hybrids that were popular from the 1940s to the 1970s, which were bred to have enormous, waxy blooms with enlarged sepals, giving the flowers a rounded appearance. These species and their hybrids prefer intermediate temperatures, especially during winter, but they are equally easy indoors on a windowsill or under lights. Some of the most spectacular Paphs, those in the *multiflora* group, produce successive spikes bear-

ing up to a dozen or more blooms. These plants have plain green leaves, but they like warmth as well as more light than the two groups mentioned above. I have found such species as *P. haynaldianum, P. glaucophyllum,* and *P. victoria-mariae* to be easy and satisfying, but I admit I've struggled with the incredible *P. rothschildianum* and its relatives, such as *P. stonei* and *P. glanduliferum.* I believe these last require the bright light and humidity of a greenhouse to really thrive.

TEMPERATURE: Warm to intermediate-cool

LIGHT: Low (1,000–2,000 fc)

HUMIDITY, WATER, AND FERTILIZATION: In general, Paphs are less demanding about humidity, though indoors a pebble tray or room humidifier will suit them. Relative humidity around 50% should suffice, combined with consistent watering when the surface of the mix has dried but the interior is still damp. Paphs let you know that they are not getting enough water—their leaves become wrinkled and droopy. In severe cases, the whole growth will topple over at the base, at which point a week's recuperation inside a plastic dry cleaner's bag is warranted. They are not heavy feeders; apply a weak solution of a balanced

Paphiopedilum Prince Edward of York, a *multiflora*

liquid fertilizer every few weeks when they're in active vegetative growth.

POTTING AND MEDIA: For the majority of the species and hybrids, 4–6-inch plastic or clay pots are suitable, though most growers prefer the moisture-retentive qualities of plastic for *Paphiopedilums*. Choose a pot that allows 2 inches from the base of the plant to the pot rim all around. The classic Paph mix is pure fine-grade fir bark, to which may be added a bit of peat moss or long-fibered sphagnum to hold more moisture or perlite, gravel, or Turface to hold less. Some growers do well with pure Turface or lava rock, though this necessitates frequent watering.

Larger plants can be divided easily when out of bloom; tease apart or sever the rhizome carefully so as not to cut into the base of the leaf fans (see p. 76). Older but still living roots will have lost their active growing tips but will be firm, not mushy or papery. As in the pleurothallids and some other orchids, if a Paph root loses its tip it cannot grow another. Dead roots pull apart easily, revealing a stringy, resilient core; these should be removed. Reset the divisions with the base of the leaves about an inch below the surface and use a pot clip to prevent upheaval. Back divisions that have no active lead growth will usually produce one within a year if their roots are still functional. Paphs benefit from yearly repotting even if you don't divide them but simply replace the old mix.

Phalaenopsis **(Taisuco Kachidian × Hisa Nasu) 'Symphony White'** HCC/AOS, a classic moth orchid

Phalaenopsis (Phal) 🏵 🍶 🏳

(*FAIL-EH-NOP-SIS*)

SUBTRIBE: Sarcanthinae

NUMBER OF KNOWN SPECIES: 48

NATIVE RANGE: Asian tropics

SKILL LEVEL: Beginner

GOOD INTRODUCTORY SPECIES: The complex hybrids involving *Phalaenopsis amabilis, P. equestris,* and *P. amboinensis* among others, which are often much more readily available than the pure species

If any genus of orchids challenges the family's reputation for being difficult, it is certainly the tongue-leaved, long-blooming, singularly resilient *Phalaenopsis*. I think one of the seminal factors leading to the phenomenal increase in the popularity of orchid-growing during the past fifteen years has been the realization by the floriculture industry that consumers will gladly pay a few dollars more for a blooming "Phal" whose flowers will still be beautiful long after cut flowers have bought a one-way ticket to the compost pile. Now that Dutch, Asian, and North American growers are mass-producing relatively inexpensive potted Phals for the florist trade, legions of would-be orchid growers are bringing home the plants to

Phalaenopsis **(Peach Boy × Ambonosa) 'Ontario'** AM/AOS

brighten the table or receiving one as a get-well gift. The majority of these folks eventually discard the plant after it stops blooming. However, for a growing minority, this seemingly innocuous ambassador administers the bite that brings on orchid fever. Anyone reading this book probably knows exactly what I am talking about.

The "classic" moth-orchid *Phalaenopsis* hybrid, with its 3-foot, branched, arching spray of rounded flowers backed one against the next like a delicate butterfly mobile set above large, flat, fleshy leaves, owes most of its genetics to *P. amabilis*, the big, white moth orchid from Australia, Papua New Guinea, the Philippines, and Java. To me the large round petals look like the ears of an African elephant raised high in alarm. The gaps between the "ears" are filled by the three smaller sepals, and the bloom is fronted not by a trunk but by a small, complicated lip with two upcurving lobes or wings and a tapered tip. The lip adds a bit of yellow-orange and red spotting to the field of white. The scooplike lip of this and related species is handed down to most of the hybrid progeny. Long considered the "true" *Phalaenopsis* among fanciers, the *P. amabilis* hybrids have been joined by the "art-shade," miniature, and novelty types that feature yellow, pink, and peach flowers, small, branched sprays, or spots, blotches, and bars, respectively. Personally, I prefer these livelier *Phalaenopsis* to the somewhat stark, minimalist blooms of the classics, but all have their place and all are equally easy to grow.

Being monopodials, Phals produce one big leaf after another along a stubby vertical stem. Chubby, pewter-colored roots with a bright green or reddish tip force their way out from the bases of the leaves and proceed either down into the potting mix or along its surface and out into the air. The moderately fleshy leaves do have some water-storing ability, but without pseudobulbs the plants are not as drought-tolerant as, say, *Cattleyas* or *Oncidiums*. The inflorescence pokes out from between the leaf bases as well, only higher up on the stem than the roots. After a two-week spell of lower temperatures (down to the low 60s at night) in the fall, the spike begins to lengthen slowly, and a few months later the first flower buds are evident. The flowers on each spike bloom sequentially over several months, and it is not uncommon for a new axillary spike or two to form after the first group of flowers fades. For this reason, never cut off a *Phalaenopsis* flower spike until it has turned brown down to the base, so you don't miss some more blooms. Occasionally, instead of additional flower spikes, an old inflorescence may produce a keiki that can be clipped off and potted separately once it has formed a couple of roots and leaves. Before tissue culture, the keikis were a handy way to produce new plants commercially, and it is still a useful technique for the hobbyist. Keiki hormone paste is available from suppliers to persuade a plant that doesn't come to it naturally. A plant on its last legs may also produce a keiki in a last attempt at self-perpetuation.

Phalaenopsis Littlefly 'Zuma Cutie', a miniature

Phalaenopsis parishii var. *lobbii*

CULTURE

Big, flat leaves are an adaptation to low light, so it is no surprise that *Phalaenopsis* are among the more shade-tolerant orchids. This does not mean they won't benefit from slightly brighter conditions. An east- or southeast-facing window or a spot under artificial lights will produce better flowering, though the plants will survive in very low light. If the plant is receiving enough light, the upper surface of the leaf will be a medium to dark green and the lower surface should have some maroon or burgundy tinting, as should the root tips, wet roots, flower spikes, and leaf bases. Though water stored in the leaves can help them through a short drought, the leaves will advertise their displeasure at chronic underwatering in several ways. Well-hydrated plants growing with adequate humidity will hold their leaves, firm and unwrinkled, up off the potting mix or pot. On a water-stressed plant, the wrinkled leaves flop listlessly on the potting mix, and although they will never regain their previous altitude, with an increase in moisture they will at least lose the wrinkles (see p. 44). Water stress may also be a sign of root loss from overwatering, so the first thing to assess—should your plant look forlorn—is the health of the roots. Do the visible roots look pewter-colored when dry

and deep red or green when wet—good signs—or do they have a dead tan/brown appearance? (See p. 99.) Are the root tips green or maroon? The tips of actively growing roots should be bare of velamen for $1/2$–1 inch and green or maroon in color. Is the plant firm in the pot? Do the roots prefer to burrow down into the pot, or do they snub the staleness for the air above? Even if some of the roots are dead, the plant can be rehydrated by removing it from the pot and gently brushing off any old mix that is not glued firmly to the roots. Then thoroughly soak the roots for thirty minutes and use sterilized scissors to clip off any brown roots, then wrap the remaining live roots somewhat loosely in very damp NZ or other long-fibered sphagnum moss (not peat moss) and drop the tangle into a new pot. If your house is dry, enclose the plant in a dry cleaner's bag to raise the humidity. Soak the moss when you notice the roots have turned silver again. When fresh, the moss has some antifungal properties that will help the roots recover. After a few weeks, the leaves should start to regain their plumpness, and new tips should appear along the old root sections. Once the leaves look plump again and the roots are growing, it is safe to remove the bag.

TEMPERATURE: Warm, then intermediate for two to four weeks in fall. (This can be accomplished by summering the plants outdoors until temperatures begin to dip into the upper 50s at night.)

LIGHT: Low (1,000–1,800 fc)

HUMIDITY, WATER, AND FERTILIZATION: Though Phals are more tolerant of low humidity than most rain forest orchids, aim for readings around 40%–50%. Water as soon as you see the roots down in the mix turn silver. Ideally, you should keep the potting mix slightly damp,

Phalaenopsis Sweet Memory 'Amy Dawn' AM/AOS, an "art shade"

Doritaenopsis Fangtastic Roslynn Greenberg 'Montclair' HCC/AOS

but it's more important to watch the root color and the leaf turgor. Phals are moderate feeders; a balanced liquid fertilizer applied once or twice a week will keep them growing vigorously.

POTTING AND MEDIA: By nature *Phalaenopsis* are epiphytes, and it is possible to raise them as mounted specimens in a humid greenhouse. But most are potted in 4–8-inch clay or plastic azalea pots (pots that are about as tall as they are wide at the rim). In a greenhouse, medium-grade fir bark suits them, but indoors a mix that holds and distributes water more evenly is preferable. Bark blends, Pro-Mix, or Pro-Mix with added charcoal, bark, or perlite are options if you let the mix partially dry between waterings (the surface will turn from chocolate to light brown when it has dried properly). NZ sphagnum can produce spectacular results, but be sure to pot with it fairly loosely and repot annually to prevent salt buildup.

When repotting, clip off any dead roots and sections of stem. If your plant is older and has produced a tall stem with many stilt roots, you can clip off and pot the top leafy section with a good complement of roots, leaving the lower section of the stem in the original pot. If this older section has viable roots, it should produce a new set of leaves in a few months if you keep it lightly watered.

Phragmipedium (Phrag)

(FRAG-MEH-PEE-dee-um)

SUBTRIBE: Cypripedioideae
NUMBER OF KNOWN SPECIES: 22
NATIVE RANGE: Mexico south to Brazil
SKILL LEVEL: Experienced
GOOD INTRODUCTORY SPECIES: *Phragmipedium caudatum,
    P. wallisii*

Phragmipediums, along with *Mexipediums* and their ancestors, the canelike *Selenipediums*, are the slipper orchids of the Neotropics. They closely resemble the *Paphiopedilums* both vegetatively and florally, producing fans of narrow, medium to light green leaves and successively flowering spikes of pouch-lipped flowers sporting very narrow, often twisted sepals and petals. The petals can grow to amazing lengths. Some forms of *P. caudatum* have dangling petals 20 inches long! Until recently, the genus has always taken a back seat to the *Paphiopedilums* among hobbyists. Most *Phragmipedium* flowers are sort of drab in color—green, greenish yellow, maroon

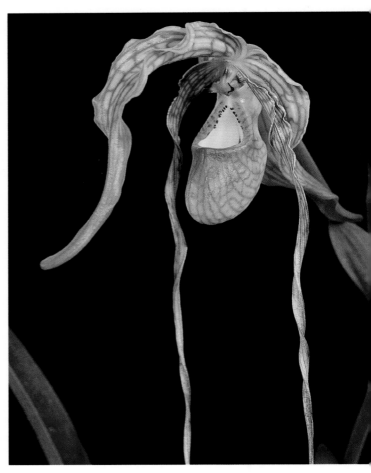

Phragmipedium caudatum 'Green Dragon'

Phragmipedium besseae 'Mount Ephirum' HCC/AOS

P. caudatum and the closely related *P. lindenii* and *P. wallisii* grow as low epiphytes or terrestrials, but the rest of the genus prefers streamsides, wet cliffs, and similar places where water is always nearby; indeed, for part of the year, some species, including *P. longifolium* and *P. besseae,* may have their roots submerged in water. All but the first three mentioned above need something akin to hydroponic culture to thrive. Many growers place the pot in a shallow saucer, while others just water liberally. The plants also require very pure water, a fact that led to their downfall in my collection. The hard well water I was using at the time resulted in all sorts of root problems among the six or eight species and hybrids I had acquired from a friend who was forced to give up her collection. They demand more light than *Paphiopedilums*—more like *Cattleya* light (but certainly possible)—and the tall spikes make under-lights culture challenging.

—but in the late 1980s a scarlet red to orange species was discovered in Ecuador and later in Colombia and Peru. The fluorescent *P. besseae* caused quite a sensation among fanciers accustomed to the drab species, and its arrival occasioned a flurry of hybridization aimed at pairing its color with the long petals of other species. Now an even more spectacular species has been discovered in northern Peru amid a storm of controversy. *P. kovachii* was smuggled into the United States by a Mr. Kovach, who recognized that it was a fantastic new species when he saw it offered for sale at a roadside stand in Peru. The smuggling and the surreptitious naming led to consternation in the orchid community. *P. kovachii* produces huge, dark pink flowers up to 6 inches across, though from photographs the blooms look a bit gangly—like a teenager who hasn't grown into his body yet. However, the unique color and size of this rare flower are sure to generate the same excitement among breeders as *P. besseae* did twenty years ago. Protected under Chapter I of CITES, *P. kovachii* cannot be legally exported from Peru until lab-raised seedlings become available. However, if past experience is a guide, unscrupulous collectors with deep pockets have probably already obtained smuggled plants at astronomical prices.

Phragmipedium schoderae

TEMPERATURE: Warm to intermediate

LIGHT: Bright (2,000–4,000 fc)

HUMIDITY, WATER, AND FERTILIZATION: Humidity should hover around 60%–70%. As I mentioned above, *Phragmipediums* need ready supplies of pure water to grow properly. Even *P. caudatum* and its ilk should never dry out completely, and the rest should remain consistently damp. If you want to try the saucer technique, use a saucer no more than an inch deep and flush the pot with plenty of water so that it washes over the sides of the saucer every time you water (see p. 43). The plants benefit from light fertilization throughout the year, as they grow and bloom almost continuously. Fertilizers designed for hydroponic culture work especially well if you are growing them that way.

POTTING AND MEDIA: Turface, rock wool, and lava rock are good media for semihydroponic culture using shallow saucers. Fine-grade bark or tree fern mixed with perlite and NZ sphagnum are possibilities for a more standard watering regimen.

Pleurothallis (Pleur)

(PLUR-OH-THAL-IS)

SUBTRIBE: Pleurothallidinae

NUMBER OF KNOWN SPECIES: 1,000 plus

NATIVE RANGE: American tropics

SKILL LEVEL: Experienced

GOOD INTRODUCTORY SPECIES: *Pleurothallis grobyi,*
P. flexuosa, P. schiedei

Hummingbird-pollinated flowers may be colorful and bee-pollinated ones sweetly scented, but the fly-pollinated orchids have achieved a diversity that surpasses those groups. This genus, with more than 1,000 species fitting comfortably within the concept of *"Pleurothallis,"* is one of the largest natural genera in the orchid kingdom. The plants are on the small side generally, with a few topping 18 inches; others, like the enormously charming but exceedingly small *P. dressleri,* creep along at a whopping ⅛ inch high. With a slender ramicaul instead of a pseudobulb, these cloud forest plants do require more careful watering than some, but their nonstop growth and flowers ranging from jewellike to cuddly to bizarre endear them to a proud minority of orchidists.

Though it is hard, when faced with such tremendous variation, to characterize an average *Pleurothallis,* I'll try to capture some of the common themes. Many bear their tightly clustered leaves on a long, thin ramicaul. The leaf may be thin or succulent, lance- or spoon-shaped, almost grasslike, or, in many cases, distinctly heart-shaped. The flowers arise at the base of the leaf blade where it joins the petiole, often emerging from a small sheath that is evident when the leaf is form-

Pleurothallis truncata

Pleurothallis nipterophylla

ing. Some flowers are borne singly, others in tight, grapelike clusters often splayed out on top of a leaf, and still others in looser, branched panicles or racemes that rise above the foliage on wire-thin stems. Flowers, in just about every color save true blue, average about $^3/_8$ inch or so from tip to top. As in most pleurothallids, the petals and lip are reduced, so it's the sepals that you first notice. The dorsal sepal forms a hood, cup, or scoop over the column, while the lower (lateral) two fuse at least partially. Often the lower sepals form a mirror image of the top, giving the flowers the unmistakable look of a baby robin with its beak stretched wide for a worm. Some species flower nearly continuously, almost to the point that you'd like to say "Give it a rest, please," lest they tire themselves out. Others flower in distinct seasonal windows governed by changes in temperature and day length.

There are also several related genera that I do not have the space to treat separately. *Zootrophion* (zoo-TRO-fee-on), *Dresslerella* (dress-ler-EL-la), *Octomeria* (ok-toe-MARE-ee-ah), *Platystele* (plat-ee-STEEL-ee), *Porroglossum* (pore-oh-GLOSS-um), *Scaphosepalum* (scaph-oh-SEEP-al-um), *Stelis* (STEE-liss), and *Trisetella* (triss-it-EL-ah) are just a few of the charming miniatures in the Pleurothallidinae. Each genus is unique in its own way, and each is worth seeking out if you are a species collector. They prefer the same cultural conditions as *Pleurothallis*.

Culture

Pleurothallis are perfect plants for someone who, like me, loves miniatures, has limited space, and is fascinated with variations on a theme. They are fairly shade-tolerant, and this, combined with their incessant growth, makes them ideal for artificial-light culture, especially in an enclosed light box or grow room. While most *Pleurothallis* relish the higher humidity of an enclosed space, a goodly number will grow and bloom quite happily on a windowsill if you have a humidifier running somewhere nearby during the drier months. Though they frequent damp forests in the wild, they can be found from sea level up to the cold *paramo* grasslands above the tree line in the Andes. In other words, it is easy to find species that will thrive in the temperatures you can provide, though I would say the largest number prefer intermediate to cool conditions. In general, they are much less particular about temperature than, say, a *Masdevallia or Odontoglossum*.

TEMPERATURE: Warm to cool, depending on the species

LIGHT: Low (1,200–2,000 fc)

HUMIDITY, WATER, AND FERTILIZATION: The ideal humidity range is 60%–80% with occasional spikes to 100% (which occur naturally after watering). Though the leaves may store some water, you should water your

Dresslerella hirsutissima

Pleurothallis once the roots begin to dry but before they dry out completely. They should be contained in rather small pots or mounted, which suggests a daily to thrice weekly schedule of watering or misting. It is important to apply a weak solution of liquid fertilizer once a week year-round, because the plants are always sending up new leaves and flowers.

POTTING AND MEDIA: I prefer 1–3-inch clay thumb pots for aesthetic reasons, though plastic pots work as well. The roots are fine but numerous, so I suggest a fine, moisture-retentive medium of equal parts tree fern, perlite, and NZ sphagnum or its equivalent. You can grow the smaller species and even some of the larger ones very successfully on a mount if you pad the roots with some moss and mist or water the plants daily. Because they grow continuously, they will become dense clumps before you know it, and this can lead to stagnation and rot in the heart of the clump, which will be signaled by rapid leaf drop. The base of the leaf often shows a watery brown infection. *Trisetellas* are especially prone to this problem, and mounted culture paired with a breezy atmosphere will help decrease the chances of its developing. Regular division and repotting or remounting is the other prophylactic for crown rot. I divide the plants every fall or winter if I have time. Make sure that each division has at least six leaves—but twice that many is safer. For the smaller, tightly clustered species, the toothpick method is very effective. Spear a new toothpick (the big, pointed ones with plastic pompoms used in delis are especially good) through the center of the clump of roots and rhizomes, working from underneath. Pull the tip through but leave

Octomeria juncifolia

Polystachya bella

a good bit of it below. Then work another toothpick up right beside it, and once it is through, pull the two pom-pom ends apart as if you were gently breaking a turkey wishbone. You may have to wiggle the clump around a bit and finish the job with your fingers, but this method should give you two nice divisions with roots intact.

Polystachya (Pol)

(POLY-STACK-EE-AH)

SUBTRIBE: Polystachyeae
NUMBER OF KNOWN SPECIES: About 140
NATIVE RANGE: Mostly tropical Africa
SKILL LEVEL: Beginner
GOOD INTRODUCTORY SPECIES: *Polystachya bella, P. piersii, P. vulcanica*

My experience with this African genus is limited to a few species, but I like what I have seen so far. Species like *Polystachya bella* are easy, self-confident, satisfying miniatures that reliably produce their 3-inch racemes of sweetly fragrant, yellow-orange flowers with little attention. Vegetatively, the different species are similar. Spindle-shaped pseudobulbs that are a bit wider toward the base and narrower at the tip grow to

2–3 inches and are topped by two to five thin leaves whose bases partially sheath the pseudobulb but emanate from near its top. The leaves are 2–5 inches long, and as they are expanding or just after they have matured, a fuzzy raceme or panicle bearing up to about a dozen flowers springs up from betwixt their folds. The blooms are either yellow, orange, white, or green, and they appear either hooded or open and down-facing. Though a bunch of them are open at any one time, the spikes flower sequentially, so the little plants stay in bloom for a month or more. Fat white roots that are large for the size of the plant grow from the base of the developing pseudobulbs, which tend to walk upward away from the pot on their ivory stilts.

CULTURE

I find this genus ideal for windowsill culture, as the plants are not too demanding in regard to humidity, temperature, or watering. To flower well indoors, they should receive the bright light of a south-facing window or the consistent illumination afforded by artificial lights. It seems impossible to contain the roots in a small pot, but cramped quarters mean they will dry well between waterings. There may be little but roots left in the pot after a year of growth, but this situation seems to suit them, provided you can really soak the roots when watering.

TEMPERATURE: Warm to intermediate

LIGHT: Bright to very bright (2,500–3,500 fc)

HUMIDITY, WATER, AND FERTILIZATION: Relative humidity of 40%–60% seems adequate. The root tips will stop growing before they hit the pot if the air is very dry, so if you notice this, step up misting to encourage them into the pot. In any case, water when the mix has almost dried. Occasional applications of fertilizer during the spring and summer growing season are helpful, but *Polystachyas* are not nutritionally demanding.

POTTING AND MEDIA: For all but the largest, 2–3-inch clay pots are advisable. As I mentioned above, underpotting allows the roots to dry out between waterings. Both NZ sphagnum plus tree fern and medium-grade fir bark are suitable media. I have not experimented with mounted culture; since many grow as lithophytes, I may try one on a rock.

Promenaea (Prom)

(*PRO-MEN-AY-AH*)

SUBTRIBE: Stanhopeinae

NUMBER OF KNOWN SPECIES: 14

NATIVE RANGE: Brazil

SKILL LEVEL: Experienced

GOOD INTRODUCTORY SPECIES: *Promenaea xanthina*

Though they resemble small *Oncidiums* or *Cochleanthes*, *Promenaeas*, surprisingly, are related to *Stanhopeas* and other big, ponderous bucket orchids. These delectable little plants are just the right scale for a windowsill or under fluorescent lights; the 4-inch-long leaves hang with cheery, hunched-forward flowers about half that size. New growths start out as leafy fans with a matte gray-green appearance. The last two leaves are the largest, and when these are just about fully expanded, you'll notice that they are supported by a flattened pseudobulb about as big as a dime hidden down among all the leaves. Each wrinkled, ribbed pseudobulb huddles tightly against the last, so after a few seasons the whole plant becomes quite a specimen in a 3-inch pot. After the summer flush of new growth has hardened off, large, pointed buds appear between their lowest sheathing leaves and pseudobulbs. Each flower has its own short stem, but a healthy growth may produce as many as four blooms. The flowers don't quite clear the fans of leaves, instead coming to rest in their midst in a well-balanced bouquet of leaf and bloom. As in many *Dendrobiums*, *Cymbidiums*, and *Bifrenarias*, the lateral sepals are held out nearly straight, so the flowers are more half-round than triangular. A proportionally sized lip rolls out like a carpet from the strutting, clawlike column rising up inside.

Many of the species produce bright yellow flowers with some red stippling. *Promenaea stapelioides* has light green flowers overlaid with deep red stippling and banding; this species has been combined with yellow ones such as *P. xanthina* and *P. citrina* to create hybrids with intermediate coloration and a bit more vigor, too.

CULTURE

Promenaeas slow down in the winter months, but they should never dry out completely. The pseudobulbs wrinkle easily; water the plants enough that the pseudobulbs retain some three-dimensionality at all times. Be careful not to let water sit in the fans of developing leaves during periods of high humidity, as this will lead to a watery rot, which will quickly strike down the pseudobulbs and can spread to adjacent older ones. All in all, though, these are very easy, very rewarding miniatures for the indoor grower, and I heartily encourage you to give one a try.

TEMPERATURE: Intermediate

LIGHT: Bright (2,000–2,800 fc)

HUMIDITY, WATER, AND FERTILIZATION: To encourage more flowers from each growth, water and fertilize more frequently when the new growths are developing; taper off the fertilizer but not the water once flower buds are evident. Humidity should be in the 50%–60% range. If your humidity runs higher, mount the plants and mist frequently but place them in a bright, well-ventilated spot.

POTTING AND MEDIA: I prefer 3–4-inch clay pots or 4-inch slatted baskets, as these keep the potting mix well ventilated during periods of more frequent watering. The fine, wiry roots rot quickly under the anaerobic conditions that develop as potting mix degrades, so annual repotting

***Promenaea* Limelight** (*ovatiloba* × *stapelioides*)

is a good insurance policy. Clumps can be divided in spring, with each piece having at least three backbulbs. I recommend a moisture-retentive mix such as NZ sphagnum or sphagnum mixed with tree fern or fine fir bark.

Restrepia (Rstp) 🏵 ♀ 🏴

(RES-TREP-ee-ah)

SUBTRIBE: Pleurothallidinae
NUMBER OF KNOWN SPECIES: 28
NATIVE RANGE: Central and South America
SKILL LEVEL: Experienced
GOOD INTRODUCTORY SPECIES: *Restrepia antennifera,*
   R. muscifera

If you find the thought of miniature orchids that are nearly always in bloom appealing, then consider growing some *Restrepias.* These dainty pleurothallids consist of no more than thickened, oval, pointed leaves supported by thin, stiffened stems completely wrapped in overlapping, papery sheaths, The sheaths make the plants look as if they've been lovingly bundled in newspaper much as you might wrap your prized stemware before a move. The uppermost sheath hides the base of the leaf, where the flowers emerge. *Restrepias* are among the longest-blooming of any orchids. An individual ramicaul may produce a dozen or more successive blooms over its life, and as new growths are constantly being formed, the flowers never stop appearing here and there above the clump. The blooms themselves are decidedly insectlike, with a big, spoon-shaped "lip" (really the synsepal—a.k.a. the fused lateral sepals) crowned by the antennaelike petals and dorsal sepal. The pink, white, or yellow synsepal ranges from $^{3}/_{4}$ inch to 2 inches in length, depending on the species, and is beautifully patterned with orange, red, pink, or magenta spots that may coalesce into distinct lines or become so numerous as to infuse all or part of the surface with their particular hue. The flowers are borne on 1–2-inch stems that usually clear the leaves, but in *R. muscifera* and its allies, the flowers barely clear the last sheath, forcing the blooms to cower under the leaf blade like scared little gnomes. The genus appears to consist of a small group of closely related species. The problem for taxonomists is that once the delicate flowers are pickled, the characteristic coloration of the different species bleeds out, and the bleached flowers often look almost identical in shape and proportion.

CULTURE

Like just about all pleurothallids, *Restrepias* are cloud forest epiphytes that thrive in a damp, breezy atmosphere and moderate shade. They thrive under artificial lights in an enclosed environment; however, they are a resilient lot and are much more satisfying to grow on a windowsill than many in their clan. Because they make keikis easily, they are good pass-along plants to share with friends; many of my plants came into the collection as gifts from orchid pals. Keikis may also develop if the roots have suffered and the plant is in decline, so don't give all of your keikis away if new leaves have stopped developing from the main rhizome.

TEMPERATURE: Intermediate to cool

LIGHT: Low (1,200–2,000 fc)

HUMIDITY, WATER, AND FERTILIZATION: Ideally, maintain humidity around 70%–80% with natural spikes to 100% after watering. However, *Restrepias* can tolerate humidity in the 40%–60% range (which you can achieve indoors with the aid of a humidifier) without too much trouble. They are nearly always putting up flushes of new leaves and flowers, so water or mist frequently to keep the medium lightly damp and apply dilute fertilizer about once a fortnight.

POTTING AND MEDIA: In a humid environment they will do well on tree-fern plaques, but most folks pot them in $1^{1}/_{2}$–3-inch clay or plastic thumb pots. They grow so quickly that you can easily run out of room in a small space, but rather than divide a big plant, it's preferable to carefully snip or pull off a keiki once it has a nest of short

Restrepia guttulata **'Willow Pond'**

Restrepia trichoglossa

Sobralia (Sob) 🏵 🏳

(SO-BRAL-ee-ah)
SUBTRIBE: Sobraliinae
NUMBER OF KNOWN SPECIES: About 100
NATIVE RANGE: American tropics
SKILL LEVEL: Beginner
GOOD INTRODUCTORY SPECIES: *Sobralia macrantha*

Out of flower, *Sobralias* are very unorchidlike indeed. They produce canes sheathed in alternate, sessile (lacking a petiole) leaves that are oval or lance-shaped and deeply pleated along the veins. Depending on the species, the canes may be 18 inches to 5 feet tall. On closer inspection, though, the fat roots that appear from the cane bases and head off into soil and duff are very orchidlike, as are the large, showy flowers—many of which bear a remarkable resemblance to fine *Cattleya* hybrids, though they are not even distantly related. Because they are terrestrial, they are easier to accommodate in a mixed collection of houseplants provide you have the space to grow them to size. The ruffled white, orange, pink, purple, or rose flowers are very pretty, but with few exceptions each lasts only a single day, opening at daybreak and withering before the next dawn. An individual cane may produce half a dozen or more in succession over a few months, so in season the plants always have

Sobralia crocea, a cloud forest species

roots and at least two mature leaves. Once the keiki is established and has put on some size, sell the older plant or pass it on to a friend. Some species or clones are freer with them than others, but you can force the hand of a recalcitrant plant by choosing a nice healthy leaf, preferably one that is about six months old, and cutting it off about halfway down the ramicaul. Stick the stub of ramicaul into some damp sphagnum so that the leaf base rests atop or just under the surface of the moss and keep the cutting damp and shaded (you can also enclose it in a plastic bag). A new leaf should appear within four to eight weeks, but if it doesn't, don't give up hope until the original leaf has browned completely. This is a good way to rescue a traumatized specimen whose roots have rotted due to a sour mix. To prevent this, repot *Restrepias* annually during the winter or early spring. I use straight NZ sphagnum loosely packed around the roots.

a few flowers open, though it's rare to see a specimen bedecked in dozens of blossoms. Because of the ephemeral nature of the blooms, you hardly ever see them at orchid shows.

CULTURE

The roots these plants produce are a sight to see—big, rope-like things that quickly fill even a 10- or 12-inch pot and force the plant up and partially out of the container. Rather than a problem to be corrected, cramped quarters seem to promote bloom, so let your *Sobralia* get comfortably potbound. I fertilize the plants fairly heavily, which they seem to appreciate, but this heavy fertilization may also explain the leaf-tip dieback, which can be a minor annoyance sometimes.

TEMPERATURE: Intermediate

LIGHT: Bright (2,000–3,000 fc)

HUMIDITY, WATER, AND FERTILIZATION: With the exception of the high-elevation species from the Andes, *Sobralias* do not require a saturated atmosphere and will perform well at a relative humidity of 50%. Keep the mix damp at all times, and once the plants become potbound, you may have to water almost daily. Fertilize moderately during the cooler months and heavily during the warmer ones.

POTTING AND MEDIA: A *Cymbidium* mix is suitable, as is Pro-Mix, or fine fir bark with about 20% added peat. Dividing a clump is a challenge. I use a bow saw (after sterilizing the blade with a torch) to saw the roots into sections. This seems like rough treatment, but the plants recover quickly enough. The largest species should be placed in a 12–14-inch pot, while the smallest are at home in one about 5 inches across. Clay is preferable, as they get quite top-heavy.

Sophronitis (Soph)

(SOPH-RO-NIGH-TIS)

SUBTRIBE: Laeliinae

NUMBER OF KNOWN SPECIES: 7

NATIVE RANGE: Mainly Brazil, but also Bolivia and Paraguay

SKILL LEVEL: Experienced

GOOD INTRODUCTORY SPECIES: *Sophronitis cernua*

Something about little plants with big, colorful flowers seems universally appealing to us humans, whether they are orchids, cacti, alpines, or temperate woodland wildflowers. So it comes as no surprise that *Sophronitis* are very desirable orchids. The species as well as the hybrids (produced by crossing them with others in the *Cattleya* alliance) are loved for their luminous flowers in shades of orange, red, purple, and, rarely, yellow—the vibrant hues that plants manufacture to attract fickle hummingbirds to their nectar. Vegetatively, *Sophronitis* are miniatures. Most stand under 3–4 inches high, and the smallest, like the species with the tongue-twisting name *S. brevipedunculata*, top out at less than half that. In form they look like miniature *Cattleyas,* with rounded or oval pseudobulbs topped with a stiff, tapered or oval leaf. The smaller ones grow tight against their mount, the new growths zigging, then zagging along slowly. Flowers appear from the expanding growths that develop at certain times of the year (usually from fall to spring). The most prized is *S. coccinea,* which in its best forms produces 2½-inch-wide flowers of the most beautiful saturated scarlet with a hint of yellow in the lip. Both in its native Brazil and abroad, many superior forms of *S. coccinea* have been bred and named, and a few growers specialize in collecting them. Interestingly, the flowers continue to expand for a few days after opening—like butterflies slowly pumping up their wings. Before you drop this book and take out your credit card, I should warn you that *Sophronitis* are not the easiest of orchids to cultivate. When they are happy, they grow and bloom spectacularly, but when they are unhappy, they sort of

Sobralia macrantha 'Voodoo Priestess' AM/AOS

Sophronitis coccinea 'Mountain Firestorm' AM/AOS

Sophrolaelia Beautiful Sunset 'Neon Light' AM/AOS

lights, but I have had trouble getting them to bloom heavily. This may be due to insufficient light or, more likely, to not enough change between daytime and nighttime temperature, especially during fall and winter, when flower buds begin to develop. A bit of this tendency is carried through into the *Sophrolaeliocattleya* and *Sophrocattleya* hybrids, though they are typically easy, compact, and floriferous orchids.

Sophronitella (SOPH-RON-IT-EL-AH) contains but a single species, *S. violacea*, a miniature from Brazil with spindle-shaped pseudobulbs less than an inch tall, each crowned with a single curved, grasslike leaf about twice that length. It is a charming little plant that grows well on a mount or in a thumb pot under conditions similar to those recommended for *Sophronitis*. I think it blooms more easily, perhaps because it requires a bit less light. The flowers are magenta with a hint of white in the center, and they appear singly or in pairs from small, pointed sheaths at the base of each new leaf.

Sophronitella violacea

limp along and rarely flower, gradually getting weaker and eventually perishing. So what makes them happy? Can a plant truly feel happiness? I'll answer the first question but leave the second to the phytopsychologists to resolve. In the wild they grow on small trees in fairly bright light (but not full sunlight) in places where fog rolls in frequently and the temperatures are never extreme. Indoors they thrive under fluorescent

In a mixed collection, cultivate *Sophronitis* in small pots or baskets, but if you grow cloud forest orchids and are thus accustomed to misting daily, a mounted position will prove more to their liking. They grow throughout the year, with new pseudobulbs coming in several flushes. Despite information to the contrary, most are not truly cool-growing orchids, though *S. coccinea* languishes in summer heat.

TEMPERATURE: Intermediate to cool

LIGHT: Bright (2,200–2,500 fc)—bright enough to keep leaves medium green with some flush of burgundy along the veins

HUMIDITY, WATER, AND FERTILIZATION: Humidity in the 60%–80% range with spikes to 100% is ideal, with frequent misting. Water when the roots are nearly dry, and fertilize regularly year-round.

POTTING AND MEDIA: Either 2–3-inch clay pots or small slatted baskets suffice for all but specimen plants of *S. coccinea;* however, the smaller, creeping species are much easier to accommodate on a cork slab or section of branch. Divide as you would a *Cattleya,* and pot in medium bark or an NZ sphagnum mix. If using sphagnum, be sure to repot annually to avoid salt buildup—*Sophronitis* are especially intolerant of salts.

Stanhopea (Stan) 🏵 🚩

(*STAN-HOPE-ee-ah*)

SUBTRIBE: Stanhopeinae

NUMBER OF KNOWN SPECIES: 55

NATIVE RANGE: Mexico to Brazil

SKILL LEVEL: Beginner

GOOD INTRODUCTORY SPECIES: *Stanhopea costaricensis, S. wardii*

Stanhopeas are marvels of evolutionary design. Their complicated dangling flowers mimic the shape and scent of female euglossine bees so perfectly that male bees attempt to copulate with the flowers, receiving a dab of pollen instead of a chance to pass along their own genes.

These are large plants, producing round, ridged, tightly clustered, lime-sized pseudobulbs, each one topped by a single big leaf. The leaf blade is broadly oblong and noticeably pleated along the veins, and a large plant may have a leaf canopy more than 2½ feet across. *Stanhopea* flower spikes originate at the base of the newest pseudobulbs, usually in summer and fall, and immediately turn downward into the roots. The spikes are tipped with pointed sheaths that help penetrate the roots and mix, and eventually the inflorescence emerges from the bottom and begins to unfurl its blooms. *Stanhopea* flowers are very short-lived (one to two days), and the flowers are timed to open concurrently. When I managed the collections

***Stanhopea inodora* 'Point Loma'** HCC/AOS

at the University of Connecticut, we anticipated the opening of these fantastic flowers as we did the yearly blooming of the orchid cacti or the ephemeral blooms of the stinking voodoo lily. Once I even managed to put a *Stanhopea* in an orchid show. It was spectacular for the judging on Friday, but the flowers were gone by Sunday. Given their size and ephemeral blooms, you may wonder why anyone takes the trouble to grow them, but *Stanhopeas* have many fans. They are easy to cultivate in a warm to intermediate greenhouse, and the flowers are simply marvelous to behold.

Once the inflorescence breaks through the roots, the sheaths part as the flower buds, numbering from two to a dozen, begin to swell. The number of flowers per inflorescense is constant enough within a species that it is used as a diagnostic characteristic in the taxonomy of the genus. The petals and sepals are white, cream, or yellow, often spotted with brown or red. The flowers hang upside down, so the corolla acts as a parasol for the column and lip. The shape and carriage of the petals on some species give the impression of birds in flight. The truly remarkable part of the flower is the complicated lip, fashioned to resemble a female bee. Though to us the lip may seem like a vague facsimile, its dimensions, curves, and, above all, pheromonal odor are irresistible to a male bee. The perfume is strong and pleasant enough — sort of a musky, penetratingly sweet smell that will fill the room. Often the lip is described in three parts: the epichile (tip) approximates the bee's abdomen, the mesochile (the middle section) its thorax and wings, and the hypochile (base) its head. This "head" may even have two realistic eyespots to complete the ruse. As a male bee lands on the lip and attempts to copulate, the tip of its abdomen swings down against the column, picking up and/or depositing pollen.

CULTURE

To accommodate their blooms, *Stanhopeas* are usually hung from the rafters of the greenhouse in moss-lined slatted or wire baskets. You can certainly grow them on a bench for ten months of the year, then suspend them around the time the spikes are first evident at the base of the newest growths. Their

Stanhopea tigrina **var. *negroviolacea* 'Predator'** FCC/AOS

large leaves cast quite a bit of shade, and at the UConn greenhouse we used them to provide a canopy over *Paphiopedilums* and *Phalaenopsis*.

> TEMPERATURE: Warm to intermediate
> LIGHT: Bright (2,500–3,500 fc)
> HUMIDITY, WATER, AND FERTILIZATION: *Stanhopeas* will be happy with average orchid-greenhouse humidity — 50%–70% — combined with ample water and fertilizer during the growing season, tapering off by half during the winter.
> POTTING AND MEDIA: Round, sheet moss–lined, galvanized wire baskets are appropriate, as are 10–12-inch slatted baskets (don't line them with wire or hardware cloth to hold in the potting mix — it may strangle the spikes). I have grown *Stanhopeas* mounted on cork with a generous moss pad, but they did not reach their full potential. Straight medium-grade fir bark works well. Though the plants are fairly tolerant of a stale mix, you should repot every eighteen to twenty-four months. The pseudobulbs can be split apart easily in spring before new growth is evident.

Trichopilia (Trpla) 🔲 🍼 🚩

(*TRIKE-OH-PILL-EE-AH*)
SUBTRIBE: Oncidiinae
NUMBER OF KNOWN SPECIES: 29
NATIVE RANGE: Mexico to Brazil
SKILL LEVEL: Beginner
GOOD INTRODUCTORY SPECIES: *Trichopilia suavis, T. tortilis*

Lavish is the best way to describe the flowers of this small genus. Vegetatively, *Trichopilias* resemble some of the *Odontoglossums* in the extremely flattened, oval or spindle-shaped pseudobulbs, and oblong or lance-shaped 6-inch leaves. However, the sheathing leaves that flank the pseudobulbs on many Oncidiinae are soon deciduous on *Trichopilias*, leaving just a single blade on each pseudobulb. Most new leads appear during the warmer months, and the plants undergo a short rest as temperatures cool in fall before launching horizontal or pendent spikes from the base of that season's pseudobulbs. These just about clear the rim of the pot before developing one to seven large flowers. An individual bloom may measure 5 inches from ruffled or spiraling petal tip to petal tip; the petals and sepals are identical in size, very narrow, and pointed. As with *Brassavolas*, it is the enormous lip that steals the show, and like *Brassavolas* and other moth-pollinated orchids, the lip on some species (*T. fragrans*, in particular) has a large white skirt and strong, sweet fragrance at night. *T. suavis* sports a tubular, ruffled lip stippled artistically with bubble-gum pink. All in all, the blooms have an over-the-top elegance that is tremendously appealing.

Trichopilia suavis

Trichopilia turialbae

CULTURE

Generally, the *Trichopilias* are easy to grow, provided you follow a few guidelines. During the growing season, they need regular watering so that the potting mix never goes completely dry; it should stay moderately damp. They are more shade-tolerant than many Oncidiinae; in fact, the leaves will easily burn or bleach in too much sunlight. I have had trouble with leaf-tip dieback when using water of borderline quality. They

will grow happily under lights or on a windowsill, provided the humidity can be raised to 50% during winter. Because the spikes head out horizontally, take care not to seat the clump too low in the pot.

> **TEMPERATURE:** Intermediate, with a cooler rest in fall and winter
>
> **LIGHT:** Low (1,600–2,200 fc)
>
> **HUMIDITY, WATER, AND FERTILIZATION:** Relative humidity should average about 60%. The pseudobulbs may rot off as they develop if high humidity is coupled with low air movement. Water before the mix becomes dry, even in winter, and fertilize moderately during the warmer months.
>
> **POTTING AND MEDIA:** A 4–6-inch clay or plastic pot or a similar-sized basket is a good choice. The common wisdom is that *Trichopilias* bloom more heavily if divided regularly, but I have never put this idea to the test. Divide plants in spring or early summer, giving each one three to four pseudobulbs. My medium of choice is NZ sphagnum plus tree fern; if tree fern is not available, fine bark, perlite, and a bit of sphagnum will suffice.

Vanda (V) 🏳

(VAN-da)

SUBTRIBE: Sarcanthinae

NUMBER OF KNOWN SPECIES: 48

NATIVE RANGE: India, Asian tropics, and Australia

SKILL LEVEL: Experienced

GOOD INTRODUCTORY SPECIES: The myriad hybrids, especially the *Ascocendas,* which take far less room than the *Vanda* species and intraspecific hybrids

Let's face it: the farther you live from the tropics, the more difficult it is to grow *Vandas* well. Sure, you can get them to bloom some, but with nowhere near the exuberance they show in southern Florida, Taiwan, or India. Why? Mostly it is a question of light. *Vandas* are high-light orchids, and while the June sun in Massachusetts more than suffices, the wan December light makes them sulk. Also, they are big plants with BIG roots that prefer to splay out into the air, so they need copious misting to remain satisfied. If you live south of the Mason-Dixon Line or have a very warm, bright greenhouse, *Vandas* will prove very rewarding. However, if you live in Minneapolis and are contemplating taking one home from your trip to Hawaii, think again. Fortunately for growers with less light and space, much breeding work has been done with the dainty *Ascocentrums,* yielding hot-colored *Ascocenda* hybrids that are easier to accommodate.

The king of *Vandas,* and one of the main parents behind all *Vanda* hybrids, is ironically no longer a *Vanda* at all. *Euanthe (Vanda) sanderiana* is a species endemic to the Philippines

Vanda tricolor 'Summerland' HCC/AOS

trasts with the white-and-brown tepals, but hybrids based on *V. rothschildiana* have a small lip that doesn't add much to the flower.

Related genera that require similar culture include ***Papilionanthe*** (*PAP-ILL-EE-OH-NAN-THEE*), a small genus from tropical Asia with terete foliage—that is, the leaves have narrowed, rolled in on themselves, and thickened in response to a life in the full tropical sun. These "terete-leaved vandas," as they are called, ramble and branch, becoming a bushy tangle of sticklike leaves and fat white roots. I have grown only *P. teres;* up in the brightest rafters at the tippity top of the warm greenhouse it grew and grew and grew, but did I ever see a single bloom? he asks rhetorically. No. The sunlight at 42°N latitude is just not bright enough to bring out any flowers. In Florida, where *P. teres* can be raised in full sun, it is a very satisfactory plant, with rosy flowers in typical *Vanda* shape and carriage.

Renantheras (*REN-AN-THE-RAH*) are spectacular in flower, sending out sprays of brilliant orange and crimson blossoms shaped like smaller, narrower *Vanda* blooms. Some of the showiest, such as *R. coccinea* and *R. storiei,* are huge plants with long internodes between the leaves, lofting vine-like stems—not a plant that's easily accommodated indoors.

Vanda Crown Fox Pink Glow 'Marie Daguia' AM/AOS, a typical *Euanthe sanderiana* hybrid

that boasts large, fairly flat flowers that are sort of a fleshy pink with darker red tessellations toward the center of the lower segments. Crossed with the stunning *Vanda coerulea,* it yielded the legendary *V. rothschildiana,* a vigorous, robust plant with blue-violet, strongly tessellated flowers that is the backbone of *Vanda* breeding to this day.

Vandas are monopodials with strap-shaped leaves that angle out from a main stem in herringbone fashion. Enormous roots erupt from the stem toward the bottom and set off into the air, eventually branching and grabbing hold of any object they may encounter. Flower spikes are produced along the upper part of the stem, usually in a predictable pattern such as every third leaf or so. Since the stubs of old spikes remain for some time, it is easy to guess where the next will originate. Spikes arch out from the stem or curve and then grow upright, lined most of the way with large, waxy flowers whose petals and sepals are spoon-shaped and roughly the same size and color. *V. tricolor* has a bright pink lip that con-

Vanda Rothschildiana 'Dawn'

These species are behind many of the *Renanthera* hybrids, which also incorporate more compact species, including *R. imschootiana* and *R. monachica*, both fine plants in their own right and much easier for most everyone to handle.

Rhynchostylis (RINK-OH-STY-LIS) look like robust *Vandas* with compact stems and curved, V-grooved leaves. They are stupendous in bloom, producing tightly packed, erect or pendulous racemes more than a foot long. Each flower is about an inch across, very fragrant and also long-lasting. *R. gigantea*'s flowers are white spotted with reddish purple, while *R. coerulea*'s spots are a sumptuous deep violet-blue.

All of these genera have been hybridized with *Vanda* and also among themselves.

CULTURE

A *Vanda* that is receiving enough water, light, and fertilizer will retain its leaves for a long time. If you see a 3-foot-high plant clothed in leaves to its base, you know it has gotten the care it needs. If you see one with a bare lower stem or, even worse, only a few leaves up top, one of these needs (most likely water) has not been met. *Vandas* are traditionally raised in slatted baskets. The basket can be filled with large chunks of bark, lava, rubber, or some other material to help anchor the newly potted plant until its roots can fasten to the slats themselves. However, you can skip the mix entirely and just wire the plant into an empty basket. In this case the basket is simply a place to attach a wire so that the *Vanda* can be hung up. Since their roots are so large and aggressive, it is difficult to maintain them on a bench, let alone in a pot. Most growers prefer to suspend the plant and let the roots hang down below.

Rhynchostylis gigantea 'Elisa' AM/AOS

TEMPERATURE: Warm to intermediate; a few species prefer intermediate to cool conditions

LIGHT: Intense (4,000–5,500 fc)

HUMIDITY, WATER, AND FERTILIZATION: Because their roots are primarily aerial, *Vandas* require a relative humidity above 60% with spikes to 90% after watering so they can absorb the droplets that cling to the roots after the velamen has initially been saturated. Mist or water daily. If your plant has become desiccated while you were away, you can soak the roots in a 5-gallon bucket for twenty to thirty minutes, or until they cannot absorb any more water (it will then pool as droplets in low spots along their length). Soaking is also a good way to administer a boost of fertilizer every few months. Vandas should be fertilized moderately to heavily during warm weather and less during cooler seasons.

POTTING AND MEDIA: As mentioned, 8–12-inch slatted baskets are the preferred container, as the roots move out easily and the basket gives you an easy way to hang the plant up. You can tie the stem to the wire basket hangers until roots have firmly attached to it. A few chunks of coarse fir bark, coconut husks, or charcoal, or even medium-grade fir bark, are all possibilities as a medium for the initial roots to gain a purchase. The medium will also trap a bit more water for the plant.

Zygopetalum (Z) 🌼 🚩

(ZY-GO-PET-AL-UM)

SUBTRIBE: Zygopetalinae

NUMBER OF KNOWN SPECIES: 16

NATIVE RANGE: South America

SKILL LEVEL: Beginner

GOOD INTRODUCTORY SPECIES: *Zygopetalum intermedium*, *Z. mackayi*

You know there is a blooming *Zygopetalum* in the house long before you see it, so penetrating is the musky-sweet perfume evaporating from its big purple-lipped flowers. *Zygopetalums* are robust, leafy plants producing fans of 18-inch-long, strap-like leaves that radiate from clusters of lime-sized pseudobulbs at their bases. The leaves are very light green and the veins even lighter, lending the foliage a noticeably striped or ribbed look. I find they grow well in a semiterrestrial potting mix suitable for *Cymbidiums* or *Paphiopedilums*. Most of the species and hybrids bloom in winter or early spring, so they are regulars at orchid shows and society show tables. The fleshy flowers are held aloft on stout vertical stems originating from the base of the pseudobulb and reaching a length of up to 3 feet. The blooms cluster toward the top, each a pretty combination of green petals and sepals covered with burgundy or brown leopard spots and a large skirted lip in light

Zygopetalum **New Era 'Green Dragon'**

pink overlaid with lines and spots of purple or penetratingly deep violet.

CULTURE

As you might expect of semiterrestrials, *Zygopetalums* prefer a water-retentive but freely draining mix kept slightly damp. They have stout roots and are overall quite large, but they are easy enough to raise on a windowsill or in a sunroom.

TEMPERATURE: Intermediate

LIGHT: Bright to very bright (2,000–4,000 fc)

HUMIDITY, WATER, AND FERTILIZATION: If you keep the humidity above 50% and provide enough water to prevent the roots from ever going completely dry, the plants will produce robust new fans every year. Fertilize heavily during the spring and summer.

POTTING AND MEDIA: Even though they are large plants, *Zygopetalums* cluster their pseudobulbs tightly one on top of the next, so an 8-inch pot will suffice for a couple of years before you need to repot. Most of the new growths are produced during spring and summer, so time repotting to coincide with the end of flowering. Each plant division should have two to four mature pseudobulbs. I use a potting mix that is two parts medium-grade fir bark, one part peat moss or chopped sphagnum, and one part perlite.

Taxonomy and Nomenclature

LATIN IS NO ONE'S FIRST LANGUAGE, and it can be a bit ponderous if you are not used to it. However, most orchids simply don't have common English names, and that's not all bad. Common names are often charming and poetic, but many of them, like "moth orchid" (for *Phalaenopsis*), are used for a number of species, so it is difficult to know which plant someone is referring to. Even more confusing is a name like "slipper orchid," which has been applied to *Paphiopedilum, Cypripedium,* and other genera. The Latin binomial refers to one species and one species only, so whether you are in Japan, Colombia, or the United Kingdom, when you see *Phalaenopsis equestris* on a label, you know what to expect (assuming it's correctly labeled, which is another story!). The Latin name can tell you a great deal because it represents a system of classification based on a plant's familial or evolutionary tree as well as its individual characteristics.

To put this family tree in perspective, briefly, the classifica-

Laelia tenebrosa 'Lora Jean' HCC/AOS

"orchidness" that most people can immediately recognize, simply because all orchids descend from a common ancestor, just as we do. All botanical family names end in "aceae," a nomenclatural convention that makes it easy to tell a family name from a genus or species.

Because the orchid family is so huge, taxonomists have subdivided it into a series of five subfamilies, whose names all end in the suffix "oideae." Each of the subfamilies is basically a "child" of the "original" orchid, and each has spawned its own line of descendants. As a point of interest, almost all of the plants covered in this book are in the subfamily Epidendroideae, the newest and most rapidly evolving group within the Orchidaceae. Three of the five subfamilies are further divided into TRIBES (names ending in "eae"), then further into SUBTRIBES (names ending in "inae"). It is really at the level of subtribe that these divisions become meaningful from a horticultural point of view, and thus in Part Four I have indicated, at the beginning of each genus entry, the subtribe it belongs to. Orchidists use the term "alliance," as in the *Oncidium* alliance, interchangeably with "subtribe." In other words, to say that *Brassia* is in the *Oncidium* alliance is the same as saying it is in the subtribe Oncidiinae.

Subtribes are further split into GENERA (GENUS is the singular). A genus is a grouping of plants with very similar characteristics. Conveniently, most plants within a genus share many of the same physical characteristics and have similar cultural needs, so I have used genera as the organizing principle for Part Four. A few genera—*Dendrobium,* for example—are so large and diverse that I have broken them down into smaller groups with similar cultural requirements. Because orchids interbreed so freely with other, related genera, hybridizers are able to combine two natural genera (occurring in the wild) to create an artificial, hybrid genus that has never existed in the wild. The first person to successfully bloom a plant created through hybridizing has the privilege of naming it, and often the name is a combination of the original two genus names: *Laeliocattleya* is an artificial genus created by combining *Laelia* with *Cattleya*. This sort of combo name can be unwieldy, but at least it lets us know who the parents are. If the *Laeliocattleya* is crossed with another hybrid, say, an *Epiphronitis* (*Epidendrum* × *Sophronitis*), a very complicated hybrid, in this case called *Kirchara*, will result. Like many of the complex hybrid genera, this one is named after a person. No offense to Mr. or Mrs. Kirch, but I find this sort of vanity name confusing because it offers no information about the parents. (For more on hybrid genera, see Chapter 14.)

Genera are further divided into SPECIES, which are distinct groups of genetically very similar plants that naturally inter-

tion system works as follows. The plant kingdom has two divisions. The first, Pteridophyta, includes all the plants such as ferns and mosses—otherwise known as bryophytes—that reproduce without flowers or seeds, relying instead on spores. The second division is the Spermatophyta, or seed plants, which includes most of the plants now on earth and which have evolved more recently than the Pteridophyta. The Spermatophyta are divided next into gymnosperms, which means "naked seeds," because the ovules, or eggs, are not enclosed in an ovary. This group includes all of the conifers and a few related plants. The other subdivision of Spermatophyta is the angiosperms, which means, in effect, "covered seeds," because they evolved coverings, or fruits, for their ovules or seeds. The biggest group of plants alive today is the angiosperms, which are divided into two classes. These are the monocots, or plants with a single cotyledon (the first or embryonic leaf), and the dicots, which have two cotyledons. Both the monocots and the dicots are split into a series of families; orchids are one of the largest families within the monocots. A family is a grouping of plants that share certain recognizable characteristics. Those in the orchid family all have, along with other shared characteristics, sexual parts united into a structure called a column. Though it is arguably the largest family in the plant kingdom, all orchids possess an

breed. Humans are a species—*Homo sapiens*—distinct from other (now extinct) species in the genus *Homo,* such as *Homo erectus.* In the binomial system, this is the standard way of writing out the Latin name of a species—*Genus* (capitalized) and *species* (lowercase), both names either italicized or underlined. The system is sort of like phone numbers with area codes and exchanges in that it allows for many more possible combinations than a single name would. Thus *Phalaenopsis violacea, Sophronitella violacea,* and *Cattleya violacea* are three very different plants with the same species epithet, *violacea,* which obviously means violet, telling you something about

Laelia tenebrosa **var.** *aurea* **'Fantasy'**, a yellow variety

the flowers, too. A latinized species name is always lowercase and italicized or underlined, but when a breeder creates a new hybrid species, he or she can give it a non-Latin name. *Ascocenda* Yip Sum Wah and *Phragmipedium* Eric Young are both artificially created hybrid species. Notice that the name is capitalized (even if it's not a surname) and not italicized. Still, Eric Young is the species name (specific epithet) for all offspring produced when *Phragmipedium besseae* and *P. longifolium* are crossed. It is common for orchid references to indicate the parents of a hybrid genus in parentheses after the name—*Phragmipedium* Eric Young (*besseae* × *longifolium*). In orchid-speak, a hybrid species like Eric Young is also called a GREX.

In plants, separations between species are more blurred than in animals, especially among the orchids. When a plant occurs over a wide range or in geographically isolated areas, often there are distinctive races, called subspecies (abbreviated subsp.), which are considered too closely related to be separate species but distinct enough from one another to be recognizable. More commonly, there are minor variations within a species, such as flower color, size, or degree of hairiness, that are not extreme enough to be given a subspecies designation. These are designated VARIETIES (abbreviated v. or var.). Botanically speaking, a variety represents a consistent, natural, minor variation that occurs within a given population of the species. In practice, the term "variety" is applied to all sorts of things, both horticultural and botanical. *Cattleya lobata* var. *alba* is simply a white-flowered variant of a species whose flowers are usually violet. The key here is that a variety differs from the "typical" member of the species in some relatively minor way, just as you might designate people with red hair *Homo sapiens* v. *aurantiaca* (meaning orange). Except for this minor difference, the redheads are just like everyone else in the species. The term "variety" was intended to refer to natural or wild variants, but it began to be used by horticulturists to refer to cultivated strains that appeared or were bred in gardens.

To keep wild and human selected variations separate, the term CULTIVAR was introduced. A cultivar is a CLONE or seed strain selected for a particular trait or traits; in orchids the term is applied only to a clone, however. The cultivar name is capitalized, not italicized and in single quotes: *Bulbophyllum sumatrum* 'Rainbow'. A variety or subspecies can have cultivars, too, like *Homo sapiens* v. *aurantiaca* 'Woody Allen' or *Phragmipedium besseae* var. *dalessandroi* 'Orange Nugget'. The key is the quotes, so when you see *Phragmipedium* 'Orange Nugget' in a catalog, you know that this is shorthand for the particular clone I just mentioned and will be exactly like every other 'Orange Nugget' out there—unless a careless nursery person mixed up their labels. Often a clone is named when it is given an award by the American Orchid Society or another institution. The award is written after the cultivar name, as in

Oncidium Twinkle (grex). Notice the distinct color forms of the three plants pictured here. Each could be given a different cultivar name — say, 'Plum Pudding' for the center one — if the grower wanted to enter the plant for an award or clone it through tissue culture.

Bulbophyllum sumatrum 'Rainbow' FCC/AOS (for more on awards, see Appendix 3). If a particular hybrid is especially fine, there are often a number of cultivars available.

The field of taxonomy is undergoing major changes. Since the time of Carolus Linnaeus, the father of the binomial system and modern taxonomy, plants have been classified according to similarities in visible characteristics, such as the number of pollinia, the shape of the seed, or the details of the flower. Until very recently, it was impossible to directly compare the genes of one species with those of another, so researchers relied on these visible *expressions* of the genes. This system can lead to problems, because similar-looking forms may have evolved independently, if unrelated plants were subject to similar environmental factors or shared the same pollinator. However, with advances in molecular genetics, it is now possible to compare species' genetic codes directly. This is a far more reliable way to establish relationships than by using expressed characteristics, and it is leading to major revisions in many of the large plant families, including the orchids. When direct comparison of genetic codes demonstrates that two species or two genera do not share a common ancestor,

they must necessarily be divided into separate entities. Conversely, if molecular evidence tells us that the two morphologically dissimilar genera are in fact very closely related, they may be combined into one. All this reshuffling is exciting for those interested in plant evolution, but for horticulturalists struggling just to remember all of the "old" Latin names, it is an endless source of frustration. Horticulturalists tend to cling to familiar names far longer than botanists, and a slow shift can be confusing as well. Thus you may see the same plant referred to as *Odontoglossum rossii*, *Lemboglossum rossii*, or (the most recent revision) *Rhyncostele rossii*. Trying to keep up with the changes is like trying to stay abreast of the rapid evolution of digital technology. However, I think that digital technology (in the form of Web sites) offers us a better way to keep up with taxonomic revisions than static references, like this book, can. There is no way around all this nomenclatural turmoil; it results from the time we live in, and we just have to grit our teeth and do the best we can to live with the confusion.

For this text I have used Dressler's *Phylogeny and Classification of the Orchid Family* as my reference, incorporating newer name changes gleaned from the Web wherever possible.

Orchids on the Web and Orchid Organizations

THE WORLD WIDE WEB and Internet search engines have completely revolutionized how we get information, do business, and communicate with one another. The exploding popularity of orchid growing is due in large part to the Web. When I began growing orchids, the only way I could hope to find a particular species or hybrid was to search paper catalogs, sales booths, and the back of the American Orchid Society bulletin; in some cases I had to search for years. Now all I have to do is type in the name in a search engine such as Google, and presto, within .00005 seconds I have a list of three or four nurseries that sell it, pictures of the plant, cultural notes from various sources, and often taxonomic or geographical tidbits to boot. In all seriousness, this digital tool has been as revolutionary for orchidists as the steam engine was for industry or the printing press for scholars. We now have at our fingertips access to an unlimited body of information about our favorite plants. I am simply astounded. The Internet also makes it easier for small backyard (or basement) nurseries to operate without the expenses of printing and long-distance telephone charges, and of course it makes communicating with enthusiasts around the world incredibly easy. Even someone who grew up in the radio generation can learn to do simple Web searches within an hour. Here, instead of offering a long list of

orchid nurseries, supply houses, and other resources, I list a few of my favorite links and let you do the rest.

BiblioOrchidea is an incredibly useful searchable database and bibliography of orchid literature. There is a membership fee for using it.
www.bibliorchidea.net/

Genera names in current use is a searchable database.
www.bgbm.fu-berlin.de/iapt/ncu/genera/Default.htm/

Jay's Internet Orchid Encyclopedia. A huge database of orchid photos and species information.
www.orchidspecies.com/

Linda's Orchid Page. All about orchids.
www.orchidlady.com/

Margaret and Charles Baker's Orchid Culture. Includes climate data and other information.
www.orchidculture.com/

Not So Green Thumb. Lists of orchid genera, photos, and other information.
www.notsogreenthumb.org/

Orchid Guide Digest. E-mail forum and listserver on orchids.
www.orchidguide.com/

Doritaenopsis 'Arian Mowlavi' HCC/AOS

The Orchid Mall. Fabulous—has links to nurseries and suppliers.
www.orchidmall.com/

Orchid Organizations

American Orchid Society
16700 AOS Lane
Delray Beach, FL 33446-4351
Phone: 561-404-2000
Fax: 561-404-2100
E-mail: theAOS@aos.org
Web site: www.orchidweb.org/

Every orchid grower should be a member of the AOS, which publishes the monthly magazine *Orchids* as well as *Awards Quarterly*. The Web site has links to sister organizations, specialist groups, and affiliated local societies.

Orchid Digest
P.O. Box 10360
Canoga Park, CA 91309-1360
www.orchiddigest.com/

A great quarterly magazine for the serious orchid enthusiast.

Royal Horticultural Society
80 Vincent Square
London SW1P 2PE, England
www.rhs.org.uk/

The RHS publishes the excellent monthly magazine *The Orchid Review*, available by subscription at the above address.

Cattleya Caudebec 'Carmela' HCC/AOS

Judging and
Showing
Orchids

BEAUTY IS CERTAINLY IN THE EYE of the beholder, as a trip to a home furnishings store will prove. Still, there are some things that most everyone finds beautiful—a colorful sunset over the ocean, a rainbow, van Gogh's painting *Starry Night*. I would hazard a guess that most folks find orchids beautiful, too, at least the sort of archetypal orchid that comes to mind when you hear the word. These flowers elicit in us a visceral response of joy and ecstasy that runs up the spine and brings tears to the eyes. The appreciation of beauty is one of the fundamental aspects of being human.

Consciously or not, we constantly evaluate our world and the people and things in it, rating them against our own ideal of beauty. Even though these standards are relative, they are at least based on some consensus—a sort of collective, unconscious aesthetic—that exists within and even across cultures. You may consider the idea of judging orchids against an imagined ideal to be a hopelessly subjective endeavor, but we all do it, whether we admit it or not, and a bloom somehow becomes more precious if others swoon over its loveliness, too. The American Orchid Society (AOS) and sister organizations around the world have set up judging organizations that establish quantifiable ideals of beauty by which a particular

Cymbidium Minipure 'Garden of Eden' CMA/CSA

that has received a combined flower quality score of 90–100 points. This is the highest award given for flower quality, and very few are handed out each year (in 2002 the AOS awarded only seventeen). It carries a great deal of prestige, and plants that receive this award are likely to be cloned or used for breeding.

Award of Merit (AM/AOS). Awarded to a plant that has received a combined flower quality score of 80–89 points. A plant with an AM/AOS after its cultivar name is a sure sign of high quality.

Highly Commended Certificate (HCC/AOS). Awarded to a plant that has received a combined flower quality score of 75–79 points. This is a much more common quality award, so it carries less prestige than the AM; a plant so recognized has been judged superior to the average representative of that species or hybrid, though with room for improvement.

A plant that has received an AM or HCC is often brought in for judging again once it has matured, and it frequently

genus or species may be judged. Much as the ancient Greeks and Leonardo da Vinci developed mathematical rules of proportion for the human form and for buildings, these panels of dedicated volunteers have instituted guidelines for judging such characters as the width of a plant's petals, the length of the lip, the intensity of coloration, and the number of flowers on a stem. The orchid judges compare each plant to an established ideal and award the plant a series of points, much as judges at the Olympics rate a figure skater's performance. If the point score is high enough, the plant is given a flower quality award.

Receiving such an award grants the plant and its grower prestige and recognition that increase the value of the plant and—let's face it—give the grower's ego a boost. Anyone can enter a plant for AOS judging, either by attending a monthly judging at one of the twenty-eight regional judging centers in the continental United States and Hawaii or by displaying it at any sanctioned orchid show in the United States or abroad. The time and location for each judging center's monthly meeting, as well as a schedule of upcoming shows, is printed in each issue of *Orchids* (formerly the *AOS Bulletin*), the AOS member magazine. The AOS publishes all awards in the *Awards Quarterly*—an invaluable reference for the serious orchidist.

The American Orchid Society's system of awards for flower quality, which has been widely adopted, is as follows:

First Class Certificate (FCC/AOS). Awarded to a plant

Odontoglossum crispum var. *xantotes* 'Sunset' HCC/AOS

receives a higher point score. That is not surprising, since the size and quality of flowers can vary depending on the conditions of culture and the maturity of the plant. You will often see the actual point score indicated after the award designation, as in *Phalaenopsis* Perfection Is 'Chen' FCC/AOS (94 points), granted in 2002 to a Taiwanese grower at an AOS-judged show in China. Flower quality awards can be given to a plant that originated in the wild, but they are usually given to cultivars developed through controlled breeding.

Fashions change, of course, and while "toad" *Paphiopedilums* received some high awards thirty years ago, these round-flowered types have been replaced by lither forms as today's ideal. Flower quality awards reflect the evolution of taste and advances in breeding, but no doubt they also recognize some intrinsic beauty that sets one flower above the rest.

The grower of a plant that received an award during the preceding calendar year is eligible to be nominated to receive one of several endowed awards.

The BENJAMIN BERLINER AWARD, given in memory of one of my orchid heroes, honors the most outstanding *Lycaste* or one of its related genera.

The BENJAMIN KODAMA AWARD recognizes the grower of the most outstanding member of the *Dendrobium* alliance.

The coveted BUTTERWORTH PRIZE honors the grower of the most outstanding plant awarded a CCM or CCE.

The CARLYLE A. LUER PLEUROTHALLID AWARD, named after the tireless taxonomist who has nearly single-handedly unraveled this difficult subtribe, is given to the grower of the most outstanding member of the Pleurothallidinae.

The FRED HILLERMAN AWARD is given to the grower of the most outstanding example of the Angraecoid alliance in honor of the man whose name is synonymous with the group.

The HERBERT HAGER *PHALAENOPSIS* AWARD, in honor of *Phalaenopsis* guru Herb Hager, is given to the grower of the most outstanding *Phalaenopsis* or a related genus.

The JAMES AND MARIE RIOPELLE *MILTONIA* AWARD, in honor of two pioneers in the genera *Miltonia* and *Miltoniopsis*, honors the grower of the most superior member of these two genera.

The MASATOSHI MIYAMOTO *CATTLEYA* ALLIANCE AWARD recognizes the grower of the best member of this alliance.

The MERRITT W. HUNTINGTON AWARD, in honor of one of the founders of the AOS, is given to the grower of the finest plant to be awarded an FCC that year.

The NAX BOTANICAL TROPHY, established in 1964, the oldest of the annual awards, recognizes the grower of the most

Dendrobium hercoglossum 'South Beach' CCE/AOS

outstanding orchid species given an award that year.

The ROBERT B. DUGGER *ODONTOGLOSSUM* AWARD, given in honor of a great *Odontoglossum/Oncidium*-alliance hybridizer, recognizes the best hybrid or species within that alliance.

The ROY T. FUKUMARA VANDACEOUS AWARD, in honor of one of the great hybridizers within the *Vanda* alliance, recognizes the best example from within its ranks given an award that year.

The W. W. WILSON CYPRIPEDIOIDEAE AWARD honors a man who received more than 550 AOS awards, including 7 FCCs. It recognizes the most outstanding *Paphiopedilum*, *Phragmipedium*, or other member of the subtribe awarded that year.

The following are other awards granted by the AOS judging committee:

AWARD OF DISTINCTION (AD/AOS). Given to a hybrid (and its breeder) that represents an interesting new breeding trend, such as leopard spotting in *Phalaenopsis*. The AD and the AQ are given to the hybrid (grex) rather than to a particular clone.

AWARD OF QUALITY (AQ/AOS). Given to a hybrid (and its breeder) that represents a marked improvement over its predecessors. A hybrid whose members have received a number of flower quality awards is often entered for an AQ. An unbloomed seedling of a hybrid that has received this award is almost guaranteed to be an outstanding performer.

CERTIFICATE OF BOTANICAL RECOGNITION (CBR/AOS). Granted to a cultivar of a new or interesting species so that it can be documented, photographed, and published in the *Awards Quarterly* for educational purposes. It is less a recognition of quality than of something new and different. I often first hear of a new species when its CBR is published in the *Awards Quarterly.*

CERTIFICATE OF HORTICULTURAL MERIT (CHM/AOS). Awarded to a cultivar of a species or natural (not human-made) hybrid that exhibits characteristics deemed of horticultural value (floriferousness, vigor, shape). For the species lover, this is a useful award to look for, as it recognizes plants that are worth seeking out.

JUDGES' COMMENDATION (JC/AOS). A catchall award that says to the grower, in effect, "We think you have something interesting here, but take it home and grow it on, then bring it back again for consideration."

The awards listed above are granted to the plant, but two other awards can be given to the grower in recognition of cultural mastery. In some ways, these last are the most rewarding, as they honor a person's skill and expertise with a particular plant. These awards are given according to a point system that measures number and size of flowers, leaves, overall health, appearance, and presentation of the plant. When you are buying a plant with a CCE or CCM, it does not guarantee that your results will be similar, but it at least implies that the plant can be grown to perfection in cultivation—something that cannot be said for all orchids.

CERTIFICATE OF CULTURAL EXCELLENCE (CCE/AOS). Awarded to the grower of a plant that receives a combined culture score of 90–100 points. This is a rare honor bestowed for extremely high cultural skill.

CERTIFICATE OF CULTURAL MERIT (CCM/AOS). Awarded to the grower of a plant that receives a combined culture score of 80–89 points.

If you are interested in exhibiting plants at an orchid show, entering plants for judging, or pursuing accreditation as an

Pleurothallis medinae 'Laguna' CBR/AOS

orchid judge, pick up a copy of the American Orchid Society's *Handbook on Judging and Exhibition,* an invaluable guide to the standards and processes by which orchids and growers are evaluated. Becoming an orchid judge takes years of training and a large commitment of time, but it offers a tremendous opportunity to study the plants and interact with other experts in the field.

Orchid Societies, Shows, and Exhibits

The American Orchid Society has 348 affiliated regional chapters in the United States and dozens more in Canada, South America, Europe, and elsewhere—a testament to the overwhelming popularity of orchids! Most chapters hold monthly meetings with speakers, and the larger ones put on annual orchid shows open to the public. I strongly encourage anyone interested in orchids not only to join the AOS or a sister organization but to attend local chapter meetings. This is the best way to exchange information with other orchidists, hear lectures by experts in the field, buy inexpensive orchids brought in by other members, and borrow books from the chapter's library.

One of the best features of an orchid society meeting is the show table, to which members bring blooming plants for others to view. Often knowledgeable members (usually AOS judges) discuss the plants or even give out ribbons for the best examples. When I first started attending meetings of the Connecticut Orchid Society, I was intimidated by the experts, and it took quite a bit of courage to start bringing in plants. However, their encouragement was truly inspiring, and their constructive comments were helpful in my never-ending pursuit of cultural excellence. The experience gave me the push I needed to start entering plants in orchid shows, and to eventually take over as show chairperson and, later, vice president. As in any volunteer society, the chapters depend on their members to fill board positions, put on shows, bring refreshments, and contribute to speakers' fees. Please support them as much as you can. These grass-roots organizations are at the heart of the hobby of orchid growing, and we are all in their debt.

Rossioglossum grande 'Otani' AM/AOS

Glossary

ACIDIC Having a pH below 7.0. A very acidic medium (below 5.0) makes most nutrients less available to the plant. Organic media such as sphagnum moss, fir bark, and peat moss have a low pH, but that is generally not a problem for epiphytic orchids. Very pure water as well as some fertilizers increase acidity (lower the pH).

AERIAL ROOT A root that has grown away from the potting mix and into the air, or a root growing on a bare mount or along the outside of the pot. If the humidity is above 50%, these roots will continue to grow indefinitely. They are physiologically different from roots growing in potting mix: they have thicker velamen and chloroplasts to carry out some photosynthesis. When repotting, do not bury aerial roots, as they will suffocate.

ALKALINE Having a pH above 7.0. At high pH, certain nutrients become unavailable to the plant. If your water is hard—very high in calcium and magnesium—these minerals will build up in the orchid medium and make it alkaline over time. Liquid fertilizers can counteract this effect, though hard water may create problems if you are using an inorganic medium, such as rock wool, with little buffering capacity. Hard water will also lead to lime buildup on the leaves, which does not seem to harm them; sponge with dilute vinegar (1 part white vinegar to 6 parts water) to remove some of this residue.

ALLIANCE A group of related genera and their hybrids—for example, the *Oncidium* alliance—that can be interbred.

ALTERNATE Arranged singly along a stem or rhizome rather than

Phalaenopsis parishii **var.** *lobbii*

opposite. The term is most often used to describe leaves but is also applied to stems, pseudobulbs, roots, and flowers.

Amendment A substance added to a potting medium or fertilizer to alter its properties in some way. Perlite, charcoal, or peat moss added to fir bark will change the nutrient- and moisture-holding capacity, pH, and appearance of the mix. Fertilizers can be amended with minor nutrients, organic compounds, and vitamins to increase their efficacy.

Anther The pollen-bearing portion of the stamen.

Anther cap A protective cover with a hinged base that lifts as the pollinator exits the flower, exposing the pollinia so they may attach to the pollinator's body.

Artificial lights Lights, such as fluorescents or HID fixtures, used to supplement or replace sunlight for orchid culture.

Backbulb An older, sometimes leafless pseudobulb with dormant vegetative buds along the rhizome that can begin growing once the backbulb is separated from newer, actively growing pseudobulbs, especially if it still has functional roots.

Bark The ground-up outer bark of various conifers, especially Douglas fir (*Pseudotsuga menziesii*) or redwood (*Sequoia sempervirens*), used either alone or with other ingredients as an orchid medium. Bark is graded by the size of the individual chunks.

Bifoliate Bearing two leaves.

Bud blast Premature loss of developing flower buds, usually caused by some drastic change in the environment.

Buffering capacity The ability of a substance to absorb acidic or alkaline ions before a net change in pH occurs.

Calyx A collective term for the three sepals of an orchid flower.

Charcoal Partially burned wood (usually a hardwood such as oak) that has carbonized. Charcoal is a decay-resistant amendment that has some antiseptic and salt- and odor-absorbing properties. Charcoal dust can be sprinkled on freshly cut plant divisions to lessen the chance of infection.

Clone An exact duplicate. When a plant is divided, the sections are clones. Clones can also be produced through tissue culture. A plant with a cultivar name, such as *Oncidium variegatum* 'Firewater', is a clone, meaning that every 'Firewater' is genetically identical to every other, so if you buy one, you know that it will look like the picture.

Cloud forest A type of high-altitude tropical forest (3,000–10,000 feet) that develops when rising damp air cools and condenses as fog, dew, or rain. Cloud forests are characterized by their moderate to cool temperatures, very high humidity (near 100% except on sunny days), and nearly constant cloud cover in afternoon and evening. In such forests, epiphytic orchids reach their highest diversity.

Coir Technically, the decomposed fibers of coconut husks, but the term is also used for the fresh fibers.

Column The sexual parts (pistil and style) of an orchid flower united into a single composite structure that has evolved for insect or bird pollination. The column juts out of the center of the bloom, with pollen, massed into two or more hard pollinia, at its tip under an anther cap. (The Cypripedioideae have pollen

in two patches on either side of the column tip.) The stigmatic surface (the receptive part of the female sexual organ) is a tacky pocket under the tip of the column.

Cool grower An orchid that prefers temperatures in the 50°–75°F range with occasional spikes to 85° or dips to 45°.

Cork The bark of the cork oak, which is harvested sustainably from orchards in the Mediterranean. Natural cork bark, which is a lightweight, very rot-resistant mounting surface, can be purchased in large sections and broken up or sawn into smaller slabs. Processed cork (wine corks or cork board) is also used for mounts occasionally. Cork does not work well in pots, for it tends to be attacked by insects and it breaks down into a thick sludge.

Corolla A collective term for the petals of a flower.

Crest A raised area on the lip of an orchid flower that helps lure or guide a pollinator to the proper position for pollination.

Cross Short for crossbreeding, usually referring to a hybrid between two natural species (interspecific cross) or between two hybrids. A cross is indicated by an × in the Latin name, with the pod parent on the left and the pollen parent on the right, as in *Cattleya* (*mossiae* × *aclandiae*). The name of an intraspecific cross (one between two individuals of the same species or same hybrid) when the parents are named cultivars gives the seedling's lineage, for example, *Masdevallia coccinea* ('Dragon's Blood' AM/AOS × 'Firefly' HCC/AOS). Since both parents have quality awards from the American Orchid Society, the offspring are likely to be superior to the wild type. Orchids in different genera can also be crossed; *see* **Intergeneric hybrid**.

Cultivar Technically, a seed strain or a clone that possesses a quality or qualities that distinguish it from a typical representative of the species. In the orchid world, a cultivar is almost always a clone; the name is capitalized and in single quotes after the species name.

Damping off A fungal disease that rots seedling stems at the soil line.

Deciduous Producing leaves that fall after one growing season or less than a calendar year.

Dorsal The upper sepal of a resupinate orchid flower, which is at 12 o'clock viewed face-on.

Enclosed light box, case, chamber, or room An artificially lit space enclosed in a material, such as plastic sheeting, that prevents water vapor from escaping and thus elevates humidity. An enclosed space is especially useful for cultivating cloud forest orchids indoors. I define a room as a space large enough for an adult to stand and work in.

Epiphyte A plant growing on the trunk or branches of a (usually woody) plant, but using the host only for support and access to higher light levels above the forest floor. It acquires water and nutrients either directly from rain or as runoff from the host's bark.

Equitant Belonging to a group of primarily Caribbean *Oncidiums* having triquetrous leaves, fine, wiry roots, and branching flower sprays.

Evergreen Producing leaves that fall after more than one growing season or calendar year.

Family A large taxonomic group of plants sharing some basic genetic and morphological characteristics.

Fir bark *See* **Bark**.

Flask As a noun, a sterile glass or clear plastic container used in orchid seed germination and mericloning (tissue culture). As a verb, shorthand for in vitro orchid seed sowing.

Footcandle (fc) The amount of light a candle casts 1 foot away. Most orchids require 1,000–5,000 fc to grow properly, which is about one-twentieth to one-fourth the strength of full tropical sunlight.

Genus (plural, **Genera**) A group of related species that can be traced back to a common ancestor. The genus name is the first, capitalized part of the Latin binomial; *Cattleya mossiae* is in the genus *Cattleya*.

Greenhouse An enclosed structure covered with translucent material such as glass or clear plastic sheeting that is designed specifically for the culture of plants.

Green pod An immature orchid seedpod or capsule, from which the seeds are harvested in a technique used to overcome seed dormancy.

Grex All of the seedlings from a particular cross—basically an artificial species created through controlled pollination. The grex name is usually capitalized, not italicized, and non-Latin, such as *Masdevallia* Angel Frost, a hybrid between *M. veitchiana* and *M. strobelii*. The seedlings of this cross are a grex, and they share a particular set of genetic characteristics obtained from their parents, though individual seedlings may express these traits very differently from others. A grex can receive an Award of Distinction (AD) or an Award of Quality (AQ) from the American Orchid Society if it has produced a number of superior seedlings.

HID High-intensity-discharge lamp, a type of bulb that emits very bright light and is used extensively in horticulture.

Hybrid A plant produced either naturally (a natural hybrid) or artificially (an artificial hybrid) by cross-pollination between two different species. The resulting hybrid species may then be cross-pollinated with another species to create a different hybrid. The barriers to cross-pollination between different species or even different genera are very weak in orchids, and it is quite easy to create hybrids by transferring fresh pollen from one plant to the receptive stigma of another.

Hydroponic Grown in a dilute nutrient solution or an inert medium regularly flooded with a nutrient solution. A few orchids—*Disas* and *Phragmipediums* come to mind—are regularly grown hydroponically.

Hyphae The threadlike filaments that form the mycelium of a fungus.

Inflorescence The flowering parts of an orchid plant.

Intergeneric hybrid A hybrid between two or more genera. Such hybrids are rare in most plant families, but orchids are famous for their promiscuity. Some artificial crosses involve as many as six genera.

Intermediate grower An orchid preferring temperatures in the 58°–82°F range (58°–62°for winter lows and 80°–82° for average summer highs, with occasional spikes to 85°–90°).

Keel A raised area, usually on the orchid's lip. *See* **Crest**.

Keiki From the Hawaiian word for "baby." A new growth (lead) produced from a flower bud along an orchid stem that has reverted to a vegetative bud in response to stress or change in temperature, or simply as a natural way for the plant to reproduce. A keiki can be artificially induced by applying a synthetic hormone (keiki paste) to a dormant flower bud.

Labellum A ten-dollar word for lip.

Lanceolate Having a shape like a lance—narrowly oval and narrowing to a point at both ends. The term is usually used to describe a leaf.

Lath house An open, unheated structure covered with well-spaced wooden laths (strips) or plastic shade cloth that protects plants from the full effect of the sun. A lath house usually blocks 30%–70% of full sunlight.

Lava rock Somewhat porous volcanic rock that is used as an orchid medium or amendment. It is fairly inert but does release some minerals as it weathers.

Lead The newest actively growing vegetative part of the plant. The term is usually applied to sympodial orchids.

Leaf axil The inner angle formed where a leaf joins a stem.

Lip The modified third petal of an orchid flower, often large and vibrantly colored to lure and guide pollinators. In a resupinate flower the lip always sits below the column.

Lithophyte A plant that grows on bare rock.

Lumen A measure of light equal to 1 footcandle spread over 1 square foot.

Medium (plural, **Media**) The ingredients used to provide a substrate for an orchid to grow on. Media for epiphytic orchids should be very free-draining, including such materials as bark chips, charcoal, or tree-fern fiber.

Mericlone A clone produced through tissue culture by proliferation of cells taken from the meristem of a plant.

Meristem The undifferentiated cells in the growing tip of a plant. Because these cells are easily multiplied, they are used for tissue-culture reproduction.

Miniature An orchid whose mature height is less than 10 inches (excluding inflorescences). Their small size makes miniatures good subjects for growing indoors.

Monopodial Producing a single or branched vertical stem lined with leaves. Each stem continues to lengthen indefinitely as new leaves are produced at its tip. Monopodial orchids do not produce pseudobulbs.

Mount As a verb, attaching an epiphytic orchid to a branch or slab to allow it to grow much as it would in nature. As a noun, the substrate (a material such as cork, tree fern, or tree branch) on which an epiphytic orchid is grown.

Neotropics The American tropics, including southern Florida, the Caribbean, Mexico, and Central and South America.

Node The point at which a flower or leaf attaches to a stem or rhizome.

NZ sphagnum A high-quality dried, whole sphagnum moss from New Zealand that wicks moisture very effectively.

Opposite Borne in opposing pairs along a stem. The term is used to describe leaves, flowers, or roots.

Osmunda fiber The root fibers of various species of *Osmunda* ferns. In the past, osmunda was a very popular orchid medium, as it is decay-resistant, drains well, and holds a fair bit of moisture. However, harvesting the fiber destroys the slow-growing plants, so its use has been greatly curtailed.

Ovate Egg-shaped.

Paleotropics Also called the Old World tropics. Tropical areas of India, Asia, Africa, Australia, New Guinea, New Zealand, and the Pacific.

Panicle A branched inflorescence.

Peat moss Partially decomposed sphagnum moss, which provides a water-retentive, sterile, highly acidic growing medium. In orchid culture, peat is primarily a minor amendment in semiterrestrial media.

Pedicel The flower stem of a single-flowered inflorescence.

Peduncle The flower stem of a multiple-flowered inflorescence.

Perlite Volcanic glass that has been rapidly heated to more than 1,600°F, which causes it to pop like popcorn as the internal water vaporizes. Perlite is used in orchid media to improve aeration and drainage. Occasionally it is used (in the form of sponge rock) as a medium by itself.

Petal In orchids, either of the two segments of the inner whorl of floral parts that, along with the lip, constitute the corolla. The petals of a typical orchid flower are positioned at about 9 o'clock and 3 o'clock.

Petiole The stem of a leaf blade attaching to a pseudobulb, ramicaul, or main stem.

pH Shorthand for potential of hydrogen, a measurement of acidity or alkalinity. A pH above 7.0 is considered alkaline; below 7.0, acidic. Every one-point rise or fall in pH represents a tenfold change.

Pleurothallid A subtribe of mostly small orchids from the cloud forests of the American tropics.

Pod A three-chambered orchid seed capsule that is green when unripe and then yellow, turning brown or tan, when ripe. The ripened pod splits open along the seams, allowing the dustlike seed to escape.

Pod parent The female parent of a cross, which passes on more genes (in the form of nonnuclear DNA) than the male parent and so may have more genetic influence on the progeny. In botanical terminology the pod parent is written first (*pod parent × pollen parent*).

Pollen parent The male parent of a cross.

Pollinium (plural, **pollinia**) A waxy sac of aggregated pollen, often with a sticky "foot" (viscidium) designed to deliver a concentrated load of pollen.

Progeny Offspring.

Pseudobulb A swollen, modified stem of certain epiphytic orchids that contains spongy tissue to hold extra water and nutrients for the plant's use in times of stress.

Raceme An unbranched inflorescence.

Ramicaul A secondary stem attaching a leaf to the rhizome of a pleurothallid (instead of a pseudobulb).

Relative humidity A measure of the amount of water vapor in the air. Humidity is relative because the carrying capacity of air increases as the temperature rises, and thus the amount of water vapor must also increase for the air to become saturated, or reach the dew point. Most epiphytic orchids prefer a relative humidity above 50%, and many like a range of 70%–100%.

Resupinate Of an orchid flower, twisting 180° during development so that the column is oriented with the stigmatic surface facing downward. The opposite orientation is called nonresupinate.

Reverse osmosis (RO) water Very pure water produced by forcing tap water through special filters under pressure to remove almost all the dissolved salts and impurities.

Rhizome A stem that grows along the ground or another surface.

Rock wool An insulating material made from lava that is melted, spun, given a water-repellency treatment, then bound together in a wool-like fleece.

Scandent Having a lax, sprawling, or weakly vining habit of growth.

Scape Inflorescence.

Seasonally wet tropical forest A type of low-elevation forest in areas with a marked and dependable shift in rainfall over the year, that is, rainy summers and dry winters or vice versa. Orchids native to such forests are often deciduous and have a strict dormant period, during which they require a reduction in watering to prevent rotting and initiate flowering.

Segment An individual petal, sepal, or lip of a flower.

Semiterrestrial Growing on the ground with shallow roots into decomposing organic material or moss rather than deep roots into the mineral soil.

Sepal In orchid flowers, any of the three outer segments, which are often brightly colored.

Sessile Of a leaf or flower, stalkless.

Sheath (1) A modified leaf base that protects the rhizome, pseudobulb, or developing leaves; (2) a modified leaf that surrounds the immature flower spike.

Sheathing leaves Small leaves with long bases that wrap the developing pseudobulb and often persist as either green leaves or a dried wrapper around the mature pseudobulb. Such leaves are found in many orchids, particularly those of the *Oncidium* alliance. Some growers remove them, for they can harbor pests such as scale or mealybugs.

Slab A flat piece of a material such as cork bark or tree fern on which an orchid is mounted.

Species A closely related group of individuals sharing many characteristics and interbreeding freely in the wild.

Spike Inflorescence. Orchids are often described as "in spike," meaning that the flower stem or buds are evident but the plant is not yet blooming.

Stamen The anther and filament of a flower.

STAMINODE A modified, sterile stamen that aids pollination by guiding or luring the pollinator and/or by producing a nectar reward.

STERILIZE To kill all living organisms, particularly those that cause disease. Orchid-cutting tools and containers can be sterilized by applying very high heat, directly with a propane torch or by baking in a 400° oven for an hour or boiling in a water bath, or by soaking in a chemical sterilant, such as a 10% chlorine bleach solution or isopropyl alcohol straight from the bottle, for 20 to 30 minutes.

STIGMA The receptive area of the female part of a flower, which collects and holds the pollen until pollen tubes grow down into the ovary to fertilize the ovules.

SUBTEND Be positioned below.

SUBTRIBE A taxonomic grouping that in the Orchidaceae includes genera that are fairly similar and are descended from a common ancestor.

SYMPODIAL Producing a series of individual, complete growths from a creeping rhizome. That is, each growth has roots, a leaf or leaves, usually a pseudobulb or stem, and dormant flower and vegetative buds.

SYNSEPAL An aggregate sepal formed when the two lateral sepals fuse along their closest edge.

TEPAL An undifferentiated sepal or petal.

TERETE Of a leaf, cylindrical, round in cross-section. The term is usually applied to the swollen leaves of drought-adapted orchid species.

TISSUE CULTURE A sterile laboratory propagation technique in which plant cells—usually obtained from the meristem, or growing tip—are multiplied through the influence of hormones. Masses of these cells can be divided and redivided indefinitely. When the propagator has obtained enough cells, he or she induces them to grow into plants by adjusting the concentrations of hormones and nutrients in the sterile medium. Large quantities of clonal material can be obtained rather quickly through tissue culture.

TOTAL DISSOLVED SOLIDS (TDS) Technically, the percentage, expressed as parts per million (ppm) or the equivalent mg/L, of dissolved salts and other solids in a given volume of water. This number represents the total ions dissolved in a tested water sample. The higher the TDS reading, the poorer the water is for orchids.

TREE-FERN FIBER A potting material derived from the chopped-up trunks of tree ferns (family Cyatheaceae) from Southeast Asia, Central America, and South America. The trunks consist of bundled conductive tubes that carry water and nutrients to the tree's crown. When chopped up, the bundles separate into individual tubes or fibers, each 1/2–3 inches long, black, and very stiff and wiry. Tree fern is a decay-resistant, fairly fine orchid medium, but concerns about overharvesting of the slow-growing plants may lead to discontinuation of its use (as has happened with osmunda).

TRIBE A subfamilial taxonomic grouping.

TRIMEROUS Having flower parts in groupings of three.

TRIQUETROUS Having three sharp, projecting angles, like the leaves of an equitant *Oncidium*.

TROPICAL RAIN FOREST Low-elevation forest that experiences consistently high rainfall (more than 150 inches annually) throughout most or all of the year. Orchids that grow in rain forests usually require warm, humid conditions under cultivation.

TURFACE A calcined clay aggregate used as a component of potting mixes.

TURGID Plump, stiff, full of water. Not wrinkled and limp.

TWIG EPIPHYTE An epiphyte, usually a miniature, adapted to living on the smallest branches of a tree, where air movement is usually livelier and the light brighter than on a trunk or main branch. Because life tends to be precarious on a twig, most of these epiphytes grow quickly from seed, bloom prolifically, and have a short lifespan.

UNIFOLIATE Bearing one leaf.

VARIETY A form of a species that differs in some small way, such as flower color or leaf shape, from the typical form. In horticulture the term is often confused with "cultivar."

VEGETATIVE Pertaining to the nonflowering parts of a plant: the leaves and pseudobulbs, roots, and rhizome.

VELAMEN The spongy white or silver outer layer of epiphytic orchid roots that aids absorption of water and minerals and protects the inner tissues.

VERMICULITE An inert, lightweight amendment used in horticultural potting mixes. It is made from a claylike mineral that in its natural state resembles mica rock, but when it is heated quickly, steam between the layers causes it to expand, rather like popcorn. Vermiculite holds some water and nutrients between its spongy layers.

VIRUS An ultramicroscopic organism consisting of strands of genes (RNA or DNA) surrounded by a protein coat. Viruses can reproduce only within the living cells of another organism. Twenty-six orchid viruses have been identified, and more will probably be discovered with further research. Incurable without sophisticated laboratory equipment, viruses cause decreased vigor in the affected orchid. They can be spread by the transfer of sap on unsterilized cutting tools or by sucking insects such as aphids.

VISCIDIUM *See* **POLLINIUM**.

WARDIAN CASE Basically a big terrarium, in which relative humidity is high compared to that of the room it is in, placed in front of a window. A true Wardian case, a Victorian invention, is a lovely piece of furniture, but I use the term rather loosely for any plastic or glass case or cabinet that encloses plants, whether lit artificially or naturally.

WARM GROWER An orchid that prefers temperatures in the 65°–85°F range, with winter lows of 65°–70° and summer highs around 85° and spikes to 90°–95°.

Bibliography

Arditti, Joseph A., ed. *Orchid Biology: Reviews and Perspectives.* Vols. 1–7. Ithaca, N.Y.: Cornell University Press, 1977–1997.

Arditti, Joseph, and Robert Ernst. *Micropropagation of Orchids.* New York: John Wiley & Sons, 1993 (out of print).

Bechtel, Helmut, et al. *The Manual of Cultivated Orchid Species.* 3rd ed. Boston: MIT Press, 1992.

Christensen, Eric. *Phalaenopsis: A Monograph.* Portland, Ore.: Timber Press, 2001.

Dressler, Robert L. *Phylogeny and Classification of the Orchid Family.* Portland, Ore.: Dioscorides Press, 1993.

Dunsterville, G. C. K., and Leslie A. Garay. *Orchids of Venezuela: An Illustrated Field Guide.* Cambridge, Mass.: Botanical Museum of Harvard University, 1979.

Grove, David L. *Vandas and Ascocendas and Their Combinations with Other Genera.* Portland Ore.: Timber Press, 1995.

Hawkes, Alex D. *Encyclopedia of Cultivated Orchids.* London: Faber and Faber, 1987.

Kyte, Lydiane, and John G. Kleyn. *Plants from Test Tubes: An Introduction to Micropropagation.* Rev. ed. Portland, Ore.: Timber Press, 1996.

Lavarack, P. S., et al. *Dendrobium and Its Relatives.* Portland, Ore.: Timber Press, 2001.

Isochilus linearis

Luer, Carlyle A. *Icones Pleurothallidarium.* Vols. 1–14. St. Louis: Missouri Botanical Garden Press, 1985–1996.

Northen, Rebecca Tyson. *Home Orchid Growing.* 4th ed. New York: Van Nostrand Reinhold, 1992.

————. *Miniature Orchids and How to Grow Them.* Reprint. New York: Dover Publications, 1996.

Pridgeon, Alec, ed. *The Illustrated Encyclopedia of Orchids.* Portland, Ore.: Timber Press, 1992.

Reeve, T. M., and P. J. B. Woods. "A Revision of *Dendrobium* Section *Oxyglossum,*" *Notes from the Royal Botanic Garden Edinburgh* 46 (2), 1989.

Schweinfurth, Charles. "Orchids of Peru," *Fieldiana: Botany* 30 (1–3), 1959.

Sheehan, Tom, and Marion Sheehan. *An Illustrated Survey of Orchid Genera.* Portland Ore.: Timber Press, 1995.

Siegerist, Emily S. *Bulbophyllums and Their Allies: A Grower's Guide.* Portland, Ore.: Timber Press, 2001.

Van Der Pijl, L., and Calaway H. Dodson. *Orchid Flowers: Their Pollination and Evolution.* Coral Gables, Fla.: University of Miami Press, 1966.

Watson, James B., series ed. *Orchid Pests and Diseases.* Delray Beach, Fla.: American Orchid Society, 2002.

Wisler, Gail C. *How to Control Orchid Viruses: The Complete Guidebook.* Gainesville, Fla.: Maupin House, 1989.

Withner, Carl. *The Cattleyas and Their Relatives.* Vols. 1–6. Portland, Ore.: Timber Press, 2000.

Bulbophyllum orthoglossum

Cattleytonia Capri 'Lea' AM/AOS

Photo Credits

Miltoniopsis **Alysen Ono 'Magic'**

Index

Numbers in italics refer to pages on which photographs appear.

Laelia milleri